THE AMAZING STORY OF REPEAL

THE AMAZING STORY OF REPEAL

An Exposé of the Power of Propaganda

By FLETCHER DOBYNS

WILLETT, CLARK & COMPANY
CHICAGO NEW YORK
1940

Manufactured in the U. S. A. by The Plimpton Press
Norwood, Mass.-LaPorte, Ind.

Contents

Foreword

IF ALL the instruments of publicity — the printing press, radio, telegraph and telephone — were used solely for the purpose of bringing to the people the truth, the whole truth and nothing but the truth, it would be possible to solve the difficult problems that crowd upon us by the orderly process of evolution, and to escape bitter and fanatical controversies, wars and revolutions. To an ever increasing extent, however, these instruments are being put to an opposite use through the uses made of "propaganda." They are being employed by great pressure groups of all kinds, motivated by selfishness and greed to deceive, mislead, inflame and regiment the people to pursue courses of action inimical to their economic and spiritual interests. Daily the truth is being buried under an avalanche of half-truths, lies and appeals to passion, ignorance, prejudice and fear.

Propaganda is not a new phenomenon. From the beginning of our history, the people have been deceived and misled by slogans and catch-phrases. Unscrupulous groups have duped and betrayed innocent and trusting people. They have seized land, forests, mines, waterways and streets that belonged to all the people, erected tariff walls, built up trusts and monopolies, put over dishonest financial schemes, destroyed their rivals and exploited the public — all through the clever use of propaganda. During the First World War the technique of public deception and regimentation was greatly perfected and the art of propaganda reached its full maturity.

Today every interest that has something to put over through the manipulation of public opinion, has on hand its corps of professional propagandists. Whether known as ministers of propaganda, public relations counsels, publicity men, or by any other name, the business of these men is to poison the wells of information. They take advantage of ignorance, engage in suppression and fabrication, excite fear and hatred, pander to prejudice and ridicule and defame honest men who endeavor to expose them.

In the totalitarian states we have seen dictators, through the artful uses of propaganda, seize, secure and retain the power to destroy the liberties of millions of people and to force on them the beliefs and practices of the pagan and the savage. Likewise, the so-called democratic nations are ruled and exploited by the economic and political groups that are most proficient in using propaganda to their advantage. So universal and effective has it become that it is now practically impossible to distinguish between honest statement of fact and opinion and dishonest propaganda.

If we are to deal successfully with the propaganda menace, the public must understand what propaganda is. This is an indispensable first step. We must become familiar with the motives, the methods and the technique of the propagandist. We must learn to detect and ignore propaganda, we must build up adequate intellectual and emotional defenses against it. This can be accomplished only by its thoroughgoing exposure. The mask of hypocrisy must be torn from the propagandist and his employer and the whole greedy and corrupt business exhibited in its stark reality. This can be done most effectively by a case study in which the facts involved are established by unimpeachable evidence and are so concrete and simple that they can be understood by everyone.

The excellent studies that have been made of war propaganda, of the Navy League, the munitions makers, the public utility companies and other interests, have not proved effective because these studies involve facts and economic theories with which the people are not familiar and concerning which they can be confused and misled. After devoting more than ten years to the investigation of the subject, I have reached the conclusion that the methods used to bring about the repeal of the Eighteenth Amendment furnish ideal material for an authentic and illuminating case study of the whole propaganda problem. From personal observation and experience, most people are familiar with the history of the liquor traffic and the evils it produces. Such a study involves no difficult economic questions that can be used to deceive and confuse. There cannot be the slightest question as to motives and methods. These were conclusively established by testimony given and documents produced by the men who created and carried on the repeal campaign propaganda, when they were under oath before congressional investigating committees. The campaign covered the entire country, it continued for many years, and it employed every method of deception, coercion and emotional distortion that professional propagandists could devise and unlimited money could pay for. It exhibited propaganda in the perfection of its technique and the depth of its disregard for moral and social values.

Stored away in the government vaults in Washington, forgotten and gathering the dust of the passing years, are five volumes containing 5,088 pages of testimony which tell an amazing story. This report (Lobby Investigation Committee, U. S. Senate, 71st Congress, 2nd session) is one of the most astonishing public documents in existence. Its perusal leaves the reader incredulous. It reveals a group of men who are recognized as the industrial, financial and social leaders of America deliberately organizing, conducting and promoting a campaign to overthrow the Eighteenth Amendment. It discloses why they wanted the amendment repealed, and how they achieved their objective. It shows that for public consumption they declared that they were seeking to promote the general welfare, to put an end to bootlegging, drunkenness, hypocrisy and political corruption, while in reality their actual motive was to get rid of their income taxes!

The presentation of the evidence before the investigating committee required many days, it was introduced piecemeal, and it was inadequately reported by the newspapers that were in sympathy with the repeal movement. The public, therefore, was not informed of the facts at the time of their disclosure and the report of the committee sank into oblivion. This volume deals extensively with the testimony in this report.

Considerable space in the report is devoted to the activities of the Association Against the Prohibition Amendment, a powerful and effective organization of which Pierre du Pont became the "directing force." The extent of Mr. du Pont's interest in the association and his influence on the repeal movement is clearly indicated by the following resolution, which was adopted by the board of directors at a meeting in the Waldorf-Astoria Hotel, New York, after repeal was an accomplished fact:

In the long and difficult fight to secure repeal of the Eighteenth Amendment, a number of different individuals have played an important part, but to none is credit due in larger measure than to Pierre S. du Pont.

For the past five years of the critical period of the battle which has at last resulted in such gratifying victory, Mr. du Pont has been in many important respects the directing force of the organization. He has given of his great abilities, his time and his money without stint. His counsel has always been wise and his suggestions constructive. He brought to the association the marked prestige which attaches to any group with which he is connected. The executive committee, with him as chairman, has held meetings at frequent intervals and has directed in a general way the policies to be pursued.

In the stringent financial conditions of the last two years, the association has experienced grave difficulty in raising the funds required to continue its work. Particularly these past six months, when the general public has accepted repeal as a practically accomplished fact, it became almost impossible to obtain the necessary funds. Except for the leadership taken by our association, in the states where elections were held this year, except for the ability to arrange for the monetary outlay incident thereto, ratification of the Twenty-first Amendment would assuredly have been delayed for several years and might have been seriously jeopardized.

The directors of this association are entitled to know that on repeated occasions, Mr. du Pont volunteered to advance the sums needed to carry forward the association's activities and thus assumed cheerfully and willingly and with superb generosity the financial burden of the completion of our work. It is no exaggeration to suggest that save for him that work must have been abandoned or at least curtailed to such an extent that it could not have proved effective.

It is generally conceded that repeal has failed to solve the liquor problem. Half a million saloons, taverns, night clubs and other retail establishments, alluring advertising and effective salesmanship, are causing a steady increase in the amount of liquor consumed. All the historic evils that brought about the adoption of national prohibition by the almost unanimous action of the states exist today in aggravated form. Public resentment is increasing and there is a rapidly growing demand for some more effective method of liquor control. A study of the propaganda by which repeal was accomplished and of that which is now being used to safeguard its results, necessarily involves a consideration of the facts in regard to the liquor problem and indicates its only possible solution.

My twofold object in writing this book is to contribute something to the understanding of modern propaganda and of the liquor problem of today.

FLETCHER DOBYNS

Pasadena, California
January 1, 1940

Part One

How Repeal Was Put Over

Chapter One

The Association Against The Prohibition Amendment

WHEN the Eighteenth Amendment was adopted and became part of the Constitution of the United States, it was believed by a large majority of the people of the country that a great victory had been won; that a social disease had been forever stamped out, and that henceforth there would be no more "liquor problem." The victory had not been easily won. It had taken years, decades, generations to educate ourselves into believing that the liquor traffic should be banished.

Yet within the short space of only a few years the supporters of national prohibition were acutely aware of the fact that the battle had been only half won with the adoption of the amendment. They were awakening to the fact that the struggle for the proper enforcement of the amendment would have to be as realistic and uncompromising as had been the struggle for its adoption. They were beginning to realize that its widespread violation was the result not only of inefficient and corrupt administration, but also of the defects of the enforcement statute. A movement to correct these conditions had started and achieved important results. Prohibition agents had been placed under the jurisdiction of the Civil Service Commission, the responsibility for enforcement had been transferred from the treasury to the Department of Justice, violations of the law had been made felonies, and it had become possible to inflict adequate penalties in all cases. In 1928 the people had elected Mr. Hoover, who had given an unequivocal pledge that he would uphold and enforce the amendment, and he had appointed an attorney general who was making a sincere effort to fulfill that pledge. Referring to the Prohibition Bureau, the Wickersham Commission said: "Since the extension of the civil service laws over it, there has been continued improvement in organization and effort for enforcement, which is reflected in an attitude of greater confidence in the prohibition agents on the part of the United States attorneys and judges. . . . Only in the last few years has enforcement been reasonably emancipated from political interference."

The manner in which the opponents of the liquor traffic were beginning to face the facts and gird themselves for a decisive battle for real enforcement, is illustrated by the statements of three outstanding leaders of the prohibition movement: Canon William Sheafe Chase, superintendent of the International Reform Federation; Bishop James Cannon, Jr., chairman of the Board of Temperance and Social Service of the Methodist Episcopal Church, South; and Dr. Ernest H. Cherrington, general secretary of the World League Against Alcoholism. These men had been in the forefront of the battle for national prohibition and had strenuously opposed the timid and temporizing attitude of many of the dry leaders. Dr. Chase said:

> The Volstead Act is full of loopholes. The wets know the loopholes. The drys generally do not know them. They have accepted the wet propaganda that the Volstead Act is very drastic and despotic and that the experience of the dry states in enforcing prohibition was incorporated into the National Prohibition Act.

After stating the deficiences of the law, he continued:

> At least twenty-six amendments to the Volstead Act are needed to prevent evasion, remedy weakness, and stop nullification by the many devices invented and developed by enemies of the Eighteenth Amendment since the Volstead Act went into effect.[1]

Bishop Cannon and Dr. Cherrington also proposed a number of radical changes in the law and the method of its administration. If these suggestions had been adopted, the result would have been an enforcible statute.

The Wrecking Crew

The most powerful factor in the defeat of this movement for the proper enforcement of the prohibition law was the Association Against the Prohibition Amendment. On January 21, 1924, just four years after the Eighteenth Amendment went into effect, the Honorable Louis C. Cramton, addressing the national House of Representatives, said:

This day there meets in Washington the Association Against the Prohibition Amendment in a so-called face-the-facts conference. I would, therefore, call attention at this opportune time to some facts deserving consideration in connection with that association which has in its aims, its policies and its methods more possibilities of evil for the future political, industrial and moral welfare of our land than any other organization now in existence. It is an organization opposed to law enforcement, promoting, thriving upon and rejoicing at triumph of crime and disorder over law and order.

From its very beginning, the Association Against the Prohibition Amendment has proclaimed its nullification program. In its prospectus issued soon after the incorporation of the organization in April 1919, *before the wartime prohibition measure had gone into effect,* but some months after the Eighteenth Amendment had been ratified in the manner prescribed by the Constitution, it declared:

"This association has two immediate aims: (1) To prevent the country from going on a bone-dry basis on July 1, and (2) to make the Eighteenth Amendment forever inoperative."

It daily prophesies failure, justifies violation of the law, opposes enforcement, throws its influence on the side of lawlessness when it ought to be on the side of law and order.

The leader in the whole movement to discredit the law and make it "inoperative," as originally promised by it, is the Association Against the Prohibition Amendment.[2]

This is an exact statement of the origin, purposes and methods of this organization from the hour of its birth until its dissolution after the repeal of the Eighteenth Amendment. The statement was also profoundly prophetic of the corrupting influence the organization was to exert upon the political and moral life of the nation. The wartime prohibition measure provided that after July 1, 1919, and until the termination of demobilization, traffic in intoxicating liquors should be prohibited. The Eighteenth Amendment was ratified on January 16, 1919, but did not become effective until January 16, 1920. After both these measures had been adopted, and before either had become operative, the AAPA publicly announced that its purpose was to prevent the enforcement of a law that had been passed by Congress and to render forever inoperative a provision of the Constitution of the United States.

The motives and methods of the men behind this organization were well understood by those acquainted with the facts and were repeatedly and authoritatively exposed. But in 1930 the sinister character of the campaign they were conducting was established beyond reasonable doubt by direct and unimpeachable evidence — their own secret files,[3] which were seized by the Senate Lobby Investigation Committee.

Knights Errant of the Constitution

It was necessary, of course, that the members of this association should conceal their real motives and operate under the camouflage of a lofty and disinterested purpose. When their great propaganda machine got into full swing, we were told that the amendment was a failure, that it was responsible for bootlegging, drunkenness and crime, that it was one of the major causes of the depression. They solemnly demanded its repeal in the interest of law and order, political purity, true temperance, prosperity. When the organization was formed, however, the amendment had not yet gone into effect, and so this line of pretense was not available. The amendment had not yet proved to be unenforcible. One thing was certain, however: it would destroy the huge profits of the brewers, distillers and saloon-keepers, and their affiliates.

If the members of the association had announced that their purpose was to save the profits of the liquor interests, they would have been greeted with the contempt they deserved. They pretended, however, that their purpose was to save the Constitution of the United States. They declared that " the principal business and object of the association shall be to educate its members as to the fundamental provisions, objects and purposes of the Constitution of the United States " and " to publicly present arguments bearing upon the necessity for keeping the powers of the several states separated from those of the federal government." The final report of the association states that " Captain William H. Stayton, nationally known as the father of the repeal movement, the first president of this organization and subsequently, until the time of its dissolution, chairman of its board of national directors, . . . had formed very definite ideas as to the encroachment by the federal government upon the powers vested in the states."

We cannot look directly into the mind of " the father of the repeal movement," but there is no record of his having shown any concern for the Constitution until the Eighteenth Amendment threatened the profits of the liquor interests. He testified that he and his compatriots who organized the association had all been employes of the Navy League.[4] Some may have forgotten the record of the Navy League. Among its founders were J. Pierpont Morgan, George Westinghouse, John J. Astor, Charles M. Schwab. Its ostensible purpose was to promote the security of " the greatest, freest and happiest nation in the world." Its actions proved that its real purpose was to induce the taxpayers of that happy nation to pour hundreds of millions of dollars into the pockets of its members. It was denounced by President Hoover for distorting facts and conducting a campaign of misinformation. The final verdict of the country in regard to it was expressed by Senator Capper as follows:

> The Navy League includes in its membership those who sell steel and others commercially interested in the profits from armament building. These have a selfish interest to override their loyalty to their country and their own regard for the truth. The fact is, we have had this same kind of fight from the Navy League — false statements, misconstructions of government reports, half-truths — every time we have

tried to hold down expenditures for the navy to a reasonable limit. . . . The pity of it is that in the past the Navy League has imposed on the public, especially along the seaboard, as a patriotic organization. The country should be grateful to President Hoover for having torn off its mask and shown it to be the greedy commercial organization that it is — seeking to make excessive profits from the government for steel and shipbuilding companies under the plea of super-patriotism.[5]

After its exposure, the Navy League fell into a state of innocuous desuetude. During its halcyon days, Stayton was its executive secretary, and Gordon C. Hinckley, who became secretary of the AAPA, was one of its employes.[6]

Further light is thrown upon the question of the sincerity of Captain Stayton by the fact that the names of the following stalwart defenders of the Constitution appear on the lists filed in Washingon of contributors to the campaign fund of the AAPA: Pennsylvania Central Brewing Company, Loewer's Gambrinus Brewing Company, The Garden City Brewery, The Buffalo Brewing Company, Perot and Son, The Superior Beverage Company, Flock's Brewing Company, John A. Trainer, The Erie Brewing Company, The Lion Brewery, The Schaefer Brewing Company, John F. Trommer, Jacob Ruppert, Gottfried Krueger Brewing Company, The Joseph Hensler Brewing Company, California State Brewers' Association, F. & M. Schaefer Brewing Company, Piel Brothers, Fred Pabst, Hugh Murray, George Ehret, Jr., W. Fred Anheuser, Obermyer and Liebman, R. A. Huber, care of Anheuser-Busch Company, Patterson Brewing and Malting Company, Chr. Heinrich Brewing Company, Daeufer-Liederman Brewing Company, L. F. Neweiler's Sons (Brewers), Hugh F. Fox (secretary, U. S. Brewers' Association), William Hamm, William Peter Brewing Corporation, Reno Brewing Company, Anheuser-Busch, Inc., Francis Perot & Sons Malting Company, Union Brewing Company, New York Malt Roasting Company, Philip Schneider Brewing Company, Julius Stroh (Products), Froedlert Grain & Malting Company.[7]

In October 1922, the Wisconsin Malters' Club sent out the following appeal for funds:

GENTLEMEN: In view of the fact that the Wisconsin division of the Association Against the Prohibition Amendment has done such wonderful work during the last primaries, having been positively instrumental in securing eight wet out of the ten congressional candidates, and all of which facts were again praised and confirmed by Mr. Dietrichs of Chicago, at our meeting held yesterday, it was unanimously decided to give them further financial aid in order that the association might be able to complete the work they have set out to do.

To this end we permitted ourselves to be assessed for half of the amount contributed at our previous meeting, namely, at the rate of five cents per 1,000 bushels of steeping capacity. In as far as the money is needed now, will you not be kind enough to forward immediately to the undersigned your check? [8]

In June 1926, the Gottfried Krueger Brewing Company, of Newark, sent out the following letter:

GENTLEMEN: We are deeply interested in the Association Against the Prohibition Amendment and have been asked to solicit donations from our many creditors who would be benefited if the present prohibition law were modified.

This money would be used for the continued support of the association, and we know of no way in which prohibition could be better combated. The association is one of the strongest of its kind in the country and we earnestly believe that it should be heartily supported by those who would be benefited if the Volstead Act were repealed. If you are interested in the work of this association, kindly return the enclosed card with your check to our office.

Trusting you may see how all would be benefited if the association were supported. . . .[9]

The final report of the association lists among its achievements "the defeat for Congress of Andrew Volstead, father of the national prohibition act," which "was also an accomplishment of the year 1922 which our membership helped to attain."

Why was Volstead marked for slaughter? Because he had drafted a law the purpose of which was the enforcement of the Constitution of the United States. Why were eight dry congressmen defeated in Wisconsin? Because they voted to uphold the Constitution and laws of their country. Why should the association be supported by "those who would be benefited if the Volstead Act were repealed"? Because this would enable them to profit by the nullification of the Constitution. These were some of the ways in which Stayton and his associates showed their deep concern for the integrity of the Constitution.

Golden Age of the Association

An adequate understanding of the significance of the repeal movement would require a knowledge of the history of the activities of this association during the first seven years of its existence. That history should be written, but there is not space for it here. It is a record of nullification, violation of law, replacement of honest public officials by those who were dishonest, repeal of state enforcement laws, intimidation, political lynchings, systematic and ceaseless dissemination of falsehoods, in every way possible creating conditions under which the amendment could not survive.

The year 1926 marked the beginning of a new era in the history of the AAPA. In that year, although Stayton remained as president, the control and management of the association were taken over by a group of multimillionaires under the leadership of Pierre, Irénée and Lammot du Pont, John J. Raskob, vice-president of the Du Pont Company, and Charles H. Sabin. The people have become familiar with the wealth and political activities of the Du Ponts and Raskob.

Mr. Sabin became chairman of the committee that raised the campaign fund, and later was elected treasurer of the association. On October 12, 1933, the New York *Times* said:

> Mr. Sabin was chairman of the board of the Guaranty Company of New York as well as of the trust company, and was president and a member of the board of the Guaranty Safe Deposit Company. He was treasurer and a director of the Sutton Place South Corporation, chairman of the board of the Intercontinental Rubber Company, and a trustee of the Mackay companies.

It then gives the names of sixteen large corporations of which he was a director.

The success of this group in raising money is illustrated by the following financial statement of the association filed with the clerk of the House of Representatives:

FINANCIAL STATEMENT
Receipts and Expenditures
January 1 to December 31, 1930

Cash in bank and on hand, Jan. 1, 1930	$ 30,725.56
Receipts	790,892.56
(Loans of $112,000.00 included)	
Total	$821,618.12
Expenditures	818,723.41
Cash in bank and on hand Jan. 1, 1931	$ 2,894.71 [10]

The source of this fund is indicated by the names of a few of the contributors.

For the year 1928

Du Pont, P. S., Du Pont Building, Wilmington, Del.	$43,332
Du Pont, Irénée, Du Pont Building, Wilmington, Del.	21,083
Fisher, Fred J., Cass and Boulevard, Detroit, Mich.	25,000
Du Pont, Lammot, Du Pont Building, Wilmington, Del.	17,083
Harkness, Edward S., 54 Madison Ave., New York, N. Y.	17,083
Raskob, John J., 230 Park Ave., New York, N. Y.	17,083
Sabin, Charles H., 140 Broadway, New York, N. Y.	10,083
Phillips, Thomas W., 205 North Main St., Butler, Pa.	4,583
Krueger Brewing Co., Gottfried, Newark, N. J.	2,700
Pabst, Fred, 917 Chestnut Street, Milwaukee, Wis.	2,000
Schaefer Brewing Co., F. & M., 2 South Ninth St., Brooklyn, N. Y.	1,550
California State Brewers' Association, 944 Russ Building, San Francisco, Calif.	1,500
Hensler Brewing Co., Newark, N. J.	1,500
Ruppert, Col. Jacob, 1639 Third Ave., New York, N. Y.	1,500
Anheuser, W. Fred, 1553 South Grand St., St. Louis, Mo.	1,000
Busch, August A., St. Louis, Mo.	1,000

For the year 1929

Du Pont, Lammot	$30,000
Harkness, Edward S.	30,000
Johnson, Eldridge R.	25,000
Crane, R. T., Jr.	25,000
James, Arthur Curtiss	25,000
Du Pont, Irénée	17,500
Du Pont, P. S.	17,500
Mather, Samuel	10,000
Phillips, Thomas W.	10,000
Sabin, Charles H.	10,000
Pabst, Fred	5,250

For the year 1930

Du Pont, Irénée	$30,000
Raskob, John J.	17,500
Du Pont, Lammot	17,500
Harkness, Edward J.	17,500
Du Pont, Pierre	12,500
Crane, Richard T.	12,500
James, Arthur Curtiss	12,500
Sabin, Charles H.	7,500 [11]

On September 5, 1928, Mr. Stayton wrote the following letter:

Maj. Henry H. Curran
New York, N. Y.

My dear Major: I fear you are a bit skeptical as to my statement that we have had recent contributions totaling $130,000 from a single congressional district.

I was referring to the state of Delaware, which is one congressional district.

The three Messrs. du Pont and Mr. Raskob are all Delawareans; they have each subscribed $25,000 to the directors' fund, which makes an even $100,000; they have each subscribed $5,000 to the two special funds, making another $20,000; and Mr. Pierre du Pont has given more than $10,000 to the recent Delaware questionnaire project; so the total is something above $130,000.

William H. Stayton

On January 24, 1930, the president of the association wrote a letter to Mr. Percy S. Straus, in which he said:

Our chief plan at present, in impressing our dry Congress with the fact that the country is mostly wet, is the holding of state-wide referendums such as we last year carried on successfully in Wisconsin, and before then in Montana, Nevada and New York. This year Massachusetts will come first, with other states afterwards as fast as we can reach them.

For this there will be required over a million dollars to be used this year, of which a little over $200,000 has already been subscribed by a few of our directors, Messrs. Pierre S. du Pont, Edward S. Harkness, Richard T. Crane, Charles H. Sabin, Irénée du Pont, Commodore Arthur Curtiss James, Lammot du Pont, John J. Raskob, Eldridge R. Johnson, and Honorable Thomas W. Phillips, Jr.

In 1929, the following letter, signed by Mr. Stayton, was mailed to " 100 Boyd's millionaires," May 13:

. . . The fight has not been won. To win it will still take time, a mighty effort, and the expenditure of much money.

I hope you will consider it a service which you can render to the welfare of our country and the preservation of our cherished institutions to contribute for the carrying on of this work. Your generous contribution may be mailed to Charles H. Sabin, treasurer, 21 East Fortieth St., New York, N. Y.[12]

At the time of the Senate investigation, Mr. Henry H. Curran had become president of the AAPA. When he was on the stand, Senator Robinson of Indiana stated that, according to the records, 75 per cent of the entire fund of the association for the previous year had been contributed by fifty-three men. The testimony continued:

SENATOR ROBINSON. Now do these 53 contributors represent this vast majority of the American people that you were talking about that were in open revolt?

MR. CURRAN. No, Senator, they do not. That is the same old thing we talked about yesterday. . . .

SENATOR ROBINSON. And you got your money, 75 per cent of it, last year, from the pockets of 53 millionaires.

MR. CURRAN. What of it?

SENATOR ROBINSON. I am only mentioning that 53 men are furnishing you the sinews of war for your campaign, and 53 men does not constitute a vast majority.[13]

The personnel of the association's general staff bears out Senator Robinson's comment. The 1931 report of the association shows that its general staff was composed of the following men:

W. H. Stayton
Chairman of the Board
Henry H. Curran
President
Charles H. Sabin
Treasurer
Emmett Dougherty
Secretary

Executive Committee
Pierre S. du Pont, *Chairman*

Robert K. Cassatt
Benedict Crowell
Henry H. Curran
Irénée du Pont
Grayson M. P. Murphy
Charles H. Sabin
W. H. Stayton
James W. Wadsworth, Jr.

Finance Committee
Lammot du Pont, *Chairman*

Matthew C. Brush
Robert K. Cassatt
Henry H. Curran
Joseph R. Hamlen
C. Wilbur Miller
John J. Raskob
Charles H. Sabin
William P. Smith

The money which these men raised directly represented only a fraction of the resources at their disposal. Through ownership, advertising and financing, they controlled the policy of a large number of the most powerful daily newspapers and widely read magazines. They were able, therefore, to command the free use of millions of dollars' worth of space in these publications for the dissemination of wet propaganda. This fact was recognized by the president of the association in his final report:

A great debt is due to the liberal press of the nation which has been a factor of overwhelming importance in the accomplishment of repeal. Referring to it, I said in a recent speech in New York: " As on no other question of modern times, without regard to partisan politics, a large proportion of the powerful and influential newspapers and periodicals of America have united in a program of education which has had profound effect. In season and out of season, by editorial and by cartoon, the press has brought home to the American people the fallacy of the Eighteenth Amendment. And with all due regard to the work done by this association under the leadership of Captain Stayton, with the highest credit to Mrs. Sabin and her group of valued women, with full recognition of the other organizations working for repeal, I do not hesitate to assert that save for what the press has done, we would not be celebrating victory tonight and the possibility of such a celebration might have been delayed many, many years."

The association was also able to obtain the free distribution of a vast amount of its propaganda through its political retainers. It was a feature of its highly developed technique to put its propaganda out in the form of statements, speeches and articles by officeholders who were the beneficiaries of its money and influence. In this way, its source and motive were concealed, it became " news " and as such was consumed by an innocent and unsuspecting public. This went on constantly in every part of the country, the sounding-boards ranging from village aldermen to United States senators and candidates for the presidency. The following instances will illustrate the technique.

James M. Beck had been solicitor general in the regime of Harding and Daugherty. He went to Philadelphia and became the vestpocket congressman of Boss William Vare. He posed as a great constitutional lawyer and, with a great affectation of sincerity, demanded the repeal of the Eighteenth Amendment. On January 23, 1930, Henry B. Joy, a director of the association, telegraphed Mr. Stayton as follows:

> Get Hon. James M. Beck to make speech in Congress in defense of Constitution. He can do it better than any other and carry tremendous weight. Wickersham's address shows for first time they are forced into defensive position. Keep them there. Assume offensive and keep it.[14]

On January 29, Mr. Stayton wrote Mr. Joy:

MY DEAR HARRY: I had a talk with Mr. Beck yesterday and he is going to make the constitutional speech as per your suggestion.[15]

On February 6, Mr. Stayton sent the following telegram to the New York *Evening Post* and the New York *Times:*

I have just read advance sheet Congressman Beck's speech to be delivered Friday. He points out that the Whig party died because it tried to perform its constitutional duty and enforce the fugitive slave law founded on the Constitution but obnoxious to the people, because it interfered with human freedom, and he warns the Republican party to beware. If your policy would permit an editorial on this matter it would greatly aid our plans.[16]

Senator James W. Wadsworth was a member of the board of directors of the AAPA. When Mr. Curran, the president of the association, was on the stand, he gave the following testimony:

SENATOR WALSH (Montana). And what magazines have you contributed articles to?

MR. CURRAN. Let us see. Senator Wadsworth contributed an article to the *North American Review* which was published about four or five months ago, and, oh — maybe this is what you have in mind, sir. . . .

SENATOR WALSH. . . . Senator Wadsworth is one of your directors?

MR. CURRAN. Yes.

SENATOR WALSH. What did your association have to do with the article?

MR. CURRAN. Why, we wrote it.

SENATOR WALSH. Who was the author of it?

MR. CURRAN. Senator Wadsworth. We wrote it.

SENATOR WALSH. What do you mean by saying, " We wrote it "?

MR. CURRAN. It was written by — this is a shame — it was written by Mr. Samuel Morse, who is of our organization, and it was corrected and revised and approved or disapproved by Senator Wadsworth and sent to the *North American Review*. . . .

SENATOR ROBINSON (Indiana). The man who wrote the article, what do you pay him?

MR. CURRAN. $6,600 a year.[17]

Mr. Curran thought that it was " a shame " that he was compelled to expose the fact that, in order to give it greater weight and publicity value, Senator Wadsworth had signed an article prepared by one of the hired writers of wet propaganda.

An outstanding achievement of the association was its capture of the national machinery of the Democratic party. This was accomplished through the influence of Al Smith. As the representative of Tammany Hall, Smith was a rabid wet and a staunch supporter of the association's program. When he was nominated for president, he appointed as chairman of the Democratic national committee John J. Raskob, one of the most powerful and influential members of the association. Raskob was a Republican but he had two qualifications for his new position: he wanted to " rid the country of the damnable affliction of prohibition " and he could open the money bags and secure the support of the millionaires connected with the association.

After the election of 1928, he appointed Jouett Shouse, who later became president of the AAPA, chairman of the Democratic national executive committee. As will be pointed out more fully later, Raskob and Shouse devoted the next four years to the work of wresting the Democratic party from the control of men of the type of Bryan, Glass, Hull, Sheppard and other dry leaders, and turning it over to the Tammany organizations of New York and other northern cities which were determined that the Eighteenth Amendment should be repealed.

Great Propaganda Machine

After the Du Ponts took over the association in 1926, it built up a great propaganda machine which for power and efficiency surpassed any organization of its kind that this country had ever known. Motives and methods will be considered later, but the magnitude of its work is indicated by the following passage from the annual report of the association for 1930:

> In the general increase of publication concerning the fight against prohibition, information from this department has retained and considerably increased its place throughout 1930. News publication, based

on our information, shows three times as many readers reached in 1930 as in 1928, and over 55 per cent more than in 1929. Available clippings on file in this office prove that six hundred millions of copies of newspapers, containing conspicuous publication of our news, were read in almost every community throughout the country during the year; 153,617,704 copies of magazines and periodicals containing articles and editorials attacking prohibition have been read by the public similarly.

Seventy news stories were issued in the year. These covered five pamphlets published by the research department, various political situations in which we were interested and statements by officers of our association. Although some of these were of purely local interest, actual clippings on file show that each of them reached an average of almost 9,000,000 readers.

Exceptional opportunities for making our information facilities available to the Washington correspondents were presented in connection with the House Judiciary Committee hearings and the Senate Lobby Committee's investigation. Every effort was made to provide the newspaper men with advance copies of statements to be made and to give them information as to the various witnesses. Published results on our side of these hearings were too voluminous to be accurately tabulated — we have on hand 15,000 clippings which we have been unable to file or record — but the number that have been checked and filed show a combined circulation of nearly 200,000,000.

More than 4,000,000 copies of books, pamphlets, reports, reprints, letters and leaflets were distributed from our office in 1930. They dealt with economic, constitutional, political, and practical sides of our work. The mailing lists used have ensured wide and effective dissemination and they also prevent waste and duplication.

The Authors and Artists Committee gained 172 members during 1930, and now numbers 578 men and women. Day after day Mr. Shuler, as executive secretary, has been called upon for information by members and other writers. He has also read many manuscripts of books, articles, plays, stories or pamphlets, whose authors have asked advice or assistance.

With the cooperation and consent of the newspapers and artists concerned, a collection of cartoons attacking and ridiculing prohibition was published and widely distributed.

As representatives of the Authors and Artists Committee, of which Irvin S. Cobb is the chairman, Channing Pollock, Owen Johnson and

Wallace Irwin went before the House Judiciary Committee and spoke most effectively at the recent hearings.

Pierre du Pont a Prohibitionist Prior to 1926

If the members of this association had thrown their ability, wealth and power on the side of law and order, the liquor rebellion would have been suppressed and the work of strengthening the enforcement statute and improving its administration would have continued. It is one of the tragedies of our history that the entire weight of their influence was cast on the side of the criminal liquor dealers, the underworld, Tammany politics, tax evasion and public deception. There cannot be the slightest doubt that it was their seven years' campaign that brought about the conditions which made it possible for President Roosevelt and his political allies to give prohibition its final and fatal thrust. We must know why and how these men accomplished this result if we would understand the liquor problem of today.

The Du Ponts were, of course, thoroughly familiar with the evils of the liquor traffic and the economic and social benefits to be derived from its suppression. In 1928 Professor Irving Fisher of Yale University wrote to Pierre du Pont a letter in which he said:

It was reported concerning the Du Pont de Nemours Company, in a hearing before the United States Senate subcommittee of the judiciary and as part of a confidential file submitted in evidence November 20, 1918, belonging to Hugh F. Fox, secretary of the U. S. Brewers' Association, that the advertising manager of the company " explained how for many years past the Du Ponts have absolutely prohibited the use of intoxicants by their employees, and, now with the rush of war orders, the prohibition ban has been drawn even closer." Camillus Kessler, employed by Mr. Fox, reported to him: " After calling on several of the men in the offices in Wilmington, I took the ferry and went across the river to Penn's Grove where one of the largest of the Du Pont factories is located. There I talked with the chief of police, some of the men who work in the high explosive department, and one of the guards. They all assured me that there was not a drink to be had in Penn's Grove. The only bar in the town had been closed by the Du Ponts, and if any workman wanted a drink of any kind, he would have to go to Wilmington or some other neighboring town.

"It is reported if a guard is seen taking a drink off duty, he is immediately discharged. If a workman comes to work with the slightest indication of liquor on his breath, he is not allowed to work. From all that I could see, prohibition could not be more effectively enforced than it is in Penn's Grove. I was informed by the officials and by men who had worked in the other factories of the company that the same conditions exist in all the Du Pont Company factories."

In response to Professor Fisher's inquiry as to his attitude since becoming the head of the repeal movement, Mr. du Pont said:

If certain work involving danger to life and property requires absolute sobriety, I cannot find fault with the employer refusing to employ a man who shows any signs of contact with alcohol, when he reports for work, and, in fact, where the employer may be held liable for the action of the man employed, he may, if he chooses, properly decline to employ a man who uses intoxicants at any time. This is no different from refusing to employ a man whose sight or hearing is in any way defective for jobs requiring great keenness in those senses. It is purely a matter of choice of the man most suitable for the job.[18]

Until 1926, Mr. du Pont was an advocate of prohibition. When Mr. Stayton was on the stand, Senator Robinson of Indiana asked if it was not true that fifteen of the twenty-eight directors of General Motors were members of the Association Against the Prohibition Amendment.

MR. STAYTON. Yes, sir; 15 of the 28.

SENATOR ROBINSON. American directors?

MR. STAYTON. Yes, sir.

SENATOR ROBINSON. Would you not think it would be a fair statement to say the association is a Du Pont subsidiary?

MR. STAYTON. I would not. Mr. du Pont for five years was on the other side. For five years after this organization was formed, Mr. Pierre du Pont was a dry.

SENATOR ROBINSON. But the Du Ponts have largely for the last three or four years financed it, haven't they?

MR. STAYTON. I should say beginning in 1928 they have contributed a large proportion.

SENATOR ROBINSON. Their interest in this is certainly as great as it is in many others of their subsidiaries.

MR. STAYTON. No; I think more.

SENATOR ROBINSON. What?

MR. STAYTON. More, sir.

SENATOR ROBINSON. More?

MR. STAYTON. I think Mr. Pierre du Pont's interest in this is greater than it is in anything else in the United States.[19]

Why the Du Ponts Went Wet

Prior to the war, the income tax was not very onerous. In 1916 the tax on individual incomes was $173,386,694, and on corporations $171,805,150, or a total of $345,191,844. After the war, however, the figures reached dizzying heights, as the following table will show:

Total Individual and Corporate Income Tax

1921	$1,420,962,538
1923	1,600,758,303
1925	1,904,886,389
1926	1,962,268,033
1928	2,348,396,179 [20]

In 1928 the income tax on individuals amounted to $1,163,254,-037, and the corporation tax was $1,184,142,142. This was a serious matter to the Du Ponts as their collective fortune was one of the largest in the world. Their company had made a net profit of $228,731,000 from 1915 to 1918, and paid salaries and bonuses of $228,015,000. These huge profits had been invested in the manufacture of a large number of other products, including chemicals, paints, varnishes, rubber goods, cellophane, rayon, and in the purchase of 10,000,000 shares of the stock of the General Motors Corporation. In 1934, the Du Pont Company owned and operated more than 60 plants in 22 states. In 1935, the Securities Exchange Commission revealed the fact that members of the Du Pont family controlled shares with an approximate market value of $310,000,-

000 in E. I. du Pont de Nemours & Company.[21] This family faced the necessity of turning over to the government fabulous sums in the form of corporation, personal and estate taxes. Something had to be done about it.

That they never permitted sentimental consideration of the public welfare or love of country to interfere with their pursuit of profits is shown by the following extract from the report of the Senate committee that investigated the munitions industry:

The War Department became convinced that there was desperate need for vast additional powder manufacturing capacity in the fall of 1917. The Du Pont Company, by its own admission, controlled "about 90 per cent of the smokeless powder producing capacity of the United States." It had constructed the large plants from which the Allied governments had been supplied during the period of our neutrality. So it had practically a monopoly of the construction and operating experience necessary for the contemplated plant. Naturally the government turned to this company for assistance. It could not do otherwise. Yet for three months the building of this powder factory was delayed because the Du Pont Company would not accept the liberal contract terms offered it. When asked about the critical character for the prosecution of the war of the period when this delay occurred, Lieutenant Colonel Harris testified:

"It is hard to say which was the most critical time of the war, but that was a very critical time."

The government offered to pay "every dollar of expense," to advance $1,000,000 on account of profit, and to pay additional profit as determined by arbitration. This was rejected by the company's board of directors upon the recommendation of Mr. Pierre du Pont. He wrote that "we cannot assent to allowing our own patriotism to interfere with our duties as trustees" for the stockholders. At the time, he was one of the ten largest holders of the company's common stock.

The government threatened to build the plant itself, but it had no real alternative to accepting the terms of the Du Ponts. A man was appointed to undertake the work who apparently had no prior experience in powder manufacture. The Du Pont Company refused to cooperate in assisting the government effort. Finally a contract was signed under which the Du Pont Engineering Company, a wholly owned subsidiary of the Du Pont Company, built the Old Hickory powder factory without risk to itself, and made a profit on operation of the plant amounting to $1,961,560. If the war had continued, the profit per year would have been about $15,000,000.[22]

A subsequent transaction proves that Du Pont and Raskob did not allow even common honesty to interfere with their pursuit of wealth. Shortly before the end of 1929 each sold stock to the other at a price below the purchase price. Immediately after the first of the year the transactions were reversed, leaving the parties precisely where they were before the sales. In their tax returns these sales were treated as losses and made the basis for large reductions in the amount of income tax owed to the federal government. After more than two years of investigation, the commissioner of internal revenue charged:

. . . that arbitrary market quotations were capriciously selected by Raskob and Du Pont for the sales; that actual market prices played no part; that sales made November 15, 1929, were antedated to November 13 to get the benefit of lower prices for loss purposes; that no actual funds were used, it being agreed that neither would be out the use of cash; that the sales to each other were intentionally made in almost the same amounts so that neither would lose cash; that their checks were matched and deposited together; that, pursuant to agreement at time of sales, they resold to each other all the identical stocks purchased from each other and the identical certificates issued therefor; that they used a pretended " short sale " transaction to balance the matter between them at the end, emerging only $46.86 apart upon cross sales totaling $29,766,754.86; that post-dated checks and letters were used to reverse on January 27 the transaction of December 26; and that a note for $700,000 given by Raskob to Du Pont in connection with the resale of January 6 was a sham, while one for $1,080,000 purportedly given by Raskob to Du Pont on a " short sale " did not exist.

After an exhaustive review of the evidence, the United States Board of Tax Appeals said:

Men do not conduct themselves and accomplish the end as did these parties toward each other, and attain an end so advantageous to their fortunes, without a common understanding. This design was too complete to be without designer. The record before us bares its transparency.

Upon consideration of all the evidence, we hold that neither of the pretended sales of stocks between Du Pont and Raskob was a bona fide complete disposition thereof, and did not possess that reality indispensable to sales contemplated by the statute as to the deduction of realized losses, but that both were contrived and consummated through mutual understanding and agreement between the two parties for the reacquisition of the stocks originally owned by each, by the reversal of the sales in the manner in which they were reversed, agreement in the first sale inhering as a part of the original plan and transaction, and in the second sale occurring at the time of the sale or within thirty days thereafter. That formula of tax escape cannot be approved. The deductions of losses from such purported sales are therefore disallowed.[23]

This means, in the language of the street, that these men made the deliberate attempt through a fake transaction to cheat the government out of approximately $2,000,000.

Why did they change their attitude toward prohibition? The record proves conclusively that it was because, as a result of cold calculation, they had reached the conclusion that if the liquor traffic were brought back and taxed, it would make possible the repeal of the federal income tax, and, as during the war, they did not intend to let patriotism interfere with profit. Their entire course of conduct proves this, but fortunately we do not have to rely on inference. In a circular which he sent out to the large income taxpayers of the country, Pierre du Pont said:

As our average tax collections for the years 1923–26 from individuals and corporations were $1,817,000,000, resulting in a considerable surplus, it is fair to say that the British liquor policy applied in the United States would permit of the total abolition of the income tax both personal and corporate. Or this liquor tax would be sufficient to pay off the entire debt of the United States, interest and principal, in a little less than fifteen years.

At the lobby hearing, Senator Caraway produced a memorandum from the files of the association, dated October 26, 1926, and read from it the following statement: " Irénée du Pont's statement that one of his companies would save $10,000,000 in corporation tax if we should have, say, the British tax on beer." Then the following occurred:

SENATOR CARAWAY. Where did you get that statement?

MR. STAYTON. I got the statement from him but what was in his mind further than the statement I don't know.

SENATOR CARAWAY. The thing I am getting to is, Mr. Irénée du Pont is one of your heaviest contributors?

MR. STAYTON. Yes.

SENATOR CARAWAY. And he thought that if you could get the Eighteenth Amendment repealed, that he could lift $10,000,000 tax off his corporation?

MR. STAYTON. That $10,000,000 of taxes would be lifted from that corporation, yes, sir.

SENATOR CARAWAY. That would be a strong consideration.

MR. STAYTON. I should think so, yes, sir; since he was an officer of the corporation.[24]

It should be recalled that this was only the tax for one year on one of the provinces of the far-flung industrial empire of the Du Ponts, and it did not include their personal income taxes.

How Big Income Taxpayers were Enlisted for the War on Prohibition

The other pillars of the association were no more altruistic than the Du Ponts. Thomas W. Phillips, Jr., president of T. W. Phillips Gas & Oil Company, was a member of the board of directors of the association, and closely associated with the Du Ponts in its work. In a letter addressed to Pierre S. du Pont, he said:

I am enclosing a copy of a letter just written to Justice Stone, which I am sure will be of interest, and wish especially to call attention to the article to which I therein referred in the April number of *Plain Talk* by J. Hopkinson Smith, entitled "Is Prohibition Constitutional?" Please regard the letter to Justice Stone as confidential beyond the executive committee of the association.

Recently Major Curran had a long interview in the New York *Tribune* in which I am glad to see he called special attention to the fact that if it were not for the expense connected with enforcing prohibition, and the loss of revenue occasioned by the Eighteenth Amendment, the income taxes could be eliminated entirely or greatly reduced. For some time past I have been intending to write to him, Captain Stayton and you suggesting that one of the most effective means of carrying on the campaign at this particular moment would be to have a well prepared letter featuring this point mailed out to either all of the income taxpayers or at least to those who are assessed with heavy surtaxes.

As I look upon this matter, I realize that prohibition has indirectly cost me already several hundred thousand dollars; and, of course, if it continues indefinitely, the amount that I will be assessed on account of this religious and reform fanaticism will mount into the seven-figure column. I do not know how this strikes other people, but it is very irritating to me. . . .

Perhaps the quickest and most effective way of bringing religious, not necessarily Christian, people to their senses, is to stage a demonstration of what their attitude is doing and will do to the financial support of their work. If, for example, all or a large part of the heavily assessed income taxpayers would take the view that the money indirectly taken from them through taxes on account of prohibition, plus the amount that their consciences compelled them to donate for the purpose of fighting prohibition, not only left very little or nothing for the churches and church work, but had a tendency to sour them and their whole families on the churches, and those responsible for the attitude of the church organizations.

I am sending copies of this letter to Major Curran and Captain Stayton.[25]

A memorandum from the files of the association which was read into the record contained the following:

October 26, 1926

Memorandum concerning suggestions of points which may properly be considered in the preparation of a series of form letters with the thought of trying to cover the whole subject in a series of, say, five letters.

Irénée du Pont's statement that one of his companies would save $10,000,000 in corporation tax if we should have, say, the British tax on beer.

In 1914 the brewers paid taxes on 66,000,000 barrels of beer. If we should have back the right to manufacture beer, if we should manufacture just as much as we did in 1914, and if we should tax it at the British rate, the income would be $1,320,000,000, or more than the net amount received from income and corporation taxes. Note too that this tax would be practically all net for it would be a stamp tax and there would be no scandals concerning rebates and no snoopers in business offices examining books.

If the taxes should be taken off corporations, there would be a rise in stock values and all owners of stocks would profit accordingly.

I suppose we might want to say something to the effect that a man would save personal income taxes.

Do you realize that Congress has power to at once legalize a glass of mild, wholesome beer? And, that the workingman and others would willingly pay a tax of three cents per glass and that that amount (based on past consumption) would enable the federal government to get rid of the burdensome corporation taxes and income taxes and to take the snoopers and spies out of offices and homes? . . .

State and municipal taxes as well as federal taxes have been greatly increased by the prohibition law. A beer tax would lead to sobriety and would be willingly paid, and it is one of the few taxes that is willingly paid. . . .

An argument that might perhaps appeal to business men is that if we had wines the purchase of them would lead to revival of prosperity in Europe and lead to the payment of the debts due us and to an increase in our trade with Europe.

Many employers expected more output on Monday morning in consequence of the prohibition law. Most of them find that they are not getting it and those that still believe they are getting it, find that their increased taxes more than eat up the profits derived from the increased output.

The Associated Press dispatches of August 25 of this year show that Great Britain collected $682,000,000 in liquor taxes and she had less than 25,000,000 barrels of beer, whereas our output at the pre-war rate would be about twice as high as that of Great Britain.

W. H. Stayton

In a memorandum dated October 25, 1926, Mr. Stayton says:

I have selected by hand-picked method the names of about 2,000 men who pay income taxes on incomes of $100,000 or more each. . . .

Wherever I have written a series of five letters, I have tried to lay the whole business out in advance so that you might in one letter, for example, let the men know who we were, and in another letter let them know what they stand for, and let them know how their pocketbook and personal interests will be involved in the hope of covering the entire scope in five letters.

The nature of the letters is illustrated by the following passage from a letter sent to Mr. Frank C. Brophy of Phoenix, Arizona:

For example, the treasury department figures show that there were nine individuals in Arizona who in 1925 had incomes of $90,000 and over. Naturally, I do not know who these individuals are, but I expect you can identify at least several of them. Based on a modification of the Volstead Act and the adoption of the proposed beer or beer and natural wine tax, each of these individuals would be relieved of the payment of an average of more than $20,000 a year tax.

In a memorandum dated October 8, 1927, Mr. Stayton says:

We are sending out, I understand, a good many letters to voluntary committees and the question now of the contents of these letters seems to me to be of prime importance.

I have not come to any conclusion at all about the matters, but I suggest for your consideration that the following things, if practicable, be mentioned in the various letters:

1. That we are now proceeding by the referendum route; that we can make our budget definite because it takes 10 cents per voter, etc.

2. I suggest that you consider whether it would be wise if you would ask a person to give us one per cent of what he pays for income tax and then give him a little income tax argument à la the Murphy plan.

Camouflage

In their struggle to save themselves hundreds of millions of dollars by substituting for an income tax a liquor tax to be paid by the masses, these men operated under carefully prepared camouflage, the nature of which is indicated by the following resolution:

RESOLUTION ADOPTED BY THE NATIONAL EXECUTIVE COMMITTEE OF THE ASSOCIATION AGAINST THE PROHIBITION AMENDMENT

Whereas, the Constitution of the United States, as established by the Fathers, delegated to the federal government only such powers as in their very nature should be federal and not state, and under that distribution of powers our country enjoyed progress and stability for a hundred and thirty years; and

Whereas, the Eighteenth Amendment is misplaced in the federal Constitution, in violation of the fundamental American right of local self-government in local affairs, and in surrender to the federal authorities of police duties over the habits and the conduct of individuals which belong of right to the states; and

Whereas, national prohibition under this amendment has been the source of intolerable wrongs, having undermined our federal system of government, robbed our citizens of constitutional rights, fostered excessive drinking of strong intoxicants, bred corruption and hypocrisy, caused ruthless killing of men, women and children, sown disrespect for law and order, and flooded our country with untaxed and illicit liquor; therefore be it

Resolved, that the Association Against the Prohibition Amendment demands redress of these wrongs through restoration to the several states of the right of their people to enact such liquor laws as they may respectively choose, the abolition of the old-time saloon having paved the way for sound and enlightened legislation by them for the control, or, if they wish, for the prohibition of the liquor trade, provided that such legislation shall not conflict with the duty of the federal government to protect each state against violation of its laws by citizens of other states; and be it therefore further

Resolved, that the Eighteenth Amendment must be repealed.

The secret files and the public performance of the AAPA brand this resolution as a swindle. Its members professed great solicitude for the Constitution while they were practicing and preaching its nullification and doing everything in their power to prevent its enforcement. They did more than any body of men in our history to destroy respect for the Constitution. They professed solicitude for local self-government while with every resource at their command they were assisting liquor outlaws to overrun states and local communities and make it impossible for them to protect the health and morals of their people. They pretended to be concerned about lawlessness while they were engaged in a vast conspiracy, the object of which was to bring about an open rebellion against the Constitution and laws of the country, in order to destroy respect for a law they did not want and thereby bring about its repeal. They pretended to be opposed to the saloon while they were secretly plotting to bring it back as an effective means of promoting the sale of liquor and the increase of liquor revenue.

Fabian Franklin, a member of the board of directors of the AAPA, said that if the law was ever repealed it would be because it had become odious to the people, and that they will not " obey a law which they don't respect." The first great objective of the association was to destroy respect for the law and its strategists knew that the surest way to accomplish this was to bring about its open and constant violation, and charge the resulting conditions to the law.

There is space here for only a few illustrations of the method and spirit of their campaign to achieve this objective. Article VI of the Constitution of the United States provides that " all executive and judicial officers, both of the United States and of the several states, shall be bound by oath or affirmation, to support this Constitution." The Eighteenth Amendment specifically conferred upon the states concurrent power of enforcement.

It was universally recognized that unless the states assumed the responsibility imposed upon them by the Constitution, the Eighteenth Amendment could not be enforced. Within a year after ratification, thirty-eight states enacted enforcement laws. Others followed later.

One of the most effective methods of bringing about the breakdown of the law and liquor chaos was to secure the repeal of state enforcement acts. Tammany Hall and the liquor interests, parading as the Association Against the Prohibition Amendment, led the way. In 1923 they forced the repeal of the New York enforcement act. The United States district attorney for the southern district of New York declared that this was "the hardest blow the enforcement of the Eighteenth Amendment had received." This was true, and not only for New York; it was the first great staggering blow to the cause of national prohibition.

After 1926 the association, with true Du Pont realism and efficiency, poured its money and its lobbyists into the various states to work with the liquor interests and the Tammany politicians of both parties to destroy enforcement laws. One instance will illustrate the spirit and method of these campaigns. When Mr. Curran was on the stand, the following occurred:

SENATOR ROBINSON (Indiana). Now, you also conducted a campaign in Wisconsin last year?

MR. CURRAN. Yes.

SENATOR ROBINSON. What was the purpose of the campaign?

MR. CURRAN. The purpose of the campaign was to try to help secure a verdict by the people of the state of Wisconsin in favor of advice to the Wisconsin legislature recommending the repeal of the Seversen Act, which was the name of the Wisconsin state Volstead Act.

SENATOR ROBINSON. Was that campaign successful from your standpoint?

MR. CURRAN. Yes; splendidly.

SENATOR ROBINSON. How much did it cost you to wage that campaign?

MR. CURRAN. About $29,000, I think the figure was.

SENATOR ROBINSON. Well, now, did the legislature repeal the law?

MR. CURRAN. They did.

SENATOR ROBINSON. Were you represented in the legislature?

MR. CURRAN. We were.

SENATOR ROBINSON. Who represented you there?

MR. CURRAN. Dr. J. J. Seelman.

SENATOR ROBINSON. How much did you pay Dr. Seelman?

MR. CURRAN. $10,000.

SENATOR ROBINSON. I read a letter here from yourself as president to Dr. J. J. Seelman, 69 East Wisconsin Avenue, Milwaukee, Wis., dated April 10, 1929:

"Dr. J. J. Seelman
Milwaukee, Wis.

Dear Dr. Seelman: You nearly knocked me over with the financial arrangement, but I understand all the circumstances, and we are going ahead with it as Mr. Wood is writing to you today.

I know how well you will cover the legislature. In this we cannot fail. I know nothing of more present importance to us, but I know also that you will carry the affair to a successful conclusion.

Let me congratulate you again on the result of the referendum and tell you personally how warmly it is appreciated by every member of our executive committee and by every director from whom I have heard.

Now give them the other barrel!

And please keep me fully and continuously informed.

Yours very sincerely,
Henry H. Curran, *Pres.*"

Now, April 10, the same date, a letter goes forward to Dr. J. J. Seelman, from which I quote, this letter being sent by the vice-president, Charles S. Wood. I take it he is one of your vice-presidents?

MR. CURRAN. Yes.

SENATOR ROBINSON. This is a copy of the letter. Was he in charge of the finances of the Wisconsin campaign for you and your organization?

MR. CURRAN. Yes. Well, we all know about it. He was in Wisconsin.

SENATOR ROBINSON. The letter reads:

"Dr. J. J. Seelman
Milwaukee, Wis.

Dear Dr. Seelman: I talked over with Major Curran very thoroughly yesterday the matter of arrangements with you to take care of the interests of the association in connection with the present session of the Wisconsin legislature. Major Curran has requested me to write you the decision arrived at, which I do, as follows:

We understand that you will give the work of the association all of your time which it may require for the above period; and also that you will secure at least $750 per month additional income for the association from the state of Wisconsin.

We are prepared, therefore, to accept your proposal that we pay you the sum of $2,000 per month, beginning with the month of April and continuing until the bill for repeal of the Severson Act is finally disposed of or the legislature adjourns. . . .

With kindest regards, I am,

Sincerely yours,
Charles S. Wood, *Vice-Pres.*"

I am curious to know why this man should be valuable to you to the extent of $2,000 a month only while the legislature was in session.

MR. CURRAN. Well, that is when the matter was up. That is when the matter that was before the legislature was up, Senator.

SENATOR ROBINSON. What was he to do to earn the $2,000 a month while the legislature was in session?

MR. CURRAN. Whatever anybody does that is interested in legislation.

SENATOR ROBINSON. That is what I am trying to find out. What does anybody do for $2,000 a month?

MR. CURRAN. They go to the capitol, they converse with the legislature. If you please, they lobby. You are familiar with that. . . .

SENATOR WALSH (Montana). Now, will you explain to us why you want the state enforcement laws repealed?

MR. CURRAN. Yes.

SENATOR WALSH. Please do so.

MR. CURRAN. When people in a state start a movement to repeal their state enforcement act, we help them, and support the repeal, because it indicates, first, that the people of that state, if the referendum carries, are unwilling to perform the gratuitous act of cooperating with the federal government.

SENATOR WALSH. Quite obviously.

MR. CURRAN. In the enforcement of this federal statute.

SENATOR WALSH. Quite obviously, but what I want to know is why you object to the state government of the state of Montana having an enforcement law.

MR. CURRAN. We are here for such a referendum and were in Montana, because it shows that the people of Montana are opposed to national prohibition, in our belief.

SENATOR WALSH. Just a test of sentiment, then?

MR. CURRAN. It is primarily that, Senator; yes.

SENATOR WALSH. Yes. Well, you take the position, do you not, that prohibition cannot be enforced?

MR. CURRAN. Personally it never has been enforced. Can't. . . .

SENATOR WALSH. Well, that is your position, is it not? You send out documents to the effect that it is impossible of enforcement?

MR. CURRAN. I believe it is impossible of enforcement.

SENATOR WALSH. And, at the same time, you are endeavoring to repeal state laws providing for the enforcement?

MR. CURRAN. It should be enforced, in my opinion, by the federal government solely. It is a federal matter. It is the only part of the whole Constitution where they talk about it concurrently being enforced by the states.

SENATOR WALSH. The real situation is that you argue that it cannot be enforced?

MR. CURRAN. Yes.

SENATOR WALSH. And you try to repeal state laws so as to make good your assertion that it cannot be enforced?

MR. CURRAN. Oh, that is not it, Senator.

SENATOR WALSH. It is not?

MR. CURRAN. No. In the states where they have state enforcement acts, it is not enforced any better than in the states where they do not have them.

SENATOR WALSH. That is entirely aside from the question. I was trying to find out why you contribute money for the repeal of the state enforcement laws, throwing the whole burden on the federal government, when you assert that it is impossible for the federal government to enforce it.

MR. CURRAN. Well, it is, Senator.

SENATOR WALSH. Really you do not want it enforced, do you, Mr. Curran, and is it not for the purpose of enforcing your argument that it cannot be enforced?

MR. CURRAN. It shows that the people are opposed to it, and where the people are opposed to a law, you cannot enforce it. You never can.

SENATOR WALSH. And, of course, if you have not any law, you cannot enforce it?

MR. CURRAN. Well, you have got a law. You have got your Volstead Act.

SENATOR WALSH. And these states whose laws you have been helping to repeal, their laws provide for additional help in the enforcement, and you take away that additional help, do you not?

MR. CURRAN. Gratuitous help. It is a breach of trust for a state to have such an act if the people are opposed to prohibition — a breach of trust. . . .[26]

Thus Mr. Curran tried to absolve the association from deliberately fomenting lawlessness when it went into the various states and worked for the repeal of their enforcement acts by saying that enforcement was a matter for the federal government to attend to. This, of course, was absurd, because Article VI of the Constitution and the Eighteenth Amendment imposed upon the states the obligation of supporting and enforcing the Constitution, of which the amendment was an integral part. That it was not only absurd, but utterly dishonest, was shown by the fact that the association and its congressional tools were not endeavoring to bring about repeal by the orderly and lawful method. They were struggling to repeal the federal enforcement act and opposing every effort to strengthen it and to secure adequate appropriations for its administration in order to cause a complete breakdown of federal enforcement. For public consumption they tried to deny this, but their files, their literature and their deeds show that this was their deliberate purpose. Mr. Walter H. Buck, a director for the national organization and president of the Maryland branch, gave an exact statement of its purpose and method in the following letter to Mr. Stayton:

> I hope, very much, therefore, that the Association Against the Prohibition Amendment will keep its face set steadily in one direction, and that is the repeal of the Eighteenth Amendment. The practical way to do this is to organize for the fight this fall in such selected districts where we should be able to put in a wet in the place of a dry member of Congress. Ultimately we should be able to cut off all appropriations to the prohibition unit of the federal government, and sooner or later by such means we will be in a position to get rid of the Eighteenth Amendment. And I believe that the way I indicated is the only way.[27]

Significance of Repeal of Enforcement Acts

Referring to the withdrawal of state support from the Constitution of the United States, Justice Kenyon said:

> There is a moral obligation on the states to assist in enforcing the Eighteenth Amendment and laws passed in pursuance thereof. They should take care of the violations coming peculiarly within the province of the state, such as intra-state violations of the law. States are a part

of the federal government. Surely there is a solemn moral duty on the states to support the Constitution. The Constitution and amendments and laws to carry them into effect are still the supreme law of the land.

Addressing the Ohio State Bar Association, William G. McAdoo said:

The inevitable logic of the repeal by a state of its prohibition enforcement laws or the refusal of a state to perform its constitutional duty to enact such laws is nullification, open and undisguised, of the Constitution of the United States. It is to the active and unabashed campaign in favor of nullification that I wish to call your attention as a part, and a very fundamental part, of the broader problem of law and order which I mentioned at the beginning of this address. . . . Constitutional government is impossible if we proceed on the principle that only those parts of the Constitution are to be observed and enforced which any given state or individual happens to like or approve. This is the slippery path which leads to anarchy. It is the negation of the principle of majority rule, it sets up that very tyranny of the minority which the opponents of prohibition assail so loudly.

In 1931, the legislature of Illinois repealed the state enforcement act. Governor Emmerson vetoed the repeal measure. In his veto message, he said:

It is apparent, therefore, that House Bill No. 1 would remove from the statutes all these laws on this subject and the serious consequences of such a situation cannot be ignored by any thoughtful citizen. The police, sheriffs, constables, and other law enforcing officers, numbering tens of thousands, could not under state law interfere with the sale of liquor to school children, the operation of stills and dramshops near schools and colleges, or any other trafficking in intoxicants.

The only protection from these evils would be the activities of a comparatively few federal agents, unless some measure of power remains in municipalities by ordinance, but this would necessarily be weak and ineffective. . . .

I would like to point out that all civil officers in Illinois are required, before entering upon the duties of their respective offices, to take and subscribe to an oath " to support the Constitution of the United States." One of the provisions of that Constitution vests in Congress and the several states concurrent power to enforce the Eighteenth Amendment. This became a part of the Constitution of the United States on January 29, 1919.

The Fifty-fifth General Assembly of this state ratified it on January 14, 1919. That same general assembly definitely accepted for the state of Illinois the joint responsibility of enforcement and exercised the concurrent jurisdiction by the enactment of the so-called search and seizure act. Two years later the passage of the Illinois prohibition act was a continuation of the acceptance.

It is now proposed that this responsibility and jurisdiction shall be relinquished and that portion of the Constitution of the United States shall not be supported.

It is quite evident to me that the repeal of these acts is not a mere gesture of disapproval of prohibition, as some would have it appear, but tends to strike at the fundamental unity of national government under the federal Constitution. I am not for nullification. Destructive principles, which do not protect the lives and homes of all of our citizens, will not afford the solution of the liquor problem. . . .

We cannot cure individual disregard for law by state disregard for the federal Constitution.

No sincere advocate of this bill holds this opinion. It has only one purpose. That is to hinder and thwart and make impossible the efforts of the federal government to execute the Eighteenth Amendment and thereby compel the substitution for it of some other system. This is not the orderly and legal method for securing this change. It smacks more of lawlessness and rebellion.

The Referendum Route

Shortly after the Du Ponts took over the AAPA, Mr. Stayton prepared a memorandum in which he said " that we are now proceeding by the referendum route; that we can now make our budget definite, because it takes 10 cents per voter." In other words, in order to finance these referendums, it would be necessary to have $10,000 for every 100,000 voters in the various states.

In 1929 Lammot du Pont, chairman of the finance committee, sent out " a letter to Republicans from a Republican " soliciting funds to finance referendum campaigns. With a few alterations, the same letter was sent to Democrats by John J. Raskob, who was the chairman of the Democratic national committee. Mr. Raskob's letter stated that " it will require heavy expenditure in many states, however, for our work in securing signatures to the necessary initiative petitions and in getting out the votes in the referenda." In 1930 Mr. Curran wrote: " Our chief plan at present, in impressing our dry Congress with the fact that the country is mostly wet, is the holding of state-wide referendums such as we last year carried on successfully in Wisconsin, and before then in Montana, Nevada and New York. This year Massachusetts will come first, with other states afterwards as fast as we can reach them. For this there will be required over a million dollars to be used this year, of which a little over $200,000 has already been subscribed. . . ." [28]

The purpose of these referendums was to induce dry legislatures to repeal state enforcement laws, to prevent a dry Congress from providing for adequate federal enforcement, and to furnish the occasion for a flood of false and inflammatory propaganda that would destroy respect for law and thereby discredit the amendment. In the letter sent out by Mr. du Pont and Mr. Raskob, they stated that their plan was to induce the voters " to unite in an organized protest state by state, that will be heard in Congress and that will secure direct political action in the states themselves." In his letter congratulating Dr. Seelman on the result of the referendum in Wisconsin, Mr. Curran wrote: " Now give them the other barrel! " The other barrel was the actual repeal of the enforcement act by the legislature, and Dr. Seelman was given two thousand dollars a month to camp at the state capitol and see that this was accomplished. The lobbyist for the association in Illinois was a Mr. Hooke. The record discloses the purpose and nature of his activities:

SENATOR ROBINSON (Indiana) (*reads*). " Mr. Hooke, our representative in Illinois, is making surprising progress in the effort to secure the eight votes we need in the Illinois senate to get the bill through." Did you just need 8 votes in the Illinois senate?

MR. CURRAN. I guess it was 9 votes we needed, Senator. It takes 26 to carry the Illinois senate. The vote was 21 for submitting to the people of the state of Illinois the question of referendum for a repeal of the Illinois Volstead Act.

SENATOR ROBINSON. What was Mr. Hooke doing at Springfield to get these eight votes?

MR. CURRAN. Well, he was doing just what you would do. He was talking to legislators. He was going back in the districts.[29]

It was the same story with all these referendums — " impressing our dry Congress with the fact that the country is mostly wet " and forcing dry legislators to repeal the enforcement laws.

The officials of the association were men of great ability; they were absolute realists and every move was the result of shrewd calculation. They were after the liquor revenue and they moved straight upon their objective. Theirs were the tactics of war. There were, therefore, very definite reasons why they should proceed " by the referendum route." What were these reasons? The Constitution contained no provision for state-wide referendums on the question of whether members of state legislatures or of Congress should obey their oaths to uphold and defend the Constitution of the United States. Such referendums were not binding upon anyone, they were without legal effect, they were open rebellion. Why then were they made such an important part of the association's strategy?

In an article which appeared in the New York *Times* of May 15, 1927, William Atherton Du Puy said:

Congress affords a correct measure of the political temper of the people. Four Congresses have been elected since the constitutional amendment was passed. There has been no retrogression. In fact, Congress gets dryer all the time. One measure after another having to do with prohibition has come up in Congress after Congress. The drys always win. They win overwhelmingly. The wet vote is but 10 per cent of Congress, 15 per cent, sometimes 20 per cent. It does not have enough strength actually to constitute an opposition.

The wets seem perennially hopeful. For a year preceding the last general election, for instance, they proclaimed that they were going to elect 200 wet members of the House and various senators. The tide had turned; the people were aroused and ready to take their vengeance.

But when the smoke of battle had cleared away, nothing had happened. There was, in fact, one more dry member of Congress than before.

In the Senate 35 members had been elected. Of these 6 were wet and 29 dry. The Congress stands today 6 to 1 in favor of the drys.

A similar result was recorded in the choice of governors. Here again 35 men were to be chosen. The wets did not do quite so well here as they had done with senators. They got 5 out of the 35 — New York, Maryland, Rhode Island, Connecticut and Wisconsin.

And what record did these 35 states write in the votes that chose their legislatures? Thirty of them, says the record, were dry in both houses. Four more split, choosing one chamber dry and the other wet. A single state, Maryland, chose a legislature that was wet in both houses.

In Illinois, two representatives at large were chosen, members of Congress for whom the whole state voted. Two of the candidates were wet and two were dry. The drys won by majorities around 340,000. The majority of the congressional delegation was dry. The governor was dry. The legislature was dry. Practically all of the state officials were dry.

In Ohio the Democrats nominated a wet for senator — he lost. They nominated a dry for governor — he won. A Democratic dry candidate for lieutenant governor won over a wet Republican. Lower down on the ticket there were dry Republicans who won and wet Democrats who lost. No wet of either party won.

Massachusetts chose a dry governor by a large majority. She elected 11 dry representatives in Congress as against 3 wets. She elected a state legislature that was dry in both houses. Practically all of the state officials are dry. Measured by these standards Massachusetts is dry.

One can run a line a hundred miles inland at the upper end of Massachusetts and follow that line down the coast until it has passed Maryland. In the territory east of the line will be included nearly all the territory in the United States that elects wets to office. Yet look at it on the map. What a slight fringe it is on the great stretch of the continent. The additional areas of Wisconsin, Louisiana, and, possibly, Missouri, are insignificant as compared to the great mass of the country.

In August 1928 Mr. Curran, with the written approval of Pierre du Pont, issued a public statement in favor of Governor Smith for president. In it he said:

On November 6, I am going to vote for Governor Smith to be president, because he is right, and Mr. Hoover is wrong, on the one great issue of this campaign — prohibition. And this I shall do as a Republican. . . .

. . . Mr. Hoover is for the Eighteenth Amendment as it stands, definitely despite his undecipherable uncertainties about "modification" and "nullification." But Mr. Smith is against the Eighteenth Amendment as it stands, definitely and without any uncertainty whatever. . . . In fact, this issue will not appear at all in many of the fights for other offices. But in the duel for the presidency, prohibition is the issue, for the other two contestants have personally made it so.

So one must choose, if he appreciates the importance of the question of prohibition. And my choice is Smith. . . .[30]

Mr. Hoover received a popular plurality of 6,300,000, the new Congress was dry by a majority of 90 to 16 in the Senate and 328 to 106 in the House, nearly every state legislature was dry, and of 48 governors, only 5 were wet.

The strategists of the AAPA knew that the issue had been squarely drawn and that the people had shown that they were behind the amendment by an overwhelming majority. The effect of these dry majorities was disastrous to the cause of repeal and had to be overcome in some way. They knew that they would have to perpetrate a swindle of some kind, and as usual they were equal to the occasion.

In ordinary elections, both parties had their candidates whose interests they protected. Republican election officials saw to it that all votes cast for their candidates were counted. Democratic officials were equally zealous for their candidates. In these elections, dry votes had to be counted. It was necessary, therefore, that some scheme be devised by which wet politicians, instead of watching each other and forcing the counting of all votes cast for their respective candidates, could work together to disfranchise dry voters. State-wide referendums furnished a perfect solution of the problem. In referendums on the prohibition question, the political machines did not have candidates to protect and could form bipartisan combinations to manipulate the elections. The daily newspapers, big business interests, machines of both parties, the liquor interests and the underworld of the cities could combine to deceive, mislead and disfranchise the people.

Another advantage was that the questions to be voted on could be so framed that they would be simply tricky devices by which the people could be completely misled. If the proposition was to repeal a state enforcement act, the people were told that prohibition was a national law and should be enforced by the federal government, and that the states should not be burdened with the trouble and expense of its enforcement. If it was to repeal the amendment, the people were not told that that meant the return of an unrestricted liquor traffic, but the " return of the problem to the states." By this deceptive phrase, large numbers of unthinking people were made to believe that the intention was to retain prohibition, but have it administered by the states. If it was to modify the Volstead Act, the people were told that this would reduce the use of hard liquor and make real prohibition more effective. Some of these propositions were plain frauds. The New York proposition was as follows:

> Should the Congress of the United States modify the federal act to enforce the Eighteenth Amendment to the Constitution of the United States so that the same shall not prohibit the manufacture, sale, transportation, importation and exportation of beverages which are not in fact intoxicating as determined in accordance with the laws of the respective states?

The use of the words " not in fact intoxicating " would have left the law without any standard for its enforcement, and would have repealed the amendment by congressional action. Not one voter in a hundred thousand had any conception of what the effect of this proposition would be.

The California measure repealed the state enforcement act and provided that when lawful under the federal Constitution, the state of California should have exclusive right to license and regulate the manufacture, sale, possession and transportation of intoxicating liquors, and prohibited public saloons. Later it was found that this measure destroyed the right of local communities to prohibit the liquor traffic, and that it legalized the saloon under other names. The result was that after repeal of the Eighteenth Amendment, many local communities that had been dry for thirty years or more were overrun by saloons under other names, and the people were helpless. Judges and prominent lawyers stated that they did not realize the significance of the language used.

The proposition varied in the different states, the form being decided upon after consultation with the politicians. The prize referendum is described in the following extract from the final report of the AAPA:

> Confident that a majority of the people of the nation were opposed to the Eighteenth Amendment, Pierre S. du Pont, in May of 1928, submitted to more than 100,000 citizens of Delaware a questionnaire to ascertain direct evidence of this opposition. Six queries were propounded by Mr. du Pont and sent to nearly every voter in Delaware by the association's Delaware division. As a result the voters of that state registered overwhelming opposition to prohibition in answer to all six questions. A typical question was: "Do you think that change in the existing prohibition law is needed?" The vote was: Yes — 32,915; No — 4,422.

The Du Ponts controlled the three leading daily newspapers of the state of Delaware; the politicians were their chattels; and it was generally conceded that changes were needed in the prohibition law!

Drys Ignored Referendums

The opponents of the liquor traffic denounced these referendums as fakes and advised all drys to have nothing to do with them. The dry forces of Illinois adopted the following resolution:

> It is not a right or function of one of the states of the United States to hold an election on the question of modification of the Constitution of the United States by nullification instead of the method provided for amending the Constitution, as contained in the Constitution itself.[31]

The national board of directors of the Anti-Saloon League adopted the following resolution:

That it is the sense of this board that the temperance forces of the United States should not be diverted from the main issues in any election to so-called wet and dry referenda on the Eighteenth Amendment or the national prohibition law, which referenda are without authority under the Constitution and which are legally futile and can have no binding effect. In any state referenda having to do with the laws or state constitutional provisions which will have a legal and binding effect the temperance forces should take an active part.[32]

The results are illustrated by the vote in New York and Illinois. In New York, with a single exception, the dry organizations of the state advised ignoring the question, regarding it merely as a straw vote, with the following results: Yes — 1,763,070; No — 598,484; Blanks and void — 546,236. Approximately 780,000 registered voters did not go to the polls at all, while many thousands more did not register. In Illinois the vote for president was 2,107,504 in 1928. In 1930 the total vote on the prohibition referendum, both wet and dry, was 1,583,134. Of the registered voters, 636,036 did not vote.

That the officials of the AAPA, when talking among themselves, recognized that these referendums were fakes is shown by their files. Mr. Curran testified that Mr. Larkin G. Mead was vice-president of the association and "head of our information department." In the files, there was a memorandum by Mr. Mead in which he said that Kenneth O'Brien was promoting a wet magazine to be called *Fizz,* and that he was trying to get a few "multimills" to underwrite it "for $300,000 as a starter." Mr. Mead then said: "O'Brien is one of the original Stayton helpers and seems pleased and pleasant about it all. His latest is for us to pay for a national referendum — à la Du Pont in Delaware. I told him I thought we'd spend more time and money than it cost originally, trying to prove that it was on the level."

How the AAPA Used the Results of the Referendums

Many of those who voted for the propositions that were submitted did so because they were dissatisfied with existing conditions, not because they wanted the amendment repealed and the

liquor traffic brought back; and millions refused to vote at all. But whatever the questions, and however the results were obtained, the officials of the association and their whole brood of propagandists and newspapers shouted, "The people have spoken"; "Legislators and congressmen now have a definite mandate from the people; will they obey it?" Their attitude is shown by the following letter from Mr. Curran to Mr. Raskob, dated June 8, 1929:

The governor [of Wisconsin] said he signed the bill in response to the mandate of the people, as shown by the overwhelming popular vote against prohibition on April 2.

To this governor the people's will meant a mandate.

It will mean that later in other states to other governors. And still later, it will mean a mandate to members of both Houses of Congress. We have a long road ahead of us, but we are on our way and moving forward.

This final mopping up in Wisconsin established definitely the following five states in revolt against federal prohibition, through their action in repealing their state Volstead acts and refusing to exercise any of their "concurrent" power in aid of federal prohibition: New York, Maryland, Wisconsin, Montana and Nevada. . . .[33]

This brings us to the gist of the whole matter. The AAPA knew that if they went before the people in an honest and lawful manner on a bona fide wet and dry issue, they would be defeated. So they decided to secure, by tricky and dishonest methods, a wet plurality on a referendum vote, and then go to the legislator or congressman and demand not that he vote wet but that he "obey the command of his constituents." That this policy was adopted shortly after the association became "a Du Pont subsidiary" is shown by the following extracts from the minutes of a meeting of policy holders held on November 17, 1927:

As to the political work to be done in New Jersey, and in other states where a referendum is in prospect, Mr. Stayton stated: "My general view is that we should proceed as we did in Nevada by getting candidates, both for legislatures and Congress, pledged in advance to abide by the result of the referendum. If we oppose a candidate, it is not because he is a dry, but on the ground that he has refused to abide by the vote of his constituents. . . ."

For example, in a state which has not had a referendum but which looks wet, we should have to go largely on the advice of the politicians. But if we should go into New York or Montana or any of the states that have had referenda, or into any district — as the Denver district — we should know that the district has already gone wet on referendum and we would then not be making our fight on the wet and dry issue, but on the issue " shall a representative obey the command of his constituents on a specific subject which has been definitely voted upon."

Why it was necessary " to go largely on the advice of the politicians " is of course evident. The association pitched the ball and the politicians had to catch it. It was essential, therefore, that there should be perfect team work.

The platform of the association solemnly declared that " the Constitution of the United States, as established by the Fathers, delegated to the federal government only such powers as in their very nature should be federal and not state," that national prohibition was a " violation of the fundamental American right of local self-government in local affairs," and demands a " restoration to the several states of the right of their people to enact such liquor laws as they may respectively choose." When we look through this smug camouflage, we see a little coterie of multimillionaire munition makers and Wall street financiers raising a huge corruption fund and sending it, together with their propagandists and lobbyists, into the various states to appeal to the cupidity of the rich, deceive and inflame the ignorant, debauch politics, override the intelligent and responsible majority, and force the repeal of laws that had been enacted to uphold and enforce the Constitution of the United States.

In some of the states the drive for repeal bore fruit quickly. The report of the AAPA for 1930 boasted of the fact that nine states " have officially repudiated the Eighteenth Amendment," stated the gains for the year, and said: " The results of plebiscites in Illinois, Massachusetts and Rhode Island were freighted with profound significance." That was true, but not in the sense in which the word "significance" was there used. The really profound significance of these plebiscites is expressed in the following statement from the 1931 report of the association:

> By the end of the year, the idea of submitting repeal of the Eighteenth Amendment to special conventions in the several states, which is our first major objective, had caught the imagination of politicians in many parts of the country, and that plan of procedure may be said now to have achieved pretty general recognition and acceptance among party leaders.

A large number of wets believed with Clarence Darrow that "repeal of the Eighteenth Amendment is pure nonsense. . . . One might as well talk about taking his summer vacation on Mars. . . . A continuation of nullification must be our method of relief." But this attitude did not satisfy the directors of the AAPA. Liquor had to be legalized, its sale promoted by high pressure methods, and the saloons brought back, if it was to be taxed and produce enough revenue to make possible the abandonment of the income tax. This could be accomplished only by the repeal of the amendment. They knew, however, that a repeal amendment would never be ratified if it was submitted to the legislatures of the states. Members of the legislature represented separate districts in every part of the state, and their voters could not be swamped by the cities. Candidates for the legislature ran as Republicans or Democrats, their interests were protected by their party machinery, and it was impossible to refuse to count dry votes that were cast for them. These men wished to be re-elected, and they knew that if they did not obey the wishes of their constituents they would be defeated. In these elections, the people were able to speak and give a mandate to their representatives that would not be ignored. For these reasons, it was through the legislatures that the American people could really decide the question of repeal. It was clear, therefore, that if the procedure that had been followed in the case of every amendment adopted since the foundation of the government, should be continued, there was not the slightest chance that the amendment would be repealed.

But through their use of the state-wide referendum, the AAPA had seen a great light. Submit the question of repeal "to special conventions in the several states," and the problem would be solved. In state-wide elections of delegates to these conventions, the city, with its wealth, daily newspapers, political machines, underworld and other resources, could overwhelm the rest of the state. But of still greater importance was the fact that the dry delegates would have no one to protect their interests and would be absolutely helpless. Bipartisan rings of crooked politicians could then control the polls, count the votes, make the return and deliver the goods. Both parties accepted the plan for "truly representative conventions," and the swindle that had proved so successful in the state referendums was worked on a nation-wide scale. The dry leaders exposed and denounced the scheme but they were unable to reach the people and prevent its consummation.

Those in control of the AAPA were men of the type that ignore the Constitution, disregard the law, corrupt public officials, and stop at nothing that will advance their selfish interests. But this was the first time that they had succeeded in striking from the Constitution a provision that blocked their antisocial designs. This significant truth was expressed by Pierre du Pont: "The great victory tonight does not concern liquor. Captain Stayton and the association have taught the American people how the Constitution can be amended by conventions." [34]

The Canadian System

In order to break down opposition and to prepare the minds of the people for the unlimited sale of liquor, a saloon was defined as a place where liquor was sold over a bar to be consumed on the premises and that this was the institution that was the cause of all the pre-prohibition evils. It was said that if there were no bar and the liquor were not consumed at the place of sale, but taken off the premises in bottles and drunk in automobiles, homes, hotel

rooms, flats and other places, such a place would not be a saloon, and therefore innocuous. The wets spoke solemnly of the Canadian system and the Swedish system, and held out a vague hope that repeal would be followed by state control, and that profits would be eliminated from the liquor business, and it would become as harmless as the hardware business. The following statement of Al Smith illustrates this aspect of the wet propaganda: "We may well learn from the experience of other nations. Our Canadian neighbors have gone far in this manner to solve the problem by the method of sale made by the state itself, and not by private individuals."

Of course, this was a fraud. In the first place, the wets did not want any such system and had not the slightest intention of working for its adoption. In the second place, they knew that it would not produce the promised results. History demonstrates the fact that at all times and under all circumstances the evil effects of alcohol have resulted not from the name of the beverage, the seller, the place where it was sold or the law governing its sale, but from the alcohol bought and consumed. Whether the drink was beer, wine, whisky or gin, whether it was obtained in taverns, saloons, dispensaries or speak-easies and sold by hosts, bartenders, barmaids or bootleggers, under license, under state control or under prohibition, the sale and consumption of alcohol have invariably been accompanied by the same brood of evils.

The truth as to the results of sale " by the bottle " in state liquor stores was fully revealed, but it was not allowed to reach the people. Earl L. Douglass, in his *Prohibition and Common Sense,* one of the authoritative volumes issued by the Alcohol Information Committee, showed that this system had been tried in South Carolina and South Dakota, had failed completely and had been replaced by state prohibition laws. He also showed that the claims made for the Canadian and Swedish systems were pure wet propaganda and false.

Mr. Ben H. Spense of Toronto, a distinguished journalist, made an impartial and exhaustive investigation of conditions in Canada. In books and magazine articles he demonstrated the fact that conditions were far worse than they had been under the old saloon system. He gives a convincing statement of the facts, and adds:

Manson Doyle, the secretary of religious education for the United Church of Canada, whose particular job it is to look after the welfare of young people, exclaimed to the writer: " My wrath blazes out at the accursed traffic which is such a negative factor in the progress of our young people." Mr. Doyle went on to say: " My interest in young people brings continued anxiety and suffering of soul, as I watch the steadily increasing place of command which the social use of liquor has come to occupy in the home life of Canada. I am quite sure that it has now become a more insidious temptation than in the days of the bar. Young people find themselves invited by a charming hostess to take liquor. Under the eyes of a group of people in whose company they wish to be agreeable, it is surely a more difficult invitation to turn down than the invitation of the old-time bartender or the urge of a nondescript crowd of men. I am appalled by the increasing number of young people who, when the question of drink comes up, arch their eyebrows and express surprise that anybody should cavil as to the absolute acceptability of a drink of liquor under any and all conditions. The children of families which have been total abstainers for three generations now take it for granted that to use liquor is the right thing because it is a product especially sponsored by the government of the land. The man who sells it is a government official, very often of good social standing. The whole influence of our way of handling the distribution of liquor has tended to break down the sense of the undesirability of drinking habits."

The United Church of Canada, the largest religious body in the dominion outside the province of Quebec, in a memorial to the recent ecumenical conference, said: " The effect of government sale upon citizens is alarming. The law forbids drinking in any public place and requires that the liquor be consumed in the home or in the hotel room. . . . It gives respectability to the traffic, breaking down the natural antipathy of the young and old toward it. It familiarizes the presence of liquor in the home, removing any sensitiveness concerning its possession. In consequence the home becomes degraded and too often the whole family participates in the use of intoxicating liquors; the pocket flask becomes common and the bottle is frequently introduced to guests. . . . The liquor traffic is a supreme lawbreaker, a ruthless home destroyer, a menace to character, to employment, and to every good thing in human life. . . . It is not possible to increase the facilities to obtain intoxicants without greatly increasing the evils which are consequent upon the beverage use of strong drink."

A few years ago, Dr. Jennie Smillie, a prominent Toronto physician, was appointed by the Women's Liberal Association as convener of a committee to inquire into the working of the liquor control act. She reported:

" Drinking among women is on the increase in Ontario because of the accessibility of liquor in the home. The effect of this is very far-reaching. It not only debauches womanhood but endangers the lives and destroys the morals of children."

The evils of alcoholism are not because of the taste or character of the beverages in which the alcohol is contained, not in the place or method of their sale, nor in the time and circumstances of their consumption. The evils are because of the drug alcohol itself. What made the old saloon a socially hurtful institution was not the proprietorship, building, equipment, location or clientele, but the stuff sold therein. What made the old license system a stench in the nostrils of decent society was the alcohol in the beverages dispensed. What makes the government liquor-selling systems of Canada a demoralizing influence, politically and morally, is that they sell alcoholic beverages. What makes the Ontario liquor system bad is the same factor, and the further fact that the home has become the drinking place.

The use of liquor cannot be rendered innocuous because of a home environment. The same amount of liquor will have precisely the same intoxicating effect when consumed in a home as if drunk in a saloon. In Ontario there are more consumers and more liquor is being consumed in the homes than was consumed in home and barroom combined in the old days.[35]

In a comprehensive article on the subject in the *International Student* for March 1932, Mr. Spense concludes as follows:

The so-called " liquor control systems " of Canada are a magnificent, stupendous success from the standpoint of men who make and seek to derive profit from the sale of alcoholic beverages, and from the standpoint of men who drink and want facilities provided by which they can obtain the kind of drink they want. Perhaps, also, from the standpoint of the politician who seeks a system that will provide jobs for party friends and business associations that will provide party funds. But from the standpoint of serious-minded citizens who seek a real solution of a grave problem, of patriots who seek to purify the life of their country and strike off shackles that hinder development, and of altruistic reformers who strive to lift humanity to higher levels, these systems are a ghastly, grim, unspeakable failure.

Bootleggers and Speak-Easies

The propaganda of the AAPA on the subject of the speak-easy and the bootlegger was false and misleading. It was said that they were the product of prohibition; that they were establishing a reign of corruption and lawlessness which was debauching our politics, destroying respect for all law and subverting our institutions. With a lofty and patriotic zeal, the AAPA piously called upon the people to repeal the Eighteenth Amendment and " destroy this prohibition Frankenstein." This was sheer hypocrisy. A large proportion of the members of the association had their bootleggers and they openly and defiantly drank and served bootleg liquor. Their real objection to the bootlegger and the speak-easy was not that they were corrupt and lawless, but that they sold untaxed liquor.

The statement that the speak-easy and the bootlegger appeared in this country with the Eighteenth Amendment was false. In 1930 the Department of Justice prepared an authentic " Factual Monograph " on *The Value of Law Observance.* It contained quotations from newspapers showing conditions before the adoption of the amendment, of which the following are examples.

The Pittsburgh *Leader* of March 14, 1907, under the heading, " Some Facts About Moonshine," stated:

From July 1, 1876 to July 1, 1905 (29 years) 30,763 illicit distilleries were seized in the United States. . . .

From July 1, 1876 to July 1, 1905 (29 years) 54 revenue raiders were killed and 94 wounded; total casualties, 148. This does not include informers or deputy marshals who were killed making arrests. Casualties were much more frequent when the service was young. From

July 1, 1876 to July 1, 1882 (6 years), 35 raiders were killed and 61 wounded; total, 96 casualties. During this period, 5,230 stills were raided, making the average casualties 1 to every 54 stills seized. Since 1876 there has been one or more casualties every year excepting 1894, 1900 and 1903. The government keeps no record of moonshiners killed.

On November 15, 1900, an editorial in the same paper declared:

At the meeting of the retail liquor dealers yesterday the statement was made that there are in Allegheny county 2,300 unlicensed dealers who sell liquor in violation of the law, every day in the year, Sundays and election days included.

In 1890 the Philadelphia *Times* said:

The police force of this city is the one cause of this flood of drunken demoralization and defiant lawlessness that now disgraces this city. There are not 100 of the nearly or quite 4,000 speak-easies in operation in Philadelphia that are not known to the police; but instead of closing them and bringing the criminals to punishment, they are protected, compelled to pay the price of protection to the police or to the party, and to vote and work at elections as the police direct them in obedience to orders from the city administration.

After the Eighteenth Amendment was repealed, Joseph H. Choate, director of the Federal Alcohol Administration, stated that

the bootleggers are now turning out from their stills alone, not counting smuggling and alcohol-divertings, a quantity of spirits which cannot be much less, and may be more than we drank before prohibition. This quantity is being consumed in addition to the entire sales of legal goods, which, ever since repeal, have run not far below pre-prohibition figures.

Gambling kings, vice lords and racketeers exist not because there are laws against gambling, commercialized vice and blackmail; they exist because there are people who are determined to make money by these means, law or no law. Bootleggers exist not because there are laws taxing or prohibiting the liquor traffic; they exist because there are people who are so devoid of a sense of social responsibility and respect for law that they will gratify their greed regardless of the law.

There was another element of dishonesty in this propaganda. In order to eliminate the speak-easy and the bootlegger, it would have been necessary to repeal all prohibition laws, abolish liquor taxes and licenses, remove restrictions against the sale of liquor on Sunday and after midnight and against the sale of liquor to children and the establishment of saloons in the neighborhood of schools and churches. In other words, it would have been necessary to remove every restriction from the business and permit it to operate twenty-four hours a day, seven days in the week, in open defiance of public decency. The Du Ponts and their associates proposed the imposition of a tax on liquor so heavy that it would make possible the repeal of the income tax. They knew that this would mean bootlegging on as large a scale as under prohibition, but they knew that it would also mean that in addition to this there would be a vast amount of liquor sold legally, which would be taxed. They were not concerned with bootleg lawlessness if it was a necessary result of a system under which their taxes would be reduced.

The Saloon Will Never Come Back

In connection with the propaganda about the elimination of the saloon and the bootlegger, there was one fraud so infamous that it would be incredible were it not conclusively established by direct, positive and unimpeachable evidence. The platform of the AAPA declares for the " restoration to the several states of the right of their peoples to enact such liquor laws as they may respectively choose, the abolition of the old-time saloon having paved the way for sound and enlightened legislation by them for the control, or, if they wish, for the prohibition of the liquor trade." It is solemnly assumed that the saloon is gone forever and the way paved for enlightened legislation governing the liquor trade that will make it harmless. Year after year, from coast to coast, the AAPA chanted, " The saloons will never be permitted to come back." Large numbers of good citizens were " taken in " by this propaganda. I remember discussing the repeal question with an intelligent woman who was prominently identified with social work. I suggested the danger of the return of the saloon, and she said scornfully, "Now you know that no one proposes the return of the saloon." The political confederates of the AAPA took up the refrain and the platforms and the candidates declared that the saloon would never be permitted to return.

The man who led the great chorus of propagandists and politicians was Pierre du Pont. During all this time, however, he was deliberately planning the restoration of the saloon. The saloon was the most effective agency for promoting the sale of liquor that had ever been devised. Its efficiency is illustrated by the following statement from *McClure's Magazine* of April 1907, which is quoted in the monograph of the Department of Justice referred to above:

> The brewers employ agents to watch continually every nook and cranny in Chicago where it may be possible to pour in a little more beer. If a new colony of foreigners appears, some compatriot is set at once selling them liquor. There is now one retail dealer to every 285 people. Every man, woman and child in Chicago drank, in 1906, two and a quarter barrels of beer — three and a half times the average consumption in the United States. Each also drank about four gallons of spirituous liquors — two and one-third times the average. The main object of the brewing business, the thorough saturation of the city, especially the tenement districts, with alcoholic liquors, is well fulfilled.

The saloon was necessary if enough liquor was to be sold to make possible, through the revenue derived therefrom, the repeal of the income tax and the payment of the national debt in fifteen years. Mr. du Pont's plan, therefore, was to lead the people on to the acceptance of repeal by promising that the saloon would not come back and then, when the movement had reached a point where it could not be stopped, to cheat them out of what had been promised and bring back the saloon. This statement is not the result of inference. On January 6, 1930, Mr. du Pont wrote a letter to Nicholas Murray Butler, in which he said:

. . . It is important to decide upon the best means of securing the ultimate repeal of the Eighteenth Amendment — the chief object of our association. . . . To meet our requirements, we must have time for planning and for gradual return to state control. I believe a guaranty against the return of the saloon will be necessary.

The saloon question has never troubled me much; its bad features will continue under one name or another as long as supporters are found. Mere selling, by the glass over the bar or on a table, does not cause the " evils of the saloon." However, we must reckon with conditions as they exist. It is certain that the saloon is a bugbear to many people, even prohibitionists might find a convenient step-down if a plan were offered to insure the continued abolition of their greatest and most fought enemy. If we are to act quickly, we must plan to keep the saloon position where it now is. Have we not a sufficient task to provide for the orderly return of the " by the bottle " trade, leaving the strictly retail or " by the glass " business for future consideration?

I have adopted the following skeleton of a plan: Return to state control with provision for sufficient time to develop detailed plans, the saloon to remain in its present existing prohibited position.

The states or any of them may, by amendment to state constitution or by authority of states initiative or referendum law, provide for the manufacture, sale or transportation of intoxicating liquors within, the importation thereof into, or the exportation thereof from, such states for beverage purposes; *provided,* that all such liquors sold shall be in packages not to be opened or consumed on the premises where sold.

Congress shall offer to every territory or political subdivision of the United States, other than a state or division thereof, a referendum law, to provide for the manufacture, sale and transportation of intoxicating liquors within, the importation thereof into, or the exportation thereof from, such territory or political subdivision for beverage purposes, provided that all such liquors sold shall be in packages not to be opened or consumed on the premises where sold. . . .

Retaining prohibition against " by the glass " sales might have a similar effect for, if satisfactory plans for " by the bottle " trade are developed, the cry for even broader state control might induce the Supreme Court to see the Eighteenth Amendment in another light. Moreover, if we should find the public more receptive to complete state control than we have at first hoped, it will be easy to strike out the words " provided that all such liquors shall be in packages not to be opened or consumed on the premises where sold." [36]

The meaning of this letter is perfectly clear; and we shall see later how Mr. du Pont succeeded in putting over on the American people every detail of his confidence game. He and his associates, through the ramifications of their influence and their power, their ability to purchase and coerce, their control of newspapers and magazines and the vast propaganda machine they set up, forced both political parties to accept his program to the letter. They gave the people the most solemn assurance that the saloon would never be permitted to return, but also agreed to submit an amendment that would provide for repeal, state ratifying conventions, complete state control and the elimination of every provision against the return of the saloon. After the election of 1932, the judiciary committee of the Senate reported out an amendment that gave Congress the power to " regulate or prohibit the sale of intoxicating liquors to be drunk on the premises where sold " and its submission to the legislatures of the states. The AAPA inaugurated a veritable reign of terror that did not cease until it had compelled Congress to provide for submission to state conventions and the elimination of the provision that would have protected the people against the return of the saloon. When the necessary number of states had acted and the Eighteenth Amendment was out of the way, Pierre du Pont and Jouett Shouse, who was then president of the AAPA, publicly demanded the return of the saloon as the best means of selling intoxicating liquor.

Du Pont's real purpose when he and his retainers were assuring the people that " the saloon shall not come back " is revealed by the following article that appeared in the press after the amendment was safely out of the way:

A policy of giving the American liquor drinker " what he wants when he wants it where he wants it," was advocated today by Pierre S. du Pont, Delaware state liquor commissioner and chairman of E. I. du Pont de Nemours & Company. The Wilmington industrialist, who has long been associated with the repeal movement as chairman of the executive committee of the Association Against the Prohibition Amendment, offered his suggestions at a hearing before a liquor committee of the federal bar association today.

The article then quoted Mr. du Pont as follows:

The people of the United States have been restricted by unpopular laws for so long that they must now be given some freedom or they will go back to evading the new laws as they did the old. Liberality is certainly the best move and the fewer restrictions upon the man who wants a drink the better.

I have never yet found anyone who has been able to tell me satisfactorily why selling over the bar is objectionable. The principal argument seems to be that the bartender is an informal host who keeps people drinking. But for myself, I see no objections to a bar.[37]

In the organization's final report, Mr. Shouse put the AAPA formally on record as favoring the return of the saloon. He said:

I maintain that if we as sensible people, with a knowledge of human nature and established habits, view the practicalities of the present situation, we are forced to the conclusion that we must provide places of retail sale in accordance with what our fellow Americans want and demand. A side door, no. A back room, no. A gambling parlor upstairs, no. But I assert that if the sale of liquor is going to be conducted through legitimate channels there must be an open place to which men can go and purchase at a reasonable price one drink or two drinks, as they may desire, and for my part I want this done under legal sanction instead of being done illicitly.

The Press

It is evident why men who control forty billion dollars are able to control the press. Newspapers are no longer organs of opinion; they are commercial enterprises. Editors of the type of Greeley, Dana, Medill and Lawson have been supplanted by business men whose object is money. They know that four things are essential to the birth and survival of a modern newspaper — capital, circulation, advertising, credit. They know that if it is to build up a large circulation, the newspaper must profess lofty motives but with absolute realism adjust its policies to the desires and prejudices of the masses of the cities. They know also that it must take orders from those who can furnish capital, advertising and credit.

Mr. Fred C. Kelly tells of the facts that were made public in connection with the failure of certain banks in Cleveland. Among other things, he says:

> As part of their technique for being the invisible government of a great city, both these big trust companies in Cleveland had a long list of loans to politicians and on scant security, or sometimes not any at all. All the important newspapers in the city owed the banks millions. Cleveland has three big daily papers. The company controlling two of these was heavily in debt to one bank, and the third paper owed millions to another bank. When it became known to insiders how serious was the condition of these banks, naturally prices of bank stocks dropped to only a fraction of their former level. Banks did not want this known to the public for it would have aroused suspicion. People would have inquired what was causing prices of bank stocks, with their double liability, to drop so rapidly. The banks therefore arranged with the local stock exchanges not to issue any statements about prices of bank stocks which changed hands. All three newspapers accepted this ruling and for many months made not the slightest effort to give their readers any idea of current values in local bank stocks. Publication of bank stock quotations would have given the public a hint as to the true situation, but the papers acquiesced in keeping such facts quiet.
>
> As I have said, it is improbable that standards of banking integrity or ability were any lower in Cleveland than in many other places. But the sins of those Cleveland bankers chanced to become public. We can now peer into the records and learn what to guard against elsewhere.[38]

The power of advertisers over the policy of newspapers was clearly shown by the evidence secured by the Federal Trade Commission when it conducted its historic investigation of the activities of the public utilities companies. The nature of the evidence is illustrated by a letter written by the industrial representative of the Georgia Railway and Power Company:

Our greatest distress before we started the committee was the printing by newspapers free of charge of propaganda written by public ownership fanatics. We answered these articles with paid advertisements and then insisted that the newspapers require the public ownership fanatics to also pay for the space they wanted. The result is that out of 250 newspapers in Georgia, only four will publish anything at all from the public ownership people. . . .[39]

An illuminating example of the technique of giving orders to the press was brought out by the Lobby Investigation Committee. The Du Ponts manufacture a large number of nationally advertised products and pay millions of dollars annually to newspapers and magazines for advertising. On March 24, 1928, Pierre du Pont wrote the following letter:

Wilmington, Del.

Mr. Wm. P. Smith
Director, Association Against the Prohibition Amendment
Philadelphia, Pa.

Dear Bill: I shall be glad if you will make known to the officials of the *Saturday Evening Post* my personal interest in the affairs of the Association Against the Prohibition Amendment, also the interest of my brothers, Irénée and Lammot. I feel that the *Saturday Evening Post* is intimately related to both the General Motors Corporation and the Du Pont Company and that the aim of this paper is to promote the welfare of the people of the United States. As I feel that the prohibition movement has failed in its original aim and has become both a nuisance and a menace, I hope that the officials of the *Saturday Evening Post* will join in a move toward better things with respect to the manufacture and sale of alcoholic beverages.

Sincerely yours,
Pierre S. du Pont.[40]

The proprietors of newspapers and magazines wished not only to satisfy subscribers, advertisers and financial backers, but also to reduce the income taxes paid by themselves and their corporations. With repeal they could also anticipate millions of dollars from liquor advertising. With a few honorable exceptions, therefore, they became sounding-boards for all the wet propaganda that was poured out by the association.

The degradation of the press has a tragic significance that does not appear on the surface. " The press " sounds impersonal but behind it are multitudes of laboring and struggling human beings. It was not only the officers, directors and publishers that had to obey orders, but also the writers who prepared all the " articles and editorials attacking prohibition." In schools and colleges young men and women studied the art of writing and the social and political sciences in preparation for a career in journalism. They hoped to expose and attack injustice and corruption, promote the public welfare and endeavor to make their ideals prevail. They found however that they were compelled to suppress and distort the news, protect those who were betraying the public, pervert the truth and ignore or misrepresent and slander those who were endeavoring to suppress evil and promote the public welfare. They knew that if they sought new positions, they would have to accept the same terms. As they had to have work, they sacrificed their ideals and their intellectual integrity, prostituted their talents, and became cynical and disillusioned cogs in greed-driven machines. Their attack upon prohibition was just one of the many " adjustments to reality " they were compelled to make.

Oswald Spengler declares that one of the sure signs that Western civilization is approaching its end is the fact that the press is owned and controlled by men who use it to accomplish their selfish and corrupt purposes. He says:

Today we live so cowed under the bombardment of this intellectual artillery that hardly anyone can attain to the inward detachment that is required for a clear view of the monstrous drama. The will-to-power operating under a pure democratic disguise has finished off its masterpiece so well that the object's sense of freedom is actually flattered by the most thoroughgoing enslavement that has ever existed. . . .

What is truth? For the multitude, that which it continually reads and hears. . . . Those who have learnt to read succumb to their power, and the visionary self-determination of late democracy issues in a thoroughgoing determination of the people by the powers whom the printed word obeys.

In the contests of today tactics consist in depriving the opponent of this weapon. . . . But in the background, unseen, the new forces are fighting one another by buying the press. Without the readers' observing it, the paper, *and himself with it,* changes masters. Here also money triumphs and forces the free spirits into its service. No tamer has his animals more under his power. . . .

The reader neither knows, nor is allowed to know, the purposes for which he is used, nor even the role that he is to play. A more appalling caricature of freedom of thought cannot be imagined. Formerly, a man did not dare to think freely. Now he dares, but cannot. . . .

And on the other side of this belated freedom — it is permitted to everyone to say what he pleases, but the press is free to take notice of what he says or not. It can condemn any " truth " to death, simply by not undertaking its communication to the world — a terrible censorship of silence which is all the more potent in that the masses of newspaper readers are absolutely unaware that it exists. . . .

This is the end of democracy. If in the world of truths it is *proof* that decides all, in that of facts it is *success*. Success means that one being triumphs over the others.[41]

Beloved Authors

The 1930 report of the AAPA stated that the Authors and Artists Committee, of which Irvin S. Cobb was chairman, had 578 members. In his testimony before the Senate committee, Mr. Curran said: " We have a committee of authors and artists, and it is a committee of about 700 or 800, including many of the most prominent and beloved authors, artists and cartoonists in the country." The 1930 report further stated that " more than 4,000,000 copies of books, pamphlets, reports, reprints, letters and leaflets were distributed from our offices in 1930. They dealt with economic, constitutional, political and practical sides of our work."

The word " author " still retains some of the glamor lent it by those men and women of the past who were able to give impressive utterance to great messages. With the improvement of the printing press and the multiplication of publications, authorship has become a money-making occupation. A great majority of authors are not oracles; they are just men and women engaged like the rest of us in the business of making a living. They must dispose of their manuscripts if they are to have shelter, clothing and food. Material, publishers and markets are obtained only by hard labor, which often has to be performed under the most discouraging circumstances.

The AAPA had a great propaganda machine that was engaged in grinding out wet material, putting it in pre-digested form and furnishing it to newspapers, magazines, congressmen, senators and others. Of course, it was the essence of good salesmanship to put it out over the signatures of " prominent " and " beloved " authors. The AAPA was also able to insure them publishers and markets. Hundreds of thousands of dollars were spent purchasing and distributing these books, pamphlets and other documents. The money was going around, and our " beloved authors " determined to get theirs while the getting was good.

Mr. Curran was asked if Mr. Cobb received a salary for his work as chairman of the Authors and Artists Committee. His answer was: " He has no salary. He doesn't need one." He didn't, of course. He was paid through the promotion of the sale of the material to which his name was signed. After repeal, his advertising value was still recognized. On November 28, 1934, the Chicago *Tribune* devoted an entire page to an advertisement extolling the glories of two brands of whisky. At the end it said: " Mix your pre-dinner cocktails with them; burn them on your plum pudding. Let them add their mellow flavor to your after-dinner highballs." Then came a picture of Mr. Cobb, and under it the following: " Irvin S. Cobb's own Recipe Book, the greatest drinking guide ever published, describes nearly 100 selected recipes and there's $100 worth of Mr. Cobb's best humor besides. Send 10¢ in stamps for your copy to Frankfort Distilleries, Dept. 23234, Louisville, Ky."

Those who are familiar with the habits of bees know that they will fly far and wide and labor diligently to obtain nectar to bring back to the hive. If, however, a plate of sirup is put in front of the hive, they will fly no more until it is deposited in the honeycomb. Our " beloved authors " imitated the prudence of the bees.

The Politicians

The final report of the association states that " at the time it was started, the sentiment of the country was dominated by prohibitionists. They controlled an overwhelming majority in both houses of Congress, they were ascendant in the organization of the two major political parties, they were the temporary masters of state officials and legislatures in many sections of the country." In glowing terms, it recounts a long succession of victories which culminated in 1933 when the politicians of both parties, from the President, senators and congressmen down to the pettiest ward-heelers, performed to the crack of the AAPA whip, parroted its propaganda, and with voice and vote supported every line of its program.

Fortunately, the record shows precisely how this result was achieved. It is a matter of common knowledge that the politics of the country are controlled by " machines." The sole purpose of these organizations is to secure office, power, money and other selfish advantages for their members. They have armies of workers who are paid by jobs or money from war chests that are filled by the contributions of officeholders, candidates for office, public contractors and recipients of special privileges, and by blackmail levied upon property owners and business men and upon people who live by vice and crime. These mercenary armies sell their services to those elements that can give them the largest amount of money and manipulate the influences and " pull the strings " necessary to keep them in power. The " public policies " which they support depend upon whether the communities in which they exist are dominated by farmers, laborers, industrialists, financiers, or a combination of these elements. In the latter case, the bosses of the machines have to be lightning-change artists or tight-rope walkers, according to the necessities of the moment.

An individual can rarely " buck the machine." If he wants to be elected to office he must obtain its support, and to do this he must play its game, whatever that may be. A refusal to " go along " is an act of political suicide. He must also have newspaper support, money for printing, postage, meetings, lithographs, flags and time on the radio. After he has learned just what he must stand for, and has made his underground deals, he blossoms forth as a tribune of the people and defends the policies of his masters in the name of superpatriotism.

When the representatives of big business reached the conclusion that it would be profitable to bring the liquor traffic back and tax it, they withdrew their active and passive support from prohibition, allied themselves with the liquor interests, the underworld and every other reactionary and subversive element, and threw the entire weight of their wealth and power into the battle for repeal. Their first move was to defeat and destroy all politicians everywhere who stood for the retention and enforcement of prohibition, and to supplant them with pliant tools who would permit liquor lawlessness, act as sounding-boards for the wet propaganda, and work and vote for repeal. The final report of the AAPA tells of " the defeat for Congress of Andrew Volstead, father of the National Prohibition Act," and " the defeat of Louis C. Crampton and Grant M. Hudson, two of the most pronounced dry spokesmen in Congress," and states that

anti-prohibition planks were written by the Republicans in Connecticut, Illinois, New Jersey, New York, Rhode Island, Washington and Wisconsin, and the Democrats expressed support of repeal in the following fourteen states: Connecticut, Delaware, Illinois, Maryland, Massachusetts, New Hampshire, New Jersey, New York, North Dakota, Pennsylvania, Rhode Island, Vermont, Washington and Wisconsin.

It states further that the report for the previous year

called attention in detail to the state referenda conducted in Arizona, California, Colorado, Connecticut, Louisiana, Michigan, New Jersey, North Dakota, Oregon, Texas, Washington and Wyoming. Each constituted a striking anti-prohibition victory.

Last year's report also called attention to the fact that our association had participated actively in the election of senators and congressmen chosen for the Seventy-third Congress. Where the issue was clear-cut as between an advocate of repeal and a defender of the Eighteenth

Amendment, we did not hesitate to do everything proper looking to the choice of the repeal candidate. In almost every instance those whom we supported were victorious at the polls, with the result that for the first time since the Eighteenth Amendment was ratified, a Congress favorable to repeal by a large majority became an assured fact.

The manner in which Du Pont, Raskob and Sabin brought the politicians of the various states to their knees is illustrated by the strong-arm methods they used in Pennsylvania. The prohibition sentiment was so strong in that state that the politicians were afraid to come out openly against it. What happened is told in the 1930 report of the AAPA:

> In the Pennsylvania primaries last May, the various Republican machines refused to recognize prohibition as an issue. The two candidates for the nomination for governor were Pinchot, the dry, and Brown, who had organization support and who straddled on the question of repeal. The candidates for the senatorial nomination, Grundy and Davis, were likewise unsatisfactory. We therefore put our own ticket in the field — Bohlen for senator, Phillips for governor, and Dorrance for lieutenant governor. They stood flatly for repeal.
>
> Our purpose was, by defeating Brown, to teach the machine leaders they could not pander to the drys by dodging the prohibition issue and still expect liberal support for their candidates. We were successful, as the vote shows:
>
> For Senator: Davis, 733,108; Grundy, 494,191; Bohlen, 249,408.
>
> For Governor: Pinchot, 632,719; Brown, 612,620; Phillips, 281,399.
>
> For Lieutenant Governor: Shannon, 602,339; Armstrong, 415,759; Dorrance, 294,826.
>
> Pinchot beat Brown by 20,000 votes. The Phillips vote did that. If Brown had come out against prohibition, instead of straddling, he would have polled practically all of the total of more than 280,000 ballots that went to Phillips.

From that time on, the politicians of Pennsylvania took their orders from Du Pont, Raskob and Sabin, who lived in other states.

The methods of these gentlemen are further illustrated by the following statements from their files. In 1928, there were two congressional districts in Wisconsin that had not been subdued.

The vice-president of the association wrote Dr. Seelman, who had charge of its activities in that state, a letter in which he said:

Dear Dr. Seelman: I have your letter of September 15, and Major Curran requests me to ask you to visit both the seventh and eighth Wisconsin congressional districts as you suggest. . . .

Our executive committee has made a number of appropriations of about $2,500 each for various districts in which we are interested, and if you think the expenditure of a little money is desirable in these two Wisconsin districts, please make a recommendation accordingly.

In 1930, Mr. C. W. Crooker, who represented the association in Massachusetts, wrote a letter containing the following:

My Dear Major Curran: I inclose herewith my itemized statement of receipts and disbursements incident to activities in the second congressional district.

The item of $710, representing disbursements through Gately, is not, as I have already explained to Mr. Sibley, susceptible to individual vouchers, as they were not obtainable from the individuals involved.

Mr. Gately is the president of the Central Labor Union at Springfield, and is a very sound, prudent, reliable person.

A few examples will illustrate the manner in which these stalwart defenders of states' rights told the people of the various states who their United States senators should be and what they should stand for. Senator Lenroot of Wisconsin was one of the great progressive leaders of the Senate, a prominent candidate for the presidency, a man of commanding influence. He was also a dry leader who could not be deceived, bought or coerced. So he had to be destroyed. Mr. Curran admitted that $40,000 had been spent in Wisconsin to defeat Lenroot and to repeal the state enforcement act.

On August 10, 1928, Mr. Stayton wrote a letter to Mr. Curran in regard to the work of Dr. Seelman who "for several years ran the Wisconsin branch" of the association, in which he said:

. . . Meantime he handled the political situation very adroitly, always playing the three political parties — Republican, Democratic, and Progressive — so as to have some one or the other with him, and I think he controlled the legislature for every year since he took charge out there. He had repeated resolutions passed by the legislature asking for modification of the Volstead Act. He looked out for the referendum there and won it by 2 to 1, and I think his organization is almost wholly responsible for the defeat of Lenroot, the dry, and the election of Senator Blaine, the wet.

Blaine was a politician who could always be depended on to perform at the crack of the association whip. He gave fanatical support to its program.

William M. Butler was a distinguished business man of Boston, an intimate friend of President Coolidge, chairman of the Republican national committee, senator from Massachusetts, and one of the most influential men in Washington. He was a dry, a thorn in the flesh of Mr. du Pont, and so had to be defeated for re-election, humiliated and destroyed. David I. Walsh had been a politician all his life. His mind and character had been formed in the fetid atmosphere of machine politics. He had the backing of the spoilsmen, liquor dealers, grafters, underworld and other elements that made up Boston's Tammany Hall. But he was a fanatical wet and so Du Pont decided that he was the man that Massachusetts should have for its senator. The statement which the association was compelled to file in Washington of the money it spent to promote his election tells us more about its methods and of how repeal was accomplished than could be learned from a volume of assertions and arguments. It showed the expenditure of $74,000. The following are a few of the items:

REPORT OF EXPENDITURES FOR PERIOD OCTOBER 1, 1926, TO DECEMBER 31, 1926, IN THE STATE OF MASSACHUSETTS

October 30, 1926, to Charles S. Ashley, New Bedford, Mass., for getting out vote in New Bedford	$2,000
October 29, 1926, William M. McCarthy, getting out vote in Rockland	300
October 29, 1926, Frank A. Manning, getting out vote in fourteenth congressional district	250
October 30, 1926, John J. Gilbride, getting out vote in Lowell	1,480
October 30, 1926, John M. Thayer, getting out vote in Worcester	1,000

October 30, 1926, Peter F. Sullivan, getting out vote in Worcester	1,000
October 30, 1926, Thomas C. Stutch, getting out vote in Boston	500
October 30, 1926, Harold S. Rurledge, getting out vote in Boston	1,250
October 30, 1926, William J. Sullivan, getting out vote in Boston	1,000
October 30, 1926, James T. Cassidy, getting out vote in Boston ..	900
October 30, 1926, Michael J. Welch, getting out vote in Boston ..	250
October 30, 1926, Edward Masters, getting out vote in Boston ...	200
October 30, 1926, Harry J. Goldberg, getting out vote in Boston	850
November 1, 1926, William M. Doherty, getting out vote in Boston	200
November 1, 1926, Michael J. O'Malley, getting out vote in Boston	200
November 1, 1926, Abraham Goldberg, getting out vote in Boston	250
November 1, 1926, Pierce J. Cronin, geting out vote in Boston ..	200
November 1, 1926, John I. Fitzgerald, getting out vote in Boston	600
November 1, 1926, Geo. J. O'Donnell, getting out vote in Boston	200
November 1, 1926, Cornelius Desmond, Jr., for getting out vote in Lowell	880
November 1, 1926, Bernard J. O'Neil, for getting out vote in Boston	100

If this money had been spent on the entire state over a period of months for literature, postage, halls, speakers, advertising and so on, it might represent selfish and dishonest propaganda, but it would not be evident from the record. But when $74,000 is dumped into a state on the three days preceding an election, and reported as given in large sums to the organization and to individuals to "get out the vote," the merest tyro in politics knows that it represents the wholesale purchase of votes.

In 1928, Senator Walsh wrote the following letter:

United States Senate
Washington, D. C.
October 15, 1928

Maj. H. H. Curran
New York, N. Y.

Dear Major Curran: I think you may know that Mr. F. G. R. Gordon of Haverhill covered western Massachusetts two years ago in the interest of my election to the Senate.

The Association Against the Prohibition Amendment paid Mr. Gordon, as I understand, his expenses, he contributing his time to our cause.

This being a presidential year with a tremendous vote to be polled, I need all the help that I can have.

After a talk with Mr. Gordon today, I am suggesting that if he was appointed a general organizer for the balance of this campaign in your association, working in the general interest of the building up of your movement, and was free to cover the same field that he covered in 1926, it would be of tremendous assistance to my campaign.

I am therefore applying to you in the interests of the cause we are all interested in, to so arrange matters that Mr. Gordon may have the opportunity to do for me this year what he did two years ago. Mr. Gordon will be glad to contribute his services, but he must have expenses.

Sincerely yours,
David I. Walsh

Mr. Curran replied that it would be a pleasure to comply with this request, and added:

I know Mr. Gordon and know about his work, and cannot suppose that there can be any hitch in his going to work at once, agreeably to us all, and carrying on until election day.

With warmest best wishes for a splendid victory to cap your campaign. . . .

Mr. Walsh repaid the AAPA in magnificent fashion. He trumpeted its propaganda and was its faithful representative in the United States Senate. His greatest act of gratitude, however, was performed at the Democratic national convention of 1932. Senator Hull and other dry Democrats insisted that the convention should go no farther than to promise to submit a repeal amendment to the states. Walsh and Mike Igoe, representing Illinois' Tammany Hall, wanted a plank declaring for immediate modification of the Volstead Act and unconditional repeal and making these measures articles of party faith binding on all Democrats. This nullification-repeal-party-faith plank was known as the Walsh-Igoe plank. The result was stated by the Chicago *Tribune* as follows:

> The wringing wet policy was written into the proposed national platform after a majority of the subcommittee of nine which drafted the platform recommended a plank which would merely urge submission of repeal without committing the party itself to repeal. This plank was rejected by the committee by a vote of 35 to 18. . . .
>
> Sunday saw the dripping wet uprising against the merely damps growing. As the easterners came in, Senator David I. Walsh of Massachusetts began conferences and by Tuesday night members of the resolutions committee from 24 states had signed up for the Walsh-Igoe plank.
>
> It became a tidal wave when the resolutions committee finally got down to the prohibition question yesterday afternoon and the wets won overwhelmingly.[42]

Where other methods failed, the association proceeded " by the referendum route " to control the United States Senate. Senator Thomas J. Walsh of Montana was an outstanding dry who could not be induced to change his mind, and could not be defeated. He was then put on the spot and forced to declare that if the question was submitted to the people of his state, he " would stand by the vote on the referendum." Then, although the total population of Montana is less than that of Milwaukee, the association " appropriated " $10,000 contributed by eastern millionaires to promote a referendum in Montana, which would instruct its senator how to vote on the liquor question. This money was used to control the election by the methods usually employed by the AAPA. Thus Senator Walsh received his instructions and crowned his long career of moral leadership by deserting his old comrades — Borah, Capper, Glass, Sheppard and others — and voted to submit to conventions an amendment that provided for the return of the liquor traffic, the open saloon, and all the other accompaniments of that traffic. By these and similar methods, nearly all the men of courage and self-respect were driven from public life or silenced.

The politicians came to realize the power of the AAPA. They learned that by the simple device of becoming wet, they could obtain the support of powerful financial interests, of the machine and of the press, and also the money with which to conduct their campaign and "get out the vote," while their dry opponents would be damned by silence or by vilification. They became concerned, therefore, about the Constitution, political corruption and true temperance, and announced themselves for repeal. They accepted and broadcast the propaganda of the AAPA just as they accepted and used its money.

The American Legion

The final report of the AAPA acknowledges its debt of gratitude to the American Legion for its "active and effective work" for repeal. Any adequate discussion of this organization and its wet activities would require a separate volume. But there are certain facts which can be treated as matters of common knowledge. During the war, the American people were justly proud of their army, and they have never ceased to have a strong feeling of gratitude for the men who composed it. After the war, a great majority of the soldiers resumed their ordinary callings, satisfied with the sentiment of appreciation of their services with which they were uniformly greeted. There was a small group of men, however, who were determined to capitalize that sentiment and cash in on it. These were the men who worked themselves into the leadership, attended all the conventions, did the strutting and big talking, and played the politics of the American Legion. They have not represented the great majority of the soldiers and they have been repeatedly and publicly repudiated by some of the bravest, most intelligent and most patriotic men that went through the shell fire of the western front. They have, however, gone up and down the land wielding the legion club. As strike-breakers, red baiters, guardians of the Constitution, infallible exponents of true patriotism and one hundred per centers generally, they have always operated under the camouflage of super-Americanism.

The militant political activities of these men were not necessary to induce the American people to be generous in their treatment of the veterans and more than fair in providing for all their legitimate needs. But one need only to examine the news index of the New York *Times,* under the heading "Veterans," to see that these

" leaders " have been constantly engaged in making baseless and exorbitant demands and in raiding the federal treasury. These raids have been fought and partially checked by the vetoes of every President since the war. They have been opposed by all competent and courageous statesmen, and by the intelligent and responsible men and women of the country. At the time of the last raid, President Roosevelt, in a vigorous veto message, pointed out that half of the men did not leave this country, that many of them had good jobs and did not need the money, that they had already received large sums from the treasury, that the country was in the throes of a great depression, that the people were being heavily taxed, that the treasury was borrowing money and the budget was out of balance, that a great strain was being put upon the public credit, that there was danger of unduly inflating the currency, and that the government needed every available dollar to sustain our economic structure and to keep millions of men, women and children from starvation. He stated that the veterans had already received $7,800,000,000, and added: " The bill before me provides for the immediate payment of the 1945 value of the certificates. It means paying $1,600,000,000 more than the present value of the certificates. It requires an expenditure of more than $2,200,000,000 in cash for this purpose. It is a new straight gratuity or bounty to the amount of $1,000,000,000."

Donald A. Hobart, national commander of the American Veterans' Association, said that the payment of these certificates " is unfair because it advocates a $2,000,000,000 hand-out without regard to individual need. It is dishonorable because it commercializes patriotism and reacts in the public mind to the great disadvantage of the truly deserving veterans." This meant nothing to our professional patriots. They descended upon Washington and at the point of the shotgun forced a cowardly Congress to pass their bill over a second presidential veto.

The greatest difficulty they encountered was the politicians' fear of imposing the additional tax burden upon the people. The wets offered them the solution of this problem. They said, " Help us bring back the liquor traffic and tax it and that will put billions into the federal treasury and we will help you to 'get your cut.'" How this bait was dangled was illustrated at the hearing before the Senate committee that investigated the national prohibition law in 1926. When Big Bill Thompson became mayor of Chicago, he announced that he was "as wet as the Atlantic Ocean" and that Chicago was a wide-open town. This, of course, was the position of Tony Cermak and his infamous Tammany organization. A number of bills had been introduced into Congress providing for the manufacture, sale and taxation of beer and wine, and a committee had been appointed to conduct hearings on the subject. Two days before the hearing began, the Chicago council, composed of henchmen of the Thompson and Cermak machines, adopted the following resolution:

> *Resolved:* That it is the sense of the City Council of the City of Chicago in meeting assembled, that the Congress of the United States of America and the State of Illinois, amend and modify existing prohibition laws under their respective jurisdiction and within their proper powers which will permit the manufacture, sale, and distribution of wholesome beers and light wines, and that all governmental revenue derived from such permission be set aside as a separate fund for the payment of bonuses to ex-service men. [43]

This was carried to Washington by Tony Cermak and put before the committee and the country to enlist the support of the American Legion leaders. After this idea had had time to germinate, a national convention of the legion declared for repeal on the ground that the Eighteenth Amendment "created a condition endangering respect for law." It is important, therefore, that we learn something of the sincerity of their pretense of respect for law.

After the legion convention of 1921, held in Kansas City, the New York *Nation* published communications and newspaper reports of this convention, and stated that the evidence showed "that the assembly was a medley of rum, rowdyism and riot." The following are some of the statements:

Very little control of any sort was manifest during the three days and nights of the convention. Liquor — of the virulent Volstead vintage — flowed freely and furiously. Bootleggers openly disposed of their wares. Not even the wildest spectacles of open saloon days could compete with this occasion. It is significant that on the day after the convention closed, the press reported an announcement by the local federal authorities that the " three days grace " was over and the prohibition law would be enforced.

The great parade on Tuesday was the occasion of a very belligerent display of the new patriotism. Down the line of march the paraders, many of whom were one hundred per cent intoxicated, knocked the hats off civilians in the front rank of spectators. One parader drew his gun on a spectator who was not sufficiently prompt in removing his hat.

The official program went through with only one hitch. The resolution approving the use of chemicals was dropped without a struggle when a member of the committee threatened to expose the committee chairman as a son-in-law of Du Pont, connected with the chemical department of the famous powder works.

The Kansas City *Post* declared that

the fighters were, for the most part, drunk. Liquor flowed like water during the three nights of the convention. Crap games were in progress in the lobby of the Baltimore and the length of Eleventh street every night. Bottles of " white mule " and " moonshine " were set up in the center of each group of crap-shooters. The authorities admitted themselves afraid to make arrests.

The St. Joseph *Gazette* said:

Illustrative of the hoodlum spirit at times present, all of the clothing was torn from a young woman who emerged from an office building near Eleventh street and Grand avenue in the very heart of the business section early Tuesday morning. When the young woman finally made her escape, she had naught of her clothing except a few torn shreds of undergarments and her shoes and stockings.

When a manager of one of the downtown hotels told a number of men to stop " shooting craps " on the floor of the lobby, he was told: " Oh, go to hell, we're running this joint now." [44]

There is not space to tell of the succeeding conventions, which repeated the same story of contempt for law and decency. Their spirit is illustrated by the following statements from an article that appeared in the *Forum* for June 1931, which discussed the approaching legion convention that was to be held in Detroit:

There have been twelve progressively bigger, noisier, more elaborate and more significant ones so far, and in between the forty-eight departments practice up on state meetings. . . .

For the great majority, however, voicing the " Aye " which results in America's spending several hundred million dollars in the coming year is a mere formality. The real business of the convention is the hell-raising. Upon the adjournment of executive sessions each afternoon, the veterans flock out on the streets again to devote themselves to serious drinking and revelry.

After the evacuation of Boston, an editorial writer in the Harvard *Crimson* said bitterly: " It was merely an excuse for a wholesale brawl, exceeding in its disgusting completeness any similar spectacle which the United States has to offer. Even Boston has seen fit to allow a total relaxation of law and order during the stay of the ' buddies ' of the legion, those glorious Americans who fought, the slogan says, to make the world safe for democracy, and who have come back to raise hell annually so no one can forget it."

S. A. High, speaking of the Omaha convention he saw, said: " There never has been a time in the history of the city when vice has been more rampant and law less regarded."

The politicians in any city are delighted to have the legion come and eager to show their friendly cooperation. They know the organization as a staunch and valuable ally, both locally and nationally.

President Hoover was invited to address the 1931 convention, and when he appeared he was greeted with the chant, " We want beer, we want beer." At this convention, the legion adopted a resolution favoring the repeal of the Eighteenth Amendment. When it was presented, the New York *Times* tells us, " immediately pandemonium broke loose on the floor, with cries of ' We want beer ' drowning the shouts of the dry forces, who were demanding adoption of the minority report." [45] The resolution was as follows:

Whereas, the Eighteenth Amendment of the Constitution of the United States has created a condition endangering respect for law and the security of American institutions, therefore, be it

Resolved, that the American Legion in this thirteenth annual convention assembled, favor the submission by Congress of the repeal or modification of the present prohibition laws to the states with a request that each state submit this question to the voters thereof.

NOTES

[1] W. C. Durant, *Law Observance* (Durant Award Office, 1929), pp. 119, 122.

[2] *Congressional Record,* Vol. 65, Part 2, 68th Congress, p. 1213.

[3] Hearings before a Subcommittee of the Judiciary, U. S. Senate, 71st Congress, 2nd Session. (Hereafter, this report will be referred to as LI.)

[4] LI, p. 4131.

[5] See the evidence presented by George Seldes, *Iron, Blood and Profits* (Harper & Bros., 1934), pp. 271 ff.

[6] Stayton's next venture as knight errant of the Constitution took place when the Du Ponts and their associates made him an officer and propagandist of the ill-starred American Liberty League, which was organized to " defend and uphold the Constitution of the United States."

[7] Ernest Gordon, *When the Brewers Had the Stranglehold* (Alcohol Information Committee, 1930), pp. 218–19.

[8] *Ibid.,* pp. 216–17.

[9] *Ibid.,* pp. 217–18.

[10] Annual Report of the AAPA for 1931, p. 17.

[11] LI, pp. 4096, 4097.

[12] These letters appear in LI, pp. 4225, 3898, 3999 respectivelv.

[13] LI, p. 3895.

[14] LI, p. 4177.

[15] *Ibid.*

[16] LI, p. 4178.

[17] LI, pp. 3914–15.

[18] Irving Fisher, *The Noble Experiment* (Alcohol Information Committee, 1930), pp. 15–18.

[19] LI, p. 4245.

[20] Statistics of Income for 1929, U. S. Treasury Department, pp. 22, 365.

[21] Report of Securities Exchange Commission.

[22] Munitions Industry, 74th Congress, 2nd Session, Report No. 944, Part 4, pp. 35, 36.

[23] 37 U. S. Board of Tax Appeals 173, pp. 32, 70.

[24] LI, p. 4167.

[25] LI, pp. 3991–92.

[26] LI, pp. 3962–64, 3912–13.

[27] LI, p. 4141.

[28] LI, p. 3898.

[29] LI, p. 3966.

[30] LI, pp. 4047–48.

[31] LI, p. 4373.
[32] LI, p. 4414.
[33] LI, p. 4063.
[34] New York *Times,* Dec. 6, 1933.
[35] *Christian Century,* Feb. 8, 1933.
[36] LI, pp. 4011–12.
[37] Chicago *Tribune,* June 30, 1932.
[38] *Esquire,* Aug. 1935, p. 95.
[39] Cited by Stephen Raushenbush, *The Power Fight* (New Republic, 1932), p. 17.
[40] LI, p. 4236.
[41] *The Decline of the West* (Alfred A. Knopf, 1926), II, 461.
[42] Chicago *Tribune,* June 30, 1932.
[43] Hearings before the Subcommittee of the Committee of the Judiciary on the National Prohibition Law, U. S. Senate, 69th Congress, p. 660.
[44] *Nation,* Nov. 23, 1921.
[45] New York *Times,* Sept. 25, 1931.

Chapter Two

Shock Troops Of The AAPA

THE final report of the AAPA gives an account of the formation of the United Repeal Council, of which "Pierre S. du Pont was named chairman." This organization was composed of the AAPA, the Voluntary Committee of Lawyers, the Crusaders, the Women's Organization for National Prohibition Reform, and the American Hotel Association. These subsidiary organizations were initiated by the AAPA, and their work was carried on by the lawyers, by the wives and sons and daughters of the association's members, and by men who wanted to open saloons in hotels. The names of the organizations were skillfully chosen not merely to conceal the motives of their members, but to lead the people to believe that these motives were the exact opposite of what they really were.

The Legal Profession

Nothing indicates more clearly the nature and extent of our national deterioration than the change that has taken place in the legal profession. Lawyers distinguished by learning and professional integrity have steadily declined in numbers and influence during the last fifty years. To an increasing extent, men go to lawyers because they want something "put over," and select lawyers not because they know the law, but because they know "the ropes." Bar associations, state and national, have solemnly denounced the ethics of ambulance chasers and lawyers who represent gangsters, racketeers and other powerful characters of the underworld. But of still more sinister portent is the fact that the

" leaders of the bar " and the " great constitutional lawyers " who are active in and dominate these associations, in their service of big business interests engage in practices that are even more reprehensible. The following carefully considered statements are impressive expressions of this fact.

Professor Calvert Magruder of the Harvard Law School has declared that

it is unfortunate that the best brains of the profession have been spent on manipulation of the corporate devices for the development of holding companies, security affiliates, mergers, nonvoting stock and investment trusts, at the behest of financial adventurers, who have thereby attained control of vast pools of wealth contributed by the general public.[1]

Professor William O. Douglas, formerly of the Yale Law School and now justice of the United States Supreme Court, said:

It is sad but true that the high priests of the legal profession were active agents in making high finance a master rather than a servant of the public interest. They accomplished what their clients wanted accomplished and they did it efficiently, effectively, and with dispatch. They were tools or agencies for the manufacture of synthetic securities and for the manipulation and appropriation of other people's money. . . . They neglected their foremost function — to create and maintain financial practices which were respectable, honest and conservative.[2]

Justice Harlan Stone of the United States Supreme Court has added his voice to the indictment:

Steadily the best skill and capacity of the profession have been drawn into the . . . service of business and finance. At its best the changed system has brought to the command of the business world loyalty and a superb proficiency and technical skill. At its worst it has made the learned profession of an earlier day the obsequious servant of business, and tainted it with the morals and manners of the market place in its most antisocial manifestations.[3]

And John T. Flynn has spoken in equally unequivocal terms:

Our vast, complicated, shameful corporate system, which, in so many of its manifestations, is deliberately designed for frauds upon stockholders and the public, is the proud invention of men who plume themselves upon being the leaders of the nation. These great law firms have guided their greedy and acquisitive clients through the mazes of trickery that the financiers had not the wit to travel alone. No cause seems to be too reprehensible for the lawyers to gild with their own sadly tarnished respectability.[4]

It was lawyers of this kind who laid the fuse for repeal. After the repeal amendment had been ratified, the *Literary Digest* said:

The American public is entitled to know the extraordinary role in this accomplishment played by the Voluntary Committee of Lawyers. The powder train had been laid over the years with the help of such powerful repeal bodies as the Association Against the Prohibition Amendment, Mrs. Sabin's organization of women, and the Crusaders. But the lawyers saw to the fuse. To them belongs the credit for the amazing precision of the rapid series of explosions which has blasted prohibition from the Constitution within the year.

At first limited in membership to New York city lawyers, the Voluntary Committee soon expanded to include eminent barristers in all parts of the country. It advanced with signal success toward its original objective, the passage of repeal resolutions by the nation's bar associations. Then, with the imminence of congressional action, it turned its attention from the agitation to the mechanics of repeal. . . .

But, as usual in such affairs, one man led the rest. He is Mr. Choate — tall, friendly, diffident, but immensely purposeful son of our former ambassador to the Court of St. James. He should take the final curtain.[5]

The final report of the AAPA is still more eloquent in its tribute to Mr. Choate and his " voluntary " associates.

The name " Voluntary Committee " was intended to convey the impression that the organization resulted from the voluntary and spontaneous action of disinterested citizens whose purpose was " to preserve the spirit of the Constitution of the United States." The facts show conclusively that their action was just as voluntary and disinterested as was that of Pierre du Pont's valet when he laid out Mr. du Pont's evening clothes.

Joseph H. Choate, Jr., was a member of the firm of Evarts, Choate, Curtin and Leon of 72 Wall street. For over half a century it had been the business of this firm to conduct millionaires through the loopholes of the law and to throw the shield of the Constitution over the liquor interests and big business whenever the people had endeavored to stop their depredations. With a lordly assumption of wisdom and of reverence for the Constitution, Mr. Choate contended that the power to deal with the liquor traffic rightly belonged to the states and that the Eighteenth Amendment was an invasion of the sacred rights of the states to handle their own police problems. But when the states were endeavoring to handle their own police problems, his firm was contending with vast array of precedents and " profound reasoning " that such endeavors constituted a violation of the Fourteenth Amendment to the Constitution of the United States. At a time when the liquor traffic was destroying individuals, wrecking homes, and spreading poverty, disease, crime and political corruption in Kansas, the decent people of the state arose and passed a law which banished it. In their fight against this law, the liquor interests chose Joseph H. Choate, Sr., as their leader, and bearing aloft the shield of the Constitution he led them to the grand assault. Representing the brewers, the distillers and the saloonkeepers, Mr. Choate appeared before the United States Supreme Court and hurled the following bomb into the camp of the people who represented the intelligence, the morality and the patriotism of Kansas:

> The thirteenth section of the liquor prohibition law of Kansas as amended in 1885, is an attempt to deprive these persons of their property and their liberty without " due process of law " and is therefore absolutely void.

This proved to be a " dud," for the Supreme Court replied:

> The power which the states have of prohibiting such use by individuals of their property as will be prejudicial to the health, the morals, or the safety of the public, is not — and consistently with the existence and safety of organized society cannot be — burdened with the condition

that the state must compensate such individual owners for pecuniary losses they may sustain, by reason of their not being permitted, by a noxious use of their property, to inflict injury on the community.[6]

In 1894, the federal income tax law was enacted. The proposition that a man's taxes should bear some relation to his ability to pay was, of course, declared an attack on property, it was communistic and an outrage upon the Constitution. Again the great business and financial interests turned to their dauntless champion, Mr. Choate, Sr., and he appeared before the Supreme Court and demanded that the "communist march" be stopped. By a vote of five to four, the court decided to stop the march. The people then had the effrontery to amend their Constitution and give Congress the power to re-establish the income tax.

When the Eighteenth Amendment cut off liquor revenue and increased income taxes, the great constitutional lawyers of Wall street informed the Supreme Court that the amendment had not been legally adopted and that the Volstead Act was unconstitutional. The court brushed aside their learned quiddities and upheld the amendment and the enforcement act. The only alternative left was to secure the repeal of the amendment, and that required the deception and coercion of the people. But big business realized that its great lawyers could be as useful in deceiving the people as they usually are in befuddling courts. The people must be told that the Constitution was being raped and that law enforcement machinery was being broken down.

The lawyers of the country must be enlisted and organized for the fight, bar associations must be "worked" and great names must be furnished for use in the wet propaganda. Pending repeal, a method of nullifying the Constitution must be found under which the courts would be stripped of their power to protect the integrity of our institutions. A uniform act providing for repeal conventions must be prepared and furnished to the legislatures of the states for immediate passage, and after repeal, liquor laws must be administered so as to insure the consumption of the maximum amount of liquor by the people and the collection of the largest possible revenue from the traffic. Joseph H. Choate, Jr., having served his apprenticeship and being in the full maturity of his powers, was ready to answer the Macedonian cry of big business. He went on the board of directors of the AAPA and organized the Voluntary Committee of Lawyers.

He had able colleagues. A member of the first board of managers of the Voluntary Committee was James H. Winston of the firm of Winston, Strawn and Shaw of Chicago. Ralph Shaw of this firm was a member of the national board of directors of the AAPA and its most fanatical worker in the middle west. His wife was associated with Mrs. Charles Sabin and Mrs. Pierre du Pont in forming the woman's repeal organization. The position of this firm in La Salle street was analogous to that of Evarts, Choate, Curtin and Leon in Wall street. Furthermore, whenever Wall street had anything to put over in Chicago, it usually turned to Winston, Strawn and Shaw. If the reader is curious to know how this firm worked with the legal lights of Wall street, the methods it pursued when serving big financial interests, and the rewards it received, let him read *The Investor Pays,* by Lowenthal, which tells the story of the St. Paul receivership. A fact of still greater importance in this connection is that for half a century this firm has been one of the most formidable legal bulwarks of the liquor interests in the United States. For a generation prior to the adoption of prohibition, it represented a number of distilleries, a dozen breweries, and the string of saloons which they owned.

It was a small group of men of the type of Choate and Winston who determined the policies and directed the work of the Voluntary Committee.

Defenders of the Constitution

In announcing the organization of this committee, the New York *Times* said:

> Banding together to bring about the repeal of the Volstead Act and the Eighteenth Amendment, several prominent lawyers have organized the Voluntary Committee of Lawyers, Inc., according to a statement issued yesterday from the committee's office at 20 Broad street.
>
> "The general purpose of the corporation is to preserve the spirit of

the Constitution of the United States," their statement read. "Its immediate purpose is to bring about the repeal of the Eighteenth Amendment." [7]

That the talk about the "spirit of the Constitution" was a smoke screen, and that the "immediate purpose" was the only purpose, was conclusively shown by the committee's action after repeal was achieved. On November 9, 1933, the New York *Times* said:

> The executive committee of the Voluntary Committee of Lawyers, Inc., announced yesterday that it had closed its offices, repeal having fulfilled the purpose of the organization.

In his book *The Dry Decade,* Mr. Charles Merz points out that in 1917 and 1918 these lawyers were not opposing prohibition on constitutional grounds. Why should they? At that time Mr. du Pont and men of his type were supporting prohibition on the ground that it would keep their workers sober, do away with blue Mondays and increase output. But after 1926, it seemed probable "that their increased taxes more than eat up the profits derived from the increased output." Of course, their great lawyers could not frankly say that they wanted the liquor traffic brought back in order to reduce the income taxes of their masters. So they went to their regular wailing wall and poured out their lamentations over the destruction of the Constitution. They solemnly declared that "the Eighteenth Amendment is inconsistent with the spirit and purpose of the Constitution of the United States, and in derogation of the liberties of the citizens and rights of the states as guaranteed by the first ten amendments thereto." Pontifical pronouncements of this kind were continually made by these "leaders of the American bar," and taken up by the propagandists of the AAPA and triumphantly broadcast to every part of the land.

That these statements were a part of a deliberate campaign of deception, there can be no doubt. In the first place, the great lawyers had remained silent during the years when the amendment was being submitted, ratified and put into operation. They became vocal only after their rich clients became repeal fanatics. In the second place, while people might believe that the amendment was a mistake and should be repealed, the question of its constitutional validity had been removed from the field of honest discussion. When the amendment and the Volstead Act were before the Supreme Court of the United States, all these considerations and many others were urged upon it with the greatest ability and ardor by Elihu Root, William D. Guthrie and other lawyers of outstanding ability and influence. Charles E. Hughes and many other distinguished lawyers argued the cases for the government. It is safe to say that no case that ever came before that court was more exhaustively presented than were the prohibition cases. When the court rendered its decision, it was not acting as the mouthpiece of private interests or helping to broadcast propaganda. This is what it said:

> That amendment, by lawful proposal and ratification, has become a part of the Constitution, and must be respected and given effect the same as any other provision of that instrument.
>
> The first section of the amendment, the one embodying the prohibition, is operative throughout the entire territorial limits of the United States, binds all legislative bodies, courts, public officers, and individuals within those limits, and of its own force invalidates every legislative act — whether by Congress, by a state legislature, or by a territorial assembly — which authorizes or sanctions what the section prohibits.
>
> The second section of the amendment — the one declaring "The Congress and the several states shall have concurrent power to enforce this article by appropriate legislation" — does not enable Congress or the several states to defeat or thwart the prohibition, but only to enforce it by appropriate means.[8]

A more solemn and unequivocal declaration that the amendment and the statute had been enacted in the manner provided by the Constitution and in entire conformity to its letter and spirit, could not have been made. But the "eminent lawyers" of the Voluntary Committee knew that not one lawyer in a hundred had read those decisions, and that none of the people had read them. They believed, therefore, that by virtue of their great reputations they could get away with anything that the interests of their clients demanded.

So they set to work. One of the first — and one of the most difficult and important — tasks assigned to the Voluntary Committee was that of lining up the lawyers and the bar associations of the country for repeal. The committee was, of course, ideally equipped for this task. The AAPA was deluging the business men of every part of the country with letters telling them of the financial advantages they would reap from repeal. Lawyers were beginning to realize that open and effective work for repeal would please the men from whom they could expect big fees. They were greatly assisted in making the necessary mental and moral readjustments by receiving from " leaders of the American bar " pompous communications, couched in language with which they were familiar, assuring them that the Eighteenth Amendment was contrary to the spirit of the Constitution, and " a source of confusion and hindrance in the interpretation and administration of the entire body of the law." These letters were also definite notice to lawyers everywhere that the attorneys for the big business and financial interests of the country had gone wet and that drys would be outside the charmed circle. There was another fact that had an important bearing on the situation. The great law firms in the big business and financial centers represent interests that extend to every part of the country. They are constantly calling upon lawyers in Dallas, Phoenix, Denver, Duluth and other cities to " look after the interests of their clients " in matters arising in those cities. If a lawyer sent back an enthusiastic reply on the question of repeal, he became favorably known to the big city lawyer. When, therefore, he went to Chicago or New York, he had a valid excuse for going into the office of Winston, Strawn and Shaw, or Evart, Choate, Curtin and Leon, and he might be taken to lunch at the Mid-Day Club or the Bankers' Club, and improve his prospects for important business connections.

The members of the Voluntary Committee, being amply financed, were able to take advantage of this situation. In April 1929 they sent out a letter, signed by Mr. Choate and other members of the board of managers, to twenty thousand members of the American Bar Association, asking them to enlist in the repeal movement. When the American Bar Association met that year, the members of the Voluntary Committee were on hand, doing everything in their power to line up the members for a repeal resolution. They found, however, that they had not yet done enough missionary work, and that it would be advisable to carry the matter over for another year, as shown by the following dispatch from the convention to the New York *Times:*

> Prohibition placed on the front doorstep of the American Bar Association by the wet wing of the organization, probably will remain there for another year, at least, under the care of the Voluntary Committee of Lawyers, Inc.
>
> Leaders of the committee said today the association was not yet ready to vote on repeal of the Eighteenth Amendment, and the anti-Volstead organization, which led successful fights before the bars of New York city, Boston and Philadelphia, will do missionary work in the south and west before making concentrated campaign in the general association.[9]

How successful that missionary work was is shown by the fact that the annual report of the AAPA for the year 1930 was able to boast of the fact that in that year the American Bar Association went on record in favor of repeal.

An incident in this missionary campaign showed the supercilious attitude of these great lawyers and their contempt for law. Marshall Stimson, a prominent Los Angeles lawyer, wrote Mr. Choate that every member of the committee should take an oath that he obeyed the law or the committee should abandon its work, since it would not be " coming into court with clean hands " unless its own members obeyed the law they sought to repeal. Mr. Choate replied: " In a free country, those who disapprove of a law are entitled to say so, whether they have obeyed the law or not."[10]

The manner in which these lawyers performed to the crack of their masters' whip is shown by a few illustrations. We have seen that one of the principal features of the strategy of the AAPA was to force the repeal of the state enforcement acts and thereby bring about a state of liquor lawlessness that would discredit the amendment. So deplorable were the results that the President called upon the states to perform their constitutional duty to co-operate with the federal government in its efforts to enforce the law. Thereupon the Voluntary Committee issued a statement, in which it said:

Our motto remains: "Hands off the State Legislatures!" For the President to determine, first that as a matter of law, states are under a duty to enact particular legislation, and then add his opinion that their omission to do so is one of the causes of grave abuses in the enforcement of a federal statute, is a plain effort to coerce the legislators of the states to adopt a policy of the President. Never should the act of a president go unquestioned when it involves, however slightly, the exercise of a power not vested in him, no matter how noble his motive may be.[11]

They could, however, permit to go unquestioned the attempt of their clients, by deception, coercion and bribery, to force the states to repeal their enforcement statutes and treat the Constitution and the laws of Congress with open contempt.

Lawyers Interpret Report of Wickersham Commission

On January 20, 1931, President Hoover submitted to Congress the report of the Wickersham Commission that had been appointed to make a "thorough inquiry into the problem of the enforcement of prohibition." As will be pointed out in a later chapter, from the standpoint of the immediate problem of enforcement, the report of the commission was not only futile but disastrous. Considered from another point of view, however, it was a forceful and important document. If it had not been garbled, distorted and falsified by wet propagandists and the wet press, if the facts it set forth and the recommendations it made had been honestly and fairly presented to the people, it would have made a significant contribution to the ultimate settlement of the liquor problem. For this reason, it was highly commended by the general superintendent of the Anti-Saloon League and the officials of the other dry organizations. Dr. John Haynes Holmes said: " As an ardent dry, I am entirely satisfied with the report as signed by the ten members of the committee." Dr. Stanley High, a prominent dry leader, said: " The Wickersham Report cuts the ground from under the present wet program."

The statement of Dr. High was fully justified. The program of the AAPA was the modification of the Volstead Act to permit the manufacture and sale of beer, repeal of state enforcement laws, inadequate appropriations for federal enforcement, repeal of the Eighteenth Amendment, the return of the liquor problem to the states, and the open saloon as the best agency for promoting sales — the exact program that it succeeded in putting over. The report of the Wickersham Commission was a devastating and unanswerable repudiation of every line of this program. Its dispassionate description of conditions, both before and after the adoption of the amendment, is a powerful and convincing arraignment of the liquor traffic. It shows that the traffic exerts a destructive influence upon the individual and society, that it corrupts our politics, and that it is inherently lawless. No person who is unbiased by financial or political considerations can study this report without arriving at the conviction that the liquor traffic is a menace to our civilization, and that the only debatable question is how it can be most effectively restrained and put on the road to extinction at the earliest possible moment.

The report was signed by ten of the eleven members of the commission. Among its conclusions and recommendations were the following:

The commission is opposed to repeal of the Eighteenth Amendment.

The commission is opposed to the restoration in any manner of the legalized saloon.

The commission is opposed to the federal or state governments, as such, going into the liquor business.

The commission is opposed to the proposal to modify the national prohibition act so as to permit manufacture of and sale of light wines or beer.

The commission is of opinion that the cooperation of the states is an essential element in the enforcement of the Eighteenth Amendment and the national prohibition act throughout the territory of the United States; that the support of public opinion in the several states is necessary in order to insure such cooperation.

The commission is of opinion that there is yet no adequate observance or enforcement.

The commission is of opinion that the federal appropriations for enforcement of the Eighteenth Amendment should be substantially increased.

All the commission agree that if the amendment is revised, it should be made to read substantially as follows:

Section 1: The Congress shall have power to regulate or to prohibit the manufacture, traffic in or transportation of intoxicating liquors within; the importation thereof into and exportation thereof from the United States and all territory subject to the jurisdiction thereof for beverage purposes.[12]

Such a revision of the amendment would have given Congress the power not only to prevent the return of the saloon, but to prohibit entirely the liquor traffic in every part of the United States. Cities dominate state-wide elections, but they cannot control legislative and congressional districts outside the cities. Even in wet states, therefore, many drys were sent to Congress who worked with the representatives of the dry states of the south and west. For this reason, the national Congress had for more than ten years been dry, and it seemed certain that the suggested revision would mean a bone-dry nation by congressional enactment. It also seemed probable that the ease with which a statute can be repealed would keep the drys of the country more alert and active and result in more effective enforcement.

The wets were enraged at the report and in their condemnation of it they exhausted their vocabulary of denunciation. In a speech which he delivered in Boston a month after the submission of the report, Mr. Wickersham said:

Curiously enough, the most vehement criticism and the most abusive articles came almost exclusively, so far as I can learn, from the wet press. In the past, there was much well founded complaint of the extreme intolerance of prohibitionists. This peculiar characteristic of late appears to have been appropriated by their opponents. Apparently, a large body of anti-prohibitionists expected the commission to find a way for them to secure liquor with ease, and were enraged when we failed to do so.[13]

When the wets abandoned sneers, ridicule and invective, and attempted to be specific, they said that the report was contradictory. They declared that the commissioners had filed separate statements which pointed out that the amendment was not being properly enforced, and had also signed a general report recommending that it should not be repealed.

The type of criticism with which the country was deluged is illustrated by the statement of George W. Merck, New Jersey chairman for the Association Against the Prohibition Amendment, that " the report is absurd when you compare the majority report with the individual opinions of the members who signed it."

The fact is that, except in the case of Newton D. Baker, there was no conflict between the separate statements and the general report. This is shown by the following extracts from some of these statements:

MR. ANDERSON. We must not lose what has been gained by the abolition of the saloon. We can neither ignore the appalling conditions which this commission has found to exist, and to be steadily growing worse, nor submit to their continuance.

MR. POUND. Federal control of what has become a nation-wide traffic, and abolition of the saloon, are great steps forward which should be maintained.

JUDGE MACKINTOSH. Civilization will not allow this nation to end the long attempt to control the use of alcoholic beverages. The necessity for such control increases as the public feels more responsibility for the protection of the home and its children, as the medical profession gives more recognition of alcoholism as a disease, as industry requires more efficiency, as the machine age demands more alert and clear-eyed operators of its swift and intricate parts.

JUDGE McCORMICK. Absolute repeal is unwise. It would in my opinion reopen the saloon. This would be a backward step that I hope will never be taken by the United States. The open saloon is the greatest enemy of temperance and has been a chief cause of much political corruption throughout the country in the past. These conditions should never be revived.

MR. WICKERSHAM. I cannot believe that an experiment of such far-reaching and momentous consequence as this of national prohibition should be abandoned after seven years of such imperfect enforcement and only three years of reorganization and effort to repair the mistakes of the earlier period. The older generation very largely has forgotten and the younger never knew the evils of the saloon and the corroding influence upon politics, both local and national, of the organized liquor interests. But the tradition of that rottenness still lingers, even in the minds of the bitterest opponents of the prohibition law, substantially all of whom assert that the licensed saloon must never again be restored. It is because I see no escape from its return in any of the practicable alternatives to prohibition, that I unite with my colleagues in agreement that the Eighteenth Amendment must not be repealed and, differing with some of them, I have been forced to conclude that a further trial should be made of the enforceability of the Eighteenth Amendment under the present organization, with the help of recommended improvements.

In their joint statement, these men said:

Hereinbefore we have given our reasons for the conclusion that repeal of the Eighteenth Amendment is not advisable. We are convinced that it would be a step backward, that it would not conserve the achieved benefits of national prohibition, and that it would be likely to lead to conditions quite as bad as those we are seeking to escape.

They differed as to the advisability of revision and as to what action Congress should take if it were given jurisdiction over the question. But, with one exception, there was nothing in their separate statements that was inconsistent with the conclusions of the report which they all signed. They agreed that the liquor traffic was a social and political menace, that there must be no relaxation in the struggle for its suppression, that the saloon must not return, that the Eighteenth Amendment must be neither nullified nor repealed, that if it were revised, Congress should be given power to control or entirely suppress the liquor traffic, and that there should be honest and vigorous enforcement of the law.

Big Business Sends for its Lawyers

The great strategists of the AAPA saw at once that the policy of denouncing the report was a mistake. They saw that they were informing the people that the former attorney general of the United States, three federal judges, two prominent lawyers, the dean of the Harvard Law School, and the president of Radcliffe College, after two years of exhaustive study of the subject, had presented an overwhelming condemnation of the whole greedy and corrupt scheme for destroying the Eighteenth Amendment and turning the liquor problem back to the states. They knew that the report was a voluminous one, that it dealt with a complicated situation in which there were many conflicting elements, that a superficial reading might lead to confusion and misunderstanding, and that a knowledge of its true meaning and significance could be gained only by a thorough and unprejudiced study. They knew that few people would have the time or inclination for such a study and, what was of still greater importance, they knew that at least a hundred and twenty million people would never even see the outside of the report, and would form their conclusions in regard to it from newspaper statements and gossip based on such statements. Why then tell the truth about the report?

It was decided, therefore, that the report of the committee should be declared to be a great document, the embodiment of the highest wisdom on the subject, and that it was a complete justification of the wet program. It was evident that the most effective procedure would be to have a statement to that effect sponsored by men who were regarded as leaders of the bar.

The "voluntary" lawyers rose to the occasion. On March 21, two months after the submission of the report and nine days after Mr. Wickersham's Boston speech, they issued a solemn statement in regard to the report. It praised the commission for its exhaustive study of the facts, garbled from the report the strongest statements in regard to failure of enforcement and the results of liquor lawlessness, suppressed the conclusions and recommendations of the commission itself, wove wet propaganda into the statement in such a clever manner that it conveyed the impression, to one who had not read the report, that the report sustained the wet program. The following passages from the statement will show why big business pays great lawyers huge fees:

> These findings of fact, concurred in by all the members of the commission, fully support the conclusions of the board of managers of the Voluntary Committee of Lawyers: (1) that the Eighteenth Amendment, being a police regulation, has no proper place in the Constitution of the United States; (2) that it is unenforceable because it has not the support of law-abiding citizens; (3) that it does not tend to bring about temperance; (4) that it tends to increase crime and corruption; and (5) that it impairs the due administration of justice and causes disrespect for law.
>
> They are practically unanimous in agreeing that the Eighteenth Amendment should be repealed or that some other plan should be adopted; and the only concrete plan suggested would require a repeal of the Eighteenth Amendment and the adoption of an entirely new amendment empowering Congress to control and regulate liquor.
>
> Some of the commissioners suggest that simultaneously with the repeal of the constitutional prohibition against intoxicating liquor, a provision be inserted in the Constitution whereby control of the liquor traffic shall be granted to Congress. We can appreciate that this suggestion may have much to recommend it from the point of view of political expediency. It is obvious, however, that the objections to the Eighteenth Amendment, being what they are, such a procedure would not eliminate them, for it would leave with Congress a power which does not belong there, and which might be exercised to perpetuate or revive substantially the intolerable situation which now exists.[14]

Even if it be conceded that the five conclusions of the Voluntary Committee of Lawyers are matters on which honest men may differ or that they are "fully" supported by some of the facts set out in the report, the statement is nevertheless a fraud, for its authors suppress the conclusions of the commission and substitute their own in such a clever fashion that the average reader, unacquainted with the report, would believe that the commission had endorsed not only the program but also the propaganda of the wets.

In view of the effrontery displayed in this statement, it need surprise no one that, when the national conventions of 1932 were about to convene, the Voluntary Committee adopted a resolution demanding that President Hoover and all Democratic candidates for the presidency declare themselves in favor of the repeal of the Eighteenth Amendment. Referring to this action, the New York *Times* said:

> Joseph H. Choate, Jr., of the board of managers of the committee, explained in a supplementary statement that the resolution expressed "the views of lawyers as lawyers," regardless of party affiliations, adding that the question of party was now subordinate to the question whether our traditional form of government is to continue at all.[15]

Defenders of the Constitution Demand its Nullification

There was not a lawyer or a well informed layman in America who did not know that modification of the Volstead Act would mean nullification of the Constitution. Ninety per cent of the liquor traffic had consisted in the manufacture and sale of beer. As its service required an elaborate cooling and pressure system, its sale in any substantial amount necessitated the saloon. The brewers owned most of the saloons. The amendment was aimed more directly at them than at any element of the community. When it was before the Senate, a motion to exclude beer from its prohibition was promptly and decisively rejected. The men who wrote it also wrote the enforcement act and specifically included beer, ale and porter in the prohibited beverages. In 1921 practically the same body of men, after an elaborate hearing, passed a supplemental act prohibiting the prescribing of beer by members of the medical profession. Walter Lippmann, an advocate of repeal, expressed the situation as follows:

> It is also true that the Volstead Act cannot be liberalized without *nullifying the intent* of this immutable Eighteenth Amendment. There is no slightest doubt that the amendment was intended to prohibit the

lightest beer and the lightest wine no less than gin and absinthe. We, therefore, arrive by irresistible logic at the conclusion that the Volstead Act itself is immutable. . . . But that the object of the movement against the Eighteenth Amendment is to nullify the intent of the authors of the amendment, no candid man can deny. They meant to prohibit all intoxicating liquors throughout the United States.[16]

There was no honest doubt that beer was an intoxicating liquor. Dr. Walter Miles of the Carnegie Institute, who conducted one of the most exhaustive researches into the subject ever made, said: "There is no longer room for doubt in reference to the toxic action of alcoholic beverages as weak as 2.75 per cent by weight."[17] Dr. Reed Hunt of the Harvard Medical School said: "I am of the opinion that beer containing 2.75 per cent by weight of alcohol should be classed as an intoxicating beverage." Dr. Arthur Dean Bevan, then president of the American Medical Association, declared: "The question as to whether or not beer containing 2.75 per cent alcohol is intoxicating is not only a matter of scientific medical opinion, but a matter of common knowledge and common sense. It is a matter of common knowledge that beer which has been heretofore sold in the United States, containing from 3.5 to 4.25 per cent alcohol, is definitely intoxicating. There can be absolutely no doubt but that beer containing 2.75 per cent alcohol is an intoxicating beverage in that an individual can become drunk on the amount that is frequently consumed."[18]

The Wickersham Commission, ten of whose members were among the most distinguished lawyers, judges and legal scholars in America, made a careful study of the question of the modification of the Volstead Act to permit the manufacture and sale of beer. Speaking not as propagandists but in their official capacity, they said:

If the beer made and sold is not intoxicating, it is unlikely to prove a substitute for intoxicating drink in communities where enforcement gives the most difficulty, while if it is, there would be a palpable violation of the Constitution. . . . Evasion of the federal Constitution by specious definitions of "intoxicating" or of "medicinal liquors" or by specious provisions for the procuring of medicinal liquor, undermining by legal action respect for the fundamental law, is quite as destructive of respect for law as the things sought to be avoided.[19]

When the bill to modify the Volstead Act was before Congress, Senator Borah, the ablest constitutional lawyer in the Senate, said:

I believe the bill is an attempt to nullify the Constitution. There is in all the literature of a constitutional republic no uglier crime than nullification. It is the stiletto that goes to the very heart of constitutional government. The man on the street will tell you that the Congress is engaged in getting around the Constitution; that while we pay lip service to that instrument which we have all taken an oath to support, both in letter and in spirit, we are, in fact, evading its plain terms and nullifying its long accepted inhibitions.[20]

President Hoover said:

Modification of the enforcement laws which would permit that which the Constitution forbids is nullification. Change in the Constitution can and must be brought about only by the straightforward methods provided in the Constitution itself.[21]

The United States Supreme Court had definitely settled the question by declaring:

The second section of the amendment does not enable Congress or the several states to defeat or thwart the prohibition, but only to enforce it by appropriate means.[22]

The most perfect expression of the truth was given by a distinguished rabbi, Stephen S. Wise. He said, "Modification is nullification without the courage of its shame."

But notwithstanding the fact that modification was both nullification and a swindle, it had to be put over. So big business called on its lawyers for a statement that could be used to deceive the people and to furnish an alibi for its congressional errand boys. The lawyers responded with the following:

We favor an amendment to legalize the manufacture, sale and transportation of beers and ales as known before prohibition.

Fundamentally, the form which the amendment would take would simply be to eliminate beers and ales from the definition of "intoxicating liquors" contained in Section 4 of the Volstead Act and to add a proviso expressly excluding from the definition beers and ales as known before prohibition.

It is impossible to estimate the amount of revenue which would be derived by the states, but for the federal government an average of a number of carefully prepared estimates indicates a revenue of over $300,000,000 a year. This would give the people an opportunity to take a long stride toward real temperance.[23]

Expressly to exclude "from the definition beers and ales as known before prohibition" was the most brazenly lawless proposition advanced by any of the spokesmen for the wets. It simply meant that any kind of beer or ale that was sold before prohibition could be sold regardless of its alcoholic content. Furthermore, in all attempts to enforce the law, what constituted "beers and ales as known before prohibition" would become a question of fact for the jury in every case and the government would have to throw up its hands.

The Lawyers Grease the Skids

Our great lawyers remained on the job to the end. After the repeal amendment was submitted to the states, it was imperative that action should be taken at once. The wet propaganda "covered the country like a blanket." The underworld and Tammany organizations of our cities, the liquor interests of our own and foreign countries, big business under the leadership of the AAPA and the wet press were in complete control of the machinery of both political parties. The depression had reached its lowest point and the people were preoccupied with financial rather than moral questions. The Democratic organization was in a position of supreme power and under the control of a wet Tammany spoilsman, and cooperating with these forces was the President, bringing all the power of his office and his personal prestige to bear in favor of immediate repeal. It was of supreme importance that repeal be accomplished before there was any change in this setup. If 1933 should pass without action, it was possible and probable that the moral elements of the nation would be able to re-form their broken lines and make a successful stand against the forces that were arrayed against them.

One of the principal dangers was that the provision for repeal conventions in the various states might be delayed by the difficulties that the legislature would encounter in drafting appropriate legislation in carrying out a new method of amending the Constitution, and the possibility of further delay by court actions based on improper procedure. It was highly important therefore that great lawyers should decide upon the proper procedure, prepare a bullet-proof bill and dispatch it to every legislature in the land in order that it might be ready for immediate passage when the whip was cracked. How this emergency was met is succinctly stated by the president of the Association Against the Prohibition Amendment in his final report. In that report he says:

> The latter part of January 1933, Joseph H. Choate, Jr., of the Voluntary Committee of Lawyers for Repeal of the Eighteenth Amendment, called me by telephone from New York to propose that effort be made to get from as many as possible of the sitting legislatures the necessary measures for the creation of conventions to act upon the repeal amendment. Mr. Choate said that he would be very glad to communicate with a representative of his committee in each of the states, if we would do likewise, with a view to expediting this legislation.
>
> I expressed appreciation of the suggestion and thorough willingness to proceed. I stated to Mr. Choate, however, that before we could get anywhere from a practical standpoint it would be necessary to have some specific legislative measure to offer. Otherwise, those with whom we communicated in the different states would immediately say that they could do nothing without a definite bill. I, therefore, requested Mr. Choate to prepare a general measure which could be modified so as to conform to the statutes of the different states but which would embody factors necessary to be taken into account in order that the conventions should be set up in the proper way and that the necessary legal safeguards should be provided. This he did. The measure which he drafted was submitted to other prominent constitutional lawyers, and after it had been corrected in such manner as to meet with general approval, it was sent to the different states. . . .

Thus prior to the submission of the repeal resolution by Congress, a suggested measure was before all sitting legislatures and interested parties were prepared to press these measures for consideration. The action of Congress immediately stimulated action upon the legislation in the states and by bringing to bear every proper influence, our association was enabled to secure the creation of conventions to be held during the year 1933 in thirty-nine states.

The value of this preliminary work cannot be exaggerated. When the bills were sent to the sitting legislatures, we believed the congressional resolution would not be presented until an extra session of the Seventy-second Congress should convene in the spring. Unless, however, we could get legislation in the states during the winter, there would be of necessity a long delay because most of the legislatures would not reconvene until 1935, and thus we would be precluded from having conventions set up in the states to pass upon the proposed amendment until 1935. In the efforts made we were striving to shorten the ratification of repeal by at least two years.

Nothing could have expressed the real motives of the members of the AAPA and the Voluntary Committee better than the manner in which they came out from under cover after repeal was accomplished. Their platform had declared that they opposed the amendment because it "undermined our federal system of government, robbed our citizens of constitutional right, fostered excessive drinking of strong intoxicants, bred corruption and hypocrisy," and had protested that they were striving to "give the people an opportunity to take a long stride toward real temperance." When, however, the thirty-sixth state had ratified the repeal amendment, they threw off their campaign make-up and dropped all talk about saving the Constitution and promoting true temperance. With absolute cynicism they demanded that no restrictions be put upon the liquor traffic, that the saloon be restored, and that private greed be left free to promote the sale of liquor and foster excessive drinking by every means that it could devise. They no longer attempted to disguise the fact that they were after revenue. In order that the repeal era might be inaugurated in accordance with their desire, they had their great lawyer, Joseph H. Choate, Jr., appointed chairman of the Federal Alcohol

Control Administration, with instructions that he retain the position until all danger was over.

At one time it became necessary to warn the administration that if " some manner of application that differs from the sane and definite ideas of Mr. Choate should be adopted, it may well be that the people of America will once more be compelled to register their protest against federal control of the liquor industry." [24] This was a thinly disguised threat that if the program as presented by Mr. Choate was not carried out, the AAPA would attack the administration with all the weapons of propaganda and political terrorism that it had used so effectively during the repeal campaign. If this statement were supported only by circumstantial evidence, it would leave the average honest reader incredulous. The president of the association, however, drunk with victory and power, lost his sense of the fitness of things and told the truth. In his final report he said:

. . . When Joseph H. Choate, Jr., was selected as chairman of the Federal Alcohol Administration, it was as happy an appointment as the President could have made. I know the views of Mr. Choate with reference to the methods that should be pursued. I know his desire to make the industry self-controlling with the least possible measure of governmental interference. I know that as long as he continues in the position which he has accepted at great personal sacrifice, these policies will be pursued, and, therefore, apprehensions which I would otherwise cherish as to the unwise application of the tremendous federal authority provided in the codes are strikingly lessened. . . .

In a speech at Philadelphia on December 8th, I made an additional comment upon the code situation as follows:

" Knowing as I do the views of Mr. Choate on the subject, knowing his fixed belief that the industry should be permitted to regulate itself with the least possible interference by the government, I am certain that he will strive in every way in his power to make the application of the codes as little objectionable as is possible. . . .

" There seems to be general recognition of the desirability of a separation of beer and wines, on the one hand, from spirituous liquors on the other. Since the resumption of the legal sale of beer last spring, there has been little restriction attached to it beyond proper licensing.

In many cities we have seen it offered in soda fountains as freely as a mineral water or other beverage without any semblance of alcoholic content. And I for one believe that we have learned a valuable lesson in this connection. I heartily approve the disposition which is apparently evident almost everywhere to continue this method as to beer and also to permit the similar general sale of light wines. . . .

"And this brings me to the point of a suggestion that relates to our large centers of population. Unless in cities like yours, and in cities like New York, provision is made for the sale of liquor by the drink without the cost of food service, there will be a continuance of the speak-easy and the blind pig."

If the purpose of the officials of the AAPA was to save the Constitution and stop excessive drinking, why did they remain on the job after repeal to insist that beer and wine be served at soda fountains where boys and girls congregate, that the saloon be legalized, and that all federal restrictions be removed from the liquor traffic? Why did they put their legal champion in a position where he could see to it that this program was carried out?

The Crusaders

Another organization which the association put into the field was the Crusaders. Its members were to be young men. What a strong appeal the name, the object, and the personnel would make to all high-minded people! In the Middle Ages, the crusaders had gone forth to rescue the holy sepulcher from the infidel. In the seventies, bands of Christian women known as the Crusaders had gone into the saloons and on their knees had prayed that the work of debauching their husbands and sons, wrecking their homes, and spreading poverty, disease and crime might cease. The young men of our colleges had organized the Inter-Collegiate Prohibition Association and had gone into every state in the Union and with high idealism had carried on a crusade against the liquor traffic that had been one of the factors in the adoption of the Eighteenth Amendment. Now here was another band of young men who had enlisted for another crusade against humanity's ancient foe. Because of the name, the object, and the idealism of youth, this organization should command the confidence of all good people. They announced that their object was temperance. As they were all young men of great wealth, surely it was a fine example of *noblesse oblige*.

The name and alleged purpose were well suited to allay suspicion and gain a hearing. The founders were, however, young millionaires whose sense of social responsibility was perhaps not overwhelming, the sons of the munition manufacturers and Wall street magnates who were financing and carrying on the work of the AAPA. Their object was not temperance, but to help their fathers get rid of their income and corporation taxes by bringing back the liquor traffic with all the inevitable intemperance. They proposed to attain this end by helping their fathers deceive the people, elect to office men who would take their orders from the liquor interests and big business, secure the repeal of enforcement statutes, charge the resulting conditions to prohibition, and work for the repeal of the Eighteenth Amendment.

They held a meeting in New York and adopted as their motto, "Join the Crusaders and substitute real temperance for prohibition intemperance." They further announced that "work of a political as well as an educational nature will be undertaken, including repeal of so-called state enforcement acts, and support of candidates for national and state offices in sympathy with the aims of the Crusaders." Fred G. Clark, a wealthy oil man of Cleveland, was made national commander, and then a dinner was given. "Among those who attended the dinner celebrating the launching of the movement were: Charles H. Sabin, Jr., C. V. Whitney, John Hay Whitney, Morton Banks, Charles S. Payson, Avery Rockefeller, Lammot du Pont III, John S. Williams, William D. Carr, Sturdevant Erdman, Charles E. Otis, John E. Newell."[25]

The national organization adopted a platform which contained the following:

> The Crusaders stand for temperance. The Crusaders believe that the control of liquor should be vested in state rather than national government.
>
> The Crusaders will work toward this goal, and believe that the most

practical method to accomplish this end is, first, repeal of the present enforcement acts, the Volstead Act and the Jones Law. Second, passage by the states of laws which will control the manufacture and sale of intoxicating liquors along lines best suited to the problems of each individual state. Third, federal legislation to protect states who may desire to remain dry from liquor importation. Fourth, repeal of the Eighteenth Amendment which any plan of prohibition reform makes essential so that no future Congress may nullify these acts. The Crusaders are unalterably opposed to the saloon.[26]

The publicity agents and other employes of these young men were as busy as bees. Wherever there was a wet running against a dry, a referendum on prohibition, a movement to repeal an enforcement statute, an opportunity to spread falsehood or create contempt for law, they were on hand. Although they had no popular following and represented only a little crowd of young millionaires, they were able, by virtue of the unlimited publicity given them by the wet press, to exert a powerful influence as they appeared in political conventions, city councils, state legislatures and the national Congress, and threatened politicians with political lynching.

Women and Prohibition

The year following the adoption of the Eighteenth Amendment, the states ratified the amendment giving the ballot to women. It was generally believed that this made national prohibition forever secure. From the very beginning, the women had been in the forefront of the battle against the liquor traffic. Their leaders had been women of the type of Frances E. Willard, Anna A. Gordon, Mary A. Woodbridge, Susan B. Anthony, Anna Howard Shaw, Jane Addams, Mary McDowell, Ella A. Boole, Mrs. Henry W. Peabody, Ida B. Wise and Carrie Chapman Catt. These women had lived in close contact with the people and knew their hopes, their fears and their needs. They had seen the broken homes, the sorrow, despair and human wreckage that invariably accompanied the liquor traffic. With genuine realism, they had pierced through the rationalizations and solemn profundities of lawyers and the specious sophisms of subsidized intellectuals, and had demanded that this scourge of our civilization be destroyed.

They fought for the adoption of the Eighteenth Amendment and, with equal determination, they fought for its retention and enforcement. Every woman's organization in the country that had come into existence as a result of the spontaneous and sincere action of a disinterested group of women, was opposed to repeal. Ella A. Boole, who had been in intimate touch with the situation and spoke with authority, said:

> In answer to the question, "Is there any possibility of knowing the collective mind of women?" the Woman's National Committee for Law Enforcement spoke through ten great national women's organizations, first in their own delegated bodies, and then through their representatives who formed the executive committee. They spoke not once but repeatedly without wavering, and they affiliated for cooperative expression and action. These are the organizations:
>
> General Federation of Women's Clubs, Young Women's Christian Association, National Congress of Parents and Teachers, Lend-a-Hand Society, International Order of King's Daughters, Federation of Women's Boards of Foreign Missions of North America, Council of Women for Home Missions, Women's Christian Temperance Union, National Woman's Democratic Law Enforcement League.
>
> The aggregate membership in these organizations is more than twelve millions of women who are above the average in character, intelligence and patriotism. Protestant church women number approximately twenty million. Considering the fact that there are some duplicates, Mrs. Peabody estimates that twelve millions of these are for the Eighteenth Amendment as indicated by the action of their church groups. Women of the Catholic Church are not represented in this list, but Kathleen Norris is typical of a great host of Catholic women, who declare with Cardinal Mercier: "If universal prohibition could be introduced, more lives would be saved than by universal disarmament. Alcohol kills more men than war, and does it less honorably."
>
> All these great bodies passed resolutions in favor of national prohibition.[27]

In addition to these, there were a large number of organizations supporting prohibition that were composed of both men and women.[28] In these organizations, there were millions of women opposing repeal who did not belong to any of the various women's organizations.

But the organizers of the AAPA seemed to feel that the methods which were used to influence the men would, of course, be effective with the women also. If coercion could not be applied to them directly, they could be reached through their interest in the positions, business connections and opportunities of their husbands, sons and friends. Yet it had become clear that because of their traditional hatred of the liquor traffic and their possession of the ballot, the women would remain a powerful obstacle to repeal. However, men of the type of Du Pont, Raskob, and Sabin do not quail before difficulties. As they had sent their sons and retainers — editors, lawyers and politicians — to the front, so, also in true Russian fashion, they ordered their wives and daughters into the trenches. These women responded splendidly. Bearing aloft a banner inscribed, "Women's Organization for National Prohibition Reform," they went forth to battle.

The president of this organization was Mrs. Charles H. Sabin of New York. She was the wife of the treasurer of the AAPA and a leader in the most exclusive social set in America. For ten years she had been a cog in the Republican machine of New York state, which in its desperate struggle for power had been in constant competition with Tammany Hall for the support of the underworld of New York city and of Wall street. In the Harding campaign of 1920, she became a member of the Republican state executive committee, and in 1924 she became the New York member of the Republican national committee and retained this position until she resigned to organize the WONPR. Her son was chairman of the executive committee of the Crusaders. Among her most active assistants were Mrs. Pierre S. du Pont, Mrs. Courtland Nicoll, Mrs. August Belmont, Mrs. J. Roland Harriman, Mrs. Cornelius N. Bliss, Mrs. John Sloane, Mrs. Coffin Van Rensselaer, Mrs. Joseph Cudahy, Mrs. Ralph Shaw, Mrs. Stanley Field and Mrs. Henry B. Joy. They had leisure, money, power and a strong financial interest in repeal, and they worked under the direction of the brilliant strategists and propagandists of the AAPA. They organized the women of their type in every city in the country and supported every part of the program of the association.

If these women had been sincere, they would have issued a statement as follows: " We have our bootleggers, we help finance the gangsters and racketeers of the underworld, we serve cocktails and champagne at our brilliant social functions in the presence of our children, our servants and social inferiors; we hold the law in contempt and by our attitude, our talk and our conduct, we are helping to destroy respect for law. Although because of our wealth and influence we can obtain all the liquor we want in spite of the law, we want it repealed so that our husbands may be relieved of their income and corporation taxes. We have, therefore, formed an organization to be known as the Women's Organization to Bring Back the Liquor Traffic and the Saloon and Save our Husbands' Profits, and we call upon the women of the country to help us out." This, however, would not have secured many votes.

These women had it in their power to make a great contribution to the cause of " national prohibition reform." They could have accomplished this without appealing to district attorneys, courts or other enforcement agencies by simply reforming themselves. The difficulties of enforcement had not come from the great body of the American people, but from the degenerate underworld and the frivolous and irresponsible upper world. If our social leaders had determined to repudiate their alliance with the underworld and, instead of breaking and denouncing the law, to respect and obey it and to cooperate with the great civic and religious organizations that were battling for law enforcement, a revolution would have been accomplished. If the ladies of the WONPR had simply decreed that obedience to law, rather than contempt for it, should be regarded as " fashionable " and " smart," the battle for " prohibition reform " would have been more than half won. If a hundredth part of the time and money which they spent in breaking down and destroying the law had been devoted to inspiring respect for the law and upholding the hands of those charged with its enforcement, the law would have been retained and upheld with all its resulting advantages to the individual and to society.

Smoke Screen

From the beginning to the end, selfishness and hypocrisy marked the activities of these women. The name which they adopted concealed their real purposes. They knew that if they used a name which honestly announced their purpose of destroying prohibition, they would have been ignored by the morally responsible women of the country. Following the example of their husbands, they announced that they were inspired by lofty motives. In their " Declaration of Principles," they state that they are concerned about prohibition

> because it conflicts with the basic American principle of local home rule and destroys the balance, established by the framers of our government, between powers delegated to the federal authority and those reserved to the sovereign states or to the people themselves. . . .
>
> We are convinced that national prohibition, wrong in principle, has been equally disastrous in consequences in the hypocrisy, the corruption, the tragic loss of life and the appalling increase of crime which have attended the abortive attempt to enforce it; in the checking of the steady growth of temperance which had preceded it; in the shocking effect it has had upon the youth of the nation; in the impairment of constitutional guarantees of individual rights; in the weakening of the sense of solidarity between the citizens and the government which is the only sure basis of a country's strength.

The birth of the interest of these women in the Constitution and in the suppression of intemperance, hypocrisy and corruption, coincides exactly in point of time with their husbands' determination to bring back the liquor traffic in order to get rid of their income taxes.

When we brush aside all high-sounding verbiage, we see that the sole object of these women was to help put over the program of the AAPA in its entirety. Mrs. Sabin made the following statement of the program of her organization:

> The Women's Organization for National Prohibition Reform was organized for and has given its support to three principles: First, the

repeal of the Eighteenth Amendment; second, the restoration to each state of its former power to regulate the manufacture, sale and transportation of intoxicating beverages within its own limits; third, that the resolution for the repeal of the Eighteenth Amendment should be submitted to conventions in the several states rather than to the legislatures thereof.[29]

That they were for "nullification without the courage of its shame" is shown by the fact that they

Resolved, that for economic and humanitarian reasons, the WONPR, while reaffirming its stand for the unequivocal repeal of the Eighteenth Amendment, pending this latter action by the Congress, lends its support to the immediate passage of a beer bill, provided, however, that such bill give to the several states, within their own borders, complete control over the manufacture, transportation and sale of such beer.[30]

That it supported the AAPA in its plan to proceed "by the referendum route" is shown by the following resolution:

Be it resolved, that the Women's Organization for National Prohibition Reform work to obtain referenda in those states where they have not yet been held on the question, "Shall the Eighteenth Amendment be repealed?"[31]

At their first national conference, they adopted a resolution

that this organization go on record as opposing state enforcement acts and pledge themselves to work for their repeal.[32]

The following year they adopted a resolution

that the executive committee of the Women's Organization for National Prohibition Reform, in meeting assembled in Chicago, Illinois, on January 22nd, 1931, protests to the Congress of the United States the further appropriation of any moneys for the enforcement of the prohibition law as suggested in the report of the Wickersham Commission.[33]

Their "Declaration of Principles" urges

the Congress to submit to conventions of the people in the several states rather than to the legislatures thereof, a resolution for the repeal of the Eighteenth Amendment.

These women joined their husbands in their work of degrading our political life. They went out to defeat every candidate for office who was opposed to the liquor traffic, no matter how intelligent and honorable he might be, or how important might be the service he was rendering to the country. They went out to elect all candidates pledged to the return of the liquor traffic, no matter how ignorant or corrupt they might be, and regardless of the fact that they were henchmen of the Tammany organizations that curse our cities. At their second national conference, they adopted the following resolution:

> . . . *Be it resolved,* that it is the sense of this conference that in order to effect the repeal of the Eighteenth Amendment the Women's Organization for National Prohibition Reform urge its members to support only those candidates for public office who have openly declared themselves in favor of the repeal of the Eighteenth Amendment.[34]

When the presidential campaign of 1932 opened, we were in the midst of the depression; there was uncertainty and confusion as to the attitude we should take toward other nations; we were confronted with a multitude of social, industrial, financial, political and international problems that presented an unparalleled challenge to the wisdom and patriotism of our people. These things meant absolutely nothing to the ladies of the WONPR. In determining which party they would support, their sole question was its attitude on the liquor question. The Republican party had declared for repeal but for retention in the federal government of power to protect dry territory and to prevent the return of the saloon. The Democratic party had declared for the unconditional repeal of the Eighteenth Amendment and, until that could be accomplished, for its nullification, and Mr. Roosevelt had declared that he was for the platform one hundred per cent. So a meeting of the national executive committee was called, and Mrs. Sabin, one of the founders of the National Women's Republican Club, offered the following resolution:

> The officers and members of the national executive committee of the Women's Organization for National Prohibition Reform, are in com-

plete accord with the platform of the Democratic party in regard to national prohibition.

We urge the members of our organization to support in the coming election candidates for both houses of the Congress who are committed to repeal. For in the last analysis it is that body who will inaugurate the repeal of the Eighteenth Amendment.

While the President of the United States has no power to veto or change a proposed constitutional amendment, he has through the prestige of his high office, the power to wield directly or indirectly great influence over legislation.

We, therefore, urge the members of this organization, because they are committed to the cause of repeal, whether they be Republicans or whether they be Democrats, to give their support to the nominee of that party which favors the repeal of the Eighteenth Amendment, Franklin Delano Roosevelt.[35]

This resolution was adopted by a vote of fifty-five to twenty-two. A few days later sixty-four members of the WONPR signed a vigorous protest against this action, which contained the following:

With millions of unemployed, widespread distress, and with the world confronted with a crisis that threatens the very foundation of civilization, to make the position of a candidate toward control of the liquor traffic the sole test of his fitness for the office of president is the very negation of our responsibilities as citizens.[36]

Mrs. Douglas Robinson, saying that she was for repeal, and fond of her cousin, Mrs. Roosevelt, declared that she regretted that the leaders of the WONPR "should have put themselves on record as repealists first and Americans second," and added, "I also feel that those members have repudiated the spirit of their own slogan — 'Patriotism before Party' — for they seem to me to have added to it another clause, namely, 'Repeal before Patriotism.'"[37]

With an air of injured innocence, Mrs. Sabin replied: "It was difficult when I read the letter, knowing Mrs. Robinson, to believe that she had written it. It was so unfair to the members of our national executive committee, who for three years have carried on the fight for repeal, and who today are largely responsible for the great wave of repeal sentiment which has swept the country."[38]

While these women were expressing their zeal for true temperance and declaring that the saloon should never come back, they were supporting Pierre du Pont's scheme to lead the people on by these pretenses but to secure a repeal amendment that would deprive Congress of the power to prohibit the saloon. This was shown not only by the fact that they declared for repeal and "the restoration to each state of its former power to regulate the manufacture, sale and transportation of intoxicating beverages within its own limits," and their support of Mr. Roosevelt, who was pledged to accomplish this result. It was also shown by an event that occurred during the 1932 campaign. A group of women who belonged to the WONPR, but were not on the inside and did not know the real game its leaders were playing, wrote an open letter to Mrs. Sabin protesting against the endorsement of Mr. Roosevelt, in which they said that this action "was not in the interest of real prohibition reform because, as the country stands, we could not hope to gain the support of the moderate dry element without a federal guarantee against the return of the saloon such as proposed by President Hoover."

In her reply, Mrs. Sabin said: "You seem to feel that Mr. Hoover has accepted the stand of this organization. He has not. He proposes to write into the Constitution a guarantee against the return of the old saloon."[39]

Mrs. Sabin, "The Voice of American Womanhood"

During the Republican national convention of 1932, there was a great gathering in Chicago of the supporters of the Eighteenth Amendment. There were present many of the ablest, most unselfish and public-spirited women in America. There were members of all the bona fide women's organizations, churches, temperance societies, social service groups and other civic bodies organized for the promotion of the public welfare. They expressed their continued faith in prohibition, recounted the great advantages it had brought to the people, told of the sacrifice of the character and happiness of individuals, the social degradation and political corruption that would inevitably result if prohibition should be destroyed, and pleaded with the delegates to declare for the retention and better enforcement of the Eighteenth Amendment.

On the eve of the convention, the wets staged a big repeal parade. In the evening, these paraders were herded into the Coliseum for a "great repeal demonstration." This seething mob of Chicago's riffraff was wildly enthusiastic as the speakers voiced its hatred of prohibition. Mayor Cermak presided and Mrs. Sabin was one of the speakers. The wet press hailed her as the "voice of American womanhood," but made little mention of Mrs. Henry W. Peabody and the other women who were in Chicago as true representatives of the intelligence and conscience of the women of America.

Al Smith expressed Tammany Hall's appreciation of Mrs. Sabin:

> When the ideas of the fanatics began to lose their hold upon the women of the country, when courageous women like Mrs. Sabin risked public condemnation by attacking the whole theory of the Eighteenth Amendment, the drys, who had had everything their own way, were put on the defensive. When women entered the fight for repeal, sanity began to return to the country.[40]

The enthusiasm of "society," big business, Tammany politicians and the liquor interests for Mrs. Sabin was not shared by the leaders of the moral and patriotic elements of the country. She was not the heroine of the churches, schools, colleges, parent-teachers associations, welfare workers, women's clubs, and social and civic organizations. The attitude of the truly representative women's organizations toward the Eighteenth Amendment was clearly illustrated by the action of two of them. The W. C. T. U. was free from the slightest taint of selfishness and dishonesty. Its formation and growth were the result of the spontaneous reaction of millions of unselfish and patriotic women to a great national need. It has members in every state, county, city and village. At its national convention, it passed a resolution requesting the two major political parties to adopt the following plank in their platform:

> Prohibition is the policy of the United States government incorporated in the Eighteenth Amendment to the federal Constitution.
>
> We pledge ourselves to carry out the provisions of the national prohibition act, to place enforcement in the hands of its undoubted friends, and to support such other legislation as may be necessary to secure full benefit of the prohibition law.

The General Federation of Women's Clubs was not organized with reference to the liquor question. It was composed of intelligent, representative and public-spirited women from every state in the Union who, with entire sincerity, had joined together to promulgate and support a great and enlightened program for the promotion of the public welfare. The ability, disinterestedness and clear social vision of these women was universally recognized. As part of their program of social betterment, they gave their unqualified support to the Eighteenth Amendment and the enforcement statutes. At their national conventions, they always included in their program a demand that the Eighteenth Amendment be honestly and vigorously enforced. This was very annoying to our little clique of rich ladies who were struggling to destroy prohibition. As they sipped their bootleg cocktails, they could lift their eyebrows and sneer at the W. C. T. U. and other temperance organizations and at the millions of women belonging to the great temperance societies of the Christian churches, and with a lofty air declare that they were fanatics. But they knew that they could not dispose of the General Federation of Women's Clubs in this manner. They decided therefore to intimidate this organization and they hoped that their efforts would prove as effective as were those of the Voluntary Lawyers with the American Bar Association. So, on February 29, 1932, their national executive committee adopted the following resolution:

> *Be it resolved,* that the national executive committee of the Women's Organization for National Prohibition Reform now assembled, urge its

state divisions in the future to ask all new members to indicate on their enrollment cards, the clubs of which they are members; that an effort be made to ascertain how many members of each state division, previous to this date, are members of a federated club; that a report on this dual membership, from time to time, be sent by the chairmen of our state divisions, to the chairmen of their state federations of women's clubs, incorporated in a letter which protests against the use and legality of any statement which quotes the total membership of the General Federation of Women's Clubs as endorsing the Eighteenth Amendment or the Volstead Act.[41]

The women, however, did not prove to be as susceptible to the influence of wealth and power as the lawyers of the country had been, and this movement completely failed. At the great national convention of the General Federation of Women's Clubs held in Seattle in June 1932, the following resolution was adopted:

Whereas, there are sinister influences seeking to undermine the efficiency of the Eighteenth Amendment to the Constitution of the United States and to render the laws for the enforcement thereof impotent; and

Whereas, individuals and organizations favoring the repeal of the Eighteenth Amendment are making strenuous efforts to destroy the faith of the people of the United States in prohibition and to promote the idea that prohibition is contrary to the principles of our government; therefore

Be it resolved, that the General Federation of Women's Clubs, through its delegate body, reaffirms its conviction that prohibition offers the best means for curbing the liquor traffic and its attendant crimes and pledges its continued support to the Eighteenth Amendment and the rigid enforcement thereof.[42]

The New York *Times* tells us that "out of six hundred delegates voting, only thirteen women opposed the motion to acquaint Simon D. Fess and John J. Raskob, Republican and Democratic national chairmen, respectively, with the federation's traditional policy."[43]

The WONPR in Action

After the repeal victory, Grace C. Root, "at Mrs. Sabin's request," wrote the official history of the WONPR. A few extracts from this book will illustrate the nature of their work. After telling the story of three years of feverish activity in every part of the country, the author reaches the presidential campaign of 1932:

> It was the nation-wide election of November, however, which represented to the organizations in all the states their peak of effort. They were determined that this should be the Waterloo of prohibition. As the great day approached, they brought into play all the political force and strategy that they had been developing during the minor battles of the preceding years. . . .
>
> Election day was a day of gruelling hard work for thousands of WONPR officers and members. Motor contingents assisted at the polls, distributed repeal buttons on the streets, climbed millions of steps and rang countless doorbells, rounding up the vote. Publicity campaigns wound up in a burst of oratory. Many a woman will remember the day of November 8, 1932, as the busiest day of her life.
>
> But aching heads, tired feet, hoarse voices were all forgotten as the returns of the election began to come in. Hope gave way to excited surprise, and then to triumphant certainty. The cause of repeal was winning beyond anyone's wildest dreams. [44]

After the repeal amendment was submitted by Congress the WONPR adopted the following resolution:

> *Be it resolved,* that the state committees, with the full force of their powers and energies, concentrate on enlarging the membership and increasing all organization activities, that they may be ready through numbers and organization, to take part successfully and conclusively in the election of delegates to the several state conventions who are committed to the unconditional repeal of the Eighteenth Amendment.[45]

The following extract from *Woman and Repeal* lifts the curtain and permits us to see the ladies in action:

> The national publicity department was responsible for presenting through the radio, moving pictures, special feature articles and daily press releases, an interpretation of the WONPR's objectives. This department of the organization also prepared news letters to go out to members of the WONPR from coast to coast, and from Canada to Mexico.[46]

There can be no doubt that the WONPR was one of the most effective organizations of the repeal fight. In December 1932, the executive committee of the Pittsburgh branch of the WONPR adopted a resolution

> that as Mrs. Charles H. Sabin, national chairman, has done more than anyone else for the repeal of the Eighteenth Amendment, be it resolved that we write a letter to Mrs. Sabin expressing to her our deep gratitude for all she has accomplished.[47]

The final report of the AAPA says that "the Women's Organization for National Prohibition Reform was a powerful ally to our Association." It is important, therefore, that we should know the real source of their influence. It did not result from the fact that the women of America had transferred their intellectual and spiritual allegiance from women like Frances E. Willard, Jane Addams, Evangeline Booth, Carrie Chapman Catt and Ella A. Boole, to such women as Mrs. Sabin, Mrs. du Pont, Mrs. Belmont and Mrs. Harriman. That influence had its origin in attitudes, desires and emotions entirely alien to those to which true moral leadership makes its appeal. Notwithstanding the fact that we boast of our democracy, there is in every community a small group of people who pose as leaders of fashionable society. The leadership is not based upon birth, culture, character or taste. Those who have the money to "entertain," exploit themselves and exert sufficient financial pressure, can "crash the gates" of the charmed circle. Those who are in and those who yearn for admittance to "society" regard the doings of its members, however frivolous and inane they may be, as of extraordinary importance. Those who are on the fringe and hope to "make the grade" will do anything to attract the favorable attention of those who can "make them" socially.

If, therefore, the members of this set have something they want to put over, they have only to issue invitations to teas and meetings at their houses, or request people to serve on committees with them, and the social climbers will fall all over themselves in the enthusiasm of their response. Some hope that when the particular movement is over, gratitude will bring invitations to real social functions, while others hope only to bask for a moment in the sunshine of social royalty. Mrs. Sabin and other members of New York's " Four Hundred " understood perfectly this psychological phenomenon. They knew that they had only to " give the tip " to the social bellwethers of the country, and multitudes of women would gladly do the " gruelling hard work " and forget the " aching heads, tired feet and hoarse voices " for the joy of mingling on terms of apparent equality with society leaders.

The officials of the national and local branches of the WONPR were able to employ a veritable army of women to do all the detailed work of the organization. They could rely on the enthusiasm and efficiency of these women regardless of the merits of the issues involved.

The greatest service which these women rendered to the repeal cause was the publicity they were able to give to the wet propaganda. The professional propagandists of the association knew that if they simply furnished wet " facts and arguments," the papers would not want to print them, and that if they did the people would not read them. They knew that if they were to sell the wet propaganda, they must dramatize it and make it news.

The women of the WONPR were ideally fitted for this role. In the first place, their zeal for repeal would convey to uninformed and superficial persons the idea that the women of the country, who had been the staunchest friends of prohibition, had become convinced of its folly and were demanding that it be abandoned. In the second place, high pressure salesmen had discovered that where one person would read a plain statement of the supposed virtues of a cold cream or a cigarette, a thousand would read a testimonial on the subject signed by a " society queen." The women of the WONPR had been exploited in the society columns of the newspapers and magazines, and because of their notoriety, the teas, meetings, parades and other stunts they staged were heralded by the press, and the wet propaganda included in their statements, resolutions and speeches was given the widest publicity and read by the people.

The nature of their publicity value is clearly illustrated by the following passage from *Woman and Repeal:*

An opening skirmish took place the morning after the endorsement resolution went through. There was a hearing before a subcommittee of the Judiciary Committee of the Senate, at which Mrs. Sabin and James W. Wadsworth, Jr., spoke against prohibition. Many delegates of the WONPR had stayed over to attend. The room was jammed to its doors and there were crowds outside in the corridor. Besides the wets and the drys, there were many outsiders. "We just came to see if this Mrs. Sabin could be as young as her pictures look," some were heard to say. What they saw was a woman smiling and apparently enjoying herself thoroughly. For Mrs. Sabin never used the tears which the drys had found so effective before senators and congressmen. Therefore, to the bitter end, her late opponents never understood why she invariably made such a vivid public appearance.[48]

It is easy to see why the newspapers gave her headlines and columns of space, and why the curious "ate it up." In other words, we can see why she made such good bait for the wet hook. As she was not speaking for enslaved and defeated men, broken-hearted women and ruined homes, there was no occasion for tears. This was all the more true since if she failed to reduce her husband's income tax, she would still not be compelled to reduce her scale of living.

The Real Purpose of the WONPR

In April 1932, when the WONPR was doing everything in its power to convince the women of the country that its real object was temperance, it made a solemn announcement to the effect that after repeal, it would remain in existence to fight for true temperance. At its third national conference, it adopted the following resolution:

Be it resolved, that this organization pledge itself to remain intact, directing its energy to the promotion of laws in the several states which will promote real temperance.[49]

In September 1933, when repeal was assured, they adopted the following resolution:

Whereas, with the repeal of the Eighteenth Amendment to the Constitution of the United States, the objective for which this organization was formed, as embodied in its Declaration of Principles, and to which its membership is pledged, will have been accomplished,

Be it therefore resolved, by the national executive committee that when the thirty-sixth state shall have ratified the Twenty-first Amendment, the national chairman be authorized to announce publicly that, the aim of the Women's Organization for National Prohibition Reform having been attained, the organization thereupon be dissolved;

Be it further resolved, that the chairman and the executive committee deem that an additional responsibility rests not only with them, but upon the entire membership of the WONPR, that having met with success in helping to rid the country of the Eighteenth Amendment and its attendant evils, they individually, in their respective states, should encourage and support the enactment of sane liquor-control laws.[50]

Thus, with the return of a taxable liquor traffic, their object was accomplished and they disbanded their organization with the pious suggestion that as individuals they " support the enactment of sane liquor-control laws." A " sane " law would not, of course, interfere with the saloons with which the nation is now infested, and against which no protest comes from these friends of temperance.

The American Hotel Association

Little need be said about the other member of the United Repeal Council, the American Hotel Association. Before prohibition, there was a saloon in nearly every hotel in the country. These saloons not only sold their goods to people generally but they furnished the liquor that was served to guests in the public dining rooms and to individuals and parties in private rooms. It was one of the most lucrative branches of the hotel business. The organizers and members of the Hotel Association were not concerned in the slightest degree with the public welfare; they were interested solely in cash. If they had intended to convey the truth to people, they would have called their organization the American Saloon-Keepers' Association, and announced that their purpose was to induce men to spend for liquor the money that they should use to purchase the necessities and comforts of life for their families. Of course, they were enthusiastic for the whole wet program of the AAPA.

The American Hotel Association exerted a powerful influence in the repeal campaign. Its units existed in every part of the country and they were able to put pressure upon their employes, the people who furnished them with supplies and others with whom they transacted business, their patrons, the politicians and many other elements. They furnished headquarters for the various wet organizations, permitted them to display their advertising matter and to have the run of the premises. Dry organizations were put under severe restrictions, and upon various pretexts they were often denied the use of rooms in the hotels as headquarters.

NOTES

[1] New York *Times,* July 1, 1932.
[2] *New Republic,* May 22, 1935.
[3] "The Public Influence of the Bar," *Harvard Law Review,* Nov. 1934, p. 1.
[4] *New Republic,* May 22, 1935.
[5] *Literary Digest,* Nov. 25, 1933.
[6] Mugler vs. Kansas, 123, U. S. 623.
[7] New York *Times,* Jan. 23, 1929.
[8] Rhode Island vs. Palmer, 253, U. S. 350.
[9] New York *Times,* Oct. 24, 1929.
[10] *Ibid.,* July 15, 1929.
[11] *Ibid.,* Dec. 16, 1929.
[12] Wickersham Report, p. 83.
[13] New York *Times,* March 13, 1931.
[14] *Ibid.,* March 22, 1931.
[15] *Ibid.,* May 31, 1932.
[16] *Harper's Magazine,* Dec. 1926.
[17] Walter R. Miles, *Alcohol and Human Efficiency* (Carnegie Institution, Washington, 1924), p. 275.
[18] Arthur Dean Bevan, *Alcohol and Prohibition* (Anti-Saloon League, 1928), p. 12.
[19] Wickersham Report, pp. 77, 78.
[20] *Congressional Record,* Vol. 77, Part 1, 73rd Congress, pp. 512, 518.
[21] Wickersham Report, p. 131.
[22] Rhode Island vs. Palmer, 253, U. S. 350.
[23] New York *Times,* Nov. 28, 1932.
[24] Final Report of AAPA, p. 40.
[25] New York *Times,* Feb. 10, 1930.

[26] *Ibid.*, July 15, 1930.

[27] Ella A. Boole, *Give Prohibition Its Chance* (Fleming H. Revell Co., 1929), p. 114.

[28] See *infra*, p. 230.

[29] Grace C. Root, *Woman and Repeal*, authorized by Mrs. Charles H. Sabin (Harper & Bros., 1934), p. 158.

[30] *Ibid.*, p. 176.

[31] *Ibid.*, p. 164.

[32] *Ibid.*

[33] *Ibid.*, p. 165.

[34] *Ibid.*, p. 169.

[35] *Ibid.*, p. 93.

[36] *Ibid.*, p. 94.

[37] *Ibid.*, p. 98.

[38] *Ibid.*

[39] *Ibid.*, p. 102.

[40] *Ibid.*, p. 8.

[41] *Ibid.*, pp. 170–71.

[42] New York *Times*, June 11, 1932.

[43] *Ibid.*

[44] Root, *op. cit.*, pp. 111, 115–16.

[45] *Ibid.*, p. 177.

[46] *Ibid.*, p. 136.

[47] *Ibid.*, p. 103.

[48] *Ibid.*, p. 73.

[49] *Ibid.*, p. 174.

[50] *Ibid.*, pp. 179–80.

Chapter Three

The Final Grand Assault

BY JUNE 1932, the AAPA had mobilized the big business and financial interests, the newspapers, magazines and movies, the radio, the lawyers, and the wives and sons and other retainers and dependents of its members. It had driven most of the drys from public life and set up a reign of terror which had made of a majority of the politicians of both parties cowards and sycophants. By years of propaganda bombardment, it had silenced the guns of the opposition and was ready for the final grand assault upon the Eighteenth Amendment. Under the high-sounding title of the "United Repeal Council," the leaders of the association and its auxiliaries went to Chicago to force both the Republican and Democratic national conventions to adopt their liquor platform. The final report of the association says:

On June 7, 1932, the United Repeal Council was organized, having as members the Association Against the Prohibition Amendment, the Women's Organization for National Prohibition Reform, the Crusaders, the Voluntary Committee of Lawyers, and the American Hotel Association. It adopted a resolution, presented by Mr. Stayton, which declared the repeal groups "associate ourselves as the United Repeal Council for the purpose of obtaining from each major political party a plank in its platform urging Congress to submit to the several states *for ratification in state conventions* a resolution for repeal of the Eighteenth Amendment and *pledging the best efforts of the party to the accomplishment of such ratification.*"

Pierre S. du Pont was named chairman of the United Repeal Council and on June 12 at the Sherman Hotel in Chicago a second meeting of the council was held with a number of invited guests present and a repeal plank was drafted for presentation to the Resolutions Committee of the Republican national convention. It is scarcely necessary to recall in detail the fight that occurred on the floor of that convention. . . .

The United Repeal Council continued its efforts. Its representatives appeared before the Resolutions Committee of the Democratic convention and the action of that convention is well known.

The Republican convention made a partial surrender. It declared for the submission of a repeal amendment to conventions, but opposed nullification and the surrender of the power of the federal government to prevent the return of the saloon. Du Pont and his associates were enraged at this act of insubordination, and denounced the plank as a "straddle" and a "fraud."

The Democratic convention and its candidate accepted every line of the association's liquor platform — modification of the Volstead Act, submission of a "straight repeal" amendment to conventions, return of the liquor question to the states, and the elimination from the amendment of any provision that would give Congress power to prevent the return of the saloon. This act of humble and complete submission was greeted with ecstasy by the members of the association.

The Presidential Campaign of 1932

After the conventions, the United Repeal Council entered the campaign with all the resources at its command to defeat dry and elect wet candidates, and insure a subservient president and Congress. Mr. Curran was replaced as president of the association by Jouett Shouse. Announcing the change, Mr. du Pont said:

While Major Curran has had the advice and support of the executive committee, and especially of our all-time leader, Captain William H. Stayton, the marked success of the cause has been due to the constant attacks upon national prohibition carried on by Major Curran and his assistants.

The executive committee of the association has felt the need of a character of guidance additional to that so successful in the past, and to meet this need has elected to the presidency of the association Mr. Jouett Shouse, a man so well known to the public as to need no introduction.[1]

Shouse had been a lawyer, a newspaper man, a congressman, and was an expert promoter and propagandist. In May 1929, Mr. Raskob had appointed him chairman of the national Democratic executive committee. From that time until the 1932 convention, he had gone to every part of the country as Raskob's henchman, endeavoring to force the Democratic party to adopt the repeal program of the AAPA. The purpose of Shouse and all the elements represented by the repeal council was concisely expressed by William G. McAdoo, secretary of the treasury under President Wilson: "Mr. Jouett Shouse and these New York interests are seeking to restore the open saloon in America. That is their backing, and that is their purpose." [2]

That Shouse was amply supplied with funds is evidenced by the fact that from June 2 to November 2, 1932, the association expended more than $300,000.[3] Some of the contributions to this fund were the following:

Irénée du Pont	$30,500
Pierre S. du Pont	50,500
Lammot du Pont	30,100
Charles H. Sabin	5,000
Eugene du Pont	350
Archibald du Pont	300
William du Pont	350 [4]

It must also be remembered that Mr. Shouse was given hundreds of thousands of dollars' worth of free space in the newspapers in which to broadcast his wet propaganda and urge the election of wet candidates. In addition, all the money contributed to the local, state and national committees of both parties was used to finance campaigns in which prohibition was constantly attacked.

The feverish activity, the lavish use of money, the social pressure and the financial coercion of the AAPA and its subsidiaries in the 1932 campaign constitute a sordid and disgraceful chapter in our political history.

The attitude of the two parties and their candidates resulted in the complete disfranchisement of the drys in the 1932 election. They could give no expression to their convictions at the polls. The result of the election did not, therefore, reflect the convictions of the people on the liquor question. Mr. Shouse, however, declaring solemnly that the "people had spoken" and that the election "constituted an outstanding mandate from the voters of the United States for repeal of the Eighteenth Amendment" which must be obeyed without delay, moved with all his cohorts upon the national capitol.

It will be remembered that in his letter to Mr. Butler, Pierre du Pont gave a confidential statement of the strategy of the repeal campaign. He stated that the people were opposed to the saloon and that it would be necessary to assure them that it would never be permitted to return, and that to give this assurance, a repeal amendment should be proposed which provided "that all such liquors sold shall be in packages not to be opened or consumed on the premises where sold." He stated that when the people had been made "receptive to complete state control" by means of this promise, in the end "it will be easy to strike out the words 'provided that all such liquors shall be in packages not to be opened or consumed on the premises where sold.'" Then, of course, the saloon would be back with its contributions to liquor revenue.

Let us see now just how this short-change swindle was worked. The Democratic party had been committed to the plan. At the opening of the short session of the Seventy-second Congress on December 5, 1932, the moment the chaplain had finished his prayer, Speaker Garner, then vice-president elect, recognized Henry T. Rainey, Democratic leader, who proposed the following amendment:

Section 1. The Eighteenth Article of Amendment is hereby repealed.

Section 2. This Article shall be inoperative unless it shall have been ratified as an amendment to the Constitution by conventions in three-fourths of the several states within seven years from the date of its submission.

Referring to this resolution, the final report of the association says:

> The resolution was a correct and proper interpretation of the plank of the Democratic national platform and embodied the aims and objectives for which this association and other repeal groups had been working. It was submitted to the officers of your association by the speaker before it was offered and was declared by them to be entirely satisfactory.

It was " entirely satisfactory " because it carried out Du Pont's scheme for cheating the people by depriving Congress of the power to prevent the return of the saloon. As it was lost by only six votes, it demonstrated the power of the AAPA.

The members of the Judiciary Committee of the Senate, remembering that the people had been given the solemn promise that the saloon would never be permitted to return, and that Congress would be given the power to make that promise effective, had the impudence to keep faith with the people and reported out the following resolution:

> The Eighteenth Article of Amendment of the Constitution of the United States is hereby amended to read as follows:
>
> The Eighteenth Amendment to the Constitution is hereby repealed. . . .
>
> Congress shall have concurrent power to regulate or prohibit the sale of intoxicating liquors to be drunk on the premises where sold.
>
> This act shall be inoperative unless it shall have been ratified by the legislatures of the several states as provided in the Constitution within seven years after the adoption of said resolution.

Shouse Warns Congress against Insubordination

In the final report of the AAPA Mr. Shouse said:

> Obviously this resolution embodied an attempt not to repeal but to modify the Eighteenth Amendment. Its two objectionable features were Section 3, which sought to give to Congress concurrent power to regulate or prohibit the sale of intoxicating liquors to be drunk on the premises where sold, and Section 4, which would have referred ratifica-

tion of the resolution to legislatures rather than to conventions in the states. . . .

Your association immediately challenged the resolution as reported by the Senate Judiciary Committee. In addition to statements to the daily press given at the time, our objections were set forth at length in a speech which I delivered at Louisville, Kentucky, on January 17th. . . . The following are quotations from the Louisville speech:

"It is with the third section of the pending resolution that I take definite issue. That section reads as follows: 'Congress shall have concurrent power to regulate or prohibit the sale of intoxicating liquors to be drunk on the premises where sold. . . .'

". . . And if the distinguished apologists for this indefensible section are right in their surmise that Congress might not at first care to exercise its jurisdiction, is it not irrefutable that there would be continuous effort by overzealous prohibitionists to induce, if not to compel, the Congress to legislate in accordance with this proposed section of the repeal amendment?"

As a matter of fact, there was no serious danger that the resolution would ever get through both houses of Congress. Even had it passed the Senate, the attitude of the leadership of the House of Representatives was so pronouncedly hostile to an anomalous and improper resolution of the kind that it would never have received the required vote in the House, if indeed it had been allowed to come before that body for an expression.

On the other hand, it was recognized that if we could get the right kind of resolution through the winter session of the Seventy-second Congress, we would probably be able to hasten the accomplishment of repeal by at least two years. . . . That was the reason it was so important, if possible, to have the Senate resolution properly corrected.

With this in view, the officers of your association and officers of other repeal groups, particularly the Women's Organization for National Prohibition Reform, contacted practically the entire membership of the Senate, urging that the Senate resolution should be changed in the two particulars specified, *and stating bluntly that if it was not changed, we would oppose the resolution if it went to the states.*

The association, supported by the wet press, conducted a campaign of extreme ferocity to force Congress to drop the provision against the return of the saloon. The threat that "we would be compelled to oppose ratification " was political blackmail. In plain language, what it said to the administration was this: " If the amendment is not submitted in the precise form we demand, we will turn our money and our hirelings loose in every state to block ratification, and you know we will be successful. You will then have the prohibition question on your doorstep. You will have to make an honest and determined effort to enforce the law or permit its undisguised nullification. If you do the former, we will fight you, and if you do the latter, the drys will fight you, and we will continue our fight for unconditional repeal. In either event, the question will plague you and endanger your success at the next congressional and presidential elections. Your only hope of getting the question out of the way is to bow to our command."

The Triumph of Pierre du Pont

Mr. Shouse induced Senator Robinson of Arkansas, " the Democratic leader of the Senate and formerly a pronounced defender of the Eighteenth Amendment," to take the lead in putting over this cheat. He said: " I consider the fight that was made by Senator Robinson the deciding factor in the battle." That this praise was justified is shown by Mr. Shouse's report of the battle in the Senate:

> After two days of debate, with votes on six amendments, the corrected repeal resolution, which is now the Twenty-first Amendment, passed the Senate on February 16th (1933). On February 15th, the Senate voted on a motion to consider the resolution with 58 yeas, 23 nays, and 15 not voting. The two crucial tests came that day, the first on an amendment by Senator Robinson of Arkansas to make conventions instead of state legislatures the ratifying agencies. The result of this was:
>
> | | |
> |---|---|
> | In favor of convention | 45 |
> | Against | 15 |
> | Not voting | 36 |
>
> Later the same day the Senate voted on another amendment of Senator Robinson of Arkansas to strike out Section 3, thus eliminating the provision for concurrent action by Congress. The vote was:

Yeas	33
Nays	32
Not voting	31

On February 16th, the Senate voted on substituting the Glass resolution, the measure with the saloon provision therein, for the so-called Blaine resolution. The vote was:

Yeas	38
Nays	46
Not voting	12

Shortly afterwards the Senate voted on Senator Reed's amendment seeking to add a section which would prohibit sale for consumption at place of sale. This vote was:

Yeas	37
Nays	45
Not voting	12

On the afternoon of February 16th, the Senate voted on the passage of the resolution as amended:

Yeas	63
Nays	23
Not voting	10

Thus Senate Joint Resolution 211, now Article XXI of the Constitution of the United States, as passed, was the following:

Section 1. The Eighteenth Article of Amendment to the Constitution of the United States is hereby repealed.

Section 2. Transportation or importation into any state, territory, or possession of the United States for delivery or use therein of intoxicating liquors in violation of the laws thereof is hereby prohibited.

Section 3. This Article shall be inoperative unless it shall have been ratified as an Amendment to the Constitution by conventions in the several states as provided in the Constitution within seven years from the date of submission herein to the states by the Congress.

The resolution thus presented, being in a form which met the situation, was endorsed heartily by our association and by the other repeal groups. It was taken up promptly in the House of Representatives and on February 20th passed the House by a vote of 289 yeas to 121 nays, with 16 not voting.

This was the consummation of Du Pont's scheme to lure the people on to repeal by promising that the saloon should not come back and then, at the last moment, cheating them by eliminating the provision that would have made it possible to prevent its return.

After Du Pont and his warriors had forced Congress to submit the repeal amendment in the exact form demanded, they launched their great campaign for ratification. They had their lawyers prepare bills providing for conventions, which were sent to the various states. The governors and members of the legislatures were told that these bills must be passed and ratification machinery set up at once, and that their only alternative was a journey to the political graveyard. Every conceivable lie, threat and false promise that would deceive, frighten and entice the voters was broadcast by newspapers, magazines, radios, movies, political orators, billboards and the mails. From coast to coast, every instrument of the great propaganda orchestra, from first violins to bass drums, went full blast without a moment's letup until the thirty-sixth state had ratified.

The Du Pont forces were not willing, however, to await the action of the states, although action was being accelerated by the lash they were applying. They demanded that Congress at once authorize the manufacture, sale and taxation of beer. They put forward this plan when they first took over the AAPA in 1926. From that time on they, their allied organizations, their politicians and propagandists, constantly insisted that it be put through. Their voluntary lawyers had declared that the plan was lawful and that it would immediately produce a revenue of over $300,000,000. It would achieve another and still more important result: it would make the liquor rebellion triumphant and insure ratification of the repeal amendment.

On February 20, 1933, the repeal resolution was adopted by Congress; a month later Congress and the President again performed to the crack of the whip, and the beer bill was enacted and approved. No one who was not sufficiently awake to realize what was going on can form any conception of the results of this action.

The voice of conscience, honor and patriotism was silenced, every pretense of law enforcement was abandoned, and nullification, lawlessness and rebellion ran riot. Then, with supreme impudence, the wet propagandists shouted: "See what a cesspool prohibition is! Will you permit preachers and bootleggers to perpetuate this tragic farce any longer?" Opposition to repeal collapsed, the gates were thrown open, and the rebels entered with flags flying and corks popping. The nation made an abject and unconditional surrender and ended the rebellion by acceding to every demand of the rebels.

Demobilization

For years the members of the AAPA, their lawyers, wives, sons, "beloved authors" and other propagandists, had professed the loftiest motives. They had declared that their purpose was to stop excessive drinking and the debauching of youth, to promote true temperance, put an end to political corruption and disrespect for law, prevent the return of the saloon, and work out a constructive solution of the problem under which all profit would be taken out of the business and liquor would be sold only by the bottle in places from which every lure and enticement to drink would be absent. Repeal was celebrated by a nation-wide broadcast. Microphones were established in bars and we heard corks popping, cocktail shakers rattling, and drunken and maudlin shouts and singing from New York to San Francisco. Saloons were opened, women were admitted, barmaids and hostesses were installed and other features were added that would encourage drunkenness and vice. Three years later the director of the Federal Bureau of Investigation of the Department of Justice declared that "crime has reached a pinnacle of appalling height." Nearly every city in the country is now in the grip of corrupt political machines that are allied with vice and crime and sharing the profits. Not one of the lofty objectives of our noble reformers has been achieved. And yet the moment repeal was accomplished, the moment liquor was taxed and the saloons were opened, the WONPR, the Voluntary Committee of Lawyers, and the Crusaders disbanded and closed their offices and disappeared from the scene. On December 31, 1933, the New York *Times* carried this news item:

Washington, Dec. 30.—The Association Against the Prohibition Amendment went out of existence today. It quietly closed its offices in the National Press Building and sent its files to the Library of Congress as the record of a great adventure in sociological legislation. Having attained its objective—the repeal of national prohibition, the first amendment to the Constitution ever excised from that document—the association resisted the temptation to linger on as a " sentinel of American liberty."

NOTES

[1] At a later time Mr. du Pont made Mr. Shouse president of the American Liberty League. Again he was to save the Constitution! But an incidental concern was expressed in a speech Mr. Shouse broadcast on May 19, 1936, in which he said: " You will remember that Congress in that act turned over to Mr. Roosevelt the gigantic sum of $4,880,000,000." This, he said, resulted in an increase of the income taxes, which were to have been abolished.

[2] New York *Times,* Sept. 29, 1932.

[3] *Ibid.,* Nov. 5, 1932.

[4] *Ibid.,* Sept. 16, 1932.

Chapter Four

The Allied Tammany Halls

IT WAS the liquor dealers together with others having financial interest in the liquor traffic — the underworld, the corrupt machines of the cities and the political tools of these elements — that made the last ditch fight against the adoption of the Eighteenth Amendment. It was these same forces that immediately organized the fight for its nullification and repeal. As we have seen, the liquor interests began the fight before the amendment had gone into operation. Prohibition became effective January 16, 1920, and within a few weeks the leaders of Tammany Hall of New York began the work of organizing the city machines of the country for its overthrow. Charles F. Murphy, grand sachem of Tammany Hall and a former bartender and saloon-keeper, assumed the position of generalissimo of these forces.

Liquor was a necessity for the elements that made up these city machines. Many of their leaders were in the liquor business, the saloons were their political headquarters, saloon-keepers, bartenders and their hangers-on were their political workers, and they levied huge tribute on the business through their power to protect it against the laws and ordinances passed for its regulation. It was perfectly natural, therefore, that these machines should at once mobilize all their forces for the nullification and destruction of the Eighteenth Amendment.

Murphy saw that the first and most important move was to force the Democratic party to nominate a wet politician of the Tammany stripe for president. This was important for three reasons: First, such a striking wet victory would begin the breakdown of the morale of the supporters of the law; second, it would arouse the enthusiasm of the underworld and other corrupt elements of the cities, entice them away from the Republican party and help to elect the local Democratic ticket; third, if successful, he would appoint district attorneys and other federal officials who would permit the nullification of the law in true Tammany fashion.

Allied Tammany Halls Capture Democratic Convention of 1920

The two most powerful Tammany leaders of the middle west were George Brennan of Chicago and Tom Taggart of Indiana. Murphy and Al Smith went west and spent the week before the opening of the Democratic national convention of 1920 in conference with Brennan and Taggart. They decided to line up the city machines in support of Governor James M. Cox of Ohio. Cox was a small-bore machine politician, a member of the Ohio Democratic gang, and had always been subservient to the liquor interests. When he was a candidate for governor, the Liquor League of Ohio issued the following statement: " Any man who sincerely believes that prohibition is a bad thing for the state of Ohio should devote his time unceasingly from now until election night and persuade as many votes as possible for Cox." Of Governor Cox's views on the other great national problems that were pressing for solution and of his capacity for leadership in one of the most critical moments of our history, little or nothing was known. But he was wet and nothing else mattered to Murphy, Smith, Taggart, Brennan and the city bosses who followed their leadership.

The New York *Times* for June 17, 1920, contains the following news item:

> On board the Tammany Special for San Francisco. — The real choice of the Tammany leaders for the nomination is Governor James M. Cox of Ohio, who is classed as an advocate of a " liberal " policy in enforcing the prohibition amendment.
>
> The best that Tammany hopes to get out of the San Francisco convention is something that will help the Democratic organization in Manhattan and the Bronx to elect the judicial ticket this year and put the party in good shape for the mayoralty campaign of 1921.

> In his talks with other Tammany leaders, Murphy has bluntly insisted that the only object he had in view was the success of the local ticket next fall and that as New York was a wet city, it was absolutely necessary that a wet plank be put in the platform. In his plan, Murphy has the backing of Governor Smith and the other New York leaders here.

Thus the first great offensive against the Eighteenth Amendment was inspired by the determination of Tammany Hall to retain its power to plunder the city of New York.

Murphy was a commanding figure at San Francisco. Tammany presented the name of Al Smith to the convention in order to camouflage its maneuvers for Cox. As stated in the New York *Times,*

> Governor Smith's position in this convention is much the same as that of Nicholas Murray Butler in the Republican national convention. He will be the base from which the Tammany delegates will operate, while their leader, Charles F. Murphy, completes his deals with other state chiefs.[1]

Having forced the nomination of Cox for president, Murphy and his allies proceeded to hand the nomination for vice-president to Franklin D. Roosevelt. Roosevelt was a member of the New York delegation and had played Tammany's game by seconding the nomination of Al Smith for president. Smith in return seconded the nomination of Roosevelt for vice-president.

> Charles F. Murphy, George Brennan of Illinois, and E. H. Moore of Ohio, leaders of the Cox forces, had voted on Roosevelt before the convention was called to order.[2]

Roosevelt was a young man, relatively unknown to the country at large, who, it appears, was nominated because he bore a name that had been made famous by another man and because he was willing to be a pawn for Tammany Hall.

The reaction of the country to this disgraceful convention is illustrated by the following quotation from the Philadelphia *Public Ledger:*

> The stain of Tammany that is upon American politics is so unsavory, the principles and practices indelibly associated with the very name

Tammany, and the character and reputation of the politicians of the Taggart type, who composed the defeat of McAdoo and Palmer, are so contrary to every ideal of true statesmanship and clean politics, that the domination of the convention and its candidates by that element can only be regarded as a colossal blunder.[3]

Big business interests have dominated political conventions of both parties. But this at least can be said: their business is legitimate and they supply the public with products that are useful and necessary. In the Democratic national convention of 1920, for the first time traditional Americanism went down to defeat before the political machines that have organized into militant fighting units the underworld, the spoilsmen, the grafters and the financial pirates of our cities. This was the convention which started the fight on the Eighteenth Amendment immediately after its adoption, and this was the convention that discovered Franklin D. Roosevelt, who, in 1933, finished the fight.

The next move in Tammany's bitter fight upon the Eighteenth Amendment and the first really staggering blow the amendment received was the repeal in 1923 of the New York enforcement act. In the Republican landslide of 1920, Al Smith and other Tammany candidates had been defeated and Nathan L. Miller was elected governor. He represented the intelligence and conscience of the state rather than the slums, the spoilsmen and grafters of New York city. For two years the state was governed by men who did not perform at the crack of the Tammany whip in the hands of Charles Murphy. It was during this interlude that the Mullen-Gage enforcement act was passed. It was the moral duty of the state to pass this act, as the amendment giving concurrent power of enforcement to Congress and the states had become a part of the Constitution, and particularly as New York had itself ratified the amendment. At the next election, Al Smith was elected governor, Tammany reassumed its sway at Albany, and the enforcement act was repealed. The cooperation of the state was withdrawn, the entire burden of enforcement was thrown upon the federal officials, and the breakdown of the law in New York state was made inevitable. The United States district attorney at New

York said this was "the hardest blow the enforcement of the Eighteenth Amendment has received."

Smith and Roosevelt Leaders of Allied Tammany Halls

In 1901, Al Smith, then a young man, became an active election-district leader of Tammany Hall. By that organization he was given six terms in the legislature, made sheriff of New York county, president of the board of aldermen of greater New York, and four times governor of the state. Four times he was candidate for president, with the solid and fervent backing of Tammany Hall. In his autobiography he says: "My intimate acquaintance and association with Charles F. Murphy bore out what thousands of people have said of him, that 'to know him was to love him.'"[4]

In 1924 Mr. Murphy determined to organize the same forces that had controlled the 1920 convention and force the nomination of Smith for president.

> In 1920 Murphy was instrumental in forcing the nomination of James M. Cox for president of the United States, and in 1922 Murphy gained Smith a renomination as governor of New York in spite of Mr. Hearst's aspirations. It was Murphy's intention to make Alfred E. Smith president of the United States, and it was with this end in view that the convention of the Democratic party was scheduled to be held in New York city in 1924. Murphy was exceedingly busy during the first months of 1924, making plans for the nomination of Governor Smith.[5]

Those old enough to remember the convention of 1924 will recall that Tammany displayed several new forms of technique in the work of influencing delegates. The hospitality to visiting delegates included wine, women and song, and the galleries were filled with a Tammany rabble instructed to coerce and stampede the convention for its candidate. For days the allied Tammany Halls of the country held the convention deadlocked in a determined effort to nominate their candidate. Finally Smith announced, "I have given to Mr. Brennan a blank check and they can fill it out to suit themselves."

In this maudlin and disgraceful convention, Franklin D. Roosevelt was Tammany's leader and spokesman. Reporting the convention for the *New Republic,* Mr. Bruce Bliven said:

> On the day when Franklin Roosevelt was to place the New York governor in nomination, several thousand ticketless Tammany workers "crashed the gates" at the garden and took places in the galleries. Shortly thereafter the police roped the vicinity of the building and the ticketholders who subsequently appeared were told, with the utmost politeness and good nature, to go chase themselves. The Smith demonstration was directed by captains placed about the hall, taking orders from a generalissimo near the speakers' platform.[6]

The New York *Times* gave the following description of the scene:

> The galleries cheered Alfred E. Smith for an hour and a half yesterday by larynx, by hand-driven instruments and by electricity. More than ten thousand shouted themselves hoarse, rang cow bells, blew fish horns and revolved rattlers, but their noise was drowned out by a few sirens and mechanical screechers connected with dry batteries and turned on and off by push buttons. "All set," roared a collarless and sleeveless man in the rear of the first of the east galleries as Franklin D. Roosevelt wound up his speech nominating the governor.
>
> His corps of helpers put their fingers on the buttons of great brass fire department and ambulance sirens which were attached to cases of dry batteries. "Go!" he shouted, as Roosevelt named his man.[7]

Upon the death of Murphy, George W. Olvany became leader of Tammany Hall, and in 1928 he marshaled the Tammany forces of the country for the nomination of Smith for president. This was important because Smith was their man, and, if elected, could be depended upon to be a Tammany president.

The gleeful confidence of the Tammany hordes as they moved upon Houston is reflected in the news dispatches of the time:

> With the departure of George W. Olvany, leader of Tammany, and a group of influential members of Tammany yesterday, practically all of the Smith leaders were en route to Houston or already there.
>
> "We'll come back with the nomination in the bag," said Mr. Hoey, as spokesman for the party. "We all feel the same on that, but I won't venture a guess as to what ballot the governor will be nominated on."[8]

George E. Brennan, picturesque leader of Illinois Democracy, arrived here today with the advance guard of his state delegation, and smilingly commented that no one should worry about the prohibition plank being the party's platform. " Al Smith," he announced, " will write the platform from stump to stump during the campaign." [9]

Frank Hague, mayor of Jersey City and Democratic leader of New Jersey, will function in the important capacity of negotiator in any deals involving the delivery of delegates to Governor Smith.[10]

No one having even a casual knowledge of our political history will need to be reminded of the fact that Hague of Jersey City is a boss of the same stripe as Murphy, Brennan and Taggart.

Franklin D. Roosevelt, Smith pre-convention manager four years ago, will function as floor manager for the Smith forces at the convention this year, according to announcement made by George R. Van Mamee, manager of the Smith campaign.[11]

Mr. Roosevelt began his speech nominating Al Smith for president as follows:

I come for the third time to urge upon a convention of my party the nomination of the governor of the state of New York. The faith which I held I still hold.

Commenting upon the convention, the Philadelphia *Inquirer* said:

A proud day for Tammany Hall! Feared, hated, despised, and denounced at national conventions heretofore, this organization has at last succeeded in bringing the Democratic party to its knees in submission.[12]

The *Literary Digest,* in its leading article, said:

A new political era dawns as Governor Alfred E. Smith, a product of Tammany, an avowed foe of prohibition, a devout Catholic, comes from the sidewalks of New York to become the national standard bearer of the Democratic party, and many political writers note, at the same time, that the control of the Democratic party passes from the farms and the small town to the great cities, from the south to New York.[13]

Surely that control had not passed to the business, educational, religious and civic leaders of New York, who had struggled for a generation to break Tammany's strangle hold on the city. The real truth is that the control of the party passed from those of its members, whether they lived in large or small cities or the country, who represented traditional American ideals of patriotism and political morals, to Tammany Hall of New York and its allies in other cities — organizations which stood for precisely the same things that Tammany had always stood for.

The convention was the complete fulfillment of the prophecy made by Mr. George F. Milton, editor of the Chattanooga *News*. Prior to the convention, he addressed to William G. McAdoo a letter in which he said:

> Apparently we are about to see a prosecution of a brazen attempt on the part of the underworld of American politics to dominate, control and debase a party made glorious by the patriotic achievements and lofty ideals of Thomas Jefferson, Andrew Jackson, Grover Cleveland and Woodrow Wilson.[14]

Alliance between Tammany and Big Business

Immediately after the convention, the Tammany leaders entered into an open and definite alliance with the most unscrupulous elements of big business for the control and use of the Democratic party. The result of the alliance was the election of John J. Raskob as chairman of the Democratic national committee. He had been intimately associated with the Du Ponts as an owner and manager of their vast enterprises. Governmental investigations have shown that he was a member of pools formed to fleece the public through gambling transactions on the stock exchange, that he was on the favored lists of the big Wall street bankers who permitted him to buy stock at a price below that paid by the public, that he and Pierre du Pont engaged in wash sales of securities to avoid paying taxes on their plethoric incomes, and that he joined the Du Ponts in taking over and using the AAPA to bring back the liquor traffic in order to reduce their income taxes. Speaking of his selection, Alfred E. Smith said:

Immediately following the convention there arose the all-important question of selecting a national chairman. This is by custom a responsibility resting on the candidate himself. I suggested John J. Raskob as an eminently successful business man with a clear mind, a broad view and a knowledge of men. He was born in the city of Lockport in my own state. Aside from my knowledge of and confidence in his ability, I believed it to be wise political strategy to let the business men of this country know that one of the great industrial leaders of modern times had confidence and faith in the Democratic party and in its platform.[15]

Boss Olvany gave this selection his blessing. He said:

I think it was a very good selection. It will show the people throughout the country that big business need not be afraid of the Democratic party when the party is willing to have its affairs in the hands of a man conspicuously identified with one of the biggest business corporations of the world.[16]

Thus through their chosen representatives the underworld, the spoilsmen and the grafters of our cities and the pirates of big business took undisputed control of the Democratic party for the purpose of destroying the Eighteenth Amendment.

Tammany and Franklin D. Roosevelt

As candidate for president, Mr. Smith was in a position to name the candidate for governor in his home state. With full approval of Tammany, he chose Mr. Roosevelt, and Tammany's other idol, Mayor James J. Walker of New York, was selected to make the nominating speech in the convention. In the course of this speech Mayor Walker said:

Ah, my friends, standing side by side, Alfred E. Smith and Franklin D. Roosevelt give notice to the world of the sincere and genuine patriotism that actuates the Democratic party. It is proper as we look back to four years primarily to that figure that stood in Madison Square Garden and thrilled your heart of hearts as he pronounced and led the cause of our distinguished governor.

This was the Mayor Walker who a little later resigned his office and took up his residence abroad after Judge Samuel Seabury had, with merciless persistence, exposed the frauds and acts of public betrayal of which he had been guilty. It was the same "Jimmy" Walker who, during the investigation, staged the great Tammany beer parade that attracted nation-wide attention.

During Roosevelt's first term as governor of New York, the entire country was shocked by revelations of the sale of judgeships and of the widespread graft in New York city, and by the refusal of John F. Curry, leader of Tammany, and of various district leaders, to waive immunity and appear before the Grand Jury to testify. The governor sounded no note of moral leadership, but maintained an attitude of aloof silence. His reward came when, in the Democratic state convention of 1930, Al Smith made the speech nominating him for re-election and he received the solid support of Tammany Hall.

The Republican candidate for governor, Charles H. Tuttle, in his speech of acceptance, referred to the disclosures that had been made of the bartering of places on the bench and the refusal of Tammany leaders to waive immunity and testify, and stated that this would be the principal issue in the campaign. Governor Roosevelt, in his speech of acceptance, answered this challenge: "When I first read this keynote address of my opponent I was puzzled, in fact, as to whether he was running for governor of the state of New York or for district attorney of New York county."[17] He thus adroitly evaded giving offense either to Tammany by condemning its corruption, or to decent people by condoning it. After a general statement on the subject of law enforcement, he insinuated that Mr. Tuttle was friendly with certain dry leaders, and said: "So today I ask him this question: If you become governor and if a state enforcement act is passed, will you sign that act or not?"[18] Thus he avoided a direct statement that might be offensive to the drys, and in the same breath assured Tammany that he would veto an enforcement act.

After Roosevelt was safely seated in the governor's chair a second time, the deepening of the depression made it practically certain that Hoover could not be re-elected. This state of affairs presented a golden opportunity for Smith to realize his ambition to become president and for Tammany Hall to secure all the federal patronage and also a president who would use his great power as head of his party to force the repeal of the Eighteenth Amendment. As for Roosevelt, the fact that he was in a position to be seriously considered as a candidate for the presidency he owed entirely to Smith and Tammany. Every consideration of loyalty and fair dealing demanded that he do everything in his power to secure the nomination and election of Smith, especially since no question of policy or principle was involved, but solely his personal ambition.

He decided, however, to become a candidate and began his hunt for delegates. He knew that Smith would have the support of Tammany politicians and of the Du Ponts and their associates because of his unequivocal endorsement of their repeal program. He believed, also, that if he should secure the nomination himself, he would have to have their support in order to be elected. He saw, therefore, that he would have to secure his delegates from states that were not controlled by Tammany machines and big business. He saw also that it was important that he should have no break with Tammany leaders, that he should give them everything they wanted except his support of Smith and be in a position to deal with them if he secured the nomination.

How he placated Tammany is now a matter of record. As the Seabury investigation proceeded, it became evident that Tammany was just what it had been under Tweed, Crocker and Murphy. When it was proved that in seven years the bank deposits of the sheriff of Kings county had exceeded his salary by $400,000, the City Affairs Committee petitioned Governor Roosevelt to remove him. The petition was signed by Dr. John Haynes Holmes and Rabbi Stephen S. Wise as officers of the committee. Roosevelt wrote a letter in which he refused to remove the sheriff and said little about the proved corruption in New York city, but accused Dr. Holmes and Rabbi Wise, two of the most intelligent, public-spirited and courageous civic leaders of New York, of caring more for personal publicity than for good government. Commenting on this action, *Unity,* a magazine edited by Dr. Holmes, said:

It is something of a spectacle when the governor of a great state, avowedly a candidate for the national presidency, with high claims to intelligence and character, goes out of his way to wax wroth not against those responsible for vile conditions in New York, but rather against those striving to correct these conditions. . . .[19]

Later on Walter Lippmann commented:

Ever since the Seabury investigation has been under way, Governor Roosevelt's friends have been explaining his aloofness on the ground that he had a judicial duty to perform. Apparently, however, it is proper for the governor to denounce those who are crusading against corruption and to impugn their motives. . . . He elected, instead, to play an intricate game with Tammany, to act against corruption only when he was forced to do so, to feed Tammany patronage, to consort with Tammany bosses, and to go along with Tammany in trying to discredit Mr. Seabury and the active forces fighting Tammany corruption. Tammany and its allies will have a large vote in Chicago.[20]

In an article in the *New Republic,* June 1, 1932, Mr. Bruce Bliven said:

It is not necessary to recite again in detail the story of Roosevelt's relation to the exposure of dishonesty and incompetence among New York city officials. He has used his power of removal from office only once, and then not until the scandal had become so flagrant that he could no longer ignore it. As he did so, he sought by every means in his power to placate Tammany regarding the action, and there is reason to believe that he was successful. He has flatly refused to remove from office, or to assist in the prosecution of, other officials who are quite as unfit as Sheriff Farley. Particularly bad is his record in regard to John Theofel, clerk of the surrogate's court in Queens county, and Sheriff James A. McQuade of Kings county. Of the absolute unfitness of the men there is no question; not even Tammany has the effrontery to defend them in public. Yet when the Reverend John Haynes Holmes and Rabbi Stephen S. Wise, acting on behalf of the City Affairs Committee, wrote to the governor to enlist his aid against these men, he made an extraordinary reply. Not only did he refuse to take any action, but he excoriated Messrs. Holmes and Wise in the most violent terms, and for reasons which any ten-year-old should have been able to see were unsound. . . . In the eyes of most people throughout the United States, his alliance with Tammany is his gravest liability.

Roosevelt Poses as Leader of the Drys

In 1931 the repeal campaign had reached the height of its intensity and the forces that were fighting desperately for repeal had evolved a definite program of procedure. On the other hand, the moral forces of the nation were fighting with equal desperation to prevent the return of the liquor traffic and they had evolved a program that was as definite as that of the wets who were backing Smith. In their ranks, there were not only members of churches, temperance societies, the Anti-Saloon League, women's organizations and social workers, but also many of the ablest senators, representatives, governors and other political leaders in the country. They knew precisely what they wanted and just why they wanted it.

They believed that the whole wet movement was reactionary and corrupt and that both parties should declare unequivocally for the retention and enforcement of the amendment. This continued to be the attitude of the dry element in the Republican party to the end, and they regarded the action of the convention and of Mr. Hoover in declaring for resubmission as a complete defeat and a capitulation to the most corrupt and subversive elements of the country. As a result of the wet propaganda and the three years' fight of Smith, Raskob and Shouse to commit the Democratic party to repeal, many prominent dry Democrats had reached the point where they were willing to agree to the resubmission of the question to the states. They insisted, however, that this should be done in such a manner that a free and honest expression of the popular will could be secured. They believed that if this were done, prohibition would win as decisively as it had in 1919 and in the election of 1928, the repeal movement would collapse, and the work of enforcement would no longer be hampered by repeal ballyhoo and sabotage. They knew that the Tammany-Smith-Du Pont-Raskob liquor program was simply an impudent scheme to defraud, and they were determined to fight it to the last ditch. They knew that if this swindle was to be blocked, resubmission would have to be accompanied by six specific safeguards. As to these safeguards, they were determined there should be no surrender. This was the program which they supported in opposition to that of Smith and the elements backing him:

(1) They knew that the modification of the Volstead Act would result in the nullification of the Constitution through a dishonest subterfuge and make repeal inevitable. They were, therefore, uncompromising in their opposition to modification.

(2) Both the wets and the drys agreed that the destruction of the saloon had been a great national gain and that it should never be permitted to return. The drys, therefore, demanded that the repeal amendment should provide against its return or give Congress the power to do so by appropriate legislation.

(3) One of the greatest difficulties encountered in the long struggle against the liquor traffic had been the shipment of liquor into dry states and territories in violation of their laws. The difficulty had been increased by automobiles, trucks, airplanes and other improvements in methods of transportation. The drys insisted that the repeal amendment should give Congress the power to protect dry states and communities against the greed and lawlessness of liquor dealers in wet states.

(4) As candidates for the legislature run on party slates, their interests are protected by their party machinery and the votes for dry candidates would have to be counted. If, therefore, the repeal amendment were submitted to the legislatures, the result would be an honest reflection of the will of the people. If it were submitted to conventions, dry candidates would have no one to protect their interests and crooked bipartisan rings could count the votes, make the returns and perpetrate the frauds necessary to accomplish their purposes, and the people would be helpless. The drys knew that the convention scheme had been concocted for the purpose of putting over this fraud and so they insisted that the repeal amendment be submitted to the legislatures of the states

according to the uniform practice since the foundation of the government.

(5) As there were millions of dry Democrats they felt that it would be a manifest outrage for the national convention to attempt to compel them to surrender their convictions and march in the wet parade. They insisted therefore that if the convention should declare for resubmission, no attempt should be made to make repeal an article of party faith binding upon all Democrats, but that every member of the party be left free to support or oppose the amendment as his or her conscience should dictate.

(6) As the President would have unrivaled command of the channels of publicity and would be the head of his party and the government, he would be in a position to exert a powerful influence either for or against repeal. The drys knew that if Smith were elected, he would use every influence at his command to force repeal upon the country. They insisted, therefore, on having a candidate who, whether he was personally for or against repeal, would remain neutral and permit the people to settle the question in a free and orderly manner.

While Roosevelt was working with Tammany in New York to secure its future support, he was gathering delegates by posing before the people of the south and west as the leader and real hope of the dry cause. As he was governor of a wet state and as he would need the votes of wet states if he was nominated for the presidency, he declared that he was personally for repeal. He made this declaration in the fewest words possible, and without argument. He then adopted unequivocally the six-point program of the dry leaders of his party and never wavered in its support until he was safely nominated.

A biography of Roosevelt, written for use in the pre-convention campaign, states that in 1930 he wrote a letter to Senator Wagner in which he advocated the repeal of the Eighteenth Amendment

> and the substitution of another amendment, prohibiting the saloon, preserving federal assistance in enforcement for the dry states, and the extension of the home rule principle so that dry communities in wet states could remain dry by local option. . . .[21]

This letter to Senator Wagner, which appeared in the New York *Times,* September 11, 1930, contained the following statements:

> The language of the Eighteenth Amendment is so direct and so clear that it seems to me that the time has come when these people should no longer try to beat about the bush. It is not merely a matter of the Volstead Act or the Jones Act or any other pieces of mere legislation, federal or state, under the Eighteenth Amendment — it is the amendment itself.
>
> The force and effect of the Eighteenth Amendment can be eliminated, of course, only by a new constitutional amendment. This would supersede and abrogate the Eighteenth Amendment and substitute therefor a new constitutional provision. . . . Furthermore, I am positive in saying that there must be some definite assurance that by no possibility, at any time or in any place, can the old saloon come back. Therefore, the control of any sale of any intoxicants should be wholly in the hands of the states or of state agencies. . . . There is no doubt that in many states the actual sale of intoxicants would continue to be prohibited at least by statute. . . . It is therefore clear to me that it must remain not only the right but the duty of the federal government to protect states which continue to prohibit the sale of intoxicants.

This was a clear and unequivocal statement that modification of the Volstead Act would constitute nullification of the Constitution, that the saloon should not be permitted to come back, and that it should be made both the right and the duty of the federal government to protect dry territory.

During the campaign for delegates, Roosevelt led the drys to believe that he was in favor of submitting the repeal amendment to the legislatures rather than to conventions. That he posed as their champion on this question until he had secured the nomination, is shown by the following dispatch from Chicago to the New York *Times:*

> Governor Roosevelt is expected to advocate the submission of an amendment calling for flat repeal to the legislatures, a plan to which his southern and western allies have generally agreed, but to avoid committing the convention to a pledge that Democrats must support sub-

mission. The Smith-Raskob forces would have repeal endorsed by the convention. They also favor modification of the Volstead Act.[22]

The most powerful factor in securing for Roosevelt the confidence and support of dry Democrats in every part of the country was the fact that it was largely through his influence that, in 1931, the plan of Smith, Raskob, Shouse and other wets to commit the party to repeal was defeated. Mr. Lindley's biography of Roosevelt states that "in 1926 he called prohibition a 'national issue but not a national party issue,' since it cut across both parties." In 1931, Roosevelt did more than make a statement; he led a victorious fight. Chairman Raskob called a meeting of the Democratic national committee to be held in Washington on Thursday, March 5, and announced that he would ask the committee to take a stand in favor of the repeal of the Eighteenth Amendment. In this move, he was supported by Smith, Cox, Ritchie and other wet leaders of the party, and was bitterly opposed by Senators Robinson, Hull, Sheppard, Morrison and the leaders from all the dry states. Senator Robinson, who was the Democratic leader of the Senate and who had been candidate for vice-president, in an impassioned appeal declared: "You cannot inscribe on the banner of the Democratic party the skull and crossbones of an outlawed trade." [23]

Prior to this meeting, Edward J. Flynn, James A. Farley and other members of the Roosevelt board of strategy caused the Democratic state committee of New York to meet and pass a resolution opposing the Raskob-Smith proposal to commit the party on the question of repeal. Speaking of this action, the New York *Times* said:

The general view is that the meeting of the state committee and the action it took were promoted by Governor Roosevelt for the purpose of discouraging the national committee from taking a stand in favor of repeal of the Eighteenth Amendment, which might plague the party in the next year's national campaign, when friends of the governor believe that he may lead the fight as its nominee for president.[24]

Mr. Farley also obtained the proxy of Elisabeth Marbury, a member of the national committee, in order that he might go to Washington and continue the fight before the committee. The popularity of this move with dry Democratic leaders is shown by the following dispatch from Washington to the New York *Times:*

> Smiles wreathed the faces of dry Democratic senators tonight when they heard that the New York state Democratic committee had officially frowned on the proposal that the national committee go on record concerning the Eighteenth Amendment when it meets here on Thursday. They praised the state committee and expressed the belief that Governor Roosevelt had initiated the resolution, or at least that it had his support.[25]

Mr. Roosevelt also wrote a letter to Mr. Smith, asking him not to press this resolution.[26] The significance of this move is shown by the following dispatches to the New York *Times:*

> Defeat of the plan of John J. Raskob, Democratic national chairman, and former Governor Alfred E. Smith, to get the Democratic national committee to declare against prohibition at its meeting in Washington, seemed assured last night when James A. Farley, Democratic state chairman, obtained the proxy of Elisabeth Marbury, member of the national committee from this state.
>
> The effect of the state committee's action, taken at the behest of Governor Roosevelt, has been to enhance greatly the governor's chance for the presidential nomination in the opinion of his supporters.
>
> It is the belief of Governor Roosevelt's friends that by challenging Raskob and Mr. Smith on the advisability of trying to commit the party to a wet policy at this time, the governor will get the credit for averting what most Democratic leaders regard as an unwise move.[27]
>
> Although obviously pleased with the result of the Democratic national committee meeting in Washington, which sustained his position and that of the state committee on prohibition, Governor Roosevelt declined last night in his home in Hyde Park to discuss the meeting. The governor said: "Even off the record I have nothing to say on national matters." [28]

On November 23, 1931, Chairman Raskob sent out a questionnaire to ninety thousand contributors who gave four million dollars to the campaign in 1928, asking their opinion as to the "expediency or advisability of the national convention making a positive decision on prohibition." The following passages from the New York *Times* of the following day show the attitude of Mr. Roosevelt on the question:

> Backers of Governor Roosevelt's presidential candidacy viewed John J. Raskob's prohibition poll as strategy to upset Roosevelt's plan for a moderate platform plank on the subject. It was recalled that when Mr. Raskob and Mr. Smith brought the question before the Democratic national committee at a meeting in Washington last March, the action was opposed by Mr. Roosevelt and the leaders of the party's dry element.
>
> As viewed by the supporters of Governor Franklin D. Roosevelt, the questionnaire on prohibition sent out by John J. Raskob, chairman of the Democratic national committee, to some 90,000 contributors to the 1928 campaign of Alfred E. Smith, was designed as a blow against the plan attributed to Mr. Roosevelt for a prohibition plank in the Democratic national platform next year, "not too dry to alienate the wets in the party, and not too wet to drive the drys away." [29]

In the convention Roosevelt was the leader of the drys in their fight to "avoid committing the convention to a pledge that Democrats must support submission. The Smith-Raskob forces would have repeal endorsed by the convention." Not only was Roosevelt heralded as the great leader of the drys in their fight upon the Smith-Raskob liquor program, but in spite of his formal declaration for repeal he was sold to the south and west as a real dry. This was accomplished by Farley and his publicity machine through a subtle and elaborate campaign of innuendo. It was said that the governor had banished liquor from the Executive Mansion, that Mrs. Roosevelt was an ardent prohibitionist, that he had a home in Warm Springs, Georgia, one of the driest states in the Union, that he was an adopted son of the dry south, and that his affiliations and sympathies were with the drys.

Wishful thinking on the part of the opponents of Smith caused them to spread and magnify these reports and establish the belief that Roosevelt was a dry. This is illustrated by two statements made by writers having exceptional opportunity for ascertaining the facts. Walter Lippmann, a wet, said: "The notion, which seems to prevail in the west and south, that Wall street fears him, is preposterous. Wall street thinks that he is too dry, not that he is too radical."[30] On April 20 of the same year, the dry *Christian Century* said that the southern Democratic leaders had "turned comfortably to Governor Roosevelt for whom plausible claims will be made on the liquor issue that he is as dry as President Hoover."

Democratic National Convention of 1932

When the convention of 1932 assembled, Roosevelt brought about the defeat of Shouse as permanent chairman, and the election of Senator Walsh of Montana, one of the outstanding dry leaders of the country and the candidate of Senator Hull and other drys in their fight to prevent the endorsement of the Smith-Raskob liquor program. By this course he kept the confidence and held the support of his dry delegates until they had secured for him the nomination.

The leaders of Tammany Hall and their allies — Hague of Jersey City, Walsh of Boston, Cermak of Chicago and the Tammany bosses of other cities, and the United Repeal Council under the direction of Pierre du Pont — devoted their entire time and strength and used every influence at their command to force the convention to endorse their liquor program. Cermak had been a delegate to the Democratic national convention of 1924 and had watched Tammany pack the galleries and attempt to stampede the delegates and control their action. He used the same methods in Chicago. As mayor he controlled the police and the police were in charge at the convention hall.[31] When, therefore, a man appeared with a "courtesy ticket" signed by the mayor, he was admitted. In this way Cermak filled the galleries with his rabble. Mr. Willis J. Abbot, writing from the convention hall to the *Christian Science Monitor* of July 1, 1932, described the system as follows:

. . . But perhaps this convention will teach politicians not to hold these gatherings in cities like New York or Chicago. Invariably the delegates debate to the accompaniment of packed galleries, and invariably the galleries are packed in the interest of the least admirable faction in the party. The big cities are in the control of the organized machines directed by politicians of the baser type. The present mayor of Chicago was, until the advent of prohibition, the head of the United Societies, an organization consisting of distillers, brewers and saloon-keepers and having for its purpose the protection of liquor interests from hostile legislation, and from the enforcement of existing laws. Such a training, which covered most of Mr. Cermak's business life, scarcely fits a man to take a detached view of prohibition.

Wednesday night the galleries of the convention hall were crowded with men who shouted down the speakers who tried to head off the Democratic party in its mad rush to prohibition repeal. Delegates could not get tickets for their wives. Public men of high standing and influence were denied admission to the hall. Persons who had bought tickets found them useless because of the crowds that blocked the doorways. And all because this mayor of Chicago issued " courtesy tickets " bearing his signature which the police at the doorways accepted. How much this sort of influence had to do with the eleventh-hour shift of many delegates on the liquor question can only be guessed.

In this way, Cermak was able to a very large extent to control the cheers, demonstrations, boos, catcalls and jeers of the thousands of visitors that packed the vast galleries of the stadium — a mob so lacking in a sense of decency that the convention could scarcely proceed except as it bowed to its dictates.

In an effort to save as much as possible from the approaching disaster, the dry leaders abandoned their opposition to submission of the repeal amendment to conventions and their demand for the retention of power in the federal government to prohibit the saloon — a compromise to which a majority of their best informed constituents would not have agreed. They made a last desperate stand, however, against a declaration in favor of modifying the Volstead Act and of making repeal an article of party faith binding upon all Democrats regardless of their convictions. When the thirteen-year fight of the liquor interests, the allied Tammany

Halls and big business reached its culmination in the presentation of their plank, the wet delegates and the occupants of the packed galleries staged a prolonged and frenzied demonstration, during which they became a veritable mob of Bedlamites. When Senator Hull endeavored to present a simple resubmission plank to oppose the nullification of the Constitution and the attempt to force dry Democrats to violate their convictions, to speak for the intelligence and conscience of America and to voice its traditional spirit, he "was greeted with a chorus of growls and boos." The disorder became so great that it was impossible for him to get his argument across to the delegates. His experience was so discouraging that the drys practically abandoned the struggle. Thus did nullification, repeal, conventions and the return of the saloon become articles of Democratic party faith.

The plank as adopted was as follows:

We favor repeal of the Eighteenth Amendment.

To effect such repeal, we demand that the Congress immediately propose a constitutional amendment to truly representative conventions in the states called to act solely on that proposal.

We urge the enactment of such measures by the several states as will actually promote temperance, effectively prevent the return of the saloon, and bring the liquor traffic into the open under complete supervision and control by the states.

We demand that the federal government effectively exercise its power to enable the states to protect themselves against importation of intoxicating liquors in violation of their laws.

Pending repeal, we favor immediate modification of the Volstead Act to legalize the manufacture and sale of beer and other beverages of such alcoholic content as is permissible under the Constitution and to provide therefrom a proper and needed revenue.

The states were urged to prevent the return of the saloon, but it was not proposed that Congress be given the power to take such action. There was a demand that the federal government exercise its power to protect dry territory, but there was no proposal that it be given the power necessary to accomplish this result. These were meaningless words thrown out to deceive the drys. Tammany and Du Pont knew their real purpose and effect. There was no question but that it was an endorsement of the program of the wets who had backed the candidacy of Smith. The New York *Times* said:

The majority plank embraces most of the policies advocated by ex-Governor Smith, who had offered to the subcommittee the following suggestions on prohibition:

" We favor repeal of the Eighteenth Amendment, and we pledge our party in Congress to subject such repeal to state convention for adoption. For immediate relief, we favor an amendment to the Volstead Act fixing a reasonable definition of alcoholic content so as to legalize light wines and beer."

The delegates that stood by Smith and fought Roosevelt to the last ditch were in a delirium of joy. The feeling of the great body of the delegates who were fighting for Roosevelt and who made his nomination possible is expressed in the following dispatch to the New York *Times:*

The resolutions committee adjourned in an uproar. Senator Glass angrily left the hall and declared to several of his constituents who awaited him that the platform was " most unacceptable."

" Has the prohibition plank been finished? " he was asked.

" Yes, it has been finished," he replied, " and it may finish the Democratic party. They have adopted a barroom plank."

Senator Hull sat gloomily in the midst of the discarded planks in the Rose Room of the Congress Hotel, where the resolutions committee held its meetings. He also told his colleagues that the prohibition plank, if it became a party pledge, gave promise of wrecking the party in November. He was very disconsolate, because he held that the platform had not adequately treated the economic questions or promised relief of distress.

" This is the culmination of four years of use of the Democratic organization, with affiliated organizations, equipped with vast moneys to quietly hand-pick many delegations and pack the Democratic national convention with reference to the anti-prohibition movement," Senator Hull said. . . .

The action of the committee was received with the greatest surprise by the delegates who crowded into the hotels after returning from the afternoon session of the convention. Some of them pronounced it the most astonishing thing that has happened in the Democratic party since the Civil War, and many of the anti-prohibitionists expressed the opinion that the party had taken too liberal a stand on this question.[32]

Roosevelt and the Wet Plank

As the adoption of this plank was a contemptuous repudiation of everything the drys had fought for in their campaign for delegates pledged to Roosevelt, the nomination of their leader became a matter of supreme importance. With them it was not a question of personal ambition or of political maneuvering. They were struggling to preserve a great moral and patriotic achievement that involved the welfare of the individual and of the home and the perpetuity of our free institutions. It did not occur to them that if they should secure the nomination for Roosevelt he would betray them and use the power they had given him to destroy that achievement.

In his campaign for delegates in 1928, Al Smith declared that he favored the repeal of the Eighteenth Amendment and the abandonment of national prohibition. His supporters insisted that the convention commit the party to this course of action. They were decisively defeated. The convention not only refused to declare for repeal but it pledged the party to the enforcement of both the amendment and the Volstead Act.

Here was an ideal opportunity for the exercise of all the arts of the self-seeker and the demagogue. As against Hoover, Al Smith was sure to receive the votes of the irreconcilable wets, but if he was to be elected, it was necessary for him to devise some means of pacifying the drys. How easy it would have been for him, with disarming smile and heroic attitude, to declare triumphantly that he had always recognized the right of the party convention to determine party principles and to bind its candidates to their support, and that, in the event of his election, he would give his unqualified support to the entire platform of his party. By taking this attitude he could very greatly have augmented his chances of success. In a telegram to the convention, however, while it was still in session and free to act, he stated that his views on the prohibition question were well known, that his convictions were not subject to change by a majority vote of a convention, that he was for modification of the Volstead Act and repeal of the Eighteenth Amendment, and, if elected, he would, as leader of his party, continue to advocate those policies.

The dry delegates in the 1932 convention had the right to expect that Roosevelt would deal as honorably with them as Smith had dealt with his wet delegates in 1928. If he had done so, he would have sent to the convention a telegram in substance something like this:

I have stated my views as to the proper procedure on the prohibition question and my attitude is well known. I believe that an amendment should be submitted to the legislatures of the states providing for the repeal of the Eighteenth Amendment and empowering the federal government to prevent the return of the saloon and to protect dry territory. If such an amendment is submitted, I shall cast my vote for candidates for the legislature pledged to its ratification. But this is a question that runs straight across party lines and millions of loyal Democrats are sincerely opposed to repeal, and I do not believe that the convention has the right to bind them to a course of conduct that would be repugnant to their profound convictions upon what they believe to be a great moral issue. If, therefore, I am nominated and elected, I shall not permit the use of patronage, party machinery, the power of my office or the personal prestige it may give me to force repeal upon the country. I shall see to it that the people are permitted to settle this question on its merits in orderly manner uninfluenced by any form of coercion.

In my letter to Senator Wagner, written in September 1930, I stated that because its language " is so direct and so clear," the force and effect of the Eighteenth Amendment can be eliminated only by a new constitutional amendment. Any effort to circumvent it by modifying the enforcement statutes would be an attempt by a transparent subterfuge to nullify the Constitution which I, if elected, must take an oath to defend. I shall oppose any such procedure.

I am restating my position at this time in order that it may be clearly understood that, if elected, I shall not betray the millions of people who have supported me in the faith that I would remain true to the convictions which I have declared and clearly expressed while seeking their support.

But of course Roosevelt came out with no such clear statement. He and Farley were playing a purely selfish game. The tactics they used in the struggle for the nomination were accurately described by the New York *Nation* in its issue of July 6, 1932:

In the confusion that besets the Democratic convention as we go to press, one thing stands out clear and unchallenged. That is the unashamed renunciation by Franklin D. Roosevelt of his last pretension to progressivism. He has joined the old guard of political sharpers. Indeed, the brazen tactics of his managers in Chicago, which the governor himself has been directing by telephone from Albany, are such as to leave even the Tammany crowd gasping. . . . We had never deceived ourselves as to his weak and vacillating statesmanship, but we had believed him honest and sincere. Instead he stands revealed as ready to lend his support to any trick or device that will advance his personal political fortunes.

Roosevelt Returns to the Tammany Fold

When his nomination was secure, Roosevelt turned with his usual alertness to the next move in the game to make himself president. He no longer needed his dry delegates, so he could safely forget them and the promises by which he had gained their support. Mr. Hoover, by proclaiming his allegiance to the Eighteenth Amendment until he had secured the Republican nomination, and then coming out for repeal, had disgusted the drys and there was no chance that they would rally to his support. Because of the depression, it was certain that the west would be against Hoover. It was also certain that the dry south would remain in the Democratic column. This fact was well expressed by the following editorial in the *Clarion Ledger* of Jackson, Mississippi:

Booze hounds and not Democrats seem to be running the convention. . . . The south will stand by the Democratic party this year, as it has always stood by it, but this plank in the platform will be a nauseous dose for them to swallow.

It may, however, serve a good purpose. It may awaken the men and women of the south to the fact that when it comes to national politics, they are mere pawns, moved about over the political board at will and in any way that serves the best interests of those far removed, with different ideas and different ideals.[33]

The greatest danger to Roosevelt's success would come from the opposition of the large wet centers, the powerful Tammany organizations and big business. They had become bitterly hostile to him because of the character of his campaign for dry delegates. He saw that if he was to secure their support, he must immediately and unconditionally repudiate every promise that he had made to his followers during that campaign. He also saw that he must swiftly and unequivocally espouse the entire Tammany-Raskob-Du Pont liquor program that he had opposed in that campaign. He was equal to the occasion. He flew to Chicago and was joyously received by Mayor Cermak, who bore him through the streets and delivered him triumphantly to the most disgraceful political convention ever held in this country.[34]

When he appeared before the convention, Roosevelt expressed no disapproval of the fact that when his enemies, the wet orators, had spoken for the underworld, the liquor interests, big business, and the dupes of their propaganda, they were greeted with frantic demonstrations of approval; that when his friends, men of the type of Senator Hull, had attempted to speak for the homes, the churches and the schools and to voice the intelligence and conscience of the American people, they were treated with contempt and disdain and booed and jeered into silence. He did not utter a word of rebuke to the mob spirit that had raged for days; he said nothing that would cause the mob, even for a moment, to engage in sober, intelligent and patriotic thought and action; he flattered it, he fawned upon it, he encouraged it in order that he might be sure of its help in the attainment of his ambitions.

James O'Donnell Bennett gives us a vivid picture of his appearance before the convention:

Behold Roosevelt in action before 20,000 onlookers. He puts his right arm around his wife and gives her a hearty hug. She laughs. He laughs. The 20,000 laugh. He leans toward his son James and presses him close to his heart. He is wearing a dark blue sack-suit, a withered red rose in the lapel of his coat. He is pale, but his searching eyes are shining.

He smiles, he nods, he chuckles.

In his speech he referred to the platform as " that admirable document " and added, " I accept it 100 per cent." When he came to the question of prohibition, he said:

> I congratulate this convention for having had the courage, fearlessly, to write into its declaration of principles what an overwhelming majority here assembled really thinks about the Eighteenth Amendment. This convention wants repeal. Your candidate wants repeal. And I am confident that the United States of America wants repeal.

He then shouted, " I say to you that from this date on, the Eighteenth Amendment is doomed! " [35]

Thus the dry delegates and millions of dry Democrats throughout the country were forced, with humiliation and disgust, to see their leader desert them on the field of battle, become the militant leader of their enemies and use the power they had given him to destroy their most cherished cause. In our entire history, there is not another such example of cynical political treachery. The bald truth is that Roosevelt was the political creature of Tammany Hall; for ten years he had been its ally, floor leader and front, and had deserted it just long enough to gather dry delegates and secure the nomination. He then returned to his old friends and gave to the allied Tammany Halls of the country, in their fight on prohibition, a type of leadership that made Al Smith look like a rank amateur.

Roosevelt's Campaign for Election

Roosevelt's treatment of the prohibition question during the campaign was not only a continuation of his policy of betrayal of his dry supporters, but in his appeals to ignorance, avarice and prejudice, and in his complete misrepresentation of both the Republican and the Democratic platforms, he descended to the plane of the worst demagoguery. When speaking in the dry south and west he ignored the repeal plank and discussed questions that made it possible for him to use language which would conform to the opinions and appeal to the emotions of the people he was addressing, and to ride triumphantly with the current. He reserved his discussion of the repeal plank for audiences whose ears would be tickled by a denunciation of prohibition. He chose Sea Girt, New Jersey, in the bailiwick of Frank Hague, Tammany boss of Jersey City, for his opening onslaught on the Eighteenth Amendment. The circumstances of the choice are told by his manager, James A. Farley, who states that after the convention he (Farley) went immediately to New York " to smoke the pipe of peace with the Tammany leaders " and that Frank Hague called him up and said that if Roosevelt would come to New Jersey to open his campaign " he would provide the largest political rally ever held in the United States." Farley says that " Frank Hague kept his word." [36]

A dispatch to the Chicago *Herald-Examiner* said:

> The gathering, arranged as a Democratic " love-feast " by Mayor Frank Hague, dynamic mayor of Jersey City, and one of Roosevelt's bitterest pre-convention foes, provided a mighty send-off for the governor's first appeal to the industrial east.[37]

The Chicago *Tribune* gave this description of the setting:

> Governor Franklin D. Roosevelt, delivering his first presidential speech on prohibition, attacked President Hoover as " evading and confusing the issue by the use of pussy-cat words " before a noisy, milling open-air crowd of more than 100,000 persons here today.
>
> The Democratic candidate had hit upon the right subject for the hordes of Jersey shore folk who had flocked to Sea Girt to give Mr. Roosevelt his greatest ovation. Each slashing attack brought a rising roar. . . . It was a difficult crowd to address and it was fortunate for Mr. Roosevelt that he was speaking on a subject dear to his audience's collective heart.
>
> All along the line of the motor parade through the Jersey shore country crowds had lined the sidewalks and streets to cheer the candidate. Mr. Hague apparently had lived up to his pledge to " go for Roosevelt." " That's the guy," someone shouted, as the governor entered the

grounds where the rally was being staged, and the crowd took up the words as a slogan.[38]

This crowd was instinctively wet and its frenzy had been raised to the highest pitch by the tom-toms of the wet propaganda. Roosevelt went with the current and told the crowd what it wanted to hear. Instead of discussing the question with the sincerity and breadth of statesmanship to be expected of a candidate for the presidency, he followed the tactics of the wet propagandists. He indulged in appeals to ignorance, passion and prejudice, misrepresented the position of his opponents and of his own party, and resorted to clever oratorical tricks that made the crowd howl with delight. Adopting the familiar technique of the wet propaganda, he began with a tribute to temperance as " one of the cardinal virtues." He then opened up the familiar chamber of horrors — " the attempt to impose the practice of virtue by mandate of the fundamental law "; " tragic failure "; " corruption, hypocrisy, crime and disorder "; " the spread of intemperance "; " a steady flow of profits . . . into the pockets of the racketeers." He sought to take advantage of the sentiment that had been created by the depression propaganda:

> This time of depression has caused us to see even more plainly than before not only the political and moral consequences of our action, but its economic results as well. We threw on the table as spoils to be gambled for by the enemies of society the revenue that our government had theretofore received, and the underworld acquired unparalleled resources thereby.
>
> Unquestionably our tax burden would not be so heavy nor the forms that it takes so objectionable if some reasonable proportion of the uncounted millions now paid to those whose business has been reared upon this stupendous blunder could be made available for the expenses of the government.

He stated that the prohibition plank in the Republican platform was

> nothing but dust, meaningless, worthless dust, at the bottom a cloud of words . . . words upon words, evasions upon evasions, insincerity

upon insincerity, a dense cloud of words. . . . The Democratic party fairly and squarely met the issue. It adopted by an overwhelming vote a plank so plain and clear and honest that no one could doubt its meaning, and the candidates accepted it 100 per cent.

It might be said that the Republican platform should not have declared for resubmission, that the measure it proposed for preserving the gains of prohibition would be ineffective, and that it was an attempt to please both wets and drys. But it could not be said that it was " meaningless " or a " dense cloud of words." It opposed nullification, it proposed the submission to conventions of a repeal amendment that would give to the federal government the power to prevent the return of the saloon and to protect dry territory. It declared against making repeal an article of party faith in unequivocal language:

The principle of national prohibition as embodied in the amendment was supported and opposed by members of both great political parties. It was submitted to the states by members of Congress of different political faiths and ratified by states legislatures of different political majorities. It was not then and is now not a partisan political question. Members of the Republican party hold different opinions with respect to it, and no public official or member of the party should be pledged or forced to choose between his party affiliations and his honest convictions upon this question.

With the single exception of the acceptance of conventions, this was the exact platform upon which Roosevelt had conducted his pre-convention campaign and to which his supporters had believed that he was irrevocably committed. The only difference, therefore, was that the platform made one capitulation to the wets, to which Roosevelt had assured his dry followers he was opposed.

An editorial in the *Christian Century* accurately characterized this speech and Mr. Roosevelt's entire attitude upon the prohibition question:

In his Sea Girt speech, Governor Roosevelt devoted himself to the prohibition question. . . . As a speech, it was a good speech — clever, witty, vivid and even winsome. But it was not a true speech, an honest and sincere handling of the subject to which the candidate addressed himself. . . . He did not publicly examine the Republican liquor plank nor expose its meaninglessness. He simply said it was meaningless and incoherent.

This might be condoned in a mere barnstorming orator intent only on making a speech that would " go over," but Mr. Roosevelt is running for the presidency, and the people have a right to expect of him a candid and honest treatment of this as of all other issues. The Republican plank is perfectly plain. If Mr. Roosevelt had read it to his audience, they would easily have understood it. It is clearer than the boasted clearness of the Democratic repeal plank. You may not like it, you may not be willing to vote approval of it, but you cannot misunderstand it. It disapproves of the submission of the prohibition question in the form of retention versus repeal of the Eighteenth Amendment, and promises that the question shall be submitted in the form of a constructive substitute for the present Eighteenth Amendment. To say that such a plank is meaningless is essentially dishonest. To say that it cannot be understood is to confess to a low order of intelligence. Any schoolboy can understand it. And any schoolboy can understand the difference between it and the Democratic plank which calls for the submission of the prohibition question in the form of an amendment repealing the Eighteenth Amendment.

Mr. Roosevelt might have argued that the difference between the two planks is inconsequential, or that the Democratic program is superior. He might have plucked the Republican proposal apart and shown the impracticability of finding " a constructive substitute " upon which Congress may be expected to agree. He might even have attacked the Republican proposal as a hypocritical device to conceal an alleged purpose to submit ultimately a proposal for naked repeal. Any of these modes of attack would have left Mr. Roosevelt protected against the charge of a dishonest handling of the issue. But to say that the Republican plank was meaningless, and to refuse to acknowledge the plain difference in program between it and the Democratic plank, was sheer and bald disingenuousness unworthy of a candidate for the presidency.

The insincerity of Mr. Roosevelt's light dismissal of the Republican plank as an incoherent pronouncement of the oracle is, however, outdone in his treatment of the Democratic plank which he quoted entire to his audience. Here he took a statement from Mr. Hoover's acceptance speech as his text: "Our opponents," Mr. Hoover had said, "pledge the members of their party to destroy every vestige of constitutional and effective federal control of the liquor traffic." This statement Mr. Roosevelt called a deliberate misrepresentation of the position of the Democratic party. "I charge," he added, "that this statement was made to mislead the people of this country, and I assert that a mere reading of the plain, unequivocal provisions of the Democratic platform will sustain that charge."

Every dry listening to these swagger words must have pricked up his ears. Is Mr. Roosevelt going to interpret the Democratic plank in terms which will do what the Republican plank promises to do, namely, to conserve the gains made by federal prohibition? That would seem to be what the candidate was leading up to. That clearly was the impression Mr. Roosevelt intended to make upon his audience. Though he had previously described the Republican plank as incoherent and meaningless, he now seems to admit that there is some virtue in it, and to put forward the claim that the Democratic plank was just as virtuous.

So he affects hot resentment toward Mr. Hoover's "every-vestige-of-constitutional-and-federal-control" statement. The Republicans have nothing on the Democrats at this point, he argues. "The Democratic platform," he declared, "expressly and unequivocally opposes the return of the saloon." Then Mr. Roosevelt reads the Democratic plank, in which he pretends to find justification for this sweeping statement. The language is emphatic — there is no gainsaying that. It was made emphatic in order to conceal its emptiness.

"We urge the enactment of such measures by the several states as will actually promote temperance, effectively prevent the return of the saloon, and bring the liquor traffic into the open, under complete supervision and control by the states."

Mr. Roosevelt did not tarry to expound this paragraph. It is much more effective to the unthinking listener when it is just read aloud unctuously than when it is examined carefully for the sake of exposition. It does not *promise* the enactment of such measures by the several states. It does not *guarantee* the enactment of such measures — it could not give any guarantee as to what the states would or would not do. It *urges* — that is all it does — it *urges* the states to prevent the return of the saloon. It is a pious exhortation, nothing more, and anybody who imagines that the state of Illinois, or New York, or any other state, will give a moment's consideration to such an exhortation once the Eighteenth Amendment is repealed, is simply naive. On the last day of Congress, July 17, Senator David I. Walsh, of Massachusetts, a leading wet, who had more to do than any other man with getting the Democratic convention to adopt its plank for outright repeal, admitted on the Senate floor the futility of trusting the states to act, to the consternation of his wet colleagues. The plank is a verbal trick, as anyone knows, and by his use of it, Mr. Roosevelt makes himself a party to its perpetration.

In the same manner Mr. Roosevelt charged that Mr. Hoover " either accidentally overlooked or deliberately misrepresented " the provision of the Democratic platform for the protection of dry states after repeal. The candidate quoted his platform on that point: " We demand that the federal government effectively exercise its power to enable the states to protect themselves against importation of intoxicating liquor in violation of their laws."

Mr. Roosevelt here reaches the nadir of his insincerity by asserting that " the Democratic platform with equal emphasis demands that there be federal control of the liquor traffic to protect dry states." He knows that his platform does nothing of the kind. It demands only that the federal government " effectively exercise " the power that it now has — apart from the Eighteenth Amendment. The platform assumes that the federal government already has sufficient power to protect dry states. It makes no " demand " at all with respect to the increase of that power. But Mr. Roosevelt knows that the federal government does not have the power — assuming the repeal of the Eighteenth Amendment — to do what the Democratic plank so emphatically " demands " it shall do. It was the constitutional impotence of the federal government to deal with the interstate aspect of the liquor traffic that helped to bring on the Eighteenth Amendment. Mr. Roosevelt knows that the federal government apart from a special grant of power from the states — that is, an amendment to the Constitution — cannot protect dry states. Without such an amendment, it will have no power to treat liquor in a special category as distinguished from other " commodities " in interstate traffic.

The Republican platform, of course, meets this situation by providing that a new amendment to the federal Constitution prohibiting the " saloon " and guaranteeing protection to dry states shall be submitted as a constructive substitute for the Eighteenth Amendment. Whatever one's opinions of this proposal may be, it is wholly different from the Democratic platform, and Mr. Roosevelt puts himself in a bad light before those of his fellow citizens who, though they may differ from him, wish to think well of him. By adopting slippery and shifty rhetorical devices to conceal and misrepresent so real an issue as that which obtains between himself and his Republican opponent on the prohibition question, he may make an effective speech, but only by sacrificing that confidence in his intellectual integrity upon which permanent public esteem is founded.[39]

Wherever he went during the remainder of the campaign, Roosevelt continued skillfully to select subjects in the discussion of which he could use language that would appeal to the emotions of his hearers. Pursuant to this policy, when he reached dripping wet Baltimore in the territory of Governor Ritchie, long-time ally of Smith and Raskob, he discussed the liquor plank and denounced prohibition. When he reached Chicago, he did the same thing and fawned on Mayor Cermak, life-long leader of the liquor forces, dance-hall proprietors and other underworld elements in their fight for a wide-open town. The only place in the west where he discussed this question was in San Francisco, one of the three or four wettest and most corrupt cities in America.

Wet Politicians Discover a Mandate from the People

As the Republican platform proposed to submit the question of repeal to state conventions, and Mr. Hoover had declared himself in favor of repeal, there was no place for those drys to go who did not wish to support the candidates of the Prohibition party, and it was impossible for them to express themselves on the prohibition question at the election. Whatever may be the verdict of history as to the policies of Mr. Hoover and Mr. Roosevelt, there cannot be the slightest doubt that the verdict of the people in the 1932 election was not the result of an accurate knowledge of the facts or of intelligent and sober reflection. For three years they had endured hardships and suffering that had raised their resentment to the highest pitch, and they were ready in their desperation to apply the torch to the party in power. With great adroitness, Mr. Roosevelt took advantage of this situation. Whatever divergent views may be held on this question, there can be no doubt whatever that the national conventions represented corrupt political machines, the liquor interests, the wet press and big business, and not the people, and that the people had no opportunity to and did not express themselves on the prohibition question at the election.

As Tammany politicians in and out of Congress, the liquor interests and big business were demanding that the liquor traffic be restored at once and heavily taxed, the Democratic leaders discovered that they held a mandate to accomplish that end without delay and they solemnly pretended that that mandate came not alone from the howling mobs at Chicago but from the American people at the polls. They proceeded, therefore, in humble submission to the will of the people, to carry out this mandate. Republican politicians, realizing that the drys were divided, unorganized and ineffective, and that the wets were organized and effective saw clearly that it was their "duty" to help "carry out the will of the people as expressed at the polls."

As we have seen, in the campaign Roosevelt "had gone the limit," and after the election he found himself in a position where he was compelled to fulfill a promise he had made and justify an attitude he had taken at a time when he believed that to realize his ambition, it was necessary for him to surrender to the most degraded, selfish and corrupt elements in American life. He knew that he was in a position from which he could not retreat and that, since to the mass mind success justifies anything, speedy repeal would be the most effective means of removing his reproach for having reversed his position and betrayed his friends. He also knew that, temporarily at least, repeal would silence the drys and give them a crushing blow from which they could not recover in time to interfere with his plans, threaten his power or become an embarrassing factor in the next presidential election.

The wet leaders believed that the best and probably the only chance for repeal was to accomplish it in 1933. The tide of wet propaganda was at its flood and would start to ebb when the people began to understand its source and character. The depression had reached its lowest point and, in their distress, the people listened eagerly to confident promises that repeal would give a new impetus to business and relief from taxation. With the return of prosperity, the potency of this argument would decline. The overwhelming victory of the Democratic party was largely the result of a blind reaction of the people against the party in power when the depression struck them, and the Democrats could not long rely on this source of strength. There were tens of thousands of jobs to be handed out and the distribution of patronage was being withheld in order that it might be used as a club. In time, however, hope would be replaced by resentment in the hearts of thousands of unsuccessful aspirants for jobs. The federal government had the arbitrary power of distributing billions of dollars for public relief. This tremendous power of persuasion and coercion would diminish as prosperity returned. Mr. Roosevelt had been swept into power by a great majority; he had spoken words of hope which a distressed people were anxious to believe. A "Stand by the President" cry had been raised that for the time stifled all criticism; he was regarded as a savior — and he acquired an influence and a power such as no other man in our history has possessed. This gave him dictatorial power over the machinery of his party, over Congress, governors, legislatures, the press and public opinion. The rapid rise in governmental expenditures and the prospect of increased income taxes had thrown big business into a panic, and caused it to bring to the aid of the repeal movement every resource at its command. The control of the machinery of a triumphant party, the power to dangle jobs and public funds, to exalt and destroy aspiring Democrats, to carry the wishes and commands of the President to congressmen, governors and legislatures, and to put behind the repeal movement the power of his personal prestige with the public, had been placed in the hands of Mr. Farley, whom Bainbridge Colby, secretary of state in the cabinet of President Wilson, in a nation-wide broadcast denounced as "a low-browed Tammany politician." With a few honorable exceptions, the Republican politicians were falling over each other in their eagerness to render service to the wet cause and thereby secure the support of the powerful influences back of it. The wet press and other propagandists were putting down a barrage of falsehood and intimidation against which truth and decency were powerless.

The wet leaders knew that this extraordinary combination of favorable circumstances could last but a short time, and that they must force repeal through while they had the moral forces of the nation at their mercy.

As has already been pointed out, the Judiciary Committee of the Senate reported out a resolution providing for the submission of a repeal amendment to the legislatures, giving Congress the power to prevent the return of the saloon. If adopted, it would have constituted a substantial performance of Roosevelt's pre-convention promises. It was defeated, and on February 15, 1933, a substitute was adopted that was a literal compliance with the Tammany-Du Pont program.

Roosevelt and his Oath of Office

All who were at their radios on March 4, 1933, will remember with what dramatic fervor Mr. Roosevelt declared: "I do solemnly swear that I will faithfully execute the office of President of the United States, and will to the best of my ability, preserve, protect and defend the Constitution of the United States."

Referring to this oath, Abraham Lincoln said: "It was in the oath that I took that I would to the best of my ability, preserve, protect and defend the Constitution of the United States. I could not take office without taking the oath nor was it my view that I might take the oath in order to get power and then break the oath in using the power."

At the time Mr. Roosevelt took the oath, the Eighteenth Amendment was a part of the Constitution, and it was his duty, under his oath, faithfully to execute it. The words of the oath had scarcely died upon his lips when he began to use all the power of his office to carry out the Tammany-Du Pont program of bringing about a state of lawlessness and nullification. Not even a pretense of an attempt at enforcement of existing prohibition laws was made. He at once, on the pretense of economy, caused the appropriation for the Prohibition Bureau to be cut from $8,440,000 to $3,360,000 and that for the Bureau of Industrial Alcohol from $4,000,000 to $2,500,000. This left to a handful of discouraged prohibition agents the work of enforcing a provision of the Constitution and a law of Congress which were sneered at and denounced by the President and the entire band of officeholders who, as one of his friends later declared, "had been carried into office on the President's coat tails." The result was that brewers, distillers, smugglers, bootleggers and speak-easy proprietors were given the run of the land.

Roosevelt's greatest contribution to the cause of lawlessness and nullification was the beer bill. Since 1926, the Tammany-Du Pont forces had been engaged diligently in the work of excavating and laying this mine under the Eighteenth Amendment and they knew that its explosion would put an end to the amendment, no matter what the people might or might not want. They also knew that only a man having the power that Roosevelt acquired could light the fuse that would cause that explosion. He immediately called a special session of Congress and, nine days after his inauguration, sent it the following message:

> I recommend to the Congress the passage of legislation for the immediate modification of the Volstead Law in order to legalize the manufacture and sale of beer and other beverages of such alcoholic content as is permissible under the Constitution; and to provide through such manufacture and sale, by substantial taxes, a proper and much needed revenue for the government. I deem action at this time to be of the highest importance.

Much was said about the fact that this was the briefest message ever sent to Congress, but it possessed other characteristics that were equally unusual. No other message ever put a mask of smug words over such a concealment of relevant facts, such hypocrisy, and such contempt for law and the Constitution. The President set out in bold relief the fact that the action he proposed would provide a "much needed revenue for the government," but he concealed the fact that it would not reduce taxes, but simply shift the burden from the incomes of the rich to the salaries and wages of the masses who bought the beer. He diverted attention from the fact that it would bring back the brewery, the saloon and the liquor lobby, with all their debauching influence on our national life, and that by mere congressional enactment it would scrap an integral part of the Constitution of the United States. He made it appear that such action would "be of the highest importance" to all the people, when the contrary was the fact, and the only ones to benefit by it would be big income taxpayers, liquor dealers and wet politicians.

The most extraordinary thing about this message is its statement that the beer should be "of such alcoholic content as is permissible under the Constitution." Every intelligent man and woman in America knew that the proposal was just what Senator Borah said it was — a method of getting around the Constitution. Mr. Roosevelt had said the same thing in unequivocal language in his letter to Senator Wagner. That he and his supporters all knew that it was a palpable violation of the Constitution is conclusively established by the facts. He transmitted his message on March 13, the bill passed both houses of Congress immediately, and was approved by him on March 22. As there were only nine days between the sending of the message and the approval of the bill, there can be no doubt that it had been thoroughly considered and put in final form, that its contents were known and agreed to by the President, that everything was set, and that his message was simply pushing the button.

Congressman Cullen, a Tammany Democrat from New York, was chairman of the committee that had the bill in charge. He and the other wet leaders of Congress and Mr. Roosevelt were perfectly certain that if a law should be passed legalizing the manufacture and sale of beer, it would be declared unconstitutional by the courts. They saw that it was necessary, therefore, to get around both the Constitution and the courts. As usual, great constitutional lawyers were called for, and they showed just how both these hurdles could be taken: Simply declare that the provisions of the Volstead Act should no longer be applicable to the manufacture and sale of beer. This would be notice to all the breweries and prospective saloon-keepers of the country that they could openly and safely flout the Constitution because Congress had repealed all penalties for its violation, and destroyed the machinery for its enforcement. This would paralyze the courts and make it impossible for them to perform their function of defending the Constitution since they had no power to compel Congress to enact another enforcement statute. Following this brilliant suggestion, the Cullen Bill provided:

> Nothing in the national prohibition act, as amended and supplemented, shall apply to any of the following or to any act or failure to act in respect of any of the following, containing not more than 3.2 per centum of alcohol by weight: beer, ale, porter, wine, similar fermented malt or vinous liquor, or fruit juices.

That it was found necessary to resort to this method of bringing back beer and the saloon proved beyond the shadow of a doubt that Mr. Roosevelt and his followers knew that this action constituted an open and cynical violation of the Constitution and that that was their deliberate purpose.

In defense of his action, Roosevelt could not say that the amendment belonged to the horse-and-buggy age, since it had been adopted by the practically unanimous action of the states only thirteen years before, and triumphantly reaffirmed in 1928. He could not say that the amendment and the enforcement act had been sustained because the members of the Supreme Court were reactionary or senile or both, since they had been unanimous in their decisions and he himself had declared that the language of the amendment was so clear and direct that its force and effect could be eliminated only by a new amendment. It would have been futile for him to have written to Cullen as he did later to Congressman Hill: "I hope your committee will not permit doubt as to the constitutionality, however reasonable, to block the suggested legislation." It would have been impossible to provide for the appointment of a sufficient number of new members of the Supreme Court to make certain that an act legalizing beer would be sustained. His only course, therefore, was simply to scrap the amendment, thumb his nose at the "nine old men" and put over on the people the falsehood that his action was "permissible under the Constitution." This conduct justified the statement made later and in a different connection by Robert A. Taft, son of former President Taft: "For the first time in my lifetime we have a President who is willing to mislead the people."

The bill was rushed through Congress under gavel rule, in the face of protests like this from Senator Borah:

> I shall undertake to show that not only is the beverage which it is now proposed to legalize intoxicating, but that no conditions are imposed which will prevent the return of the institution which has not only been condemned by the President, but has been condemned by every right-thinking man and wholesome woman on the face of the earth. . . . It was the most hideous institution with which civilized authority ever had to deal.

After the passage of the bill by the Senate, the Chicago *Tribune* exultantly declared:

> The senate tonight sent the brewers' big horses stamping victoriously through the second great breach in the prohibition wall.
>
> By a vote of 43 to 30 the senate passed the beer bill, assuring the 73 million Americans living in wet territory legal beer and perhaps legal wine within the next three weeks. . . . By the first of next week, it is expected, the two houses will have agreed upon senate amendments placed in the bill and the signature of the President will have been attached. . . . Two weeks after the bill becomes law legal beer may begin to flow from the breweries down arid throats, and the second victory against prohibition since the recent passage of the repeal resolution will have become a reality.[40]

The success of the Democratic party was notice to the country that the machinery for law enforcement would be scrapped, all efforts to enforce the prohibition laws would be abandoned, and the lawless liquor element invited to go the limit. The passage of the Cullen Act completed the work. It assured this lawless element that it might go its way unembarrassed by the fear that somewhere in the country some federal marshal, district attorney or judge might run amuck and endeavor to enforce the Constitution, since the power to do so had been taken from their hands by the Congress and the President.

The ruthless disregard of the moral interests of the nation, the cowardly surrender to the brutal forces of appetite and greed, the supercilious contempt for orderly and constitutional procedure, the nauseating hypocrisy and deceit that marked the passage of the Cullen Bill, brand it as the most infamous act of our entire political history. There cannot be the slightest doubt that when we emerge from the morass in which we are now floundering and recover our sense of moral value, as we surely will, this will be the verdict of the American people.

President Supports Repeal Amendment

The passage of this act produced the intended effect. The fighting drys were scattered and dazed and millions of men and women who had always voted dry became discouraged and decided that since the liquor traffic was actually back and they could not help it, they might as well legalize it so that it could be taxed. On the other hand, the wet hordes were fired with hope and courage and thus prepared for the last great battle in the war for repeal. They were also especially fortunate that in the President they had a leader who was a supreme political strategist and a master of popular psychology. He knew just how to divert the attention of the people from the real moral, social and political questions involved, and completely to conceal the hook by the kind of bait that would be the most attractive to the people at the particular moment.

On May 17, he sent to Congress a message in which, as a part of his recovery program, he asked for the appropriation of $3,300,-000,000 to be expended on public works. He stated that this would require $220,000,000 additional revenue to service contemplated borrowings, and thus would " of necessity involve some form or forms of new taxation " which would be reduced or eliminated first, as fast as increasing revenues from improving business become available to replace them; second, whenever the repeal of the Eighteenth Amendment now pending before the states shall have been ratified and the repeal of the Volstead Act effected. The pre-prohibition revenue laws would then automatically go into effect and yield enough wholly to eliminate these temporary re-employment taxes.

What a ray of hope in the darkness to learn that repeal would help the recovery program and automatically remove vexatious and burdensome taxes. On May 24, 1933, the Associated Press sent out from its Washington office a dispatch which contained the following:

The Roosevelt administration today gave another shoulder punch to the movement for repeal, with Postmaster General Farley declaring that unless the Eighteenth Amendment is written off the books every income taxpayer will have to hand the government $6 to $10 out of every $100 he earns this year. . . . In the matter of increased taxes, word came directly from the White House that President Roosevelt intends automatically to end the far-reaching new levies now under consideration in the House as soon as the Eighteenth Amendment is repealed.

Farley's words today came during a discussion of a disclosure made last night that the full weight of the administration would be thrown behind the movement to ratify the prohibition repeal amendment through the writing of letters to Democratic workers, throughout the nation, urging such a step.

The postmaster general, who is chairman of the Democratic national committee and chief dispenser of patronage, pointed out today that under the pending public works industrial control bill, income taxes would be boosted from 4 to 6 per cent on incomes up to $4,000 and from 8 to 10 per cent on all above $4,000. He estimated that the increases would affect from 4,000,000 to 6,900,000 taxpayers this year.

Farley said that his plan, announced last night, of sending letters to every Democratic worker in the country, urging them to work for repeal, will be followed as the time comes in each state to elect delegates to the state convention. He said this plan was used in New York state with the result overwhelmingly in favor of removing the amendment.

On July 8, President Roosevelt made public the following telegram which he had sent to Leon McCord, Democratic national committeeman from Alabama:

I have received your telegram of July 3 in reference to the repeal of the Eighteenth Amendment.

I think I have made it abundantly clear that the platform of the Democratic party adopted last year should be carried out in so far as it lies in our power. The special session of the Congress has already translated into law a great majority of the pledges made.

One of the pledges of the platform read as follows: "We advocate the repeal of the Eighteenth Amendment. To effect such repeal we demand that the Congress immediately propose a constitutional amendment to truly representative conventions in the states called to act solely on that proposal."

The Congress has acted on this and many of the states are now engaged in holding elections for the conventions proposed.

Finally, I have made it clear ever since my nomination a year ago that I subscribe to the Democratic platform 100 per cent.

In view of the fact that I have had so great a number of telegrams similar to yours, not only from your state, but from Tennessee, Arkansas, Kentucky and others, I am taking the liberty of giving this message to you to the press.

On July 10, the Washington correspondent of the Columbus (Ohio) *Citizen* stated that

recalcitrant governors are expected to fall in line with the spirit of President Roosevelt's message to the Democracy of Alabama, pointing to the repeal plank in the party platform. . . .

Dry Governor Pollard of Virginia, responding to pressure from within and without the state, has agreed to a special session of the legislature August 17, to consider repeal and beer legislation.

Dry Governor Murray of Oklahoma, who vetoed one repeal bill last Saturday, yielded to the demands of his legislature and permitted repeal legislation to go on the program of the special tax session.

Dry Governor Johnson of Colorado also has relented his repeal veto, and is reported ready to call a special session of the legislature.

Dry Governor Conner of Mississippi is reported to be wavering in his earlier determination not to permit the legislature to meet this year.

Governor Laffoon of Kentucky is said to have weakened under the crossfire bombardment from Postmaster General Farley and state Democratic leaders, and may place repeal on the agenda of a special session.

If we may judge from the press reports, Mr. Farley devoted most of his time to the repeal campaign. He went up and down the land speaking, writing letters, holding conferences, and supporting the cause of repeal with all the influence and power that were at his command by virtue of the fact that he was the personal representative of the President and the chairman of the national committee, and held in his hands a vast and as yet undistributed patronage. The character of the public appeals which he made in various parts of the country is well illustrated by his speech in Florida on the eve of the repeal election in that state. In reporting the meeting, the New York *Herald Tribune* of October 11, 1933, said:

> Mr. Farley called upon Florida to join " the parade of states marching toward early accomplishment of repeal." He said Florida should favor repeal to show confidence in President Roosevelt, and to hasten the return of prosperity so more persons " can take Florida vacations."

In addition to the glamor of presidential prestige and authority, the lure of rich patronage, the ability to promise reduction of taxes and the power of political extermination, Mr. Farley was in a position to create the impression that he could influence the allotment of federal funds to the various states and municipalities. It was reported that when a governor objected to calling the legislature together to submit the question of repeal, he was told that the object of repeal was to help raise funds for public relief, and that if any state refused to do its part in securing repeal and thus providing needed revenue, the fact would be taken into consideration when the money was distributed. With multitudes of people unemployed and facing starvation, with the resources of individuals, municipalities and states exhausted, this was a threat that could not be ignored even by dry governors and legislators.

In his autobiography Mr. Farley gives the following statement of the part he and Mr. Roosevelt took in the campaign for ratification of the repeal amendment:

> During the hot summer months of 1933, while public attention generally was focused upon the recovery efforts of the Roosevelt administration, I was busily engaged in making sure that another very essential

part of the program was put into effect without a slipup. My efforts were largely centered on trying to make certain that enough states voted for repeal of the Eighteenth Amendment to insure its demise, a position written into the party platform by a vast majority of the delegates at the previous year's convention. Sentiment for repeal was still very strong, but Roosevelt and I, and a number of other party leaders, were afraid that the tide might start turning the other way before definite action was taken. That was especially true of the southern states where dry sentiment had been particularly strong. At the request of local leaders, I stumped a number of these southern states, asking the voters to stand by Roosevelt in his recovery program and to help it along by voting for repeal. We felt that this line of argument would be most effective in getting the desired action. The President entered into the drive personally by sending a letter to Leon McCord of Alabama, in which he pointed out that he was most anxious to see the Eighteenth Amendment taken out of the Constitution. The result was that before the end of 1933, the necessary three-fourths of the states had voted to remove the prohibition amendment from the organized law of the land, a show of speed that even those connected with professional repeal organizations believed impossible a few months earlier. We have always looked back with pride upon this ending of the prohibition era as a major accomplishment of the Democratic party. I know that my efforts helped a trifle, at least, because one disgusted fellow in Pennsylvania wrote in that, although he was a lifelong dry, he was going to support repeal just to get me off the air. He said that every time he turned the dial, I was appealing for repeal votes.[41]

The Result

The dry leaders were unable to reach and rally their forces; they were misrepresented and vilified; the air was filled with every kind of falsehood that highly paid wet propagandists could invent; the people were absorbed by questions growing out of the depression. The drys were therefore utterly discouraged, and feeling that struggle against such a seemingly invincible combination of forces was futile, millions of them did not vote at all. The wets, on the other hand, were lavishly financed, able to broadcast their propaganda, their slogans and their rallying cries instantly to every part of the country. They were supported by the machinery of both political parties and were led by the President of the

United States at a moment when he possessed almost wartime prestige and influence. They were, therefore, filled with confidence and courage and, flushed with the hope of victory, they not only brought to the polls every wet voter in the country, but they were joined by large numbers of drys who had been convinced that repeal would hasten recovery and reduce taxes.

What was the result? In answering this question, let us assume that the wets were entitled to every vote given them in the official reports and that the dry vote was honestly counted. In the thirty-nine states in which elections were held there were 61,770,908 persons of voting age exclusive of aliens. According to the official reports 15,207,639 voted for repeal and 5,332,992 voted dry. Of those eligible to vote 41,230,277 voted against repeal or did not vote at all. Only 24.7 per cent or less than one-fourth of the total vote was cast for repeal. In only one state was 40 per cent of the vote for repeal. In thirty-two of the thirty-nine states less than 30 per cent of the total possible vote was registered for repeal. The percentages for repeal of the total vote in some of the leading wet and dry states were as follows:

Pennsylvania	34.7
New York	24.7
Illinois	26.5
Florida	11.8
Texas	10.1
Tennessee	9.3
Virginia	8
Alabama	7.7
Arkansas	7.3
South Carolina	4.2

The magnitude of "the popular uprising against the Eighteenth Amendment" is still better illustrated by comparing the number of those who voted for repeal in these states, with the number of those who could have voted for repeal but did not. The following table shows the number of votes for repeal and the combined dry and stay-at-home vote:

STATES	VOTING FOR REPEAL	NOT VOTING FOR REPEAL
New York	1,946,532	5,928,891
Pennsylvania	1,864,411	3,507,813
Illinois	1,228,668	3,395,221
Texas	310,710	2,765,231
Tennessee	126,983	1,227,345
Alabama	100,269	1,187,454
Virginia	99,459	1,142,898
Florida	98,247	728,973
Arkansas	67,622	857,039
South Carolina	33,074	752,441

Thus the country was freed from " the damnable affliction of prohibition," Mr. Roosevelt had saved his face and rendered it impossible for the drys to recover in time to be a disturbing factor in the next presidential election, and the way was opened for large revenues from a legalized liquor traffic. On December 5, he issued his proclamation repealing the amendment that had outlawed the liquor traffic, suppressed liquor advertisements, banished the saloon and given the federal government the power not only to protect dry territory but to destroy the liquor traffic everywhere within its jurisdiction.

In exchange for these historic achievements, the President, in his proclamation, gave the people a sweetly solemn sermon. He concludes as follows:

> I ask the wholehearted cooperation of all our citizens to the end that this return of individual freedom shall not be accompanied by the repugnant conditions that obtained prior to the adoption of the Eighteenth Amendment and those that have existed since its adoption. Failure to do this honestly and courageously will be a living reproach to us all.
>
> I ask especially that no state shall by law or otherwise authorize the return of the saloon either in its old form or in some modern guise.
>
> The policy of the government will be to see to it that the social and political evils that have existed in the pre-prohibition era shall not be revived nor permitted again to exist. We must remove forever from our

midst the menace of the bootlegger and such others as would profit at the expense of good government, law, and order.

I trust in the good sense of the American people that they will not bring upon themselves the curse of excessive use of intoxicating liquors, to the detriment of health, morals and social integrity.

The objective we seek through a national policy is the education of every citizen toward a greater temperance throughout the nation.

In witness whereof, I have hereunto set my hand and caused the seal of the United States to be affixed.

The philosophy of Mr. Roosevelt and the forces he led to victory is concisely expressed by the poet Cowper. Speaking of the taxation of the liquor traffic in England, he said:

> The Excise is fattened with the rich result
> Of all this riot; and ten thousand casks
> Forever dribbling out their base contents,
> Touched by the Midas finger of the State,
> Bleed gold for ministers to sport away.
> Drink and be mad then; 'tis your country bids;
> Gloriously drunk, obey the important call;
> Her cause demands the assistance of your throats;
> Ye all can swallow, and she asks no more.[42]

Roosevelt, the Saloon and the Bootlegger

From the time of the proclamation sermon, Mr. Roosevelt never lifted a finger or uttered a word to promote the policy he proclaimed. On the contrary, he is in large measure responsible for the collapse of the opposition to the saloon and the return of that vile institution. In 1917, Congress had banished the saloons from the District of Columbia. Immediately after the repeal of the Eighteenth Amendment, members of both houses of Congress endeavored to secure the passage of a law providing for the District a dispensary system similar to the one that existed in Canada, which would serve as a model for the states. All through the repeal campaign, it was constantly asserted that this was to be the substitute for the saloon and the solution of the liquor problem. In the letter to Senator Wagner previously referred to, Mr. Roosevelt stated that the saloon should never be permitted to come back and that "the control of any sale of any intoxicants should be wholly in the hands of the states or of state agencies." Two bills were introduced, one providing for the dispensary system, the other for the return of the saloon. With Roosevelt in complete control of Congress, the dispensary bill was defeated, and the saloon bill passed just one month after repeal was proclaimed and before any of the states had acted. He not only permitted the bill to pass but affixed his signature to it. The significance of this action is illustrated by the following passages from the debates in Congress:

REP. BLANTON. I am not in favor of filling the nation's capital with liquor saloons. Under this bill there would be hundreds of whisky saloons all over Washington. This bill prevents bars and brass rails, but the places where this hard liquor will be sold will, nevertheless, be saloons.

REP. PATMAN. May I suggest that the only difference between the saloons under this bill and the saloon under the old system is that in order to be served a drink in one of the new saloons you must sit down at a table? . . . The Democratic platform of 1932 provides this: "We urge the enactment of such measures by the several states as will actually promote temperance, effectually prevent the return of the saloon, and bring the liquor traffic into the open, under complete supervision and control by the states." . . . I understand that many of the states are waiting on the District of Columbia bill; that is, they are holding their bills in order to find out what sort of a model bill will be passed by the Congress of the United States in order to carry out the Democratic platform pledge to prevent the return of the saloon. They will then consider measures in the various states.

REP. STALKER. The Eighteenth Amendment has been repealed, and promises were made by both party platforms that the saloon would not return. It seems to me that any license system whereby intoxicating liquors are permitted to be sold by the drink does return the saloon. I believe that the only safeguard is to have a dispensary system so rigidly controlled that no hard liquor can reach the consumer except through stores controlled by the liquor board. This bill repudiates the platform of both of the major parties.

REP. SMITH (Virginia). The bill I am going to seek to get a vote on in the Committee of the Whole is fundamentally the Canadian or Quebec system. That system has the approval of both wets and drys in our state as being the best and most practical way to control the situation. There are two ways to control the liquor question. One is sale by the drink for private profit, to be consumed on the premises. This is inherently and necessarily a barroom. You cannot find any reasonable distinction between this bill and the old system of the saloon. The only difference is the difference between standing up and sitting down.

Both parties promised that we would not have a return of the old open saloon, and when the proclamation was made by the President on December 5, he recalled that promise and said: " I hope that no state will adopt any system of liquor control that would bring about the return of the saloon, either in its old form or in any modern guise."

SENATOR CAPPER. I do not believe this measure carries out the will of the majority that supported repeal of the Eighteenth Amendment. Avowed advocates of repeal all urged that repeal was to be in the interest of sobriety and temperance, not for the purpose of rebuilding the liquor traffic and the return of the saloon.

The profit incentive was to be taken out of the liquor business. Liquor control was to be in the public interest. . . . That is not the idea in the measure before us. Instead of dispensaries, mere places of sale, what have we here? We have what I think is a return to the saloon system. The bill provides for the licensing of 2,000 drinking places in the District of Columbia. If the license system proposed is to be the model for the cities of the United States, then all I can say is we have learned nothing from the past.[43]

If Mr. Roosevelt had vetoed this bill and insisted that a law be enacted that fulfilled the promises that had been made to the people, it is safe to say that a large proportion of the states would have taken similar action. The results for Washington are stated by a columnist in the Charlotte (N. C.) *News* as follows:

Washington is wet. I mean it is wringing, dripping wet. Intoxicants are sold in cafés, drugstores, hotels and almost everywhere. Sold by the drink, the bottle, the jug or the hogshead. Said a local watchmaker to me: " The old saloons were bad. If a man wanted to take his sweetheart to one for a drink they had to slip into a back room, go upstairs, or get a bottle and carry it off; now everybody goes into these taverns and can drink without being looked down upon." And so it is. I have seen women with snowy hair and wrinkled faces sipping cocktails with " purty gals " who looked to be still in their teens, and have watched them walk unsteadily from the table after using a few whisky sours and a bottle or so of beer to hold down the cocktails they had imbibed. Both parties told us that we would abolish the old saloon . . . and it has been done. No brass rails here. No longer is the grogshop a man's institution. Under soft lights, to the strains of dreamy music, the boys and " gals " sit at tables, are waited on by uniformed youngsters, and, oh, well. . . .

The President soon found that repeal of the Eighteenth Amendment would not banish the bootlegger if legal liquor was taxed and dealers were made to pay a license. The bootlegger remained in business and made his money by violating the revenue laws. The President then declared that the tax on liquor should be reduced to the point where violation of the law would become unprofitable and the bootlegger thus automatically eliminated. But this involved a threat to the large revenue and the income tax reduction that had been promised. The situation could be met by measures that would greatly stimulate the sale and consumption of liquor, but this would run afoul of the wet promise that repeal would " reduce drinking," " promote true temperance," " protect dry territory " and " prevent the return of the saloon." Again the great corporation lawyers came to the rescue. Joseph H. Choate, Jr., had been appointed federal liquor administrator. Publicly he had been greatly concerned for the integrity of the law and the cause of true temperance. Behind the scenes, he was an astute Wall street lawyer representing his millionaire clients. The way in which he solved the problem confronting the President is clearly shown by the following special dispatch from Washington to the Chicago *Tribune:*

In a last determined effort to force down the prevailing high prices of booze in the United States, President Roosevelt today decided to open wide the gates to admit foreign liquors from any part of the world.

Mr. Roosevelt announced at this afternoon's press conference that for a 30 or 60 day experimental period, all quotas will be dropped and liquors, wines and beers will be received without limit. At the present time, quotas have been set for each exporting country limiting the volume of shipments.

The import taxes on the liquors imported will be unchanged for the present, but the President's attitude on this point indicated that he may even propose a lower tariff unless prices respond favorably.

Mr. Roosevelt also announced that a large number of small distilleries which had neglected to file applications for permits in time to be qualified for production of American rye and bourbon whiskies would now receive permits without delay.

These distilleries, some of which the President says were owned by old families which since days of yore had manufactured whiskies in the United States, were prevented from operating under the rule which limited permits only to those distilleries for which application for permits had been filed at a certain date.

The President, said Joseph Choate, federal liquor administrator, had recommended both the temporary abandonment of import quotas and the licensing of all applicant distillers. When all applications have been acted upon, Mr. Roosevelt declared, the potential production of whisky in this country, based upon a 24-hour activity in all plants, will be 44 million gallons a year.

In some quarters the administration's effort to bring down the retail prices of liquors has been criticized as tending to encourage widespread drinking and resultant drunkenness.

But Mr. Roosevelt made it plain today he is anxious only that the liquor which is sold and consumed in this country shall be honestly made and tax paid. His chief concern, it was said, was to defeat the bootleggers who are still operating on a wide scale in some parts of the country, selling synthetic and cut liquors. The bootleggers, it was pointed out, are able to attract customers because of their relatively much lower prices than legitimate dealers.[44]

Abolish all quotas, throw our ports open to the liquor interests of the entire world, lower tariffs, grant a license to all applicant distillers, stimulate twenty-four-hour activity in all plants, bring our domestic production of rye and bourbon whiskies up to forty-four million gallons a year, permit all breweries and wineries to run full blast, reduce prices by lowering taxes, and drown the bootlegger in a flood of cheap liquor — this was the new deal on the liquor question. As a moderate tax on an unrestricted traffic would produce a larger and more dependable revenue than a high tax on a restricted traffic, this solution was ideal from the standpoint of the underworld that wanted unlimited booze, the liquor interests of the world that wanted unlimited profits, and big business that wanted unlimited liquor revenue. As the repeal movement had been launched, carried on and brought to a successful conclusion by a combination of elements determined to have booze, profits and revenue, their great objectives were now achieved.

How Dry Territory Was Protected

When seeking the support of dry delegates to the 1932 convention, Roosevelt declared " that it must remain not only the right but the duty of the federal government to protect states which continue to prohibit the sale of intoxicants." The Democratic platform, " that admirable document " of which he declared, " I accept it 100 per cent," demanded that the federal government should protect the states " against importation of intoxicating liquors in violation of their laws."

Section 2 of the Twenty-first Amendment reads as follows:

> The transportation or importation into any state, territory, or possession of the United States for delivery or use therein of intoxicating liquors, in violation of the laws thereof, is hereby prohibited.

In proclaiming that amendment, Mr. Roosevelt said:

> I call specific attention to the authority given by the Twenty-first Amendment to the government to prohibit transportation or importation of intoxicating liquors into any state in violation of the laws of such state.

This provision of the amendment would, of course, have not the slightest meaning or significance until Congress passed an act providing penalties for its violation and setting up the machinery for its enforcement. Although Mr. Roosevelt was in complete control of Congress and constantly sending in his " must " bills which had to be enacted often without even being read, he never made the slightest effort to have Congress carry out the solemn pledge to protect dry territory that had been given both by himself and his party.

In July 1937, five years after Mr. Roosevelt became President, the Judiciary Committee of the House, on its own initiative, reported out a bill for the enforcement of this provision of the amendment. The report said:

> It is apparent that no existing legislation makes effective the second section of the Twenty-first Amendment and provides a penalty for the importation into states of intoxicating liquors " for delivery or use therein . . . in violation of the laws thereof."
>
> One of the principal arguments used for the repeal of the Eighteenth Amendment and the adoption of the Twenty-first was that the liquor question should be left to the decision of the people of the various states and that, with the second section of the Twenty-first Amendment made effective, the people of states which did not desire to permit the manufacture or sale of intoxicating liquors would be better able to enforce their prohibitory laws because the government itself, through the enforcement of this portion of the Twenty-first Amendment, would protect them from the transportation into their borders of liquors whose sale they desired to prohibit, from other states.
>
> This promise both expressed and implied has not been fulfilled and it is the purpose of the proposed bill to make it effective. While there are only a small number of states who still maintain any form of prohibitory laws, these states, nevertheless, are entitled to the protection promised in connection with the repeal of the Eighteenth Amendment, and it would be afforded by the second section of the Twenty-first Amendment when it is made effective as herein contemplated.

Representative Tarver, when answering objections to the bill on the floor of the House, defined the purpose of the legislation as follows:

> This is merely saying that the thing prohibited by the second section of the Twenty-first Amendment shall be made criminal and a means provided for enforcement of that provision of the Constitution by pro-

viding that its violation shall be punished as for a misdemeanor. I cannot conceive of any reason why any member should object to such a provision. Without it we have the constitutional prohibition against the importation of intoxicating liquors into states for use or sale in violation of their laws without any penalty for its violation.[45]

At the time of this writing, this bill has not been enacted and its passage is being obstructed by the wets. The result of this long delay has been that dry states have had no protection; they have been rendered powerless to enforce their laws and have been flooded with illegal liquor. The dry forces in these states have become demoralized; many of them have been made to feel that the struggle is hopeless, and have accepted the policy of legalizing and taxing the liquor traffic.

NOTES

1 June 25, 1920.
2 New York *Times,* July 7, 1920.
3 Quoted in *Literary Digest,* July 17, 1920.
4 Alfred E. Smith, *Up to Now* (Viking Press, 1929), p. 280.
5 W. E. Werner, *Tammany Hall* (Doubleday, Doran & Co., 1928), p. 563.
6 *New Republic,* July 9, 1924.
7 July 7, 1924.
8 New York *Times,* June 21, 1928.
9 *Ibid.,* June 24, 1928.
10 *Ibid.,* June 22, 1928.
11 *Ibid.,* June 26, 1928.
12 June 30, 1928.
13 July 7, 1928.
14 *Literary Digest,* Oct. 1, 1927.
15 Alfred E. Smith, *op. cit.,* p. 383.
16 New York *Times,* July 12, 1928.
17 *Ibid.,* Oct. 1, 1930.
18 *Ibid.*
19 1931.
20 New York *Herald Tribune,* June 7, 1932.
21 Ernest K. Lindley, *Franklin D. Roosevelt* (Bobbs-Merrill Co., 1931), pp. 275–76.
22 June 23, 1932.
23 New York *Times,* March 6, 1931.
24 March 3, 1931.
25 March 3, 1931.
26 *Ibid.*
27 March 4, 1931.

[28] March 6, 1931.

[29] Nov. 24, 1931.

[30] New York *Herald Tribune*, Jan. 8, 1932.

[31] In my book *The Underworld of American Politics* I have given the history of Chicago's Tammany Hall and described the way in which Cermak became the boss of that organization and the ruler of Chicago and Illinois.

[32] June 30, 1932.

[33] Quoted in New York *Times*, July 1, 1932.

[34] In an article entitled " A Decadent Institution," which appeared in the *Saturday Evening Post* for Aug. 27, 1932, Samuel Blythe gives a vivid description of this convention.

[35] Chicago *Tribune*, July 3, 1932.

[36] James A. Farley, *Behind the Ballots* (Harcourt, Brace & Co., 1938), pp. 156–58.

[37] Aug. 27, 1932.

[38] Aug. 28, 1932.

[39] Sept. 7, 1932.

[40] March 16, 1933.

[41] Farley, *op. cit.*, p. 222.

[42] Quoted by Raymond Cowper, *Drama of Drink* (Drama of Drink Distributors, Andover, Mass., 1932), p. 37.

[43] *Congressional Record*, Vol. 78, Part 1, 73rd Congress, 2nd Session, pp. 264–72 *passim*, 786–87.

[44] March 9, 1934.

[45] *Congressional Record*, Vol. 81, Part 7, 73rd Congress, 1st Session, p. 7220.

Chapter Five

The Results Of Repeal

THE TRIUMPH of the liquor interests, the underworld, Tammany politics and the unscrupulous elements of big business, produced the precise results that had been foreseen by all intelligent and responsible people who had not been deceived and blinded by the wet propaganda. Our ports were thrown open to the liquor manufacturers of the world; breweries, distilleries and wineries sprang up rapidly; vast quantities of liquor were produced and thrown upon a market that was practically unrestrained. The country was soon filled with saloons, cocktail lounges, taverns, beer gardens, dance halls, night clubs, roadhouses and other places where liquor was sold. The ban on liquor advertising was removed and all the methods of modern high-powered salesmanship were employed to induce people to buy and drink. By denouncing prohibition as fanaticism and acclaiming "true temperance" and "civilized drinking," the wet propaganda had largely undone the work of generations of education as to the effects of alcohol. The debauchery of youth by liquor, which had been confined during prohibition largely to the upper classes, spread to the youth of every class. Dry territory everywhere was flooded with bootleg liquor.

The following are typical of reports that have come constantly from every part of the country since repeal became effective. The Los Angeles *Times* for February 12, 1934, stated that the head coordinator of the division of attendance and employment of minors made a report to the superintendent of schools in which he declared conditions to be appalling and said his investigations indicated that at least 30 per cent of the patrons of beer and wine parlors are under 21 years of age. . . .

Cliff Hellyer, former police officer and one of the investigators, told Hoyt and Superintendent Bouelle that harking back " to the good old days of the saloon," he never saw such conditions then, and characterized the present outlook as dangerous in the extreme.

" It is the conclusion of the investigators, after visiting these 209 places selling beer, wine and hard drinks," the report said, " that there is an appalling number of young people who are patronizing these establishments and are drinking heavily."

Early in the same year, three of the leading newspapers of Chicago made an investigation of conditions in that city. Their columns were filled with statements like the following, which appeared in the *Herald-Examiner* for March 6, 1934:

Shocking evidence of how Chicago's high school girls and boys — children ranging between 13 and 18 years of age — are being lured into depravity by plying child patrons with liquor has been . . . discovered during a fortnight's survey of the city's unregulated saloons. . . . Orgies which outrivaled the debauches of Paris' notorious Quartier Latin. . . . Drunkenness and laxity of morals are common in the dimly lit back rooms of these saloons, many of which carry on their vicious trade in the very shadows of the city's schools.

Sprawled on the floor and asleep at the long tables were a dozen boys and nearly as many girls. Some were obviously 14 and 15 years old. The older ones were 17 and 18. These children were students at Lake View school. . . .

A blond child of about 16 is dancing for the crowd at the bar. Her skirts are to her hips. She is drunk. . . . They're raffling off a pint of bonded whiskey for a dime a chance . . . a 16-year-old girl screams with pleasure when she wins it. . . .

Dr. Alice Phillips Aldrich, welfare superintendent of the Illinois Vigilance Association, declared:

The ancient and blood-stained commerce in agonized souls of girls has been revived since the return of the licensed tavern and promiscuous drinking between sexes. . . . As now operated, many so-called taverns have a most deplorable effect on girls. Nothing like it on so open and broad a scale was heard of in the days when the segregated vice districts were in full blast here. . . . It doesn't make much difference whether there are bars or counters, stools or tables, whether sandwiches are served or not, or whether the drinking is done perpendicularly, the effect is the same.[1]

Addressing the Senate on May 2, 1934, Senator Borah read from reports of the Chicago investigation and said:

One of the great arguments in the campaign against the Eighteenth Amendment was that the bootlegger and the speak-easy were to be done away with and the saloon was not to be permitted to come back. Much worse than the saloon has returned and is apparently here to stay. I say worse than the saloon. It is worse. It is a legalized dive, a protected rendezvous of crime.[2]

The 1935 report of the Chicago Juvenile Protective Association says:

No provision of the law is more disregarded than the article banning the sale of intoxicating liquors to drunken patrons.

Vice in Chicago's saloon-taverns flourished. Some saloons are simply houses of prostitution, having adjacent rooms used for vice; hostesses solicited at the bars and tables, thence repairing to connecting quarters with the patrons. In other cases, streetwalkers came into the saloons to solicit. . . . Cab drivers routed their fares from the liquor resorts to the houses of ill fame. . . .

Repeated instances of children in saloons came to our notice. . . . Boys and girls under age were patrons of these places. . . . Many followed regular routes from saloon to saloon during late hours of the night. Children in liquor resorts watched prostitutes openly offering themselves to men, and witnessed appalling scenes of intoxication and debauchery. They were familiar with, and impressed by, the suggestive entertainment provided in such places.

A writer for the Columbus, Ohio, *Citizen*, who had advocated repeal, wrote the following, in October 1936:

. . . I went to a game between my alma mater and its lifetime gridiron foe and came away more than ever convinced that something is very wrong about college football as it is now managed. It's more than a racket. It's becoming a public disgrace.

I never saw so many drunks in one place in my life. The old grads were back in full force with a pint on every hip. Some of the mammas had had too many cocktails. Far too many boys and girls were liquored up and unable to follow the game. Several men were sick all over the best clothes of the people who sat in front of them.

" The Day of the Game " is certainly beginning to resemble too much a Roman orgy. Everything's wide open. The bars are down and on that occasion we excuse all drinking in a burst of holiday tolerance. It seems to me that college professors and business men and parents should begin to put the question to themselves quite seriously.

In July 1935, Governor Frank G. Fitzgerald of Michigan said:

The situation today with respect to the legalized liquor traffic is worse than it was in the darkest days of the saloon. . . . The beer and liquor joint with its windows obscured, its lights dimmed, its booths to afford privacy — with a dance floor as one adjunct and tourist facilities as another — is a combination as vicious as any that has ever been devised to debauch the morals of a rising generation.[3]

The New York *Times* for January 2, 1936, carried the following dispatch:

Philadelphia, Jan. 1. — Cardinal Daugherty, speaking at his New Year's reception to representatives of the Catholic diocesan societies, criticized young women who drink intoxicants and mothers who encourage it as a means of enhancing their daughters' chances in society.

Decrying modern practices in regard to the drinking and serving of intoxicants, he urged the immediate establishment of total abstinence societies in all parishes under his jurisdiction where they do not now exist and the strengthening of those now functioning.

" Now, in too many cases," he went on, " young women drink publicly and sometimes have to be carried out in an intoxicated condition from hotels, taprooms and private dwellings. Worse still, there are not wanting mothers of families who encourage their daughters to drink in order that they may conform to modern usage and pass for up-to-date members of so-called aristocratic society. No wonder broken marriages, divorce and shameful scandal abound."

In a sermon preached in May 1936, Dr. Harry Emerson Fosdick said:

The repeal of prohibition did not solve our problems. It simply plunged us back to the *status quo ante,* plunged us once more into the intolerable situation which our fathers faced two generations ago when they rose up in indignation against the liquor traffic. Once more we face that traffic, everywhere antisocial, not to say criminal, in its consequences. . . . This present loose, tipsy, cocktail-party generation cannot be the last word in the story of alcoholism. As surely as history repeats itself, a revolt is due, a change of public attitude born out of disgust with and fear of the intolerable estate we now are in.

In an article that appeared in *Zion's Herald* in October 1936, Bishop Edgar Blake of Detroit said:

The saloon has returned in forms a thousandfold more vicious and destructive than in the old days of unrestricted freedom. The beer garden, the cocktail lounge, the night clubs, the wayside brothel, have arisen in our midst to debauch our youth. Never have we witnessed such drunkenness and debauchery on our streets and in public places as we are witnessing today. Never have our homes been so ruthlessly invaded. Never has our American womanhood fallen so low as since repeal. According to the president of the General Federation of Women's Clubs, as reported by the United Press, " repeal of prohibition has posed a new problem for hotel men — how to handle increasing numbers of drunken women." According to the secretary of the Keeley Institute, a " race of feminine barflies, standing with one spiked heel on the rail and a wobbly elbow on the bar, has evolved from the free and easy operations of saloons." " The problem of the lady drunkard," he says, " is rapidly becoming as serious as that of the male. . . ."

Almost at the moment the President was appealing to " the good sense of the American people that they will not bring upon themselves the curse of the excessive use of intoxicating liquors, to the detriment of health, morals and social integrity," thirty Detroit high school children, 14 to 17 years of age, were " laid out " dead drunk at a beer party where they were guests. " The girls were so intoxicated it required three hours to get them sober enough to go home." . . . According to the police records of Detroit, in the first five months of repeal, traffic accidents attributable to liquor increased 164 per cent. . . .

Crime has not lessened. On the contrary, the director of the Federal Bureau of Prisons says in a recent report: "The relief which we expected from the repeal of prohibition has not materialized." Crime has increased everywhere throughout the land.

The federal prisons are full to overflowing with criminals. The Department of Justice has been forced to ask Congress for increased appropriations to cope with the rising tide of crime. . . . And so the story goes — in Detroit, in Michigan, in all America. Our sense of shame is numbed. Our capacity for indignation and anger is atrophied. The spirit of moral protest is smitten with apathy. . . . Is repeal a success? Let Colonel Knox and his Chicago *Daily News* answer:

"Repeal was urged by its sanguine supporters as the remedy for all the ills of the dry regime. The saloon was never to return; liquor was to be taken out of politics; bootlegging was to be ended; drinking was to decrease; temperance was to be promoted; furthermore, unemployment was to be mitigated greatly; new revenue was to roll into state and federal treasuries in vast sums, and the nation was to be saved many millions in the cost of enforcement.

"None of the promises has been fulfilled. The saloon is back, liquor is in politics, bootlegging continues, drinking has increased, unemployment is worse, the revenue returns to the state treasury are far below the hopeful estimate of 1933, and the cost of fighting the illicit trade is still burdensome."

You can't control the liquor traffic. It recognizes no limitations. It defies all restrictions. It will not be bound by any law of God or man. It is criminal by nature. There is only one way to deal with it, and that is to kill it.

On May 14, 1936, the General Conference of the Methodist Episcopal Church adopted a resolution which contained the following:

Repeal has been a more ghastly failure than even its most consistent enemies predicted. After less than three years, this "ignoble experiment" stands indicted and convicted before the bar of public opinion. No promise upon which repeal was secured has been kept. Temperance has not been promoted. Official records prove that drinking is steadily on the increase. Repeal has added to the economic disaster. Crime and liquor violations have increased. The new saloon in its various guises is attended by shocking evils unknown to the old saloon days. . . .

One of the most tragic features of the whole debacle is the fact that the toll of disaster falls most heavily on our youth. Thousands of young girls are yielding to the advice to "learn early how much liquor they can stand," often to be brought home lifeless or virtueless, and sometimes both.

Another tragedy of this hour is that funds from the liquor traffic are being turned into public school treasuries, that thus may be stilled the voices of educational leaders that should be raised in an aggressive campaign to acquaint our youth with the facts concerning this habit-forming drug. *We protest against the use in this way of money so acquired.*

Unless the Christian people of America rally in united warfare against these and all the evils attendant upon the legalized liquor traffic, we are facing an era of debauchery and degradation such as this nation has never experienced.

In the *Christian Century* for November 25, 1936, Dr. John Haynes Holmes, one of the outstanding religious and civic leaders of America, had an article entitled "The Third Year of Repeal," in which he said:

The third year of repeal is drawing to a close. The record of this year, as told from day to day in the newspapers, is worse than ever. And this in spite of the fact that this record is not a half, nor even a quarter, told! The wet press, fattening on its liquor advertising, is publishing only what it has to publish about the ravages of alcohol. There is now no flamboyant exposure of rampant evils, no front-page featuring of drunkenness and crime and death, no editorial howling to high heaven over "appalling conditions." Yet if the liquor news were handled today the way the liquor news was handled yesterday, this nation would get a shock that would carry us back to prohibition in a year. . . .

The most impressive clippings of this current year have to do with the startling increase in drinking both moderate and excessive, occasional and regular. It used to be argued by the wets that repeal would lower the tide of consumption — that people were drinking heavily under prohibition as an act of bravado, to defy an unjust law. Make it easy and proper to imbibe and the incentive will be gone, and drinking, therefore, reduced to a minimum. This idea never made sense to me. It never was so in the old days before prohibition. Why should it be so in these new days of high-power advertising, organized publicity and general mob psychology? Now we know it isn't so! Drinking is increasing to such an extent as to break all the records of the trade. . . .

What wonder that the liquor interests are alarmed, and the dry forces elated! The campaign for the return of prohibition is now well under way. . . .

We have given repeal three years to prove itself, and it has failed, just as every sane and instructed mind knew it would fail. The moment the Eighteenth Amendment was repudiated, the floodgates were opened for the return of the same intolerable conditions of civic corruption, social debauchery, moral collapse and general public peril, which led to the enactment of the amendment in the beginning. What idiocy to think that the licensed liquor traffic, uncontrolled and uncontrollable, would do anything other than what it has already done — namely, overwhelm society with indecency, misery and crime. Now the record is written once again. The facts are in. There waits only that action upon the facts which will drive liquor from point to point till the land once more is free.

The grand jury of Cuyahoga county, Ohio, made an exhaustive investigation of conditions in Cleveland. In the report which it submitted to the court on April 21, 1937, it said:

During our term an overwhelming body of evidence was submitted to us in robbery cases indicating that beer parlors occupy an importance out of all relationship to their numbers as the places in which robberies originate. . . . At the time of our empanelment, your honor charged us to look into the serious problem of traffic manslaughter and to bring before the citizenry of Cuyahoga county any suggestions for the mitigation of this evil which might be suggested by our jury experience. The jury was impressed with the testimony which tended to indicate that in every one of the distressing cases of death caused by a motor vehicle, which came to our attention, liquor was an important element, if not the chief factor, leading to the accident.

Mr. J. Harkey Reiter is a member of the liquor control board of the state of Pennsylvania and Mr. D. Frederick Burnett is state commissioner of alcoholic beverage control for the state of New Jersey. Both are in constant touch with liquor conditions in every part of their states. In an address delivered at a banquet of the Philadelphia Retailers' Association in April 1938, Mr. Reiter said:

I am sorry to say that the public of Pennsylvania is absolutely disgusted with licensed conditions and will demand at the next session of the legislature drastic limitations on the granting of licenses. The number of licenses continues to increase at a rate of 200 a month even though liquor sales by the drink have dropped over 25 per cent in recent months. There is a place selling liquor by the drink for every 600 Pennsylvanians or a bar for not more than 150 customers when children and abstainers are excluded. This gives no consideration at all to the 5,200 beer parlors.

In 1933 if 26 per cent more of the voters had balloted against repeal, Pennsylvania would be as dry as the Sahara. Today I would not like to bet on how these same citizens would vote on the question of sale by the drink in taprooms.

In a radio address delivered on February 27, 1937, Mr. Burnett said:

Four of the major police problems from time immemorial have been immorality, gambling, narcotics and liquor. This department, which is essentially a police department, cuts across each of these fields. So far as non-licenses are concerned, the work of this department is concerned exclusively with liquor. This is why stills are seized; speak-easies are raided; poisoned liquor ruthlessly tracked down; bootleggers, hijackers and racketeers arrested. So far as licenses are concerned, our duty extends to everything that occurs on licensed premises, that is, not only liquor but gambling, immorality, intemperance, noise, brawls, in fact the whole gamut of human conduct and its extraordinary manifestations under the exhilaration of alcohol. That is why this department is concerned with slot machines and dice and betting against the house; with seductive sirens masquerading under and defiling the name of hostess; with the insidious back room evil; with music and dancing and amusements in general; with those who drink copiously and then vaingloriously drive to show how well they can hold it; with the sales to minors; with everything that deals with decency, sobriety and law and order.

It must be recognized that liquor is a commodity inherently dangerous. But that conclusion is not a terminal but merely the beginning point. The big question is, what are we going to do about it? . . .

You, friends of the radio audience, as good citizens are an integral part of the man power necessary to the success of control. It is you who see and hear first-handed those things which the police could never approach because their uniforms give warning, and which my men, roughly only four to a whole county, cannot, because of their small number, even hope to patrol, let alone control. It is you who see cheating saloons doing business on election day while polls are open or after closing hours; or on prohibited Sunday hours. It is you who see young girls and young boys plied with liquor till they reel, or sold the pocket flasks which anoint wild orgies in automobiles of indulgent parents. The sale of liquor to minors in these days of high-powered engines with which the public highways are crowded is the greatest curse of liquor. It is you who stumble into disgusting scenes at bars, in back rooms, in booths, on public dance floors, and in places that have the outward appearances of decency but are sinks of debauchery. If you want to lighten your own tax burden by making others bear their full share, if you want decency, if you want law and order, if you really want to help keep liquor in its place and broken legs and broken lives out of your homes, then obey that impulse! Do your duty, take your pen in hand and tell the department of what you know, what you have seen, and who, where and when.

In the *Country Home* for April 1938, Mr. Paul T. Sturges tells of an investigation he made of liquor conditions in six farming states:

I have just completed a trip that took me through six farming states and into dozens of stubble-field dance halls and cornstalk casinos. I was appalled at conditions, both as a reporter and as a rural father of a 16-year-old daughter and 14-year-old son.

Drinking among the younger crowd, I am convinced, is worse than it was during prohibition, and gambling and vice, I found, are traveling in its wake. I have talked with parents, business men, ministers, teachers, yes, even bootleggers. All agree that highway hot spots which are not decently operated are so damaging to the morals of rural youth that continuation of abuses will lead to another prohibition movement. Some communities are indignant, with farmers on the verge of "night-riding," as they sometimes do in the south. And it isn't just the menace to morality that is arousing them. It's also the alarming increase of rural motor car accidents, and the fear that a new " joint " may spring up right across the road from their farmhouse. Most townships don't have zoning laws. . . .

I am not a prohibitionist. I like my glass of beer as well as the next man, but, after investigating these places, I feel like a crusader, ready to fight against this widespread invasion of the countryside by the lowest sort of city vice.

Items like the following are constantly appearing in the daily press. As a result of driving a car while under the influence of liquor, a young man was convicted of manslaughter. In passing sentence the judge said:

I realize fully that this boy has sent one man to eternity, and he undoubtedly realizes that. I realize also that he has caused very serious injury to a young woman, and I presume he realizes that. If he doesn't, his presence in the sickroom the other day ought to convince him. I realize also that up to this time he has borne an excellent reputation. I have talked to his former employer and I have talked to others concerning him. I have done in this case as I have done in other cases; I have listened to those who have comments to make about the young man, both for and against. In this case, none have been against him, but he is going to carry to his dying day the fact that he sent one man into eternity by his carelessness. He is going to carry also with him the fact that this whole thing arose because of his association with evil companions, and more than all things else, because he swung away from the path of rectitude and has gone into the dens of vice, these so-called cocktail parlors.

On June 15, 1939, Mr. Chapin Hall, columnist for the Los Angeles *Times,* wrote:

It's a sad commentary on the modern youth's outlook on life when high school principals in seven cities of the metropolitan district find it necessary to confer on ways and means to curb drunkenness and reckless driving among pupils celebrating graduation week, and when police must " check " the boys and girls embarking in water taxis for liquor or evidence of intoxication.

On June 17, 1939, the following editorial appeared in the Chicago *Tribune:*

THEY LEARN NOTHING

The only thing that ever made the arguments of prohibitionists plausible to the nonfanatic majority of the population was the greed, venality and gross stupidity of saloon-keepers and the politicians who played ball with them. Neither the saloon-keepers nor the politicians have learned a thing from their tribulations. They are as selfish and stupid as ever.

Both the city council and the state legislature are running hog wild on liquor regulation, or more properly, in the direction of making regulation impossible. Of these two programs, however, that in the legislature is the more vicious.

The saloon-keeper lobby is trying at Springfield to kill local option. It appears that unless the legislators hear from their constituents the lobby may succeed. The house now has at the passage stage three amendments to the local option law.

The first requires a majority of all registered voters to vote a precinct dry. . . . A second amendment would make local option area boundaries those of existing precincts instead of those that existed in 1932. . . . The third amendment permits the attack of local option petitions in court after the voters have signified their will in an election. This is a scheme to disfranchise voters by technicalities. Each of these amendments is extremely objectionable. The bill should be killed without delay.

Meanwhile our bumble-footed city fathers, inspired by the yammering of lawbreaking saloon-keepers against enforcement of the closing ordinance, are doing their best to help the liquor business commit suicide. . . .

Of the six amendments that the council passed, the one extending the saloon closing hours to 2 A.M. through the week and to 3 A.M on Saturdays is utterly bad. The noise and disorder in and about saloons in residential districts was an insufferable nuisance at 1 A.M. . . . The Tribune led the fight against national prohibition because the rule of the dry tyrants was intolerable. . . . But those who fought prohibition didn't do so in order to turn the city or state over to the saloon-keepers.

Getting people drunk has never been an exalted occupation. The saloon-keeper is allowed to do business because he is slightly less objectionable than the rum runner, the bootlegger and the gangster. Most of the gentry can best be tolerated when they are treated like pariahs. The cause of temperance will be served if the saloon-keepers are given a kicking around. They have learned nothing and they presume too much.

An editorial in the Chicago *Daily Times* of June 21, 1939, said:

The solicitude of the city administration and most aldermen for the tavern trade is as shocking as it is puzzling. The welfare of 3,500,000 citizens, the desire of the great majority of those citizens for decent moderation in the liquor business, were flagrantly disregarded. . . .

Saloon-keepers and their political allies brought about prohibition by an arrogant disregard of the rights of the great majority of decent people. Prohibition should have taught them a lesson. But from last week's performance there is no sign that it did. The public can be pushed around just so long before it again will use drastic measures. The tavern-keepers and city council went a long ways toward that point by their latest action.

NOTES

[1] Chicago *Daily News*, Feb. 28, 1934.

[2] *Congressional Record*, Vol. 78, Part 7, 73rd Congress, 2nd Session, p. 7898.

[3] *American Issue*, Sept. 1935.

Part Two

Repeal Propaganda

Chapter Six

The Technique Of Propaganda

THE TECHNIQUE of the propaganda that swept us into the first World War consisted in diverting the attention of the people from the destruction, the barbarism and the futility of war and making them hate the Germans. The criminal Kaiser, the unspeakable Hun, German frightfulness, German spies, the rape of Belgium, mutilated babies, ravished women, bleeding France, submarine horrors, insults to the flag — these " emotion-detonating phrases " were used in such a way as to make the people hate, but never think. By the same method, our entry into the war was associated with self-respect, courage, patriotism, sanctity of treaties, freedom of the seas, rights of neutrals, national honor and lofty humanitarianism. Those who questioned this propaganda were called yellow and denounced as pacifists, cowards, pro-Germans, men who did not possess the courage of their ancestors and were willing to be safe and comfortable while humanity was being crucified. While the people were being lashed into a fury by this modern war dance, those who were inspiring and financing it remained completely under cover.

The men who launched, financed and perfected the technique of the war propaganda found that, through the income tax, they would have to help in a substantial way to pay for the war that had made the world safe for their capital and their profits. They determined to escape this burden and throw it upon the people by bringing back the liquor traffic and taxing it. They knew that this would be a more difficult undertaking than had been the creation and sustaining of the war frenzy. There is a glamor about war. Many of the greatest heroes of the race have been military leaders and a call to the colors awakens an age-old thrill. In times of war, however sordid may be the underlying causes of the conflict, the people, acting in good faith, are performing deeds of loyalty, sacrifice and heroism that for a time lift them above all that is petty and drab into the realm of great, soul-satisfying emotions in which life finds its complete validation. The people had banished the liquor traffic with such decisiveness not alone because of their intellectual conviction that it was a national menace, but also as a result of physical repulsion and moral revulsion. The very name suggested the stench of the corner saloon, the staggering drunk, poverty and disease. There were no heroes and there was no glamor.

The wet leaders knew that the restoration of the liquor traffic would require, in the language of the final report of the Association Against the Prohibition Amendment, "the most marked overturn in public sentiment that the history of our nation records." They also knew that to effect this overturn, they would have to conduct the greatest and most unscrupulous campaign of propaganda that our history records. But the stakes were large, they had the money, and they had perfected the technique; so with characteristic energy and efficiency, they embarked upon this campaign.

Everything conceivable was done to divert the attention of the people from the inevitable consequences of repeal and to make them hate the Eighteenth Amendment. The moral laxity, the political corruption and the crime of the post-war period, unemployment and the depression, and other things of which people disapproved or from which they suffered, were charged to what Mr. Hearst called "the cesspool of the Eighteenth Amendment." The principles of their strategy were these: "Never argue," use "emotion-detonating phrases," achieve "fixation by repetition." In less technical terms, use language that would simultaneously state a lie, arouse a prejudice in its favor, blind the eyes and close the mind of the hearer to the truth and make reflection impossible; repeat that language incessantly until the lie is exposed or becomes stale; then invent a new one and repeat the process, always making sure that the truth never catches up with the lies. Let the lie, the emotional poison and the tear gas strike the victim at the same instant and all take effect together.

A corps of professional propagandists was maintained to prepare "facts," "statistics," arguments, pamphlets and other documents suited to every interest, point of view, taste and emotional state. They began with those who had a direct financial interest in repeal. Income taxpayers were told that annulment of the Eighteenth Amendment would do away with the income tax; hotel owners that it would restore their bars; makers of barrels, bottles and similar articles that it would increase the demand for their products; farmers that it would create a market for their grain; laborers that it would furnish employment and increase wages; leaders of the American Legion that it would provide the money for the bonus; lawyers that it was demanded by those who paid big legal fees. Newspapers and magazines were informed that their support was demanded by the men to whom they looked for advertising and financing; and "prominent and beloved" writers and artists were promised material, publishers and markets for their articles and books. The Crusaders made their special appeal to youth and to the protagonists of personal liberty, the Constitution and red-blooded Americanism. The Women's Organization for National Prohibition Reform was assigned the task of making the women and the moral elements of the country believe that the object of repeal was to do away with political corruption, hypocrisy, bootleggers and drunkenness, and to promote true temperance. The entire country, every interest and every element of the population, was covered thoroughly.

When the great propaganda machine, complete in every detail and perfectly lubricated, went into action, it was a marvel of efficiency. Governor Pinchot has said that the wet propaganda covered the nation like a blanket. It would be more accurate to compare it to a bombardment. For seven years without ceasing, false and inflammatory statements were used with devastating effectiveness to destroy the intellectual and spiritual defenses against the liquor traffic that had been built up in the minds and hearts of the American people by generations of education. The social pressure, financial coercion, political corruption, lawlessness and sabotage exercised by the repeal forces were protected by an impenetrable smoke screen of fakes and falsehoods. Future generations will be able to gain only the faintest conception of the manner in which the truth was distorted. Reading the files of newspapers and magazines cannot reproduce the quality of the propaganda that was constantly pouring from the radio and from the lips of subsidized politicians, the nightly glorification of drinking by the movies, and the manner in which millions of people, having no personal knowledge of the facts, were induced to take up the catch phrases that were put in circulation to make rational thought and action impossible.

The wet propagandists went into action disguised as knights errant of the Constitution, the rights of the states and personal liberty, as crusaders for law, order and political purity, and as apostles of true temperance. We were told that those whose duty it was to enforce the law were spies, snoopers, tyrants and murderers, and that convicted bootleggers and speak-easy proprietors were martyrs in the cause of human liberty, John Browns in a war against a new form of human slavery. Intelligent, social-minded and courageous men and women who insisted upon the retention and enforcement of the law were subjected to misrepresentation, vilification and persecution. Cartoons appeared daily representing them as illiberal, hypocritical, unsociable, neurotic, obnoxious people with hip flasks protruding from their pockets. A man in a clerical robe, with side whiskers, retreating chin, weak face and piously uplifted eyes, Bible in hand; a man with a long nose, sharp chin, mean sour face, battered stovepipe hat, long black coat and tattered umbrella — the enemy of happiness and joy; a detestable, implacable spy, leering over transoms and peeking through keyholes at honest, kindly citizens enjoying a friendly and harmless drink; a repulsive criminal with a mask over his eyes and a machine gun in his hand — these were a few of the many ways in which law-abiding citizens were ridiculed and held up to the scorn of their neighbors. Under the title, *How They*

Draw Prohibition — A Book of Reprinted Cartoons, the AAPA gathered up this journalistic garbage and circulated it widely throughout the country.

They told us that the evils of the liquor traffic had resulted first from the saloon and then from prohibition, and that with repeal we should have neither of these sources of evil, but a new and magic device for dispensing liquor, one under which it would become only a source of comfort, cheer, prosperity and revenue; that the evils that have always accompanied the traffic would be avoided by the neat device of changing the name of the place where liquor was sold and the title of the seller. They talked blithely about light wines, wholesome beer, the relaxing and socializing effect of alcohol, civilized drinking, true temperance, the Canadian system, the Bratt system, and prated about taking the profit out of the business.

They did everything in their power to discredit prohibition and give color to their propaganda. They served liquor openly, lavishly, defiantly, in their homes, in their city clubs and their country clubs, before their children, their servants, their dependents, and the public. They decreed that it was bad form not to drink and serve liquor, and within the portals of fashionable society the man who refused to drink either because he did not want to or because he believed in obedience to law, was made to feel queer and uncomfortable. They and their sons carried hip flasks and made them the emblem of warm and genial hospitality. They patronized and protected the bootleggers they were so solemnly denouncing, and through them poured their millions into the underworld to finance the smugglers, rum runners, hijackers and gangsters about whom they expressed such righteous indignation. Nothing was left undone that would contribute to bootlegging, drinking and contempt for law. With unspeakable effrontery, they declared that prohibition had caused all the lawlessness, corruption and crime for which they themselves were responsible. Everywhere and constantly prohibition was attacked by high-sounding academic arguments, by misrepresentations, and by sneers and ribald jests.

When the wet propaganda had reached the zenith of its recklessness, the Alcohol Information Committee was organized. Among its seventy members were many nationally known economists, scientists, educators, sociologists, philanthropists, physicians, journalists, lawyers, judges, business men, statesmen, clergymen and rabbis. Their distinction was based not alone upon the fact that they had demonstrated the highest ability in their chosen calling, but also on the fact that they were known to be disinterested, socially minded and unpurchasable. The committee elected as its president Thomas Nixon Carver, head of the department of political economy of Harvard University, and announced that it was "educational, nonsectarian, nonpolitical," and that its purpose was "to promote, sponsor and distribute information on problems concerning beverage alcohol and the working of the Eighteenth Amendment." Under its auspices, books and pamphlets were published covering every aspect of these problems. The evidence was assembled and stated in a careful and scientific manner. The reasoning showed intelligence and conscience functioning at their best, and the statements were restrained and conservative. The American Business Men's Research Foundation made an impartial and exhaustive survey of conditions and issued statements containing authentic information. A study of this literature would have convinced every candid and disinterested person that the whole wet propaganda was born of selfishness, greed and corrupt politics, that it was being promoted by sophistry, fraud and coercion, and that in spite of lax enforcement and sabotage, prohibition was succeeding and advancing the economic, social and spiritual welfare of the people. The wets, however, through their control of the instruments of publicity, were able to lay down a barrage so heavy and so effective that the truth could not break through and the people were permitted to hear only the ceaseless rat-tat-tat of the wet propaganda.

Chapter Seven

How And Why America Went Dry

ONE OF the methods used to make the people hate the Eighteenth Amendment was to falsify its nature, its purpose and the method of its adoption. It was said that it was a sumptuary measure, a blue law, an interference with personal liberty, the destruction of local self-government and the rights of the states, a police measure having no place in the Constitution; that it was the result of a mania for legislation, of Wilsonian idealism and of war hysteria; that the people had not been allowed to pass upon it, that it was forced through by pressure groups, by organized minorities, by fanatics from the corn belt, and that it was slipped over by the Anti-Saloon League "while the boys were at the front." The people were continually bombarded with statements of which the following are typical: "Prohibition was sneaked over under cover of the prevalent hysterical tendency of the people of the United States to save and sacrifice to defeat the Kaiser"; "The Eighteenth Amendment, bootlegged into the Constitution in a time of stress, finds no justification in the conscience of the American people, but only in the peculiar conscience of moral reformers"; "What bayonets and Thaddeus Stevens did to bring about the ratification of the reconstruction amendments, the Anti-Saloon League and allied organizations for the reform of the habits of man did to write the prohibition amendment into the Constitution"; "If prohibition is right, then liberty is wrong. The two could not have dwelt together in any era of our country's history."

The introduction to the book of cartoons circulated by the AAPA contained this sentence:

"Thou shalt live, not according to thy conscience, but according to mine," is carrying on the traditions of Torquemada and of the Spanish Inquisition, of the Massacre of St. Bartholomew, of the burning at the stake of Protestant by Catholic and Catholic by Protestant, of Cotton Mather's letter urging that Penn and his Quaker crew be captured on the high seas and sold into slavery, of Deodat Lawson and Nicholas Noyes urging on the persecution of the Salem "witches."

These assertions, made without evidence or argument, were intended to deceive and prejudice the hearer. Centuries ago sumptuary measures regulated the expenditures of the people. This is illustrated by a sumptuary ordinance of the city of Strassburg. It declared that "almost no difference between upper and lower ranks has been observed" and that "we shall keep a watchful eye upon men and women, young and old, who wear improper, luxurious clothing, and boldly despise our well meant reminders." In present-day popular usage, a blue law is one prohibiting Sabbath breaking, swearing, dancing, card playing and theatergoing. The wet propagandists liked especially to quote a medieval law that forbade a man to kiss his wife on Sunday. These measures of a day long past were associated in the minds of the people with religious bigotry and with the paternalistic and arbitrary government from which they had freed themselves by centuries of struggle. To make them believe that the Eighteenth Amendment was a revival of ancient sumptuary and blue laws was to turn loose upon that amendment age-old resentments and hatreds. To connect the amendment with the overthrow of personal liberty, local self-government and state rights, was to visit upon it the hatred the people had come to feel against George III as they read the Declaration of Independence.

These statements had not the slightest foundation in fact. National prohibition was not forced upon the American people; it originated with them and was their achievement. The movement started in neighborhood meetings, in schools and churches, and was carried on by innumerable temperance societies, churches, colleges, women's organizations, social workers, philanthropists, physicians, laborers and leaders of industry. In the end, it had the support of practically every element except the liquor interests, the underworld and liquor addicts, and politicians desiring their support. After more than a century of experiment, discussion and struggle, the people forced the adoption of the Eighteenth Amendment. Their purpose was not to regulate morals or abridge liberty, but to destroy a lawless, antisocial business that was injurious to the public welfare and a menace to their institutions.

Early Struggles with the Liquor Traffic

There is not space here for an extended history of the prohibition movement, but a few characteristic events and statements will illustrate its origin and the character and motives of its supporters.[1]

Writing in his diary on February 29, 1760, John Adams drew a graphic picture of the social and moral evils of the liquor traffic, and continued:

> But the worst effect of all, and which ought to make every man who has the least sense of his privileges tremble, these houses are become the nurseries of our legislators. An artful man, who has neither sense nor sentiment, may, by gaining a little sway among the rabble of a town, multiply taverns and dramshops and thereby secure the votes of taverner and retailer and of all; and the multiplication of taverns will make many, who may be induced to flip and rum, to vote for any man whatever.

Half a century later, in 1811, Adams wrote to Dr. Rush of having been

> fired with a zeal amounting to enthusiasm against ardent spirits, the multiplication of taverns, retailers, dramshops and tippling houses, and grieved to the heart to see the number of idlers, thieves, sots, and consumptive patients made for the physicians in these infamous seminaries.[2]

On February 27, 1777, the Continental Congress adopted the following resolution:

> That it be recommended to the several legislatures of the United States immediately to pass laws the most effectual for putting an immediate stop to the pernicious practice of distilling grain, by which the most extensive evils are likely to be derived, if not quickly prevented.

In 1785, Dr. Benjamin Rush of Philadelphia, a signer of the Declaration of Independence, published his celebrated essay, *The Effects of Ardent Spirits upon the Human Mind and Body*. Summarizing the evidence he had presented, he said:

Thus we see poverty and misery, crimes and infamy, disease and death, are all the natural and usual consequences of the intemperate use of ardent spirits.

After giving a list of diseases caused by the use of alcohol, he continued:

Most of the diseases which have been enumerated are of a mortal nature. They are more certainly induced, and terminate more speedily in death, when spirits are taken in such quantities, and at such times, to produce frequent intoxication; but it may serve to remove an error with which some intemperate people console themselves, to remark that ardent spirits often bring on fatal diseases without producing drunkenness. I have known many persons destroyed by them who were never completely intoxicated during the whole course of their lives.

Following the publication of this essay, temperance societies were organized throughout the country and every year the agitation against the use of liquor became more widespread and effective. In 1826, the American Temperance Society was formed and Lyman Beecher published his famous six sermons on intemperance.

By the close of 1829, eleven state temperance societies had been formed and there were 1,000 local societies and 100,000 members. By May 1831, there were state societies in 19 states and 3,000 local societies which were reported to number 300,000 members. By the end of 1833 there were 5,000 societies with more than a million members and by 1835 the reform had advanced with such momentum that the Eighth Annual Report of the American Temperance Society stated that more than 8,000 temperance societies had been formed, embracing, it was thought, more than 1,500,000 members. The total population of the United States, according to the census of 1830, was less than 13,000,000. . . . In 1837 the Eighth Annual Report of the New York City Temperance Society reported a membership of 88,076 out of a total population that year of 290,000. Nearly one-third of all the people of the nation's largest city were enrolled members of temperance societies.[3]

Originally the agitation was against the use of distilled liquor. It was found, however, that the use of wine and beer increased, and that intemperance and all the other evils of the liquor traffic resulted from the use of these beverages. To meet this situation, the second national temperance convention held in 1836 declared for total abstinence from all intoxicating liquor.

As experience had demonstrated that alcohol was injurious to the individual and that the places where it was sold were centers of drunkenness, vice and crime, the responsible people of the country began to arrive at the very definite conclusion that the liquor traffic was not a legitimate business that should be licensed, but an antisocial and criminal business that should be suppressed. In 1829, Lyman Beecher said that "the traffic in these liquors is wrong and should be abandoned as a great national evil is evident." In 1833, President Wayland of Brown University wrote: "I think the prohibition of the traffic in ardent spirits a fit subject for legislative enactment and I believe the most happy results would flow from such prohibition." In the same year, President Humphrey of Amherst College said: "It is as plain to me as the sun in a clear summer sky that the license laws of our country constitute one of the main pillars on which the stupendous fabric of intemperance now rests."

In 1837 the legislature of Maine appointed a joint special committee to consider the license system of the state. Its report, presented by its chairman, General James Appleton, is one of the classics of the prohibition movement. It was not a statement of theories but of facts that had been established by generations of experience. General Appleton said:

> We shall not question that it was the design of the license law to regulate and restrict the sale of ardent spirits and even to prevent its abuse; but our present inquiry is not with the design, but the actual tendency of the law. This, we believe, has been to promote intemperance, to give it being and to continue it down to the present time.

It first assumes what the united testimony of physicians and thousands of others has proved false, that alcohol is necessary for common use, and then makes provision that there shall be no deficiency, by making it the interest of a select few to keep it for sale. The mere circumstance, whether few or many keep it for sale, is unimportant, provided those who are licensed keep sufficient to supply the demand. It is the inevitable tendency of the shop and barroom to decoy men from themselves and from their self-control; and our whole experience under the license laws of the state has proved how hopeless it is that such places should exist and men not become intemperate. If the poison were not freely offered for sale under the sanction of the law, it could not — it would not be purchased. . . .

Your committee is not only of the opinion that the law giving the right to sell ardent spirits should be repealed, but that a law should be passed to prohibit the traffic in them; except so far as the arts or the practice of medicine may be concerned. The reasons for such a law are as numerous as the evils of intemperance. Such a law is required for the same reason that we make a law to prevent the sale of unwholesome meats; or the law for the removal of any nuisance; or any other laws which have for their object to secure the good of the people of the state in the quiet and peaceable enjoyment of their rights, and against any practice that endangers the health and life of the citizens, or which threatens to subvert our civil rights and overthrow our free government. We would prohibit the sale of ardent spirits because intemperance can never be suppressed without such prohibition. There is no more reason for supposing that this evil can be restricted without law, than for supposing that you can restrain theft, or gambling, or any other crime without law.

The Independent Order of Good Templars was organized in 1851 and by 1874 had 617,000 members. In 1859 it adopted the following platform:

1. Total abstinence from all intoxicating liquor as a beverage.

2. No license in any form, or under any circumstances, for the sale of such liquors as a beverage.

3. The absolute prohibition of the manufacture, importation and sale of intoxicating liquors for such purposes — prohibited by the will of the people, expressed in due form of law, with the penalties deserved for a crime of such enormity.

4. The creation of a healthy public opinion upon the subject by the active dissemination of truth in all the modes known to an enlightened philanthropy.

5. The election of good, honest men to administer the law.

6. Persistence in efforts to save individuals and communities from so direful a scourge, against all forms of opposition and difficulty, until our success is complete and universal.

In 1853, Abraham Lincoln signed his name to a request that an address by the Reverend James Smith of Springfield, Illinois, be published and circulated. That address contained the following:

> The liquor traffic is a cancer in society, eating out its vitals and threatening destruction; and all attempts to regulate the cancer will not only prove abortive but will aggravate the evil. No, there must be no more attempts to regulate the cancer; for until this is done all classes must continue to be exposed to become victims of strong drink. . . . The most effectual remedy would be the passage of a law altogether abolishing the liquor traffic, except for the mechanical, chemical, medical, and sacramental purposes, and so framed that no principle of the constitution of the states or of the United States be violated.

Prior to 1850, a number of the states had passed laws for the purpose of restraining the liquor traffic. Certain of these laws were challenged in the United States Supreme Court, and in 1847 that court definitely established the right of the states in the exercise of their police power to destroy the traffic in intoxicating liquors. Mr. Justice Grier said:

> The true question presented by these cases, and one which I am not disposed to evade, is whether the states have a right to prohibit the sale and consumption of an article of commerce which they believe to be pernicious in its effects, and the cause of disease, pauperism and crime. . . . Without attempting to define what are the peculiar subjects or limits of this power, it may safely be affirmed that every law for the restraint and punishment of crime, for the preservation of the public peace, health and morals, must come within this category. . . . It is not necessary, for the sake of justifying the state legislation now under consideration, to array the appalling statistics of misery, pauperism, and

crime, which have their origin in the abuse or use of ardent spirits. The police power, which is exclusively in the states, is alone competent to the correction of these great evils, and all measures of restraint or prohibition necessary to effect the purpose are within the scope of that authority.[4]

The Problem of Enforcement

So widespread and intense was the popular feeling against the social and political evils caused by the liquor traffic that in the four years from 1851 to 1855, thirteen states enacted prohibition laws and the movement gained great headway in many other states. It was found, however, that both drinkers and sellers of liquor were utterly lawless and would obey the law only to the extent they were forced to, and that those engaged in the liquor traffic were able, by mobilizing for political action the lowest elements of the community, to elect public officials who would make no attempt to enforce the law. It was evident, therefore, that the next move in the fight would be to arouse the moral forces of the nation to the necessity of electing to office men who would both enact and enforce prohibition laws. A study of the history of the period leaves little doubt that if the attention and moral energy of the people had not become absorbed by the slavery question, they would have gone forward to the solution of the enforcement problem, the purchase and sale of liquor would have been confined to those belonging definitely to the criminal class, and the question would have been settled.

The spirit of the time is illustrated by the action of New York. In 1854 a prohibition law was passed by the legislature and vetoed by Governor Seymour. In 1855, the friends of prohibition, including such men as Horace Greeley and Henry J. Raymond, editor of the New York *Times,* called a state convention and adopted the following resolution:

> We regard the enactment of a prohibition law as the greatest and most vital issue of state policy now before the people. . . . We cannot subordinate this question to any other or defer its settlement to a more convenient season.

We ask a legislature that will enact such a law, a governor who will approve it, and magistrates and other officers who will enforce it; and to these ends, we solemnly pledge our influence and our suffrages.

Candidates pledged to prohibition were nominated and elected in spite of one of the most intense and highly organized campaigns the wets had ever conducted up to that time. Governor Seymour, who was given the solid support of the liquor interests, received only one-third of the votes. A prohibition law was passed and went into effect on July 4, 1855. An unfavorable court decision, opposition of the liquor dealers, and the slavery agitation, resulted in the failure of the law.

The story in the other states was similar. The prohibition movement was temporarily brought to a halt by the Civil War and the moral lapse that resulted from it, and by the increase in the foreign-born population, its concentration in cities and its manipulation by politicians.

Two events of far-reaching importance were the passage of the Internal Revenue Act of 1862, imposing a tax upon alcoholic liquors, and the organization in the same year of the United States Brewers' Association. The Internal Revenue Act met with vigorous opposition. Senator Wilson of Massachusetts pointed out that it would give respectability to the liquor business and enable those engaged in it to feel that they were acting under the protection of the federal government. Senator Pomeroy of Kansas said that the man who has paid his license " can go about the community with perfect impunity and can make as many widows and orphans and produce as much poverty, degradation and crime as he chooses," since he has " paid for the privilege of doing it." The act raised the manufacture and sale of liquor from the status of a low, disreputable trade to that of a recognized, legitimate business that could, with absolute assurance, form a national organization for its protection and promotion. All the methods which selfishness and greed could devise for creating an appetite for alcoholic drinks and spreading drunkenness and vice in the community took on an aspect of legality and respectability.

From another point of view, the Internal Revenue Act proved

to be a major moral disaster. Although passed to help meet the extraordinary expenses of the war, it was found to be a convenient form of taxation and was retained and became a permanent and fruitful source of revenue. It thus put the government into partnership with the liquor traffic and enabled it to share in the profits which increased as the drink habit spread and fastened itself more firmly upon the people. This meant that the taxpayers of the country obtained a direct financial interest in the liquor business and that its retention and extension would decrease their federal taxes, whatever its toll might be in other fields.

Five months after the passage of the Internal Revenue Act, the United States Brewers' Association was formed. The objectives and methods of the association are shown by statements of its officers and resolutions adopted at its annual meetings.

In 1868, the association's president stated that its object was

> to secure candidates for the legislature, who would, without regard to political party, promote and protect the brewing interest. Neither means nor money were spared. The entire German population was enlisted. Editorials were published in sixty different newspapers; thirty thousand campaign circulars were distributed.

In 1871 the association adopted the following resolution:

> The committee on agitation is hereby authorized and directed to select in each congressional district three brewers residing therein as a local and provisional organizing committee for such district, whose duty it shall be to organize by means best suited to the locality all the defenders of the rights of man . . . in order to defeat at all elections any candidates for office whose success might give encouragement to temperance fanatics and religious hypocrites to carry out their proposed proscriptive, injurious and dangerous plans.

From the date of its organization to the present time, it has been the business of the members of this association to organize the dregs of the country for political action, and with the power thus acquired, and by the use of money, to terrorize and debauch politicians and secure the nomination and election of public officials who would be subservient to their demands, and to compel legislative and administrative officials to oppose the enactment and enforcement of laws that would in any way restrain their business.

During this period, many other organizations were formed, such as the National Wholesale Liquor Dealers' Association, the National Retail Liquor Dealers' Association, the National Association of Wine and Spirit Representatives, the United States Manufacturers' and Merchants' Association, the Personal Liberty League, and others. All these organizations worked together to control the politics of the country and to protect and extend the traffic in intoxicating drinks.

But there were forces on the other side also. The Sons of Temperance, founded in 1842, the National Temperance Society, founded in 1865, and other organizations, waged a vigorous warfare on the liquor traffic during the sixties. The sixth national temperance convention, held in Cleveland, adopted the following resolution:

Whereas, the liquor dealers of our country have declared the traffic in intoxicating drinks to be a legitimate part of American commerce, and deny the right to prohibit or restrict the same, and through their leagues and congress have repeatedly avowed their purpose to vote for no man in favor of total abstinence, and have constantly used their political power for the continuance of their trade, and have in the past received the countenance of political parties in support of the positions thus assumed; therefore,

Resolved, that, in behalf of the public peace and welfare, we accept the issue, and will meet them at the polls in resistance to these iniquitous demands.

Resolved, that temperance, having its political as well as moral aspects and duties, demands the persistent use of the ballot for its promotion; and the convention urge the friends of the cause to refuse to vote for any candidate who denies the application of the just powers of civil government to the suppression of the liquor traffic, and exhort the friends of temperance, by every practicable method in their several localities, to secure righteous political action for the advancement of the cause.

The Churches and Prohibition

In every rural community, village and city in the United States, the churches of all denominations carried on a vigorous and ceaseless fight against the use of alcoholic beverages. Father Mathew, Archbishop Ireland and other prominent Catholics, were leaders in the movement. Speaking to American Catholics in 1887, Pope Leo XIII said:

> We have rejoiced to learn with what energy and zeal, by means of various excellent associations and especially through the Catholic Total Abstinence Union, you combat the destructive vice of intemperance. For it is well known to us how ruinous, how deplorable, is the injury, both to faith and to morals, that is to be feared from intemperance in drink, nor can we sufficiently praise the prelate of the United States who recently in the plenary council of Baltimore, with weightiest words condemned this abuse, declaring it to be a perpetual incentive to sin and a fruitful root of all evils, plunging the families of the intemperate into direst ruin, and dragging numberless souls down to everlasting perdition; declaring, moreover, that the faithful who yield to this vice of intemperance become thereby a scandal to non-Catholics, and a great hindrance to the propagation of the true religion.
>
> Hence we esteem worthy of all commendation the noble resolve of your pious associations by which they pledge to abstain totally from every kind of intoxicating drink. . . . Let pastors, therefore, do their best to drive the plague of intemperance from the fold of Christ by assiduous preaching and exhortation, and to shine before all as models of abstinence, that so many calamities with which this vice threatens both church and state, may, by their strenuous endeavors, be averted.[5]

Other statements by distinguished Catholic leaders were equally vigorous. Cardinal Manning declared:

> The chief bar to the working of the Holy Spirit of God in the souls of men and women, is intoxicating drink. I know of no antagonist to the Holy Spirit more direct, more subtle, more ubiquitous. The drink trade is our shame, scandal and sin, and unless brought under by the will of the people, it will be our downfall. The ever increasing alcoholism is the open wound from which the race may bleed to death.[6]

Archbishop Ireland also expressed himself unequivocally:

We have seen there is no hope for improving in any way or form the liquor traffic; there is nothing now to be done but to wipe it out completely. The state alone can save us. Would God place in my hand a wand with which to dispel the evil of intemperance, I would strike the door of every saloon, of every distillery, of every brewery, until the accursed traffic should be wiped from the face of the earth.[7]

A few statements will illustrate the position taken by every Protestant denomination in the land. In 1855, the General Assembly of the Presbyterian Church said:

The experience of two hundred years proves that this evil can never be removed or effectively resisted while the traffic in intoxicating liquors is continued, it being necessary, if we would stop the effect, to remove the cause. . . . Laws prohibiting the sale of intoxicating drinks can interfere with the right of no man; because no man has a right of any name or nature inconsistent with the public good, or at war with the welfare of the community; it being a well known, universally acknowledged maxim of law that " no man has a right to use his own to the injury of his neighbor." [8]

And in 1883 it declared:

In view of the evils wrought by this scourge of our race, the assembly would hail with acclamations of joy and thanksgiving the utter extermination of the traffic in intoxicating liquors as a beverage by the power of our Christian conscience, public opinion and the strong arm of the civil law.[9]

In 1892 the Methodist Episcopal Church issued the following statement:

Attitude toward the Traffic. — We reiterate the language of the episcopal address of 1888: " The liquor traffic is so pernicious in all its bearings, so inimical to the interests of honest trade, so repugnant to the moral sense, so injurious to the peace and order of society, so hurtful to the home, to the church and to the body politic and so utterly antagonistic to all that is precious in life, that the only proper attitude toward it, for Christians, is that of relentless hostility. It can never be legalized without sin."

We concur in the episcopal address of 1892, where it is declared: " In our judgment, the saloon is an unmixed evil, full of diabolism, a disgrace to our civilization, the chief corrupter of political action and a continual menace to the order of society and the peace and purity of our homes."

Political Action. — We recommend all members of the Methodist Church who enjoy the elective franchise, to so use that solemn trust as to promote the rescue of our country from the guilt and dishonor which have been brought upon it by a criminal complicity with the liquor traffic.[10]

In 1890 the Baptist Church resolved:

That we declare ourselves among its [the liquor traffic's] most pronounced and relentless foes, believing that it has no defensible right to exist, and that it can never be reformed; and that it stands condemned by its unrighteous fruits as a thing unchristian, un-American, and perilous utterly to every interest of life.

That we stand pledged by every legitimate means to work and pray and vote for the absolute abolition and overthrow of the iniquitous traffic in state and nation.[11]

The Prohibition Party

In 1869, the Prohibition party was formed and for sixty years carried on a vigorous, nation-wide campaign for national prohibition. The members of this party were largely of pre-revolutionary stock and represented the highest ideals of individual character and social responsibility, and among their leaders were some of the most effective campaign speakers in the country. The party was organized in all the states, nominated candidates for offices local, state and national, conducted vigorous and effective campaigns, and exerted an influence out of all proportion to the number of votes polled at particular elections. Multitudes of people were converted to the principle of national prohibition who did not believe that the way to achieve it was through the Prohibition party.

Its position on the liquor question is shown by the following plank of its national platform adopted in 1876:

The legal prohibition in the District of Columbia, the territories, and in every other place subject to the laws of Congress, of the importation, exportation, manufacture and traffic of all alcoholic beverages, as high crimes against society; an amendment to the national Constitution to render these prohibitory measures universal and permanent; and the adoption of treaty stipulations with foreign powers to prevent the importation and exportation of all alcoholic beverages.

In 1887, Senator Blair of New Hampshire introduced into the Senate the following proposed amendment to the Constitution of the United States:

Section 1. The manufacture, importation, exportation, transportation and sale of all alcoholic liquors as a beverage shall be, and hereby is, forever prohibited in the United States and in every place subject to their jurisdiction.
Section 2. Congress shall enforce this article by all needful legislation.

The amendment was favorably reported to the Senate by the committee on education and labor. In the House, it was referred to the Judiciary Committee, which agreed to an adverse report.

Other Organizations against the Liquor Traffic

The liquor traffic aroused the deepest resentment on the part of the women of the country because of its destructive influence upon their husbands, their sons, their homes and the communities in which they lived. In 1873, they launched the movement known as the Woman's Crusade. They formed visitation committees and went to the saloons and pleaded with the keepers to abandon their debauching traffic. The appeal to the liquor dealers that was used throughout the country was as follows:

Knowing, as you do, the fearful effects of intoxicating drinks, we, the women of Washington Court House, after earnest prayer and deliberation, have decided to appeal to you to desist from this ruinous traffic that our husbands and brothers, and especially our sons, be no longer exposed to this terrible temptation, and that we may no longer see them led into those paths which go down to sin and bring both soul and body to destruction. We appeal to the better instincts of your hearts, in the name of desolate homes, blasted hopes, ruined lives, widowed hearts, for the honor of our community, for our happiness, for the good name of our town, in the name of God who will judge you and us, for the sake of your own souls which are to be saved or lost. We beg, we implore you to cleanse yourselves from this heinous sin, and place yourselves in the ranks of those who are striving to elevate and ennoble themselves and their fellow men. And to this we ask you to pledge yourselves.

Although many saloons were closed, they soon reopened and it was found that such appeals were futile.

As a result of this movement, the Woman's Christian Temperance Union was formed in 1874. This organization enlisted in the prohibition movement the best and most intelligent women in every community in America. Their attitude is clearly indicated by the following statements of their great leader, Frances E. Willard. Addressing the union's national convention of 1881, which met in Washington, D. C., she said:

Here, then, at the nation's capital, let us turn our faces toward the beckoning future; here, where the liquor traffic pours in each year its revenue of gold, stained with the blood of our dearest and best, let us set up our home protection standard in the name of the Lord! [12]

And in her presidential address in 1883, Miss Willard said:

We have seen that the principle of prohibition must be grounded in organic law beyond the reach of demagogues and that this must be done through non-partisan methods by means of a constitutional amendment. We have seen, however, that *enforcement* can only be secured by *the election of officers who will enforce.*[13]

Before the platform committee of the Republican national convention of 1884, Miss Willard declared:

I come on behalf of millions of women, good and true, but grieved and sorrowful, to ask that the guarantees and safeguards of law shall be stripped from the saloons of my country; that their tarnished gold shall no more pollute our treasury and that the land we love may at once and forever go out of partnership with the liquor traffic.[14]

The story of the labors and the achievements of this great body of intelligent and patriotic women is one of the most inspiring chapters in the moral history of humanity.

In 1887, the Intercollegiate Prohibition Association was founded and by 1893 local organizations had been formed in one hundred forty-six colleges. The movement grew steadily until practically all the colleges of the country were organized. Courses of study covering every aspect of the liquor problem were prepared and carefully and systematically pursued by the members of the association. The organizations in the different colleges promoted the use of these study courses, held meetings for the discussion of the question, and sponsored local, state, interstate and national oratorical contests. It was estimated that between 1900 and 1917, ten thousand original orations were prepared and delivered by members of the association. Every year hundreds of well informed, highly trained and earnest college men and women spent their summer vacations participating in prohibition campaigns and speaking and working for the cause in every part of the country. After their graduation, they became leaders in the movement in the communities in which they located. As a result of the initiative of the association, courses on the liquor problem were introduced into the curricula of more than a hundred colleges and universities. This movement among the colleges furnished the prohibition cause with many of its most effective workers.

The Anti-Saloon League was formed in 1893. This organization fought the liquor traffic on every front. It engaged in educational and political work; it advocated local option, state-wide and national prohibition. Its principal function, however, was not to create prohibition sentiment. As a result of a century of education and agitation, that sentiment had become nation-wide and had attained overwhelming strength. The league was a product of that sentiment which it made effective. It united the members of temperance societies, churches, colleges, the medical profession, industry, and all political parties into an effective fighting organization whose single object was the destruction of the liquor traffic. It investigated the records and ascertained the attitudes of candidates for office, determined which of them would be of greatest service to the cause of prohibition, made this information public, urged support, regardless of their party affiliations, by all who were opposed to the saloon. It was only after years of experience had demonstrated to the moral forces of the nation that they could repose absolute confidence in the intelligence, political sagacity and integrity of the leaders of the league, that it rose to a position of power.

Because of the fact that it was practical and effective the league was made the object of every form of abuse, slander and falsehood that the venom of the liquor interests could inspire. It was said that it was a highly organized and fanatical minority which achieved its results by the ruthless methods of the powerful lobbies it maintained at the seats of government. This was the exact opposite of the truth. As Professor Peter Odegard says, "It should be kept in mind that whatever power or influence the league developed in legislative lobbies is attributable to the votes of the people back home who take their political advice from the league." [15]

Numerous other organizations have been engaged in the fight against the liquor traffic. Every Protestant church in the country had its board of temperance. Among the other organizations were the following: World League Against Alcoholism, World's Woman's Christian Temperance Union, International Congress Against Alcoholism, World Student Federation Against Alcoholism, Scientific Temperance Federation, National Temperance Council, International Reform Federation, World Prohibition Federation, National Civic League, National Temperance Bureau, Flying Squadron, Templars of Honor and Temperance, Irish Temperance Society of America, Association in Support of National Prohibition, Committee on Promotion of Temperance Legislation in the National Congress, Native Races Anti-Liquor Traffic Committee, Citizens' Committee of One Thousand, National United Committee for Law Enforcement, Woman's National Committee for Law Enforcement, National Women's

Democratic Enforcement League, Catholic Clergy Prohibition League, Catholic Total Abstinence Union of America, Association of Catholics Favoring Prohibition.

The Professions and the Press

Bodies of disinterested and public-spirited men and women, who were working for the improvement of social conditions, found that alcohol was the most effective ally of vice. Extracts from the reports of two such bodies reflect the findings of all.

In 1911, the Chicago Vice Commission, which was composed of leading business and professional men of Chicago, after exhaustive investigation of the subject of vice, rendered its report to the mayor and the city council. In this report it said:

> In the commission's consideration and investigation of the social evil, it found as the most conspicuous and important element in connection with the same, next to the house of prostitution itself, was the saloon, and the most important financial interest, next to the business of prostitution, was the liquor interest. As a contributory influence to immorality and the business of prostitution there is no interest so dangerous and so powerful in the city of Chicago.

In 1914, the legislature of the state of Wisconsin appointed a committee to investigate the white slave traffic and kindred subjects in that state. In its report to the legislature the committee said:

> The reports of the investigators indicate that in each city the most extensively used institution for the fostering of prostitution is the saloon; that in each city visited certain saloons appear to be the headquarters and meeting place for men and women seeking immoral relations; that of all men connected in any way with commercial vice, bartenders are the best informed and best able to direct customers to women and resorts where prostitution may be had. One madam examined by the committee acknowledged that when the sale of liquor was prohibited in her resort her customers fell off fully one-half. . . .
>
> The committee finds that the chief direct cause of the downfall of women and girls is the close connection between alcoholic drink and commercialized vice. Women obtain liquor in palm gardens, wine

rooms, saloons and dance halls. To these places they are frequently taken by their companions and given liquor until their senses are deadened, after which the evil design sought is accomplished. After the first offense the career of a woman is apt to be downward at a rapid rate.

No one can read the reports of investigators or the testimony of witnesses taken at the hearings, as to the cause of the downfall of girls, and not be convinced at once that more women have fallen on account of their use of liquor, and because of frequenting wine rooms, palm gardens or saloons with bed accommodations, than from any other cause.

The leading physicians of the country officially condemned the use of alcohol for beverage purposes. In 1914, the national convention of alienists and neurologists unanimously adopted the following resolutions:

Whereas, in the opinion of the alienists and neurologists of the United States, in convention assembled, it has been definitely established that alcohol when taken into the system acts as a definite poison to the brain and other tissues; and

Whereas, the effects of this poison are directly or indirectly responsible for a large proportion of the insane, epileptic, feeble-minded and other forms of mental, moral, and physical degeneracy; and

Whereas, the laws of many states make alcohol freely available for drinking purposes, and therefore cater to the physical, mental and moral degeneration of the people; and

Whereas, many hospitals for the insane and other public institutions are now compelled to admit and care for a multitude of inebriates; and

Whereas, many states already have established separate colonies for the treatment and re-education of such inebriates, with great benefit to the individuals and to the commonwealth; therefore be it

Resolved, that we unqualifiedly condemn the use of alcoholic beverages and recommend that the various state legislatures take steps to eliminate such use; and be it further

Resolved, that we recommend the general establishment by all states and territories of special colonies of hospitals for the care of inebriates; and be it further

Resolved, that organized medicine should initiate and carry on a systematic, persistent propaganda for the education of the public regarding the deleterious effects of alcohol; and be it further

Resolved, that the medical profession should take the lead in securing adequate legislation to the ends herein specified.

At its annual meeting in 1917, the American Medical Association adopted the following resolutions:

Whereas, we believe that the use of alcohol as a beverage is detrimental to the human economy; and

Whereas, its use in therapeutics as a tonic or stimulant or as a food has no scientific basis; therefore, be it

Resolved, that the American Medical Association opposes the use of alcohol as a beverage; and be it further

Resolved, that the use of alcohol as a therapeutic agent should be discouraged.

The statements of two men who were prominent in public life will illustrate the attitude of the political leaders of the prohibition movement. William Windom was for many years a leading senator of the United States and was secretary of the treasury in the cabinets of Presidents Garfield and Arthur. In 1887, he delivered an address in which he described conditions to which he had long been an eye-witness. He said:

The saloon creates a demand where none before existed that it may profit by supplying that demand. It artificially stimulates an evil habit that it may thrive by pandering to it. It methodically breeds debauchery, poverty, anarchy, and crime for pay. It purposely seeks to multiply the number of drinkers, and hence of drunkards. It invades every new community, demands tribute from every home, and lies in wait with fresh enticements for each new generation of youth. . . . Each one of our two hundred thousand drinking places forms a distinct center of aggressive forces and skillful devices for spreading the drink habit among men. Every plausible temptation and solicitation that trained talent can suggest are used to entrap the young, the ignorant, the toiling, the homeless, with the knowledge that a customer once secured is usually a customer for life. . . . Experience indicates that four-fifths of American drinking and drunkenness is due in the first instance not to any natural appetite of our people, but to the presence and sleepless efforts of this gigantic enginery, working seven days a week and twenty-four hours a day, unrestrained by any scruple and everywhere contemptuous of public and private right.

In 1912, Governor Hooper of Tennessee said:

When I appeal to the people for a legislature free from saloon domination, my appeal is not based alone upon grounds of temperance and morality. I want to say to the business men and taxpayers of this state that no valuable reform measure of any character can be secured at the hands of a legislature controlled by the whisky power. Why do I say this? Because the saloon lobby will always be found in alliance with every other corrupt and evil influence that infests the legislative halls. It cannot win alone. It wins in combination with other interests, political and financial, which have legislative axes to grind. This is not a fine-spun theory. It is a plain statement of a fact well known to every observer of politics and student of legislative history. A state and legislative ticket elected without the assistance of a whisky campaign fund will afford the people the greatest possible assurance of clean and progressive and reformatory legislation.

The press contented itself with describing some aspects of the situation. In its issue of March 2, 1884, the New York *Tribune* gave the following description of the liquor traffic:

It is impossible to examine any subject connected with the progress, the civilization, the physical well-being, the religious condition of the masses, without encountering this monstrous evil. It is the center of all social and political mischief. It paralyzes beneficent energies in every direction. It neutralizes educational agencies. It silences the voice of religion. It baffles penal reform. It obstructs political reform. It rears aloft a mass of evilly inspired power which at every salient point threatens social and national advance; which gives to ignorance and vice a greater potency than intelligence and virtue can command; which deprives the poor of the advantages of modern progress; which debauches and degrades millions, brutalizing and soddening them below the plane of healthy savagery.

On July 11, 1917, the following editorial appeared in the Chicago *Tribune:*

If the secret records of the brewing and distilling industry were ever brought to light they would tell a story of social and political corruption unequaled in the annals of our history. If the veritable narrative of the American saloon were ever written, it would make the decadence of Rome look like an age of pristine purity in comparison.

Whisky, wine and beer never caused half as much injury to society as the manufacturers and purveyors of these beverages. If these men have not made a practice of committing murder and arson, it is because these crimes did not seem immediately profitable. The liquor business has been the faithful ally of every vicious element in American life; it has protected criminals, it has fostered the social evil, and it has bribed politicians, juries and legislatures.

The inherent corruption has extended even to the so-called decent saloon. There are few that do not serve adulterated products and it is an unusual proprietor that is not more pleased when his patrons are getting drunk than when they keep sober. Philip Drunk stays longer and spends more money than Philip Sober. That is one reason why the saloons would rather sell ardent spirits than beer; they are more intoxicating.

We have been speaking of the "decent" saloons; the other variety is almost unspeakable. The smallest count in the indictment against the evil barroom is its persistent evasion of the law. We are not surprised to read that numerous Cook county roadhouses are operating without licenses, that they keep open on Sunday, or that they seem to exercise a mysterious control over public officials. Yet these are only minor offenses in the calendar of saloon iniquities.

The brewers have at times tried, or said they would try, to clean up the saloon business. The head of a great St. Louis brewery often told his confreres that it was the brewers' only salvation. The theory was accepted but the practice was always to expend every energy to sell one more keg of beer, even if it had to be sold to bootleggers and resort keepers.

It is for this reason that the prohibition movement has gained such strength. The demand for the abolition of the liquor traffic is the expression of a ripening conviction that it is conducted by nefarious means for nefarious ends.

"After the deluge" seems to have been the philosophy of the liquor men — but now the deluge seems to be on the point of breaking.

In 1890, the United States Supreme Court in the case of Crowley *vs.* Christensen declared:

By the general concurrence of opinion of every civilized and Christian community, there are few sources of crime and misery to society equal to the dramshop, where intoxicating liquors in small quantities, to be drunk at the time, are sold indiscriminately to all parties applying. The statistics of every state show a greater amount of crime and misery attributable to the use of ardent spirits obtained at the retail saloons than to any other source. The sale of such liquors in this way has therefore been, at all times, by the courts of every state, considered as the proper subject of legislative regulation.

Not only may a license be exacted from the keeper of the saloon before a glass of his liquors can be thus disposed of, but restrictions may be imposed as to the class of persons to whom they may be sold, and the hours of the day and the days of the week on which the saloons may be opened. Their sale in that form may be absolutely prohibited. It is a question of public expediency and public morality, and not of federal law. The police power of the state is fully competent to regulate the business — to mitigate its evils or to suppress it entirely. There is no inherent right in a citizen to thus sell intoxicating liquors by retail; it is not a privilege of a citizen of the state or of a citizen of the United States. As it is a business attended with danger to the community it may, as already said, be entirely prohibited, or be permitted under such conditions as will limit to the utmost its evils.[16]

Industry and Labor

As the machinery used in transportation and industry became more complicated, more powerful and more dangerous, it was imperative that it should be operated by normal men with clear heads and steady nerves. Total abstinence was required of practically all men engaged in the transportation business and a determined effort was being made to stop the use of alcohol by men engaged in other industries. The attitude of the industrial leaders of the country is illustrated by the action of the National Safety Council at its third annual congress, held in Chicago in 1914. There were present at this congress representatives of many of the leading industrial enterprises of the country, and among the many questions considered was the relation of the use of intoxicating drinks to accidents. At the conclusion of the discussion, the conference unanimously adopted the following resolution:

Whereas, it is recognized that the drinking of alcoholic stimulants is productive of a heavy percentage of accidents, and of diseases affecting the safety and efficiency of workmen; therefore, be it

Resolved, that it is the sense of this round-table meeting at the third annual congress of the National Safety Council, that it places itself on record as being in favor of eliminating the use of intoxicants in the industries of the nation.

Mr. Charles Merz states that the only element, in addition to the liquor interests, which opposed the Eighteenth Amendment was organized labor. He says:

It was the Distillers' Association of America which carried the fight to the state legislature in an effort to prevent ratification, organized emergency committees and attempted unsuccessfully to force a referendum vote in fourteen states. It was the United States Brewers' Association, and not an association interested in the theory of the Constitution or the Bill of Rights, which briefed the case against the Volstead Act and submitted its brief to the President with a petition for his veto. It was the firm of Feigenspan, New Jersey brewers, which employed Elihu Root and William D. Guthrie to carry a last desperate appeal to the Supreme Court of the United States.

Throughout the whole controversy over national prohibition from the time that Senator Sheppard's resolution for a constitutional amendment first appeared in Congress to the June day in 1920 when the Supreme Court upheld the Volstead Act, the opposition to this legislation had no funds, no organization and no real leadership except in so far as these elements were supplied by the liquor interests of the country.

With the exception of union labor, there were no important organizations arrayed in opposition to this program. There were no independent organizations in the field whose motives were disinterested and whose constituents were drawn from the rank and file of ordinary citizens.[17]

This opposition on the part of labor was more apparent than real. The unions from which it was supposed to come represented only a small portion of the laborers of the country and it was not based upon any reasoned conviction that the amendment was not socially desirable. In 1926, Mr. Charles Stelzle, an authority on labor questions, testifying before the Senate committee that investigated the national prohibition law, said:

The liquor men predicted that if the prohibition amendment was adopted, a million workingmen would lose their jobs. At first I was greatly impressed by this statement and I took measures to organize a committee which would find work for the men who would be thrown out of employment. I had had experience in this field because during the winter of 1914 and 1915 when nearly half a million people were out of work in New York city, I served as director of relief and emergency measures for Mayor Mitchell's committee on unemployment. But when I made my investigations as to the number of wage earners who were actually involved in this matter, I found that according to United States Census figures, only 69,620 wage earners were employed in breweries, distilleries and wineries, and of this total less than 15,000 were employed as brewers, distillers, maltsters and rectifiers.[18]

The brewers and distillers held before the laborers the bogy of a million idle men competing for their jobs. But the most important factor in the situation was labor politics. Samuel Gompers and other labor leaders held powerful and lucrative positions which they wished to retain. They were realists and they knew that the brewers and distillers, through their employes, could stir up trouble and compel them to defend their jobs or lose them. Their action in fomenting opposition to the Eighteenth Amendment among their members was simply the work of politicians "tending their fences." In no real sense did they represent labor and the opposition they secured was worked up rather than spontaneous and had no relation to the merits of the question.

When the amendment was before the lower House, Congressman Cooper of Ohio, who had been a laborer all his life and was a member of the Brotherhood of Locomotive Engineers, said:

I desire to say a word about the relation of the liquor traffic to organized labor. There is at this time an effort being made by the representatives of the liquor interests to give the impression that the labor unions of the country are opposed to the prohibition of the liquor traffic, and the members of this Congress are being threatened and flooded with numerous memorials, telegrams and petitions by these men, protesting against the passage of this resolution and pretending to speak for the workingmen of this country. I deny and challenge the statement that the laboring people and the thousands of members of organized labor are in sympathy with the un-American, licensed liquor traffic and that the beer keg and whisky bottle are their emblem. It is true that certain labor organizations are opposed to prohibition, but these men represent various crafts that are engaged in manufacture, sale and distribution of alcoholic liquors.

In 1915, the delegates to the triennial convention of the Brotherhood of Locomotive Engineers, representing about 70,000 members, unanimously adopted a resolution pledging this organization and its best efforts in support of the abolition of the liquor business. In a letter recently made public, Mr. Warren S. Stone, grand chief of the Brotherhood of Locomotive Engineers, has this to say concerning the question:

"We fight the liquor evil perhaps as hard as any of the churches. Liquor has no place in modern railroading. I never expect to be manager of a railroad, but if I were, a man could not work for me who would take a drink of liquor, either on or off duty. I would not make a difference between the two, because a man who will take a drink off duty is not fit to go on duty when his time comes. I fail to understand why our men do not come out in the open in certain localities and fight this enemy. It tends to destroy the home life, to lower the tone of the citizenship of the community, and the morals of the individual as well, to say nothing of his mental and physical health." [19]

The Demand for National Prohibition

By 1919, the liquor interests, the underworld, and politicians in wet communities stood practically alone in their defense of the liquor business. On the other hand, the intelligence, the realism, the moral idealism and the plain common sense of the American people had condemned it as a criminal that should be destroyed. But the intellectual and moral forces of the nation had not confined themselves to speeches and resolutions. In every part of the land they had been engaged in a desperate struggle to accomplish the extermination of the liquor traffic by governmental action. Prior to the adoption of the Eighteenth Amendment, the District of Columbia, Alaska and Puerto Rico were dry by congressional action; thirty-three states were dry by state action; and large portions of the remaining states were dry by local option. Fosdick and Scott state the situation as follows:

The thirty-three prohibition states in 1919, prior to the adoption of the amendment, comprised approximately 80 per cent of the area of the United States and 52 per cent of the population. If dry local option areas in nonprohibition states are included, the total dry area at this time comprised 95 per cent of the country and involved 68 per cent of the population.[20]

In 1911 Mr. Purley Baker, general superintendent of the Anti-Saloon League, said:

The states are helpless to enforce their own laws because the federal government persists in backing the speak-easy keeper and the blind-tiger keeper. If this present Congress, like its predecessors, refuses to hear the appeal of the people and give adequate relief, it is time to stop state legislation while we devote ourselves to the specific task of creating a Congress that will give relief. It is time our league attorneys and others . . . agree upon a bill that will be effective, and in their judgment constitutional . . . and let everybody get behind that bill and never stop . . . until it is a law upon the statute books.

To meet this situation, the Webb-Kenyon Bill was introduced into Congress in 1912. It provided

that the shipment or transportation in any manner or by any means whatsoever of any spiritous, vinous, malted, fermented, or other intoxicating liquor of any kind, including beer, ale, or wine, from one state, territory or district of the United States . . . to be received, possessed or kept, or in any manner used, either in the original package or otherwise, in violation of any law of such state, territory or district . . . is hereby prohibited.

In discussing the necessity for the law, Senator Kenyon said:

The need of such an act was expressed by the distinguished senior senator from Georgia, who has presided over the Senate with such ability and fairness, in his views submitted to Congress some years ago when Congress had under consideration a number of similar bills: "Briefly stated, the conditions which demand the passage of this or some similar bill are these: Every state in which the traffic in liquors has been prohibited by law is deluged with whisky sent in by people from other states under shelter of the interstate commerce law. There are daily trainloads of liquors in bottles, jugs and other packages sent into the state consigned to persons, real and fictitious, and every railway station and every express company office in the state are converted into the most extensive and active whisky shops, from which whisky is openly distributed in great quantities. Liquor dealers in other states secure the names of all persons in a community, and through the mails flood them with advertisements of whisky with the most liberal and attractive propositions for the sale and shipment of the same. Freed from the expense of the middleman, the distiller or dealer in other states is enabled to sell to the individual in the prohibition state at a less price than the purchaser formerly paid to the domestic whisky dealer. It is evident that under such circumstances the prohibition law of a state is practically nullified, and intoxicating liquors are imposed upon its people against the will of the majority." [21]

The bill was passed, receiving in the House 239 yeas and 64 nays. President Taft vetoed the bill on the ground that it was unconstitutional. The bill was passed over the President's veto by a vote of 63 to 21 in the Senate and 246 to 95 in the House.

That the wets understood the significance of this act of Congress is indicated by the following statement which appeared in the *National Liquor Dealers' Journal* for April 2, 1913:

The passage of the Webb-Kenyon Bill, its veto by President Taft and its victory over the veto by more than two-thirds majority apparently mark the climax of a movement that has been active for half a century. If the Supreme Court declares the act unconstitutional, it does not change the impressive fact that in the face of the united effort of all branches of the alcoholic liquor trade, the national Congress voted for the bill.

When the law came before the United States Supreme Court, it was sustained.

In spite of the Webb-Kenyon law, the liquor forces poured their liquor into dry states and communities and sent in money to bribe public officials and make a dead letter of the law. It became perfectly clear to the people that the liquor problem could be solved only by an amendment to the Constitution of the United States that would outlaw the liquor traffic on every foot of American soil and make available for its enforcement all the powers of the federal government. They saw that this was the only alternative to abject surrender. As they had no intention of giving up the fight, they settled down to work in grim earnest. In 1913, at a great national convention attended by prominent men and women from all walks of life and from every state in the Union, the dry forces launched their drive for a national prohibition amendment.

That the liquor dealers realized the meaning of this movement is shown by the following statement in the *National Liquor Dealers' Journal* for September 10, 1913:

> To us there is the handwriting on the wall and its interpretation spells doom. The liquor business is to blame. It seems incapable of learning any lesson of advancement or any motive but profit. To perpetuate itself it has formed alliances with the slums. . . . It deliberately aids the most corrupt political powers. . . . There are billions of property involved . . . but when the people decide that the truth is being told about the alcoholic liquor traffic, the money value will not count. . . .

On December 10, 1913, the following resolution was introduced in both houses of Congress:

> *Whereas,* exact scientific research has demonstrated that alcohol is a narcotic poison, destructive and degenerating to the human organism, and that its distribution as a beverage or contained in foods lays a staggering economic burden upon the shoulders of the people, lowers to an appalling degree the average standard of character of our citizenship, thereby undermining the public morals and the foundation of free institutions, produces widespread crime, pauperism and insanity, inflicts disease and untimely death upon hundreds of thousands of citizens, and blights with degeneracy their children unborn, threatening the future integrity and the very life of the nation; therefore be it
>
> *Resolved:* By the Senate and House of Representatives of the United States of America in Congress assembled (two-thirds of each House concurring therein), that the following amendment of the Constitution be, and hereby is proposed to the states, to become valid as a part of the

Constitution when ratified by the legislatures of the several states as provided by the Constitution:

The sale, manufacture for sale, transportation for sale, importation for sale, and exportation for sale, of intoxicating liquors for beverage purposes in the United States and all territory subject to the jurisdiction thereof, are forever prohibited. . . .

On December 22, 1914, the resolution passed the House by a vote of 197 to 190, but failed because it did not receive the necessary two-thirds vote. In 1916, the year before we entered the war, the opponents of the liquor traffic asked every candidate for the Senate and the lower House of Congress to give a pledge that he would vote to submit to the states a national prohibition amendment. They then conducted a vigorous campaign to elect men who had given that pledge and to defeat those who had not. The moment the results of the election were known, it was certain that the amendment would be submitted. Mr. Wayne B. Wheeler stated the situation:

On election night the lights burned late in our Washington office. Elsewhere our state workers were getting the returns. . . . We knew late election night that we had won. Many hours before the country knew whether Hughes or Wilson had triumphed, the dry workers throughout the nation were celebrating our victory. We knew that the prohibition amendment would be submitted to the states by the Congress just elected.[22]

This was five months before we entered the war and more than a year before any of " our boys were at the front."

The character of the discussion in Congress is illustrated by the following extract from a speech delivered by Senator Sherman of Illinois on the day the amendment was submitted:

It [the liquor traffic] has grown to astounding proportions. The longer it continues the greater its evils and the more potent its strength. . . . The men who have made it their instrument of pecuniary gain have assumed to control political parties, to threaten candidates, to decide elections, to administer civil government, to make new laws, to promote profitable evils, and contemptuously to break laws they cannot repeal.

The liquor interests have written their own indictment and accumulated the evidence justifying their own extinction. . . . A business whose system is lawlessness and whose finished product is a drunkard ought to have no lawful abiding place in this republic. It is an outlaw measured by its practices and a criminal tested by its results. A business that will not be regulated by law must at last be destroyed by law. The traffic in intoxicating liquor has refused to be regulated and therefore has earned the penalty of legislative extinction.[23]

In June 1917, the Judiciary Committee of the Senate recommended the passage of the amendment. In its report it said:

Deciding upon grounds like these, your committee are impressed by the overwhelming importance of the subject to the nation and to the world, and by the vast number, not to say the majority of the moral and intellectual forces of the country, which demand the submission of this joint resolution to the consideration of the states. We therefore report it favorably and recommend its passage.

In its report recommending the passage of the amendment, the Judiciary Committee of the House of Representatives said:

There is probably no other constitutional amendment that has been submitted to the states in the past that has been petitioned for so largely, and it would seem that whatever may be the individual views of members upon the merits of the moral question involved, the legislative duty to submit it is plain.

On December 18, 1917, the amendment was submitted to the states by a vote of 65 to 20 in the Senate and 282 to 128 in the House. At this time, none of the boys were at the front, and the action was taken by a Congress they had helped to elect. The amendment was promptly ratified by every state in the Union but Connecticut and Rhode Island. Eighty-five per cent of the members of the upper, and 79 per cent of the members of the lower houses voted for ratification. In twenty-one state legislatures not a single wet vote was cast. In a number of states, in which the wet sentiment was strongest, such as New York, Pennsylvania, Illinois and Wisconsin, action was taken by legislatures elected in 1918 after the amendment was submitted. In these states, ratification was made an issue in every legislative district and directly approved by the people.

The men who submitted and ratified the amendment were hard-headed, practical politicians who knew that if they were to be re-elected, they must comply with the wishes of the people of their states and districts. As prohibition had been a burning issue for years, they had gained an intimate knowledge of the sentiments of their constituents on that question and their action was dictated by that knowledge. There can be no question that it showed conclusively that the overwhelming majority of the people were determined that the nation should be purged of the liquor traffic and that the adoption of the amendment was the result of the irresistible pressure of public sentiment.

NOTES

1 Full and authoritative histories of the movement are given by D. Leigh Colvin, *Prohibition in the United States* (George H. Doran Co., 1926) and Ernest H. Cherrington, *The Evolution of Prohibition in the United States of America* (American Issue Press, 1920). A good short history of the movement is given by Earl L. Douglass, *Prohibition and Common Sense* (Alcohol Information Committee, 1931).

2 Quoted by Colvin, *op. cit.*, p. 14.

3 *Ibid.*, pp. 15–16.

4 License Cases, 5, Howard 504.

5 Quoted by Colvin, *op. cit.*, pp. 268–69.

6 Quoted by Mabel Willebrandt, *The Inside of Prohibition* (Bobbs-Merrill Co., 1929), p. 343.

7 *Ibid.*, p. 344.

8 Colvin, *op. cit.*, p. 265.

9 *Ibid.*

10 *Ibid.*, pp. 266–67.

11 *Ibid.*, p. 267.

12 *Ibid.*, p. 279.

13 *Ibid.*, p. 280.

14 *Ibid.*, p. 147.

15 Peter Odegard, *Pressure Politics* (Columbia University Press, 1928), p. 105.

16 137, U. S. 86.

17 Charles Merz, *The Dry Decade* (Doubleday, Doran & Co., 1930), p. 209.

18 Report of Hearings, II, 1288.

19 *Congressional Record*, Vol. 56, Part 1, 65th Congress, 2nd Session, pp. 428–29.

20 Raymond B. Fosdick and Albert L. Scott, *Toward Liquor Control* (Harper & Bros., 1933), p. 4.

21 *Congressional Record*, Vol. 49, Part 1, 62nd Congress, 3rd Session, p. 761.

22 New York *Times*, March 30, 1926.

23 *Congressional Record*, Vol. 55, Part 6, 65th Congress, 1st Session, p. 5646.

Chapter Eight

The Eighteenth Amendment

THE WET propagandists continually denounced the Eighteenth Amendment and the Volstead Act as rigorous, harsh and drastic. Their purpose was to deceive and inflame the people and further the campaign of hatred against the amendment. They had another very important strategic objective. They wanted to spread abroad the impression that any attempt to improve and strengthen the law would be futile, that the most thoroughgoing and rigorous law conceivable had been tried and had failed, and that every road of advance was blocked except that which led to repeal.

Statements of this nature were at the very opposite pole from the truth. The Eighteenth Amendment and the Volstead Act did not crystallize the experience of a hundred years nor make any adequate provision for the execution of the mandate of that great majority of the American people that had forced their adoption. They were not in any real sense prohibition measures at all. They were half-way measures and were filled with emasculating concessions, compromises and loopholes and with palpable absurdities. They were so weak and unadapted to their purpose that they could have been enforced only if all enforcement officials from the President down to the policeman on his beat had been honest and efficient and determined that the law should be obeyed.

The wet propagandists continually harped upon the absurdities and monstrosities of the Volstead Act and their disastrous consequences, but they did it in such a way as to further their campaign of deception and hatred. They did not point out that the trouble with the law was not its strength but its weakness. They did not frankly admit that the trouble resulted not from prohibition but from a statute that failed to provide for prohibition, and that the cure was not the return of the liquor traffic but a new enforcement law which would make the will of the people effective. By a skillfully deceptive use of the words they identified prohibition with the Volstead Act and its consequences and drew the sweeping conclusion that the Eighteenth Amendment and the Volstead Act should both be repealed and prohibition abandoned.

A number of the ablest leaders of the dry cause were familiar with the deficiencies of the law and insisted that it be revised and made effective for its purpose. Many others, however, either did not recognize these defects or feared that to admit them would be a confession of weakness and injure their cause with the people. So they minimized these defects — the embarrassment they caused enforcement officials and the corruption and lawlessness that resulted from them — and treated the amendment and the enforcement act as sacred. By this attitude they played directly into the hands of the wets, who were doing everything in their power to discredit its supporters and make them appear ridiculous. In permitting themselves to be maneuvered into a position where they had to fight a sham battle on a false front, the drys committed one of their greatest tactical blunders.

A clear understanding of this phase of the repeal campaign is essential if the renewed fight upon the liquor traffic is to be marked by realism and finality. In the first place, it affords further proof of the dishonesty of the whole wet movement. In the second place it shows how, when after generations of struggle the moral forces of the nation had won an overwhelming victory, gained the power to destroy the liquor traffic and settle the question for all time, their leaders in Washington accepted an amendment and enforcement act that were incapable of effective administration and so played directly into the hands of their opponents.

The hindsight thus obtained should not be regarded as a reflection on the intelligence or the sincerity of the dry leaders. They believed that with prohibition embedded in the Constitution, the power of the liquor forces to pursue their usual methods would be destroyed. Only through experience could they discover the manner in which these forces would continue to charge through the loopholes of the law and take advantage of every exception, concession and compromise it contained. Only by experience could they learn how the politicians of the country who were protecting gambling, commercialized vice and organized crime, would absorb into their system the bootlegger and the speak-easy and their criminal affiliates. Only experience could enable them to realize the extent to which fraudulent propaganda could deceive and mislead the people. Only experience could convince them that large numbers of men and women of wealth and prominence who pretend to be good citizens and demand the enforcement of all laws that protect them and their property, will not hesitate to treat with contempt laws that interfere with their self-indulgence and their greed.

There is not space here for the consideration of all the defects of the amendment and the enforcement act, but exhaustive and authoritative discussions of these defects are accessible to those who wish to pursue the subject further. In 1926, a committee of the United States Senate investigated the administration of the national prohibition law.[1] The committee was, of course, deluged with dishonest propaganda by senators, congressmen and other politicians from wet states and districts and by the attorneys and other hired men of the big business and financial interests eager for liquor taxes. But there was also a large amount of sincere and searching criticism of the whole situation. This came from public officials, charged with the responsibility of administering the law, who were honestly endeavoring to do their duty, and from citizens who were giving such officials their full cooperation. The discerning reader will have no difficulty in distinguishing the criticisms of those who were interested in the solution of the liquor question from those offered by men who were interested in the solution of their personal, political and financial problems.

In 1929 Mabel Walker Willebrandt, who, for eight years, as assistant attorney general of the United States, had been in charge of the enforcement of the prohibition law, published a book in which she gave a clear and unequivocal statement of defects in the law and the regulations, the blighting effect of corrupt politics, and the changes that would have to be made if proper enforcement was to be secured.[2]

In 1928 Mr. W. C. Durant, head of the Durant Motor Company, offered a prize of twenty-five thousand dollars " for the best and most practicable plan to make the Eighteenth Amendment effective." By the terms of the offer, discussion of the question of repeal was excluded and answers were restricted to the single question of enforcement. There were 23,230 plans submitted, of which 102 were published.[3] In his introduction to his book, Mr. Durant says:

> Herein I have collected the plans submitted by over a hundred law enforcers; judges, district attorneys, prohibition administrators, policemen, governors, police chiefs, justices of the peace, coast guard captains, under-cover agents, and a dozen other types of men and women actually engaged in enforcing the prohibition laws. Their contributions are the result of years of thought based on thousands of personal experiences in the public service.
>
> My collaborators are, as it were, delegates from 37 states and Hawaii and Alaska. The list includes 34 public officials in the service of the United States, 23 state officials, 15 county officials, 30 town and city officials. . . . These contributors are not theorists but hard-headed officials up against the daily difficulties of enforcing this law.[4]

The statements included in the two volumes cited point out clearly the defects of the law, the manner of its betrayal by corrupt politicians and the devastating effect of dishonest wet propaganda and of liquor lawlessness in high places.

Compromise

There can be no doubt that it was the intention of the people that the amendment should provide for the complete prohibition of the liquor traffic, that it should be made effective by an enforcement act which would make it a crime to engage in that traffic, and that its violation should subject the offender to adequate penalties and the same public odium that attaches to other criminals. The people had decided that the liquor traffic was a crime and that it should be dealt with as such, and they had given their representatives a mandate to make their purpose effective. At the time the amendment was passed they believed that this had been accomplished. But the amendment itself represented a compromise with various forces.

Any compromise with crime is fatal. It is the slippery path that leads to lawlessness and anarchy. If it is decided that the public welfare and safety require that any course of conduct be made a crime, it should be done with such certainty and finality that every person having regard for his reputation will scrupulously avoid such conduct, and penalties must be provided that are adequate to deter the criminal classes. There must be no uncertainty as to the meaning of the law, no confusion in its administration and no question as to the social and legal status of anyone who violates it. Under no other circumstances will law-abiding people respect it and criminals fear it.

If those charged with the duty of establishing national prohibition had provided for the immediate and complete prohibition of all alcoholic beverages and had made it perfectly clear that anyone who in any way or for any purpose produced, handled *or used* such beverages, was as definitely a member of the criminal class as if he had made or passed counterfeit coin, and would be treated as such, there would have been created in the great body of the American people a spirit of respect, acquiescence and obedience for the law. Those charged with its enforcement would have had to deal only with liquor addicts and lawless and criminal elements who do not have the sympathy and support of the public and whom juries and courts are willing to convict and punish. If this course had been followed, there would not have been engendered in the people such a spirit of confusion, levity, disrespect and disobedience as would make the enforcement of any law impossible.

The amendment read as follows:

Section 1. After one year from the ratification of this article the manufacture, sale, or transportation of intoxicating liquors within, the importation thereof into, or the exportation thereof from the United States and all territory subject to the jurisdiction thereof for beverage purposes is hereby prohibited.

Section 2. The Congress and the several states shall have concurrent power to enforce this article by appropriate legislation.

It will be noticed that the amendment did not become operative until one year from the date of its ratification. The people had declared the liquor traffic to be an antisocial, criminal business and had decreed its destruction, and yet it was given full legal permission to continue in existence for a year. This provision was dictated neither by justice nor by common sense. In Mugler *vs.* Kansas, the Supreme Court had declared that the power of the government to suppress the liquor traffic was not "burdened with the condition that the state must compensate such individual owners for pecuniary losses they may sustain, by reason of their not being permitted, by a noxious use of their property, to inflict injury upon the community." [5] With 95 per cent of the country dry and national prohibition having won a great popular victory in 1916, liquor dealers had unmistakable warning of approaching doom. Furthermore, they had the period between submission and ratification to get out of a business in which they had never had any moral right to engage.

The insertion of this provision in the amendment sacrificed the opportunity to accomplish the one thing most essential to the success of the law. It made it impossible to launch it in a manner that would impress the people with its seriousness and finality and command for it their respect, obedience and support. The spectacle of the business pursuing its usual course after both the Constitution and the statute had pronounced it a crime, made many people feel that after all it was not as bad as it was said to be, and engendered in them a feeling of unreality, indifference and reaction. This provision was used by the wets later as a justification for their lawlessness. They said that it showed that the prohibition movement was tainted with hypocrisy and that the liquor traffic was not criminal by nature, but only by virtue of a statute which was not binding on those who had not consented to it.

Again, the amendment did not forbid the possession and use of alcoholic beverages. Upon its becoming effective, therefore, if a man possessed liquor, he could retain it and he and the members of his family could drink it and serve it to their guests. If he was without a supply, he had a year in which to " stock up."

Only those who at the time were old enough to realize what was going on can have any conception of what took place in this country between January 1919 and January 1920. Everywhere large numbers of people proceeded to fill their cellars and warehouses with liquor. In so doing, they had no feeling that their conduct was illegal or morally reprehensible, because it was sanctioned by law. They did not act as if the purpose of the law was to suppress a demoralizing, narcotic drug, but rather as if its intention was to create a famine in an article that was a source of relaxation and pleasure, and it gave them a year of plenty in which to follow the advice of Joseph to Pharaoh and provide for that famine. As liquor and drinking paraphernalia were installed in the homes, they ceased to be thought of as means for the enjoyment of the men only; the women and children became familiar with them and learned to use and enjoy them. The degradation of women and the debauching of youth that has now reached such appalling proportions had its origin in this transference of the saloon to the home.

When the law went into effect and " the famine was sore in the land," these stores of liquor acquired a scarcity as well as a narcotic value and their owners acquired an adventitious popularity. Adler has shown that the desire to escape from feelings of inferiority and to achieve a sense of importance is as universal and as powerful as the desire for sexual satisfaction. These possessors of liquor found that they had two means of such escape — the narcotic effect of the alcohol and the ability to serve something desirable that could no longer be legally obtained. Well stocked homes came to be regarded as oases in a desert, places which were pervaded by a spirit of liberality and good cheer. If a man did not serve liquor, it was supposed that he was too poor or too fanatical and it was felt that a party at his house would be a frost. An ample supply of liquor came to be regarded as a badge of social standing, like a fine house, a large car, membership in clubs or a writeup in the society column. Those who were nervous about their social position came to consider liquor as essential to their happiness as dinner coats. The next step was natural and inevitable. Those who had failed to stock up before the law went into effect proceeded to do so — through bootleggers — and as stores were exhausted, they were replenished. Thus, the bootlegger became a respected member of " society." He was protected and defended by his patrons.

This moronic, lawless situation would not have developed if the law had provided for the immediate and complete suppression of every phase of the traffic in alcoholic beverages and the destruction of all existing stores of liquor. This would also have deprived the repeal propagandists of one of their most effective arguments.

In still another way, this year of plenty helped to discredit the amendment and contribute to its overthrow. In the past, the liquor traffic had at least been democratic. The man of ordinary means could go into a saloon and get a cold glass of beer for a nickel or a " shot " of standard whisky for ten or fifteen cents. When, however, he saw the rich filling their cellars and warehouses with choice liquors, he realized that they would continue to indulge their appetite while he would be forced to become a total abstainer. This caused widespread resentment and dissatisfaction with the amendment. The use that was made of this situation is illustrated by a statement of Samuel Gompers. Treating the amendment and prohibition as synonymous, he said:

> Class hatred is another progeny of prohibition. It is generally believed the cellars of the idle rich were overflowing with cases of wines and barrels of whisky. These supplies may last during the lifetime of many of these people. At the same time, the workers who have no cellars and have not the opportunity of gratifying a normal even though temporary rational desire, learn to hate their more fortunate fellow citizens more bitterly and uncompromisingly.[6]

This state of affairs was of the greatest assistance to the wet propagandists in their campaign of deception and hatred. It enabled them to divert the attention of the people from the great and beneficent purpose of the prohibition movement and to center it on an incidental absurdity of the amendment and its vicious consequences. Concealing the truth, that appropriate measures should be taken to remedy the situation, they beat their breasts and continually shouted, "Prohibition deprives the workingman of his beer and gives to the rich man his cocktails and his champagne."

On the day that the Senate voted on the question of submission, a motion was made that the language of the amendment be so changed that it would prohibit the purchase as well as the manufacture and sale of liquor. The motion was defeated, and when the vote on it was recorded the doom of the amendment was sealed. It then became only a question of time when it would be either nullified or repealed.

Judge William S. Kenyon, who as senator, justice of the United States Circuit Court of Appeals and member of the National Commission on Law Observance and Enforcement, had made a profound study of the liquor problem, in a statement filed with the report of the commission, said:

> People who buy bootleg liquor are assisting in violating the law and are contributing money for purposes of bribery and corruption, for they know that the system of illicit sale of liquors cannot be carried on to the extent that it is without bribery and graft. They are moral accessories to the illegal business of the bootlegger. They are assisting in breaking down law in the nation. One of the greatest of American manufacturers is reported by the newspapers to have recently said: "That portion of 'high society' that buys bootleg liquor is just a part of our underworld." A truth well stated.

According to the law, when a man purchased liquor, his act was legal and he retained his social position, while the other party to the transaction, the bootlegger who sold it to him, had committed a crime for which he could be sent to the penitentiary. To large numbers of people, this simply did not make sense. They refused to get excited about the manufacture, transportation and sale of an article that it was perfectly legal to purchase, possess and use. In time they lost respect for the law, refused to obey it and protected their bootleggers. This not only gave a sense of security to those who had been made criminals by the law, but furnished them the opportunity for a theoretical justification of their conduct. The reaction of the underworld was given classic expression by Al Capone:

> I make my money by supplying a public demand. If I break the law, my customers, who number hundreds of the best people in Chicago, are as guilty as I am. The only difference between us is that I sell and they buy. Everybody calls me a racketeer. I call myself a business man. When I sell liquor, it's bootlegging. When my patrons serve it on a silver tray on Lake Shore Drive, it's hospitality.[7]

Protection of the purchaser resulted in the same kind of resentment that had been caused by the provision for a year of plenty. The rich man who could afford a high-priced bootlegger could safely purchase and consume all the liquor he desired, while others had to do without simply because they could not afford the price. It seemed to be a scheme to discriminate in favor of the rich and against those who were not rich. There were many people of limited means who had been accustomed to drink, but were able and would have been perfectly willing to give it up and forget about it if the law had applied to all alike. They bitterly resented a law that did not put an end to the liquor traffic, but simply made drinking the exclusive privilege of those who could afford the luxury of an expensive bootlegger.

This exemption of the purchaser from penalty was a travesty on justice and common sense. The purchasers created the demand, furnished the market and supplied the funds for the whole criminal business. They made possible the existence and they maintained the whole army of moonshiners, smugglers, hijackers, bootleggers and other criminals who manufactured, transported and sold the outlawed liquor. They poured into the underworld the money that gave it wealth and power, enabled it to corrupt our politics, bribe public officials and carry on its operations in insolent defiance of the law. Their part of the transaction was morally the more reprehensible. The sellers were making a living while the purchasers were making criminals of their fellow citizens and destroying respect for law merely that they might indulge an appetite. Those who furnished the liquor had to exercise intelligence, resourcefulness and courage, and take the chance of going to jail, while the purchasers in the smug enjoyment of their immunity simply handed over the cash.

A large majority of the American people not only obeyed the law but did not abet its violation by encouraging others to commit the crime of selling. The frivolous and morally irresponsible purchasers were a small percentage of the whole population, but they financed all the lawlessness and made all the noise. If they had been subject to the same penalties as the sellers, their cowardice and their vanity would have prevented them from taking the risk of being arrested, finger-printed and sent to jail, and the pages of our history would not be marred by the sordid story of their conduct. In that case, enforcement agencies would have had to deal only with the type of people who violated the laws against other kinds of narcotic drugs, and their task would have been comparatively simple. The way this exemption was regarded by the men who were actually engaged in the administration of the law is shown by the following statements from plans submitted in the Durant contest:

JUDGE JAMES L. COOPER. Adopt a law, or laws, *making the purchaser equally guilty with the seller*. . . . The bootlegger cannot exist without customers. If his customers were equally guilty with him, and each compelled to disclose the transaction, *many citizens who now purchase would cease to do so rather than become violators of law,* and others would hesitate to take the chance. . . . It would stigmatize the purchase and consumption of intoxicating liquor and hasten the day when consumers of intoxicating liquor would lost caste in society.[8]

FREDERICK C. DEZENDORF, head of plant control, Prohibition Unit. It takes two or more persons to effect a sale or purchase of liquor, and both or all parties thereto should properly be treated alike. Therefore, the several sections governing the sale and manufacturing of illegal liquors should be amended to include the other party to the transaction — the purchaser — and apply the same penalty to him. If there were no purchasers, there would be no sellers.[9]

The wet propagandists used this situation to deceive and inflame the people. They did not tell them that the evils were the result not of prohibition, but of the omission from the law of an essential element of prohibition.

The evils of alcoholic liquors resulted from their use, the vice of the liquor traffic was that it made provision for their use, and the purpose of the people in putting prohibition in the Constitution was to put an end to their use. This purpose was expressly recognized by Congress when it put in the enforcement act the statement that "all the provisions of this act shall be liberally construed to the end that the use of intoxicating liquor as a beverage may be prevented."

In Samuels *vs.* McCurdy, the United States Supreme Court said:

> The ultimate legislative object of prohibition is to prevent the drinking of intoxicating liquor by anyone because of the demoralizing effect of drunkenness upon society. The state has the power to subject those members of society who might indulge in the use of such liquor without injury to themselves to a deprivation of access to liquor in order to remove temptation from those whom its use would demoralize and to avoid the abuses which follow in its train.[10]

The supreme court of Maine said that "it is common knowledge that it is the use of intoxicating liquor as a beverage that is deemed hurtful and is the mischief sought to be prevented by legislation."[11]

When, through use, a man has learned to crave alcoholic euphoria, he becomes blind to the evil effects of alcohol; he will deny their existence, rationalize his conduct, and defend the means by which he secures his liquor, however sordid, corrupt and even criminal they may be. It is because alcohol is a narcotic, habit-forming drug that its use is responsible for the whole complex of evils symbolized by the phrase, "the liquor traffic." The great objective of the long struggle that culminated in the adoption of the Eighteenth Amendment was to put an end to the use of alcohol. Notwithstanding this fact, the amendment did not prohibit or even mention the use of alcohol, but left it as it was, both legal and respectable. Its authors, of course, believed that by prohibiting the manufacture and sale of liquor they would stop its use. This was the equivalent of a law to prevent murder by prohibiting the manufacture and sale of deadly weapons, and yet leaving the act of murder both legal and respectable. It furnished opportunity for those who did not wish to be classified as criminals, but were willing to act as moral accessories to crime, to participate in the breakdown of the law.

If we are to profit by experience, it is essential that the people of this class be clearly identified and their exact status fixed. After the law went into effect, there were those who did not use liquor because they never had used it and did not care to do so. There were others who gave up the use of liquor because they knew that it was contrary to the spirit of the law, and because they did not wish to deal with criminals and abet the commission of crime. A large majority of the American people belonged to these two classes. But there was another perfectly distinct class. It was composed of those who openly and complacently used liquor, although they knew that it was the very purpose of the law to stop such use; that all the acts by which their liquor was furnished to them were crimes, which they not merely encouraged, but for which they were financially and morally responsible; that they were bringing into existence and maintaining a new and sinister type of criminal who committed his crimes openly in broad daylight in the homes of the people, upon the solicitation of men and women who smugly pretended to be good citizens; that they were contributing to the corruption of politics and the bribery of public officials, and helping to bring the Constitution and the laws of their country into contempt. They were satisfied that they were exempt from arrest and retained their classification as members of good society. If the use of liquor had involved the same stigma and penalties as the manufacture and sale thereof, people of this class would have obeyed the law rather than jeopardize their liberty and their social standing.

In the plan which he submitted in the Durant contest, Mr. J. R. Taylor, speaking out of his experience as a prosecuting attorney charged with the enforcement of the law, said:

> If the evils of intoxicants come from their use as a beverage, *the user is the most guilty of all the actors in the liquor tragedy*. The making of it is the beginning, the consumption the unending climax.
>
> Instead of this feature being emphasized by the lawmaking bodies by the passage of laws calculated to deter the consumer, the stress has been laid on the acts leading up to but stopping short of him. The consumers outnumber the bootleggers at least twenty-five to one, and while they are regarded as more respectable, they have created practically all sentiment against enforcement.[12]

If the law had prohibited the use of liquor, its proper administration would not have required that enforcement officials pry into homes in search of the few people who would secretly make and drink it. But it would have given them the power and made it their duty to stop all that open and public drinking that destroyed respect for the law and made its effective administration impossible. They could have given their attention to addicts and criminals who would have been unable to arouse popular sentiment against the law.

If the law had made the use of liquor a crime, its educational and moral influence would have been far more effective than its penalties. When a course of conduct becomes so obnoxious and so injurious to the public welfare that the government solemnly declares it to be a crime, all normal people wish to avoid it. This creates an atmosphere in which people instinctively shun such conduct because of a feeling of repulsion rather than from a fear of punishment. It is this public attitude toward a particular type of conduct that is the most effective instrument for its suppression. If, therefore, the man who used liquor had been placed in the same class as the bootlegger who sold it to him, it would have made a powerful contribution toward the creation of a public attitude that would have made enforcement not only possible but imperative.

A majority of the people would have obeyed the law from inclination and a sense of social responsibility; others would have done so to guard their social standing; and the penalties would have been used to deter the criminal classes. In no other way could enforcement have become merely a matter of dealing with the underworld, the policy of the law removed from the realm of significant debate, and the results of the great prohibition victory made final and secure.

Intoxicating Liquors

For generations, the liquor traffic had been the football of politics. When the disgust and indignation of the people had reached a certain point, they would force the passage of a law for its suppression, think the matter was settled, and turn to other things. The liquor forces of the particular community or state would be joined by those of the entire country and a concerted effort would be made to break down the law and force its repeal. When, by aid of their money, bootleggers, lobbyists and other emissaries, they had brought about an intolerable state of corruption and lawlessness, the people would submit to repeal. When they found that conditions became still more intolerable, they would force the enactment of another prohibition law which would, in its turn, be destroyed by the same corrupt and ruthless methods. This is what is meant by the statement so often made that the history of the prohibition movement is the story of a succession of "prohibition waves and periods of reaction."

As a result of countless bitter struggles and humiliating experiences, the moral forces of the nation saw clearly that they must either make a cowardly surrender, or completely destroy the liquor traffic in a manner that would remove the question forever from the political arena. They also saw clearly that this could be accomplished only by an amendment to the national Constitution outlawing the liquor traffic as completely and finally as the Thirteenth Amendment had outlawed human slavery. There cannot be the slightest doubt that the resistless wave of public sentiment that swept the Eighteenth Amendment into the Constitution was an expression of the people's determination that the prohibition question should be settled forever.

The Eighteenth Amendment surrendered the precise advantage which the people intended to obtain and believed they had obtained when they made prohibition a part of the Constitution. By the use of the words "intoxicating liquors," the liquor question was left in politics and the whole prohibition cause at the mercy of politicians. Generations of experience had proved that if a law prohibited the traffic in intoxicating liquors, it was unenforcible. If a man was charged with its violation, he would plead not guilty and allege that the liquor he sold was not intoxicating, and that question would have to be submitted to a jury. A crooked lawyer and dishonest "experts" would harass the prosecutor, befuddle and prejudice the jury, and create a "reasonable doubt" as to whether the liquor was in fact intoxicating. As this was an essential element of the crime, the defendant would escape. The attention of court and jury was diverted from the *real* crime, which was the act of sale, and became lost in a fog of dishonest controversy over the meaning of the word "intoxicating." The meaning of the law was made to depend not upon its language, but upon the resourcefulness of lawyers and experts and the intelligence of jurors. As each sale was a separate offense, the dockets of the courts were crowded and the law had a different meaning in each case. The result was confusion, failure, general disgust and ultimate repeal. The difficulties created by the use of the word "intoxicating" were pointed out by the United States Supreme Court in Ruppert *vs.* Caffey:

> Legislation and decisions of the highest courts of nearly all of the states established that it is deemed impossible to effectively enforce either prohibitory laws or other laws merely regulating the manufacture and sale of intoxicating liquors, if liability or inclusion within the law is made to depend upon the issuable fact whether or not a particular liquor made or sold as a beverage is intoxicating.[13]

This meant, of course, that the enforcement act would have to contain a definition of the word "intoxicating." This was clearly pointed out by the attorney general of the United States in 1919, when the Volstead Act was under consideration. He said:

It goes without saying, I think, that if a law merely prohibits intoxicating liquors and leaves to the jury in each case, from the evidence produced to determine whether the liquor in question is in fact intoxicating or not, its efficient and uniform administration will be impossible. The term " intoxicating " is too indefinite and uncertain to produce anything like uniform results in such trials. Of course, there are certain liquors so generally known to be intoxicating that any court would take judicial notice of that fact. But in the absence of a definition by Congress there will be innumerable beverages as to which the claim will be made that they do not contain enough alcohol to render them intoxicating. These contentions will produce endless confusion and uncertainty. These, I think, are substantially the reasons why Congress should itself provide a definition.

The importance of this matter has been very much emphasized by our present efforts to enforce the war prohibition act. The claim is being made that beer containing as much as 2.75 per cent of alcohol is not intoxicating. And if this must be made a question of fact to be decided by each jury, but little in the way of practical results can be expected.[14]

Congress defined intoxicating liquor as any beverage containing more than one-half of one per cent of alcohol, which was the percentage that had been agreed upon by the liquor dealers and treasury officials for the purpose of administering the Internal Revenue Act. But if Congress could adopt this definition, could it not adopt another that would name a percentage high enough to permit the return of the liquor traffic with all its evils without a technical violation of the language of the amendment? When the Du Ponts took over the Association Against the Prohibition Amendment, it declared that Congress could and should adopt a definition that would permit the manufacture, sale and taxation of beer. Al Smith, Tammany Hall's candidate for president, said:

I recommend an amendment to the Volstead Act which should contain a sane and sensible definition of what constitutes an intoxicating beverage, because upon its face the present definition does not square with common sense or with medical opinion. Each state could then provide an alcoholic content not greater than that fixed by Congress. It must be borne in mind that the Eighteenth Amendment does not prohibit alcoholic beverages, it prohibits intoxicating beverages.[15]

In 1926, Senator Edge, representative of the liquor-controlled state of New Jersey, sought to defeat the purpose of the Eighteenth Amendment and bring back the liquor traffic by congressional action by sponsoring an amendment to the Volstead Act,

striking out the words " containing one-half of 1 per centum or more of alcohol by volume " and the words " containing more than one-half of 1 per centum of alcohol by volume " wherever they appear in such act and inserting in lieu thereof the words " intoxicating in fact."

Defending this proposal, he continued:

As to the constitutionality, as I have said, there is absolutely nothing to discuss. The very words used in the bill are the words of the Constitution. The Constitution prohibits intoxicating liquors. This bill likewise prohibits intoxicating liquors. If this bill is unconstitutional, then the Eighteenth Amendment itself is unconstitutional, which, of course, would be a ridiculous assertion.[16]

Thus it was proposed by congressional enactment of a single sentence, the effect of which few people understood, to remove from the Constitution an amendment that had been ratified by forty-six states and declared by the Supreme Court to be a part of our fundamental law. This was to be accomplished by the trick of leaving the law without any standard for its enforcement, which would have made it a dead letter.

The action of Congress in using the words " intoxicating liquors " in the amendment, is difficult to understand, in view of the fact that nine months previously it had enacted the District of Columbia prohibition law which contained the following:

Wherever the term " alcoholic liquors " is used in this act it shall be deemed to include whisky, brandy, rum, gin, wine, ale, porter, beer, cordials, hard or fermented cider, alcoholic bitters, ethyl alcohol, all malt liquors, and all other alcoholic liquors.

This was the distillation of the wisdom gained from years of experience — a product of the best type of intelligent and courageous statesmanship. Each kind of liquor was specifically named and the words " all other *alcoholic* liquors " were added. This left not the slightest opportunity for confusion or evasion. If these few simple words had been incorporated in the Eighteenth Amendment, the question would have been taken out of politics and the nullification of the Constitution by legislative action would have been impossible.

The dishonest subterfuge of defining the phrase, " intoxicating liquors," was approved by the Democratic national convention of 1932, and later made the basis of the Cullen Bill, which authorized the manufacture and sale of beer, the reopening of the saloons, and the return of 90 per cent of the liquor traffic and its evils. Thus by congressional action, prohibition was destroyed and a provision of the Constitution nullified. History had repeated itself.

NOTES

[1] The National Prohibition Law. Hearings before the Subcommittee of the Committee of the Judiciary. U. S. Senate, 69th Congress, 1st Session. (Hereafter, this report will be referred to as NPL.)

[2] Willebrandt, *op. cit.*

[3] Durant, *op. cit.*

[4] *Ibid.*, p. 15.

[5] 123, U. S. 623.

[6] In a letter to President Wilson, Oct. 20, 1919. Quoted in NPL, p. 217.

[7] Quoted by Walter Nobel Burns, *One Way Ride* (Doubleday, Doran & Co., 1931), p. 32.

[8] Durant, *op. cit.*, p. 158.

[9] *Ibid.*, p. 197.

[10] 267, U. S. 188.

[11] State vs. Bass Publishing Co., 104, Me. 288.

[12] Durant, *op. cit.*, p. 472.

[13] 251, U. S. 264.

[14] NPL, p. 854.

[15] Quoted by Fisher, *The Noble Experiment*, p. 401.

[16] NPL, pp. 5, 31.

Chapter Nine

The Volstead Act

CONGRESS had the power to pass an enforcement law that would have made the success of national prohibition a certainty. The amendment prohibited the manufacture, transportation and sale of intoxicating liquor, and conferred upon Congress the power to enforce that prohibition "by appropriate legislation." If, in order to accomplish the express purpose of the amendment, it was necessary that Congress should prohibit the purchase, possession and use of such liquors, give a definition that would make evasion impossible, and provide appropriate and adequate penalties, it had the power, and it was its duty, to take such action. As a large majority of the members of Congress represented prohibition constituencies, it had the actual as well as the legal power to make the amendment completely effective.

But instead of using this opportunity to carry out the will of the people and bring the long struggle against the liquor traffic to a finish, Congress passed a weak and unenforcible law embodying every absurdity that had been omitted from the amendment and made it practically certain that national prohibition would end in a debacle.

A criminal statute should be short, clear, unequivocal, and easily read and understood by all who are likely to incur its penalties. It should contain no provisions that may result in discriminations between the rich and the poor or render its administration complicated or difficult. Its penalties should be adapted to the prevention of forbidden conduct.

The national prohibition act, the so-called Volstead Act, was declared to be

> an act to prohibit intoxicating beverages, and to regulate the manufacture, production, use and sale of high-proof spirits for other than beverage purposes, and to insure an ample supply of alcohol, and promote its use in scientific research and in the development of fuel, dye and other lawful industries.

The act contained sixty-seven sections, to which six were added by a supplemental act, making seventy-three in all. An elaborate permit system was established under which the entire alcohol industry of the country was to be minutely supervised. Provisions for the enforcement of the law and the administration of the permit system were intermingled in a manner to create hopeless confusion. There were exemptions, exceptions, cross references, modifications of ordinary criminal procedure, and a mass of rules and regulations. Enforcement agents, district attorneys, and judges differed in their interpretation of the Volstead Act, and the meaning of many of its provisions became known only when the Supreme Court had decided what they must mean. The people were bewildered, and in time became either indifferent or hostile to the law.

Those charged with the enforcement of the law agreed that the attempt to provide for the suppression of the illegal traffic in alcoholic beverages and the supervision of the production and distribution of alcohol for lawful purposes in one statute resulted in confusion, irritation and inefficiency. Their attitude is illustrated by the statement of Mr. L. H. Hampton, assistant chief counsel for the Prohibition Unit, in the plan which he submitted in the Durant contest:

> Separate the enforcement of the criminal provisions of the law from the administration of the permit system.
>
> Reasons: Enforcement of the national prohibition act requires two distinct types of official functions: (a) enforcement of its criminal provisions, and (b) administration of its permit system. Those functions are distinctly different in the service and policy required. A man who

has the type of ability and temperament to judiciously administer the permit provisions of the law ordinarily does not possess the genius for investigation and vigor of action essential for successful direction of criminal investigation. . . . As long as these two incongruous functions are committed to one organization, consideration for legitimate business interests concerned in the administration of the permit system will continue to be a major factor in the selection and removal of supervising officials, to the disadvantage of effective enforcement of the criminal provisions of the law.[1]

Difficulties of Administration

It used to be a tradition among lawyers that an indictment in a federal court was equivalent to a conviction, and that the punishment would fit the crime. This was a result of the extraordinary efficiency of the law enforcement agencies of the federal government. The men engaged in the detection of crime and the preparation and presentation of evidence were not political appointees. They were chosen upon their merits through civil service examinations; they were highly trained; they moved in an atmosphere of integrity and efficiency, and their positions were permanent. They had the absolute confidence of district attorneys, juries, courts and the public, and the underworld held them in awe. If no permit system had been established, if the production and distribution of alcohol for lawful purposes had been left in the same position as every other legitimate business, if every part of the traffic in alcoholic beverages had been made a crime, and if the enforcement of the law had been entrusted to the established enforcement agencies of the federal government, the liquor traffic would occupy the same position in this country today as does the traffic in dope.

Instead of pursuing this course, which was dictated by experience and common sense, the work of enforcing the criminal provisions and administering the permit system was assigned to the treasury department. The act provided that

the commissioner of internal revenue, his assistants, agents and inspectors, shall investigate and report violations of this act to the United

States attorney for the district in which committed . . . swear out warrants before United States commissioners or other officers or courts . . . and . . . conduct the prosecution at the committing trial for the purpose of having the offenders held for the action of a grand jury.

The commissioner and his assistants were charged with the duty of supervising the production and distribution of alcohol to be used in industry and the arts and for other lawful purposes, and it was provided that persons appointed "to have immediate direction of the enforcement of the provisions of this act, and persons authorized to issue permits, and agents and inspectors in the field service," should be exempt from the provisions of the civil service act.

When the liquor traffic was legal and subject to a tax, it was proper that the agents of the treasury department should secure evidence of the evasion of that tax. When, however, the liquor traffic was made a crime and the tax was abolished, to assign the enforcement of a purely criminal law to that department was a patent absurdity. While the enforcement act was pending in Congress, the commissioner of internal revenue called attention to the fact that his department was already burdened with the fiscal and revenue problems of the government. In 1921 a committee consisting of two members of the cabinet and an assistant secretary made a study of the subject and recommended that the prohibition enforcement unit be transferred to the Department of Justice. In 1924 the same recommendation was made by a conference of federal circuit judges called by Chief Justice Taft. It was again made by the Wickersham Commission in a preliminary report submitted in 1929.

Summarizing the proposals suggested in the plans submitted in the contest sponsored by him, Mr. Durant said:

Of the major proposals for improving prohibition enforcement, the most frequent is the plan to take enforcement away from the treasury department and give it to the Department of Justice.

Today the prosecuting arm of the government, the United States district attorneys, are under the Department of Justice. Cases are brought to them, ostensibly ready to try, by the treasury prohibition agents. An improperly prepared case must often be thrown out by the most honest district attorney; a wet prosecutor sometimes turns down the best prepared case. Treasury and Department of Justice can now blame each other for lax enforcement. The proposal is to center in the Department of Justice responsibility for arresting lawbreakers and for both preparing and prosecuting all prohibition cases.[2]

If the commissioner of internal revenue had handled the whole liquor problem in the manner prescribed by the act, it would have been necessary for him to have a force of assistants and agents large enough to supervise all distilleries, denaturing plants and bonded warehouses and all manufacturers of cereal beverages, the distribution of alcohol to industry, the arts, druggists, physicians and churches and for all other lawful uses. They would have had to guard a border 18,700 miles long against smuggling; they would have had to search for illicit stills, breweries and speak-easies; arrest and prosecute numerous bootleggers and other criminals; prepare evidence; summon witnesses; appear before commissioners, district attorneys, grand juries and courts, and perform innumerable other duties. The difficulties of their task were increased a hundredfold by the fact that while they were endeavoring to prevent the diversion of lawfully manufactured alcohol into the bootleg trade and to suppress the illegal traffic, the very law under which they operated protected a vast and lucrative market for this contraband liquor by giving immunity to those who purchased and used it. They were called upon to administer a law that held out a seductive invitation to its violation and made it possible and easy for its enemies to obtain hundreds of millions of dollars with which to corrupt politics, bribe public officials and carry on dishonest propaganda, and render enforcement of the law difficult. To have carried out the program proposed by the act in the face of the difficulties involved would have required a large, carefully selected, highly trained and well paid force of men.

Emory H. Buckner, United States district attorney for the southern district of New York, in his testimony before the Senate committee that investigated the national prohibition law, gave a graphic picture of the magnitude of the work to be performed, and stated that a conservative estimate showed that " we should certainly have a minimum of 1,500 agents in the southern district of New York." He said that

> these 1,500 agents would have to handle all this important inspection work. They would have all these denaturing plants. They would have 1,200 drugstores, 5,100 doctors, and perhaps there are 7,000 people in my district holding some kind of government paper that permits them either to buy or sell liquor.

He also pointed out that these agents should be paid enough so that they would not be constantly tempted to accept bribes in order to provide for their families.[3] R. Q. Merrick, prohibition administrator for Virginia, North Carolina and South Carolina, in the plan which he submitted in the Durant contest, stated that the proper enforcement of the law would require a force of 12,000 field agents and an appropriation of not less than $50,000,000.

In view of this situation, what action did Congress take? It appropriated $2,000,000 for 1920, the year the law went into effect, and at the end of that year the number of agents totalled 2,239, of whom 1,512 were charged with the enforcement of the law. The appropriation for 1921 was $6,350,000, and at the close of the year there were 1,372 agents in the enforcement branch of the service. In subsequent years, there were slight increases in the appropriation and in the number of agents, but not enough to make any change in the picture. In 1926, General Andrews, head of the Prohibition Department of the treasury, told the Senate Investigating Committee that for the prohibition district which included all of New England except Connecticut, there were 91 agents. For the district which included the eastern and southern judicial districts of New York and Connecticut, there were 190 agents, and 129 for Indiana, Illinois, and the eastern judicial district of Wisconsin. In his statement, which was made in 1929, Mr. Merrick said: " I have 246 counties in the three states to be policed by 80 men, and they can only scratch the surface." [4]

The salaries were so small that it was impossible to secure competent men as agents. The report of the Wickersham Commission stated that

> of the 943 prohibition agents in the service on July 1, 1920, the salaries of 839 ranged from $1,200 to $2,000 per annum. Of the remainder, 89 were paid from $2,000 to $2,500; 12 from $2,510 to $3,000 and only three received more than $3,000.

Mr. Buckner pointed out that in 1926 salaries ranged from $1,800 to $2,000, and said:

> General Andrews told you that the average was $2,000. Stop and think, gentlemen of the committee — $2,000 for a man, wife and child in New York city, with even a three-room flat or tenement to live in, is not a living wage. . . . I have put down here 1,500 agents for my district, which is certainly very conservative, and I put them down at $3,000 a year. I think they ought to have $3,500.

The agents had not only to live on these small salaries, but to face the constant temptation to make much larger amounts by simply closing their eyes.

There was no examination to test the fitness of agents, they received no training, and they could be discharged at any time. They were a part of the spoils system in an era of unparalleled political corruption. The evidence shows that many were appointed at the request of wet congressmen and senators, whose object was the breakdown and destruction of the law. The results are pointed out by the Wickersham Commission:

> The enforcement agents, inspectors and attorneys, as was authorized in section 38 of the national prohibition act, were appointed without regard to the civil service rules. A force so constituted presented a situation conducive to bribery and official indifference to enforcement. It is common knowledge that large amounts of liquor were imported into the country or manufactured and sold, despite the law, with the connivance of agents of the law. . . .
>
> From statements furnished, it appears that from the beginning of national prohibition to June 30, 1930, there were 17,972 appointments to the prohibition service, 11,982 separations from the service without prejudice, 1,604 dismissals for cause. These figures apply only to the prohibition organization and do not include customs, coast guard, and

other agencies directly or indirectly concerned with the enforcement of the prohibition laws. The grounds for these dismissals for cause include bribery, extortion, theft, violation of the national prohibition act, falsification of records, conspiracy, forgery, perjury, and other causes which constitute a stigma upon the record of the employe.

Henry W. Anderson, a member of the commission, in a statement filed with its report, said:

> Men have moral as well as physical limitations. If the people provide a law of this character and then send into action for its enforcement, throughout the territory of the United States, a small field force of from 1,000 to 1,500 underpaid men against a lawless army running into tens of thousands, possessed of financial resources amounting to billions, ready to buy protection at any cost, the people must expect unsatisfactory results and heavy moral casualties. These conditions, to the extent that they have existed, have naturally tended to discredit the law.

In his book, *Prohibition Inside Out,* Roy A. Haynes, first prohibition commissioner, makes it clear that there were many honest and loyal men in the service who struggled valiantly to enforce the law. General Andrews and Mrs. Willebrandt have given testimony to the same effect. But they had to share the odium that was cast upon the force by its inadequacy and the inefficiency and corruption of so many of its members. In time, it came to be regarded with suspicion and hostility by other law-enforcing officials of the government and was unable to secure their proper cooperation. Inadequate, incompetent, and discredited with juries, courts and the people, the force was unable to perform the task assigned to it, and widespread disregard for law was the inevitable result.

The wet propagandists did not tell the people that these evils were not the result of prohibition. They beat their tom-toms and fairly screamed that these evils, which resulted from an absurd statute and their own lawlessness, were caused by prohibition, and solemnly demanded that the reign of hypocrisy, corruption and crime be brought to an end by the repeal of the Eighteenth Amendment.

The enforcement act did not forbid the purchase and use of liquor, but it did prohibit its possession "except as authorized in this act." It then provided that if liquor had been lawfully obtained, it should not be unlawful to possess it

> in one's private dwelling while the same is occupied and used by him as his dwelling only, and such liquor need not be reported, provided such liquors are for use only for the personal consumption of the owner thereof and his family residing in such dwelling and of his bona fide guests when entertained by him therein.

As the law was enacted months before the amendment went into effect and the year of plenty was ended, the people knew that it was perfectly safe to stock up their homes, and those who wished to and could afford it proceeded to do so, in the manner and with the consequences already described.

Another exception protected a man in possession of liquor, although he had manufactured it or obtained it from a smuggler, a speak-easy or a bootlegger, and by the terms of the act, that possession was a crime. The federal statute relating to search warrants contains the following provisions:

> A search warrant cannot be issued but upon probable cause, supported by affidavit, naming or describing the person and particularly describing the property and the place to be searched. The affidavits or depositions must set forth the facts tending to establish the grounds of the application or probable cause for believing that they exist.

This law, which centuries of experience had shown to be indispensable to law enforcement, protected every right guaranteed to the citizen by the Fourth Amendment to the Constitution. It was clear, just and effective, it contained no loopholes, it extended no invitations to evasion or subterfuge, and it was a powerful agent for the prevention and detection of crime. After making this statute applicable to illegal liquor, the Volstead Act added the following exception:

> No search warrant shall issue to search any private dwelling occupied as such unless it is being used for the unlawful sale of intoxicating

liquor, or unless it is in part used for some business purpose, such as a store, shop, saloon, restaurant, hotel or boardinghouse.

Under this exception, it made no difference how much liquor a man had in his house, how he got it or what he was doing with it, so long as prohibition agents had no positive evidence that he was selling it. Another disastrous consequence was that it established the "home" distillery, brewery, winery, storage place and speak-easy. All that was necessary was to secure a building, and then, as General Andrews said, "put a family in there and a still for commercial purposes, but instruct the family under no circumstances whatever to sell liquor."[5] Agents might have probable cause to believe that the "home" was being used for the manufacture, storage and sale of liquor; their evidence might be such that in the case of any other crime, they could have taken prompt and effective action; and yet because they did not have direct evidence of an actual sale they could not obtain a search warrant and secure the evidence necessary to suppress the crime and punish the criminals. As the agent could not enter the "home" without a search warrant and the occupant would admit only those whom he knew, the agent would have to spend days and weeks establishing the connections necessary to obtain entrance and secure evidence of a sale. In order not to arouse suspicion, he was compelled to spend money, drink the liquor he purchased, and become a part of the whole lawless scene. This gave the wets the opportunity to crowd their chamber of prohibition horrors with drunken, lawless agents and snoopers, deception, subterfuge, entrapment, and so on to the end of the list.

The following are typical of the statements that came from every part of the battlefield. Mr. Charles L. Case, prohibition agent for southern California, in the plan which he submitted in the Durant contest, said:

Section 25 authorizes the issuing of search warrants to search private dwellings only upon an affidavit of a sale there. This has resulted in the use of private dwellings as wineries, breweries, distilleries and liquor warehouses. Search warrants should also be issued upon an affidavit showing reasonable cause for belief that the premises are being used for the manufacture of distilled spirits. The national prohibition act alone places limitations upon the issuance of federal search warrants in excess of those provided by the federal Constitution — reasonable grounds for belief that the law is being violated. No other federal officers are thus limited in their activities.[6]

Mr. L. H. Hampton, assistant chief counsel for the Prohibition Unit, said:

Repeal that portion of Section 25, Title II, of the national prohibition act, which forbids the issuance of a search warrant for private dwelling " unless it is being used for the unlawful sale of intoxicating liquors."

Reason: The effect of the present provision has been to afford legal asylum for illicit distilling, manufacture of wine and beer, and storage of stocks of liquor for illegal sale. No similar special protection to criminal activities within a dwelling exists in relation to any other federal offense.

The requirement that " probable cause " be established for the issuance of search warrants in connection with other offenses always has been held a sufficient observance of the constitutional guaranty against unreasonable searches.

Illicit distillers and vendors of liquors have seized the advantage given by this provision and are using " private dwellings " for the operation of small stills and the storage of stocks of liquor, secure from search as long as they abstain from making sales within or directly from the " dwelling."

Repeal of the portion of the section above suggested would permit search warrants to be issued for such places upon proof of circumstances, legally constituting " probable cause " coming to the knowledge of the investigating officer by means of his natural senses, as commonly practiced and upheld by the courts as to places other than dwellings.[7]

The Near-Beer Loophole

As has already been pointed out, experience had proved that a law which prohibited the manufacture and sale of " intoxicating " liquors was unenforcible because of its uncertainty. Many of the states therefore defined as " intoxicating " any beverage containing more than one-half of one per cent of alcohol. While this was an improvement, it was far from satisfactory because it diverted attention of the court and jury from the act of making or selling to the question of alcoholic content. In the case of distilled liquors, it was impossible to make the claim that they contained less than one-half of one per cent of alcohol. With malt liquors, however, the situation was entirely different. If a "near-bear" could be put upon the market that looked and tasted like real beer and differed from it only in its alcoholic content, the opportunity for subterfuge and evasion became practically unlimited. The claim could always be made that the alcoholic content was within the legal limitation and this raised a question of fact and gave criminal lawyers and "experts" an opportunity to confuse the jury and precipitate a farce. This brought into existence a horde of greedy and lawless brewers and bootleggers who were able to elude the officers of the law and render enforcement impossible. The result was that a majority of the states that had enacted prohibition laws forbade the manufacture and sale of all malt liquors. This provision destroyed the illegal beer business at its source and removed one of the greatest difficulties to enforcement. There was little demand for malt beverages except as a cover for the illegal beer trade. But, however that might be, the people believed that it was more important to protect the public health and morals and suppress lawlessness than it was to foster the near-beer business.

This policy met with popular approval and was upheld by the courts of the various states and by the Supreme Court of the United States. In upholding such a law, the supreme court of North Dakota said that "it is a matter of common knowledge that liquor of this description while not actually intoxicating . . . presents a constant opportunity and temptation to the criminal classes to make it a vehicle of subterfuge, fraud, and a means of evading the penalties of the prohibition law."[8] In sustaining a similar statute enacted by the state of Mississippi, the Supreme Court of the United States said:

> It was competent for the legislature of Mississippi to recognize the difficulties besetting the administration of laws aimed at the prevention

of traffic in intoxicants. It prohibited, among other things, the sale of "malt liquors." In thus dealing with a class of beverages which in general are regarded as intoxicating, it was not bound to resort to a discrimination with respect to ingredients and processes of manufacture which, in the endeavor to eliminate innocuous beverages from the condemnation, would facilitate subterfuge and frauds and fetter the enforcement of the law.

That the opinion is extensively held that a general prohibition of the sale of malt liquors, whether intoxicating or not, is a necessary means to the suppression of trade in intoxicants, sufficiently appears from the legislation of other states and the decision of the courts in its construction. . . . We cannot say that there is no basis for this widespread conviction.[9]

Profiting by this experience, Congress, when it passed the Alaska prohibition law in February 1917, and the District of Columbia prohibition law in March of the same year, included "all malt liquors." This phrase was omitted from the Volstead Act, passed two years later, and the confusing and discredited one-half of one per cent was re-established. As if its purpose was to make the breakdown of the law a certainty, Congress inserted the following clause:

A manufacturer of any beverage containing less than one-half of 1 per centum of alcohol by volume may, on making application and giving such bond as the commissioner shall prescribe, be given a permit to develop in the manufacture thereof by the usual methods of fermentation and fortification or otherwise, a liquid such as beer, ale, porter or wine, containing more than one-half of 1 per centum of alcohol; *provided, however,* that such liquid may be removed and transported, under bond, and under such regulations as the commissioner may prescribe, from one bonded plant or warehouse to another for the purpose of having the alcohol extracted therefrom. And such liquids may be developed, under permit, by persons other than the manufacturers of beverages containing less than one-half of 1 per centum of alcohol by volume, and sold to such manufacturers for conversion into beverages. The alcohol removed from such liquid, if evaporated, and not condensed and saved, shall not be subject to tax; if saved, it shall be subject to the same law as other alcoholic liquors.

This was the door through which Al Capone and all the "beer barons" of the prohibition era made their appearance. It enabled the brewers to keep their plants and their financial structures intact and carry on their campaign to bring about the breakdown of the law. Some of the brewers who kept their plants in operation for the manufacture of near-beer remained within the law because of the size of their investments, but others operated in defiance of the law. For appearance' sake, a part of their product would be de-alcoholized and sold in a legal manner. At the same time, they would attach pipes to vats containing real beer and draw it off to garages and other buildings on near-by lots, where it would be put into bottles and kegs and sent out to the bootleg trade. Some of these methods of operation are described by Mrs. Willebrandt:

> After the regular beer is manufactured such a brewer sends out "spotters" who determine the location of government officers. Sometimes they bribe an agent and get him to ride the trucks. The high-percentage beer is quickly "shot" out to what are termed "drops" — garages, or other convenient hiding places, located about the community. Another method breweries have utilized in other sections to defeat the law is the supplying to near-beer establishments of products conforming to the one-half of one per cent limitations, but accompanied by secret supplies of alcohol to be "needled" into the glasses of near-beer served.[10]

If they were discovered, and their permit to make real beer was withdrawn, they would

> secure the aid of three or four citizens, generally individuals with good reputations but perfectly willing to place the same — for a consideration — at the disposal of the beer specialists. This legally respectable group of straw men assembles, organizes a corporation, creates capital stock, promulgates by-laws, elects officers, "purchases" the brewery, on paper of course, secures a permit and starts working, with the discredited former permittees directing operations behind the scenes.[11]

Finally scarcely a pretense was made of obeying the law; "wild cat" and "alley" breweries sprang up everywhere; the country was flooded with illegal beer and gangsters indulged in mutual slaughter as they battled for control of the beer trade and its huge profits. Discussing this provision of the law, Dr. Colvin says:

> The provision permitting breweries to make regular beer with the supposition that before sale they would reduce the alcoholic content to below one-half of one per cent was the colossal blunder of prohibitory legislation. It contravened the first object of prohibitory legislation, which is to stop the traffic at its source. Permitting brewers to make regular beer with the supposition that they would de-alcoholize it was something new in prohibitory legislation. In the congressional debate, Mr. Volstead stated: " For the first time we have written into a prohibition bill the permission to make near-beer."
>
> What has been the result? The breweries have been left almost intact as a fighting force striving to come back. Although of about 1,332 breweries operating in 1916, something over 200 were dismantled, the large majority remain.[12]

In adopting the one-half of one per cent standard, Congress emphasized the blunder it committed when it used the phrase " intoxicating liquors " in the amendment. The wets used this action as an authority for their contention that Congress had the power to fix a percentage that would be high enough to permit the return and taxation of the beer traffic. This provision was one of the principal factors in bringing about the nullification of the Constitution by " modifying the Volstead Act."

Home Wine-Making

It was universally conceded that the provision of the Volstead Act relating to the home manufacture of wine was an absurdity. Referring to it, the report of the Wickersham Commission said:

> Home wine-making involves an anomalous provision of the national prohibition act. The last clause of Section 29 of Title II reads: " The penalties provided in this act shall not apply to a person for manufacturing nonintoxicating cider and fruit juices exclusively for use in his home, but such cider and fruit juices shall not be sold or delivered except to persons having permits to manufacture vinegar." . . . As the matter stands, then, when wine is produced in the home for home use,

whether or not the product is intoxicating is a question of fact to be decided by the jury in each case. If this view stands, it becomes impracticable to interfere with home wine-making, and it appears to be the policy of the government not to interfere with it. Indeed the government has gone further. Prepared materials for the purpose of easy wine-making are now manufactured on a large scale with federal aid. Much of homemade wine gets into circulation. The possibilities of leakage, when there is pressure on other sources of supply, are always considerable. Moreover, it would seem that Section 29, as its construction is now acquiesced in, is a serious infringement of the policy of Section 3.

The result was that if it were proved or even admitted that a man had manufactured wine and that it had an alcoholic content equal to that of beer or wine of pre-prohibition days, the government could do nothing about it until a jury had found that it was intoxicating in fact. All the culprit had to do, therefore, was so to deceive and prejudice the jury that it would find that his wine was nonintoxicating in fact, and he could continue to do what the Constitution prohibited. Prosecutors and judges were helpless and the meaning of the law was determined by the cleverness and dishonesty of lawyers and witnesses and the gullibility of jurors in particular cases. This meant that the law was unenforcible and the government threw up its hands. Large quantities of wine were manufactured in "homes" for the bootleg trade and tens of thousands of gallons of grape juice were manufactured and sold in such a state that they would develop a high alcoholic content shortly after delivery to the home.

Results of the Permit System

There is a short, crisp federal statute which provides that anyone who uses the mails in furtherance of a scheme to defraud shall be sent to the penitentiary. This law is respected and its strict enforcement has the approval of the people. It is easy to see how absurd it would have been if, in order to prevent the fraudulent use of the mails, Congress had provided that every mail-order house and every other business enterprise making use of the mails should take out a government permit and be subject to inspection and supervision by government bureaucrats, whose function it would have been to prevent business men from becoming criminals. But this was the philosophy of the Volstead Act. There was a large demand for alcohol to be used in industry and the arts and in scientific and other pursuits, and its manufacture and sale for such purposes was as legitimate as the manufacture and sale of shoes or any other article of commerce. If the business had been put upon that basis, those engaged in it would have been anxious to preserve their status as honorable business men, and to avoid any connection with bootleggers, gangsters and others engaged in the outlawed traffic in alcoholic beverages. They would have kept within the law in the same manner and from the same motives as do other business men. They were, however, put under suspicion and treated as potential criminals. They were forced to take out government permits and conduct their business under the supervision of bureaucrats whom they regarded as officious and obnoxious. They felt, therefore, that as long as they were following the letter of the law, they were justified in making all the alcohol they could dispose of, and in leaving it to prohibition agents to prevent it from passing into criminal channels.

The law was ideally adapted to the encouragement of this irresponsible attitude. In the past distillers had been permitted to denature alcohol and sell it tax-free for other than beverage purposes. There had been no independent denaturing plants. The situation was entirely changed by the following provision of the Volstead Act:

> Section 10. Upon the filing of application and bond and issuance of permit denaturing plants may be established upon the premises of any industrial alcohol plant, *or elsewhere,* and shall be used exclusively for the denaturing of alcohol by the admixture of such denaturing materials as shall render the alcohol, or any compound in which it is authorized to be used, unfit for use as an intoxicating beverage. Alcohol lawfully denatured may, under regulations, be sold free of tax either for domestic use or for export.

The two words " or elsewhere " were words of doom for both the law and the amendment. They opened the way for the independent denaturing plants. This enabled the distiller to make not only all the alcohol he could denature and sell in that condition, but all that he could sell to these independent plants in its natural state. His permit did not limit the amount that he could sell and it made no difference to him what was done with it after it left his control. It was the duty of the government to see that it was properly used. The independent plant had a permit to denature and sell the alcohol, but it would divert it through a " cover house " to the bootlegging trade. The government had neither the authority nor the men necessary to follow the transaction through.

The results are shown by the statements of those engaged in the administration of the law. Major Chester P. Mills, prohibition administrator for the metropolitan district of New York, in his plan submitted in the Durant contest, said:

These distilleries are required to maintain denaturing plants and will not, as a rule, sell grain alcohol to a competitor at a price that will enable the competitor (the independent denaturing plant) to manufacture and compete with them.

The independent denaturing plant has no economic reason for existence. Since the independent plant cannot usually compete for legitimate business, it is often driven to make a living by delivering unlawful supplies to the bootlegger.

We come now to the very serious evil of diversion under cover of permits authorizing firms to manufacture from specially denatured alcohol. The principal method of diversion may be illustrated by an example. A perfume manufacturer as a permit holder receives specially denatured alcohol, for whose use he must account to the government in records of perfume manufactured and on hand or shipped out. The crooked permit holder pretends to ship his manufactured product to a wholesaler known as a " cover house." The wholesaler receipts for perfume but actually receives or diverts specially denatured alcohol for the bootlegger.

To disguise the transaction, the " cover house " receives from the permit holder invoices and in many cases bills of lading. It acknowledges these invoices and even pays for them as well as acknowledging the bills of lading.[13]

General Lincoln C. Andrews said:

> Before prohibition [alcohol] was denatured at the distillery. As a result of prohibition, there grew up the thirty special denaturing plants, which, frankly, I feel are nothing more or less than bootlegging organizations because they give opportunity for diversion. There seems to be no economic necessity whatever for a special denaturing plant away from a distillery. It never did exist in the economy of alcohol.[14]

Mr. Buckner said:

> Apparently 60,000,000 gallons of industrial alcohol in the United States went into the bootleg trade. . . . The denaturing plant buys from the regular distillery 10,000 gallons of pure alcohol. The distillery has the right to sell. It is a bonded distillery. The denaturing plant has the right to buy, because it has a permit. The owner of the denaturing plant buys it. The theory is that he is going to poison it. . . .
>
> Then what the denaturing plant really does is to take the 10,000 gallons, does not put a drop of poison in it, and sells it to a bootlegger. The prohibition agent comes around to inspect. He says, " Have you sold this? " and they say, " Yes, here is the invoice, John Jones & Company." The prohibition agent does not go to John Jones, does not bother with him, does not go to the district attorney, does not take it to the grand jury, because the whole inspection business is so woefully undermanned that nothing effective can be done more than this.[15]

There can be no doubt that it was through the diversion of industrial alcohol under this absurd permit system that the illegal traffic in hard liquor got its start and finally reached such huge proportions that it passed beyond control. Major Mills, whose essay was published in 1929, states that less than two per cent of the liquor consumed was smuggled across the borders. He further said: " Diversion of alcohol and liquors under cover of indiscriminately granted permits controlled by unreliable persons provides the vast majority of liquor consumed today." [16] Mrs. Willebrandt, whose book was published in the same year, said:

"My judgment, based upon eight years' experience, is that the greatest single source of liquor supply today is alcohol diverted illegally in the form of a government permit."[17]

Medicinal Liquor

Among the strange blunders of the Volstead Act were its provisions for the prescription of alcoholic beverages by physicians and their sale by druggists. In the past it was believed that when taken internally, alcohol acted as a stimulant and had a therapeutic value in connection with certain diseases. About the beginning of the present century, it was definitely established by exact laboratory experiments that alcohol is not a stimulant but one of the narcotic drugs and that its action is that of a depressant. It was proved that the excitement and euphoria resulting from its use are only the first stage of paralysis that progresses with increased consumption until a state of complete paralysis is reached. It was also proved that although alcohol could be used as a narcotic, there were other drugs that were safer and more convenient and effective — that for every internal use that had been made of alcohol, there was a more satisfactory substitute. This discovery brought about a revolution in the attitude of scientific medicine toward the internal use of alcohol. The result is that physicians of genuine scientific attainments now use alcohol freely as an antiseptic and astringent and for other external purposes, and in the preparation and preservation of pharmaceutical products, but only in rare instances prescribe it for internal use.

In support of this fact it would be possible to fill a volume with statements by the outstanding representatives of scientific medicine in this country and Europe. In 1932 physicians connected with Harvard, Yale and Columbia universities and the Rockefeller Institute for Medical Research and a representative of the New York Life Insurance Company published a book in which they presented the results of the latest scientific investigations as to the effects of alcohol on man. It was a scientific work and had no connection with promotion or propaganda of any kind. It says:

The immediate effects of the systemic absorption of alcohol resemble those of any of the anaesthetic agents used in surgery. There is first the so-called " excitation stage," due to the removal of the inhibitory influences of the higher centers of the brain. This is followed by the stage of incoordination, in which the mental and muscular balance is upset and cerebral confusion and physical ataxia result. The subject gradually becomes oblivious to his surroundings and insensitive to ordinary stimuli and lapses into a state of stupor from which he will react only to strong stimuli; finally he passes into a state of true anaesthesia in which consciousness is entirely lost and the patient lies in a state of absolute coma from which it is impossible to arouse him. Thus the different degrees of drunkenness, as acute alcoholic intoxication is commonly called, parallel those which develop under ether or chloroform. . . .

As a solvent of various medicaments alcohol performs a useful, perhaps indispensable, function and the pharmacist requires it to compound many of our widely used therapeutic preparations. The therapeutic part played by alcohol in these preparations is very limited.[18]

Dr. Arthur Dean Bevan, professor in Rush Medical College and former president of the American Medical Association, says:

Viewed from the standpoint of modern scientific medicine, alcohol belongs to the groups of narcotics which consist of alcohol, ether, chloroform, chloral and similar drugs, such as sulphonal and veronal. The general actions of all the members of this narcotic group are very much the same. They produce a first stage of imperfect consciousness and confused ideas, followed later by a stage of excitement, and if the dose is large complete unconsciousness which may, if the dose is sufficiently large, terminate in death.

There has been some dispute as to whether these drugs are stimulants or are paralyzing agents. Scientific men who have studied this problem for the most part regard them as not being stimulants at all, or if they have a stimulating action, the stimulating action is very temporary as the main action is that of depressing agents. . . .

Alcohol has little place in modern scientific medicine as a therapeutic agent. At the Presbyterian Hospital in Chicago, where we take care of more than twelve thousand patients a year, we have not yet prescribed through the drug room of the hospital a single bottle of alcoholic liquor since the passage of the prohibition amendment, and this is not due to any regulation against the use of alcohol. Any one of the attending medical men has the privilege of using alcohol if he sees fit in the handling of his cases. It is due to the fact that there is little or no logical or scientific reason for the internal administration of alcohol in the modern treatment of disease. On the other hand, the external use of alcohol has increased very markedly. . . .

Alcohol is no longer used by scientific physicians in acute inflammatory diseases, such as pneumonia and grippe. It is not only not beneficial but definitely harmful in such conditions. It is no longer used in septic conditions. Its only use, outside of its external use, in modern scientific medicine is found in cases of individuals who are chronic users of alcohol and who are brought to the hospital suffering from some accident or some disease in which a moderate amount of alcohol is continued for a time in order to prevent the development of delirium tremens. . . .

My experience in the practice of medicine in Chicago covers the period from 1894 to date. I have never had any fixed opposition to the use of whisky in medical practice but I have never employed it, or seen it properly employed, except in just such cases that I have cited. My very considerable experience in the practice of medicine cannot have been so very different from that of other men in the medical profession.[19]

Dr. Haven Emerson has been commissioner of health of New York city and professor of preventive medicine in Cornell University, and is now professor of public health practice in Columbia University. He is also a member of the National Advisory Health Council of the United States Public Health Service and a member of the Commission of Expert Statisticians of the Health Section of the League of Nations. In a book published in 1934, he says:

Passing over the uses of alcohol as an external dressing, solvent, astringent, antiseptic, etc., which are generally and intelligently made use of, it is important to consider the reasons which still influence the laity and some members of the medical profession to use alcohol for medicinal purposes by internal administration, without a scientific reason in fact.

Alcohol is used unreasonably as a medicine on the ancient and quite erroneous assumption that its use can be relied upon to stimulate the heart, to improve respiration, and to add to the vigor and vitality of the body in general.

Alcohol, like many another familiar and powerful drug, has genuine use as a medicine, but none that cannot ordinarily be better served by other substances. It is in no sense an indispensable drug or unique in its properties so that it is essential to good medical care of the sick. Its widespread use by the laity and by physicians, in former times more than in the twentieth century, was due more to its almost universal availability and the familiarity of the laity with its strength and effect in beverage form than to particular or especially desirable drug properties.

Alcohol is not a specific or cure for any disease, unless one considers " worry " to be a disease, and a drugged indifference a cure. . . . Alcohol is prescribed as a narcotic by some physicians in the belief that it is a boon of value to the aged who suffer from the annoyance and lack of entertainment of their years. Such a makeshift management of age by dulling the wits is not generally endorsed by physicians or the laity.

Alcohol is to be avoided in snake-bite. The use of alcohol in childbed fever, blood poisoning, sepsis and in the infective fevers of childhood has been almost entirely abandoned as of no value.

A well reasoned statement from a leading American medical authority is to the effect that " much of the use for alcohol and alcoholic beverages of the past no longer exists, for better therapeutic measures have replaced them." It seems a fact that in both private and hospital practice the utilization of alcohol and alcoholic beverages by the better trained physician has decreased greatly and is continuing to decrease.[20]

Dr. George Blumer, professor in the medical school of Yale University, says:

I do not believe that alcohol is a stimulant, and if I want to use a narcotic, there are others that are more dependable than alcohol. . . . I find the advocacy of alcohol as a remedy decreasing quite distinctly.

Dr. Howard Kelly of Johns Hopkins University says:

There is no single disease in the world of which alcohol is the cure. This fact is well known to science, is now generally admitted by progressive members of the medical profession, but is rarely made clear to the layman. The purpose of medicine is to cure disease. Since alcohol cures no disease, it is not a medicine. It has no place in medical practice.

Professor A. R. Cushny of the University of Edinburgh says:

The use of alcohol in medicine is not of great importance. If it were a new drug, invented perhaps in some laboratory, it would have a vogue as a narcotic for a short time, and then would be forgotten or in consideration of its habitual and unnecessary use it might be put under the same restriction as morphine, or cocaine, each of which is, of course, far more important in medicine.[21]

These facts were well established prior to the adoption of the Volstead Act. Dr. T. D. Crothers, superintendent of the Walnut Lodge Hospital for Inebriates at Hartford, Connecticut, in the March 1914 number of the *Journal of the American Institute of Criminal Law and Criminology,* said:

Within the last ten years a revolution of theories and opinions concerning alcohol has taken place. Scientific researches in the laboratory and clinical experience confirmed by exact measurements with instruments of precision, have proven that the effects of alcohol on the body are anaesthetic and paralyzing.

The so-called tonic and stimulant properties which have been claimed for centuries, and incorporated in textbooks and literature as facts beyond question, are contradicted by modern research.

Theories that alcohol in any form gives new power and force to the brain activities, bringing out latent qualities and new energies, and in some way giving the person greater efficiency and power, must be put aside. The display of excitement, activity and mental force by persons under the influence of spirits is really the first stage of a paralysis. Thus the five senses, and the ability to reason, the rapidity of thought, the capacity to memorize, the muscular output, are all *depressed,* lowered and actually numbed by the use of alcohol in any form.

These are facts that are verifiable by measurements and can be expressed by figures, showing the loss with absolute certainty. While some alcohols are more powerful than others (by alcohols I mean any drink containing alcohol), and some have a special action on the brain, on the heart, the muscular system and the senses, they are all evidence of one great pathological effect of paralysis.

In 1917, Dr. Charles H. Mayo said: "Medicine has reached a period when alcohol is rarely employed as a drug, being displaced by other remedies. Alcohol's only place now is in the arts and sciences."[22] In the same year, Dr. Frank Billings, dean of Rush Medical School, said that the use of alcohol in medicine "is permissible only in the preparations and preservations of pharmaceutical products."[23] Of still greater significance is the fact that in 1914 the National Convention of Alienists and Neurologists and in 1917 the American Medical Association adopted the resolutions heretofore set out.[24]

The states had found that if they were to solve the liquor problem, they would have to accept the teachings of science and universal experience. In twelve states, no intoxicating liquor of any kind could be prescribed, and in nine states, pure alcohol only could be prescribed.[25] Thus in twenty-one states, physicians were forbidden to prescribe, and druggists to sell, whisky, brandy, gin, beer or any other alcoholic beverage. In 1917, Congress in the Alaska prohibition law had forbidden physicians to prescribe or druggists to sell alcoholic beverages under any circumstances. Druggists were permitted to obtain and dispense "pure alcohol for scientific, artistic or mechanical purposes or for compounding, preparing, or preserving medicines only." After a century of experience and consideration, the people had put into the Constitution an amendment prohibiting the manufacture, sale or transportation of intoxicating liquor for beverage purposes. Notwithstanding this history and the terms of the amendment, Congress legalized the manufacture, transportation and sale of alcoholic liquors for beverage purposes, and in such fashion that it made many doctors bootleggers, many drugstores speak-easies, and the law a farce.

Section 7 of the Volstead Act read:

No one but a physician holding a permit to prescribe liquor shall issue any prescription for liquor. And no physician shall prescribe liquor unless after careful physical examination of the person for whose use such prescription is sought, or if such examination is found impracticable, then upon the best information obtainable, he, in good faith, believes that the use of such liquor as a medicine by such person is necessary and will afford relief to him from some known ailment. Not more than a pint of spirituous liquor to be taken internally shall be prescribed for use by the same person within any period of ten days, and no prescription shall be filled more than once. Any pharmacist filling a prescription shall at the time indorse upon it, over his own signature, the word "cancelled," together with the date when the liquor was delivered, and then make the same a part of the record that he is required to keep as herein provided.

Section 2 of the Supplemental Act provided

that only spirituous and vinous liquor may be prescribed for medicinal purposes, and all permits to prescribe and prescriptions for any other liquor shall be void. No physician shall prescribe, nor shall any person sell or furnish on any prescription, any vinous liquor that contains more than 24 per centum of alcohol by volume, nor shall anyone prescribe or sell or furnish on any prescription more than one-fourth of one gallon of vinous liquor, or any such vinous or spirituous liquor that contains separately or in the aggregate more than one-half pint of alcohol, for use by any person within any period of ten days. No physician shall be furnished with more than one hundred prescription blanks for use in any period of ninety days, nor shall any physician issue more than that number of prescriptions within any such period unless on application therefor he shall make it clearly apparent to the commissioner that for some extraordinary reason a larger amount is necessary, whereupon the necessary additional blanks may be furnished him. But this provision shall not be construed to limit the sale of any article the limitation of which is authorized under Section 4, Title II, of the national prohibition act.

It was impossible to prove that the physician did not believe that the liquor was needed and all the druggists required was a prescription. It was therefore easy for dishonest and border-line physicians to make money by writing bootleg prescriptions or by furnishing dishonest druggists with books of signed prescriptions.

The result was that although the procedure was different and the expense greater, the stuff obtained and the use made of it was the same as when it had been obtained at the corner saloon.

Physicians Become Bootleggers

A still more tragic result was the fact that large numbers of normally honest and law-abiding physicians and druggists felt that the law was so drawn that its violation was forced upon them. Their success depends not alone upon their skill, but also upon their good will. If a man asked for a liquor prescription, it was the duty of the physician to refuse it unless he honestly believed that the man was suffering from "some known ailment" for which an alcoholic beverage was a proper remedy. He knew, however, that if he took this course, the man would not only resent it but also go to some more accommodating physician for his liquor supply. He feared that he would not only lose the money which he would have received for the liquor prescription, which he was willing to do, but that he would also lose the man's legitimate patronage, which he was unwilling to do. So he said to himself, "Well, he will get his liquor anyway, and I am not going to sacrifice my practice to a sentimental and futile obedience to a foolish law," and he lapsed to the status of a bootlegger.

As it was practically impossible to compare the amount of liquor withdrawn by druggists under their permits with the amount called for by the prescriptions in their possession, there was no effective limitation upon the amount of liquor which they kept in stock. It was comparatively safe, therefore, for the druggist to furnish liquor to those of his customers upon whose discretion he could rely. He also knew that if he refused to do so, the customers would go to his rival on the opposite corner and that he would lose both his liquor and his legitimate patronage. So he turned his drugstore into a speak-easy.

Eventually, in every part of the country, many physicians and druggists who were naturally among the most intelligent and law-abiding people in their communities, became bootleggers and proprietors of speak-easies. They lost all respect for a law which they felt they were forced to violate and their attitude and conduct spread contempt for law to every class.

Dr. Bevan expressed the attitude of the physicians who were too honest and courageous to be forced into this disreputable business. In a carefully considered statement which he published in 1928 he said:

> It, of course, has been a matter of common knowledge that the prescribing of whisky by physicians since the passage of the prohibition amendment has been grossly abused. I think very few of us realize how gross this abuse really has been and what a disgraceful situation has been brought about by the provisions of the prohibition amendment for the prescribing of whisky. I have taken pains to investigate this matter with a good deal of care, and desire to submit to you some of the important results of that investigation. The figures which I shall present to you are accurate in the sense that they give a correct picture of the situation in gross figures.
>
> Year before last there was issued from the government warehouses a total of 1,800,000 gallons of hard liquor. This was almost entirely whisky. Approximately 90 per cent of this was issued on physicians' prescriptions. This would make 1,630,000 gallons — there are eight pints in a gallon — making approximately 13,000,000 pints. At $3 a pint, which is the ordinary price obtained by physicians for these prescriptions, the total amount of money received by the medical profession (all of these prescriptions paid for at that rate) would be about $39,000,000. I desire to emphasize this point showing the enormous possibility of graft involved in this situation.
>
> I desire to submit two main facts:
>
> First, that there is an enormous amount of graft, probably in the neighborhood of $40,000,000, in the writing of prescriptions by the medical profession for whisky.
>
> The second point I desire to make is that in the modern scientific practice of medicine there are very few cases in which whisky can be properly and scientifically employed as a medical agent. . . . Before the days of prohibition, no honest doctor ever prescribed 100 pints of whisky to his patients in a few months; as certainly today no honest doctor ever prescribed 100 pints of whisky every three months, or to make it more emphatic, no honest physician ever prescribed 400 pints

of whisky to his patients in a year. The prohibition administrator in this district informs me that approximately 90 per cent of the physicians who have been issued prescription books regularly prescribe their full allotment of 100 prescriptions every three months. Almost all of these prescriptions are bootlegging prescriptions. Very few of them are bona fide scientific medical prescriptions.

There can be but one meaning to this situation. The man on the street knows what that meaning is; the public, generally, know what this situation means. It can mean but one thing, that the men who are prescribing and selling 100 prescriptions every three months, their full allotment, are a disgrace to the medical profession.

It is obvious that the existing state of facts carries with it an enormous abuse of this whisky prescribing. It is clearly the duty of the organized medical profession of this country to do everything in their power to secure such change in the government regulations as will make it impossible for the bootlegging members of the profession to continue their present practices.[26]

The Drugstore Speak-Easy

Foreseeing the degrading effect upon the drug business of making it the only legal source of supply for intoxicating beverages, the National Association of Retail Druggists, while the Volstead Act was pending before Congress, adopted a resolution disapproving such action:

Resolved: That in view of the pending and proposed legislation to prohibit the sale of alcoholic liquors, the N. A. R. D. in convention assembled, is of the opinion that such legislation should not provide for the sale by the pharmacists of the country of such alcoholic liquors for any purpose and urges every retail druggist to refrain from taking out a liquor permit.

The character of men now seeking to enter the practice of pharmacy and to conduct retail drugstores is a matter that is giving serious concern to leaders of pharmacy in the United States, and the situation is attributed largely to the fact that the retail drugstore has the legal right to dispense liquor and narcotics upon prescription.

The *Druggists' Circular,* one of the oldest and leading drug journals in the country, in its March 1926 issue publishes the result of a nationwide referendum taken among the retail druggists of the country, which shows that more than 80 per cent of the retail druggists favor petitioning Congress to relieve them of responsibility of dispensing liquor on prescription.

The New York State Pharmaceutical Association adopted a resolution at its annual convention in June 1925, in which it declares that many of the current ills in pharmacy have resulted from the fact that the prohibition law designates retail pharmacists as the only legitimate distributors of medicinal liquor to the public and petitioned Congress to relieve pharmacy of that responsibility.[27]

In his statement, Mr. Buckner showed the results in the New York district:

In our district there are 1,200 drug stores having permits to sell liquor. There are 5,100 doctors having permits to issue prescriptions. The permit that the druggist gets to sell liquor is theoretically to enable him to distribute liquor that the doctor orders. There is a little extra there for compounding prescriptions, but I think we may disregard that.

After stating that he assigned one of his assistants to investigate the situation, he continued:

For instance, looking up the government records he finds that the amount of liquor which the prescriptions would justify in our district would be 240,000 gallons a year. In other words, that the druggists should have drawn out 240,000 gallons of whisky in order to supply the very maximum amount that the doctors can prescribe for their patients under their prescriptions. . . . He found that instead of 240,000 gallons being withdrawn by druggists, 480,000 gallons were in fact withdrawn, exactly two to one! [28]

The permit to manufacture, prescribe and sell alcoholic beverages provided the supply, the temptation, the means of obtaining it, and the alibi. It was an important factor in breaking down enforcement and creating contempt for law. If the act had simply prohibited the manufacture and use of alcoholic liquors for beverage purposes, and provided adequate penalties for its violation, it would have been clearly understood by doctors, druggists and the public, there would have been neither loopholes nor alibis, and it would not have provided a source of illegal liquor nor an invitation to lawlessness and crime. At the same time, physicians and druggists would not have been subjected to temptation and to offensive bureaucratic espionage, nor would there have been any interference with their use of alcohol for all legitimate purposes.

Sacramental Wine

Another absurdity of the Volstead Act was its provision for "sacramental wine." For a hundred years, the churches, both Catholic and Protestant, had declared that alcohol unleashed the lower appetites and passions, arrested the reason and enslaved the will; that it ruined the home, was a source of drunkenness, disease, vice and crime, and that it was the greatest enemy of the Kingdom of God on earth. Denouncing it as "a veritable brew of hell," they had been in the forefront of the fight for the suppression of its manufacture in beverage form. Cardinal Manning said: "The chief bar to the working of the Holy Spirit of God in the souls of men and women is intoxicating drink. I know of no antagonist to the Holy Spirit more direct, more subtle, more ubiquitous." [29] The General Assembly of the Presbyterian Church said: "In view of the evils wrought by this scourge of our race, the assembly would hail with acclamations of joy and thanksgiving the utter extermination of the traffic in intoxicating liquors as a beverage." [30] These are typical of the statements that had been made by church groups for generations. And yet at the very time that in every part of the land they were offering up prayers of thanksgiving for the adoption of the Eighteenth Amendment, Congress was enacting an enforcement statute which reserved to the churches the right to manufacture or purchase and to use intoxicating beverages as part of their religious ceremonies. It provided that "wine for sacramental purposes may be manufactured, purchased, sold, bartered, transported, imported, exported, delivered, furnished, and possessed, but only as herein provided, and the commissioner may, upon application, issue permits therefor."

That this provision was the result of misinformation and a

strange blindness, there can be no doubt whatever. The rite of intoxication, in which alcoholic beverages were of course necessary, had been a part of primitive and pagan religions. Walter R. Miles, professor of experimental psychology in Yale University, says:

> According to current thinking, alcohol is an enemy to religion but it has not always been so considered. In primitive cultures intoxication had a close psychological connection with religious forms and practices. The close relationship between bodily excitement and mental exaltation was early discovered and so fasting, self-torture, violent and prolonged dancing, and finally, stimulating drugs were employed to heighten religious experience. Partridge in his *Psychology of Intemperance* reports how uncivilized man prizes ecstatic feelings, and the sense of increased joy, power and well-being induced by intoxicants, and how he strives for these god-given and god-pleasing states as expressions of divine favor. The cult of intoxication has existed since the earliest times. It has occurred in many forms, and numerous drugs, including alcohol, have been repeatedly designated as divine. . . . Certain primitive bands have tried to arrange for the practical affairs of life and also the " religious ecstasies " by dividing themselves into two or more companies, one of which might enjoy intoxication while the other remained sober, ready if need be to fight the tribal enemies.[31]

Not a suggestion of this rite survived in Christianity. Christ taught that man finds his true joy when he is in the complete possession of all his faculties and fulfilling the law of love. Whether the ceremony of the Lord's Supper be regarded as a sacrament or as a memorial, its complete divorcement from any idea of alcoholic excitement is clearly indicated by the language of the Gospel, on which it is based. In the Revised Version it is stated by Matthew as follows:

> And he took a cup, and gave thanks, and gave it to them, saying, Drink ye all of it; for this is my blood of the covenant, which is shed for many unto remission of sins. But I say unto you, I will not drink henceforth of this fruit of the vine, until that day when I drink it anew with you in my Father's kingdom.

Many modern churches use a fruit of the vine that has not been put through the process by which it becomes intoxicating. Those that use ordinary wine do so as a result of custom and convenience and not because of its intoxicating effect.

That this provision of the law furnished an opening through which large amounts of intoxicating liquor poured into illegal channels, was definitely established. Edwin A. Olson, United States district attorney for the northern district of Illinois, told the Senate committee that in his district " sacramental wine withdrawals in 1923 were 885,000 gallons. They dropped to 60,000 gallons in 1925 — after prosecution had been commenced against those charged with illegal diversion." [32] District Judge A. T. Cole, in the plan he submitted in the Durant contest, said: " At present there are certain ecclesiastics who obtain sacramental wines in great bulk, and distribute much of them among parishioners, to be used by them for claimed sacramental purposes. This practice, which is more common than most people are aware of, should be stopped by stringent laws." [33]

In 1925 the Department of Research and Education of the Federal Council of the Churches of Christ, conducted an exhaustive investigation of the subject. In its report it says:

> One phase of the wine question is undoubtedly serious. The withdrawal of wines on permit from bonded warehouses for sacramental purposes amounted in round figures to 2,139,000 gallons in the fiscal year 1922; 2,503,500 gallons in 1923; and 2,944,700 gallons in 1924. There is no way of knowing what the legitimate consumption of fermented sacramental wine is, but it is clear that the legitimate demand does not increase 800,000 gallons in two years. It is probably safe to say that not more than one-quarter of this wine is sacramental — the rest is sacrilegious. " Literally hundreds " of fictitious Jewish congregations, Commissioner Haynes testified before the Senate committee which investigated the Bureau of Internal Revenue, had been found engaged in fraudulent schemes to secure the release of " sacramental " wine.[34]

The provisions for alcoholic beverages for medicinal and sacramental purposes became serious obstacles to enforcement because of the opportunities they afforded for evasion and the encouragement they gave to bootlegging. Their psychological effects were even more serious to the cause of prohibition. The American Medical Association and the churches had condemned the use of alcoholic beverages and the Eighteenth Amendment had been adopted on the theory that alcoholic beverages were physically and morally destructive, and yet it was provided that physicians, rabbis, priests and clergymen might purchase and use them on the theory that they were physically and spiritually beneficial. This enabled the wets to taunt the advocates of prohibition with inconsistency and hypocrisy and to create disrespect for the law. A single incident will illustrate their technique.

In 1926, amendments to the Volstead Act had been proposed that would have rendered it completely unenforcible and in effect would have repealed the Eighteenth Amendment by congressional action. Hearings were being held by a committee of the Senate and hordes of wet lobbyists were demanding the enactment of these amendments. Among them was Tony Cermak, the Tammany boss of Chicago. His statement contained the following sneer: "The law is inconsistent with itself, prohibiting liquor as a beverage and yet authorizing its use as a beverage for medicinal, sacramental and religious purposes."[35]

The Volstead Act prohibited the manufacture and sale of alcoholic liquors "which are fit for use for beverage purposes," except under the elaborate permit system which it set up. If it had simply prohibited the manufacture and use of alcoholic liquors for beverage purposes, it would have been complete and adequate and free from invitations to evasion. If any church desired in good faith to make or have made, purchase, and use intoxicating beverages for strictly sacramental purposes, there would not have been a district attorney who would have suggested, or a judge who would have held, that such action constituted a violation of the law. The churches could have used fermented or unfermented wine in connection with their religious rites without interference by governmental officials, and there would have been no loopholes through which bootleggers might escape.

The Law of Conspiracy

There were two brief statutes that did much to give criminal trials in the federal courts an air of dignity and fateful solemnity and to inspire respect for and obedience to the laws of the United States. They read as follows:

1. If two or more persons conspire either to commit any offense against the United States, or to defraud the United States in any manner or for any purpose, and one or more of such parties do any such act to effect the object of the conspiracy, each of the parties to such conspiracy shall be fined not more than ten thousand dollars, or imprisoned not more than two years, or both.
2. Whoever directly commits an act constituting an offense defined in any law of the United States, aids, abets, counsels, commands, induces, or procures its commission, is a principal.

That simply means that if men conspire to commit an offense against the United States and any one of them performs a single act in furtherance of the conspiracy, they are all equally guilty, and receive the same punishment, whether they succeed or fail in accomplishing their object. It means that if a crime has been committed against the United States, everyone who has aided or abetted its commission in the slightest degree, is a principal and is punishable accordingly. "Good citizens" and "social leaders" did not openly patronize and fraternize with criminals engaged in the commission of crimes to which these statutes applied, nor did they denounce, sneer at or joke about those laws.

The Volstead Act withdrew the enforcement of national prohibition from the operation of these two statutes. Not only were the teachings of experience disregarded, but the zenith of absurdity was reached. As has been pointed out,[36] the purchaser was the principal, the fountainhead of liquor lawlessness and crime. And yet the act not only exempted him from all the penalties which it established, but also from punishment as a co-conspirator or for aiding and abetting. Those charged with the administration of the law soon found that this provision rendered it completely unenforcible. They sought, therefore, by various indirect methods, to reach the purchaser. But the courts held that since it was obviously the intention of Congress to exempt the purchaser, that intention could not be defeated by any form of indirection.

The farcical character of the situation thus created is illustrated by the following case: A New York banker ordered liquor from a bootlegger in Philadelphia. He was indicted and the trial court held that while he could not be punished for purchasing the liquor, he could be for conspiring with the bootlegger to transport it. The United States Circuit Court of Appeals, however, held that transportation was an element of sale and not of purchase, and reversed the conviction. In its opinion, the court said:

> While the seller of liquor, who delivers it to the purchaser, is liable under the law both for the sale and transportation, the purchaser to whom the goods are delivered is chargeable with neither the purchase nor the transportation. . . . It thus appears that while the legislative department of the government has deliberately and intentionally made the purchaser of liquor guiltless of any offense under the prohibition law, the executive department of the government seeks here, by indirection, to make of the same fact, namely, the purchase, a crime subjecting the purchaser to a maximum fine of $10,000 and imprisonment for a term of two years. Such a situation is scarcely conceivable, and yet that is the position of the government.[37]

It has been the proud boast of lawyers that the law is the "perfection of common sense." Here surely we see it as the perfection of nonsense. This state of the law helped to engender a strange intellectual epidemic. It was a combination of mental blindness, rationalization and hypocrisy that seized large numbers of people. They would openly and defiantly purchase, use and serve liquor, when they knew that every transaction by which it was produced and delivered to them was criminal, that they purchased it from criminals and that their money went into the underworld to finance criminal gangs. They would then declare that they were good and law-abiding citizens and with solemn indignation denounce their creatures and partners, the racketeers, gangsters and bootleggers, and with moral and patriotic fervor demand that these be destroyed by the simple device of making their part of the transaction legal also. This was to be accomplished by the easy method of repealing the Eighteenth Amendment. It should be added that this spiritual malady usually originated and assumed its most violent form with big income taxpayers, eager for liquor revenue.

Padlock Provision

It has been well said that one of the greatest advantages of our federal system is that it provides forty-eight separate laboratories for social and political experimentation. It had been established in these laboratories that the most effective method of enforcing laws against gambling, prostitution, intoxicating liquors and other forms of vice from which large profits were derived, was to proceed directly against the property used in connection with them. A gambling establishment, a brothel, a speak-easy or a dope joint could not exist unless it had rooms or a building in which to operate. The man who rented his property for these purposes and shared the profits was precisely as guilty as his tenants, the gamblers, prostitutes, bootleggers and dope sellers. But he was not subject to any of the penalties applicable to his partners in crime. If they were arrested and forced to hire lawyers and pay fines, they had to bear all the expense. If they were sent to prison, he calmly rented his property to another set of criminals and there was no interference with his income.

In their fight against these forms of social disease, some of the states enacted laws which provided that a building used for these illegal purposes might be declared to be a public nuisance and such use perpetually enjoined. This was a step in the right direction, but the lawless gangs would simply rent another building, and the officers of the law would have to start all over again.

The next step was the enactment of laws providing that if it were found that a building was being used for illegal purposes, the court might enjoin its use for any purposes for the period of a year. This was another story. A man might be willing to have his property used as a harbor for criminals and a source of human degradation and social disease; he might be indifferent to the stigma of an injunction forbidding such use; but if he was forced to let the property remain idle for a year, he was hit at a sensitive point, which was the region of his pocketbook. Faced with this possibility, he would refuse to rent it for illegal purposes and he would be very vigilant in his efforts to prevent such use without his knowledge. So he was transformed from a partner of criminals into an ally of the state in the enforcement of the law.

Students of the problem agree that this procedure is the most effective instrument yet devised for the suppression of commercialized vice. The famous Committee of Fifteen, which for years led the fight against this evil in Chicago, said in its report of May 1921:

> The injunction law is the most effective weapon that can be used against vice promotion. Owners do not want their property tied up for a year against its use for any purpose, nor do they want a record of an injunction against it, even though the injunction may be vacated by a bond conditioned that the owner will keep it free from immorality.[38]

States which incorporated this "padlock" provision in prohibition laws, found it their most powerful weapon for the suppression of the illegal liquor traffic. In 1887, the United States Supreme Court in the case of Mugler *vs.* Kansas [39] considered the objections to this procedure and stated that the abatement of nuisances was one of the historic functions of courts of equity. It held that the state had the right to prohibit the liquor traffic, to declare any building used in connection with it a nuisance, to enjoin such use, and, if necessary to accomplish the purpose of the statute, to forbid its use for *any* purpose for a period of a year.

Recognizing the lawless character of those engaged in the liquor business and their readiness to defraud the public by evading their taxes, for more than half a century the federal government has proceeded against the property directly in the enforcement of its revenue laws. The statute provided that if an attempt was made to defraud the United States of taxes, "the distillery, distilling apparatus, and the lot or tract of land on which it stands, and all personal property used in the business, shall be forfeited to the

United States." Construing this statute, the Supreme Court said: "Nor is it necessary that the owner of the property should have knowledge that the lessee and distiller was committing fraud on the public revenue, in order that the information of forfeiture should be maintained." [40]

The laws also provided that if, to defraud the United States of tax, any liquor should be deposited or concealed in any boat, carriage or conveyance of any kind whatsoever, the liquor and the conveyance "and all things used in the removal or for the deposit or concealment thereof respectively shall be forfeited." Here again there was no requirement that the owner have guilty knowledge, no return of the property on the giving of bond for costs, or any other legal red tape or concession. The property was seized and forfeited.

In this way, the government announced that it did not intend to employ an army of revenue agents to roam the country to prevent property from being used in connection with schemes to defraud the United States of liquor revenue. It served notice on property owners that that was their job, that they must take whatever precautions were necessary to prevent their property from being used to make, transport and conceal liquor upon which the tax had not been paid, and that their failure to do so would result in the swift and irrevocable forfeiture of the property so used. This law did not invite violations, evasions, argument, sneers or jokes. It was an expression of simple common sense, and it inspired respect and obedience. That is why few people have even known of its existence.

The Volstead Act provided that any vehicle or building used for the illegal manufacture, sale or storage of intoxicating liquor should be declared to be a common nuisance and that courts of equity should be given power to abate it. It provided that

on finding that the material allegations of the petition are true, the court shall order that no liquors shall be manufactured, sold, bartered or stored in such room, house, building, boat, vehicle, structure or place, or any part thereof. And upon judgment of the court ordering such nuisance to be abated, the court may order that the room, house, building, structure, boat, vehicle or place shall not be occupied or used for one year thereafter.

It was the unanimous testimony of those charged with the administration of the law that this provision was the most powerful weapon available to the government for its enforcement. They also agreed that the provision's usefulness was largely destroyed by senseless and paralyzing restrictions, and by the failure to provide the men and machinery necessary to make it effective.

The act did not provide that the building *shall*, but that it *may*, be closed for a year. It further provided that "the court may, in its discretion, permit it to be occupied or used if the owner, lessee, tenant or occupant thereof shall give a bond . . . of not less than $500 nor more than $1,000," on condition that the illegal use should cease. This enabled the property owner to encourage crime, to make it possible and to share its proceeds, and if he was caught, by financial and political pressure to influence prohibition agents, district attorneys and judges to permit him to give a bond of five hundred dollars and remain in full control of his property. When the storm blew over, the criminal business would usually be resumed.

While these loopholes made it possible for incompetent and dishonest public officials to render the action against property ineffective, another loophole was provided through which criminals could escape in spite of the vigilance of honest and efficient officials. Section 39 of the Volstead Act read:

In all cases wherein the property of any citizen is proceeded against or wherein a judgment affecting it might be rendered, and the citizen is not the one who in person violated the provisions of the law, summons must be issued in due form and served personally, if said person is to be found within the jurisdiction of the court.

In U. S. *vs.* McCrory, the court said:

Prior to a decree that the premises are a nuisance, rendered after such service [personal], there could be no basis for closing them. This is because the prohibition act contains no provision for any preliminary seizure of the premises. . . . The suit is therefore originally in personam and personal service or appearance is the basis of jurisdiction.[41]

What does all this mean? The statute should have provided that where property was being used for criminal purposes, it could be seized, and that fact should constitute notice sufficient to give the court authority to enter a decree binding upon the interested parties. Under this procedure, the government would not have been compelled to engage in a long, expensive and futile search for property owners who were concealing themselves to evade service. Such owners would have been compelled to enter their appearance immediately and make their defense, if they had any under the law. This is the usual proceeding in an action in rem and would have been fair, adequate and effective. It was not made available.

In actions in personam involving real estate, where interested parties conceal themselves, cannot be found or for any reason cannot be served with summons, it is the universal rule in both state and federal courts to obtain service by publication. Even this usual procedure in civil case was denied the government by the Volstead Act. The result was that owners could permit their property to be used in open and contemptuous defiance of the law, and the courts were powerless to act because of lack of jurisdiction.

This restriction had such demoralizing results and was so productive of contempt for law that the Wickersham Committee brought it to the attention of the President and the Congress in a preliminary report submitted in January 1930, in which it said:

Long before the national prohibition act, it had been found that the jurisdiction of courts of equity to abate nuisances could be made a most effective way of dealing with many forms of vice. Nearly two generations ago this jurisdiction was applied to violations of state liquor laws, and it was later applied with good results to violators of laws against prostitution.

The national prohibition law took advantage of this experience and provided for injunctions in cases where property was habitually used in connection with violations of that law.

These provisions are well conceived and are capable of doing much toward making the law effective in action. But means of evading them have been discovered in certain limitations of procedure growing out of the need of serving process upon persons interested in the property.

By conveying some small fraction of the title to a nonresident or by resident owners, landlords or tenants concealing themselves and evading the service of process, said proceedings are increasingly rendered nugatory. We are advised that open, persistent and extensive violators of the law have been enabled to escape so-called padlocking of their property in this way.

After citing the case of U. S. *vs.* Waverly Club,[42] the report continues:

There is testimony before us that this Waverly Club has been an open, persistent and extensive violator of the prohibition laws; that on November 11 last it was still operating, and that all efforts to obtain service upon the interested owners or proprietors have been futile, so that the place is constantly conducted in open defiance of the law.

Also a federal judge who has been hearing padlock cases in New York says:

"I am not only concerned about the inadequacies of the law to enforce padlock proceedings against nonresident defendants, but I have observed its failure to control effectively situations where resident owners, landlords and tenants were concealing themselves and successfully evading service of process.

"Many cases that I have heard were distressing because of the inability under the law to close places that were flagrant and persistent violators because of the cunning, strategy and resourcefulness of the owners of such places in disabling the authorities from making the necessary service of process."

We recommend meeting this situation by making available to the government the course of procedure regularly made use of in the states where private claims to property were concerned.

Although this senseless restriction made it necessary, if the law was to be enforced, that there should be a sufficient number of agents, marshals and courts to play a perpetual game of hide-and-seek with these lawless property owners and their pestiferous lawyers, the act made no provision for such machinery. The results in every part of the country are illustrated by conditions in the southern district of New York. Mr. Buckner stated that he had only twenty-three men to handle padlock cases, which made enforcement impossible. "There are," he declared,

6,000,000 or 8,000,000 people in the 28 counties, and first we have to get the evidence, and then follow that up. . . . However, for lack of prohibition agents and deputy United States marshals to see that every order is obeyed, and to get the men in court for contempt of court, and to abolish the place by contempt proceedings, we simply have not the men to do it.

Out of 198 men that General Andrews said are over there, there are so many different things for them to do, for what you might call criminal enforcement, for getting stills in tenement houses, for getting substantial transportation cases on the streets, for legal enforcement of padlock cases, and so on, we have now only 23 men. And how can we expect 23 men to do all that work? . . . You appreciate what a powerful weapon the injunction is. . . . But, you understand, that weapon, powerful as it is, we are almost denied because of lack of effective machinery.[43]

Proceedings against Personal Property

The statute provides that if an automobile, boat, airplane or other vehicle shall be used for the unlawful transportation of liquor, the "person in charge thereof" shall be arrested, "but the said vehicle or conveyance shall be returned to the owner upon execution by him of a good and valid bond . . . conditioned . . . to abide the judgment of the court. The court upon conviction of the person so arrested shall order the liquor destroyed and unless good cause to the contrary be shown by the owner, shall order a sale by public auction of the property seized," and after deducting the expenses and costs, the proceeds shall be applied to the payment of liens according to their priorities which were "created without the lienor having any notice that the carrying vehicle was being used or was to be used for illegal transportation of liquor." Upon the payment of costs, the owner of the boat, truck, automobile or other conveyance could retain his property by asserting that he had no knowledge of the illegal use. Rum-runners and bootleggers, therefore, by using cars the titles to which were held by finance companies or others, could render the forfeiture clause nugatory.

The importance of the provisions for proceedings against property and the results that might have been achieved had the terms been dictated by the teachings of experience and had adequate machinery for their administration been erected, are clearly shown by the following statements contained in plans submitted in the Durant contest. Mr. Guy W. Cheney, a district attorney in the state of New York, said:

> Anyone familiar with the attitude of the bootlegger toward prohibition enforcement knows that he fears padlock proceedings much more than he fears the usual raids and the subsequent indictment.
>
> There can be no question that the thorough use of the padlock in every assembly district in the state of New York (again merely used as an illustration) would create an immediate halt in the now almost open violations throughout the length and breadth of the state.
>
> When it became evident that the plan was to continue and not be merely a temporary gesture, both landlords and tenants would realize the futility of anything but the most secret and occasional violation. The danger would be all out of proportion to the possible profit and the incentive to remain in such a precarious business would cease. Ninety percent of the so-called soft drink places would be forced out of business.[44]

United States District Judge Richard J. Hopkins, formerly justice of the supreme court of Kansas, said:

> One has but to examine the decisions of the federal and state courts to ascertain the far-reaching effects of the nuisance acts. For instance, the federal court may padlock a resort for a year if necessary. The placing of a sign upon a hotel, club or other building worth millions of dollars, that it has been closed for a year by order of the court for violation of the prohibition act, will go far toward deterring those inclined to disregard the law.
>
> For illegally carrying on the business of a distiller not only one's personal property but the real property on which the distillery is operated may, under the revenue act, be forfeited to the government. If this forfeiture clause is used wherever the facts justify, or is extended

to the national prohibition act and actually enforced in the metropolitan centers of the country, owners of valuable property will prevent such violation on their premises.[45]

Mr. A. P. Wilson, a prosecuting attorney in the state of Washington, said:

Up to this time the law has spent nearly all its force prosecuting those who directly engage in the forbidden acts. However, the illicit traffic in liquor cannot exist without the use of tangible property, both real and personal. Back of this property is a property owner. Every bootlegger is known locally. If he cannot buy from the property owner and use his land and buildings, he cannot function.

While the property owner takes no part in carrying on the trade he gathers to himself rents and profits from those that do. . . . We now suffer intoxicating liquor to come into existence and then try to suppress it. The more effective plan would be to so control property and the uses that may be made of it that intoxicating liquor cannot be manufactured or dealt in, and there will then be no liquor to suppress.

When laws are so made that they will affect property and its owner, and when the wrongful use of it brings losses to the one holding its title, the whole matter of law enforcement will change. Whenever the property owner denies the bootlegger the latter cannot exist. The merchant carries supplies intended for the liquor traffic and sells them, well knowing the use to which they will be put. The landlord rents his building to one he well knows will use it as a place to supply liquor or suffers him to continue therein after he has knowledge. The Volstead Act, in addition to prosecuting the bootlegger, should reach past him and take hold on the property owner and his property and inflict penalties upon both.

Our plan is to exercise such control over property, in behalf of public interest and welfare, that the property owner, in order to protect himself and to receive benefits from his property, will turn against the bootlegger and refuse to furnish him supplies, transportation or housing.

Make it unlawful for property of any kind, either real or personal, to be used or suffered to be used for the purpose of manufacturing, transporting, storing, serving or selling intoxicating liquor to be used as a beverage.

Make it unlawful to use any means or method of conveyance for the purpose of transporting intoxicating liquor to be used as a beverage. Declare any means or method of conveyance, when so used, a public nuisance, which shall be confiscated.

Declare all lands, buildings, or premises in any way used for the storing, serving, selling or manufacturing of intoxicating liquor for beverage purposes a public nuisance, which must be closed for one year.

Make all property owners special prohibition agents, charged with the duty of keeping their own property free of, and from being used for the purpose of storing, serving, selling, transporting or manufacturing intoxicating liquor to be used as a beverage.

No bailee or conditional buyer of personal property shall have such an interest therein as will relieve the owner thereof from liability for suffering his property to be used in violation of the prohibitory law.[46]

Louis Lightner, district judge in Nebraska, said:

An effective form of force is the padlock, orders of abatement, and injunctions. Capital is notably timid and as soon as the owner of property realizes that the property may be closed, because his tenant is violating the liquor laws, it will add to the other means of enforcement the powerful assistance of capital.[47]

The enforcement act should have provided that if a man knowingly permitted his property, whether personal or real, to be used in connection with the outlawed traffic, he would be subject to the same penalties as the man who manufactured or sold liquor and that such unlawful use of property should be *prima facie* evidence of the guilty knowledge of the owner. It should have provided that all property, both personal and real, so used should be forfeited to the United States and the lack of knowledge of such use on the part of the owner should be no defense to the action of forfeiture. It should have provided that personal service on the owner should be unnecessary and that seizure of the property by the government should be sufficient notice to all interested parties to appear and defend their rights. Forfeiture should have been made both mandatory and final in all cases. The opportunity should not have been created for a man who had knowingly or negligently permitted his property to be used for criminal purposes to come in when caught and through social, financial or political influence, escape the consequences of his act.

If the law had contained these provisions, property owners, tenants, renting agencies, mortgagees, investment houses dealing in real estate bonds and owners of the bonds would have become diligent and determined allies of the government in the enforcement of the law. It is safe to say that such a law would have caused them to perform a large part of the work necessary for prohibition enforcement.

The wets denounced padlock proceedings as an invasion of the sacred rights of property, and they will renew this din when it is proposed that these proceedings be restored and made truly effective. They were, of course, indulging in their usual solemn hypocrisy. They were not interested in sacred rights. They were interested in liquor profits, liquor taxes and liquor votes, and they were trying to camouflage their real motives. A man has a sacred right to own and use property for honest and lawful purposes but he has no sacred right either to own or to use it for the purposes of public debauchery or as a harbor for criminals. If any man feels that these proceedings are severe, he can escape their rigors by the simple device of taking the necessary precautions to prevent his property from being used as what an experienced federal judge has described as " an outlaws' camp." Such a law will inflict no injustice on honest and law-abiding citizens.

The Volstead Act provided that " it shall be unlawful to have or possess any liquor or property designed for the manufacture of liquor intended for use in violating this title or which has been so used, and no property rights shall exist in any such liquor or property." Rooms, houses and buildings were as indispensable to the lawless liquor business as were liquors, bottles, cocktail shakers, stills and other articles used in connection with the manufacture and sale of liquor. The owners of these properties were just as much a part of the criminal business as were the operators of stills or the proprietors of speak-easies. Why should the latter have been made criminals and have their property confiscated while the former remained respectable citizens and retained their property and their income from its criminal use?

The use of property in connection with the liquor business has another and far more sinister aspect. There is no natural desire for alcohol as there is for food and sexual gratification. If a man uses liquor, it is because he has been induced in some way to take it a sufficient number of times to establish a craving for its narcotic effect. This is as true of the man who says that he can " take it or leave it alone " as it is of the drunkard. The use of liquor results from an unnatural desire and a morbid habit that have been created by external influences. Serving drinks at social functions, especially to the young and immature, the example of those who are supposed to be worthy of imitation, cocktail parties, cocktail hours, seductive advertising, personal solicitation, dance halls with bars attached, public drinking places equipped with bright lights, music, free lunches, pornographic pictures, barmaids, hostesses and prostitutes, are some of the environmental features through which people are induced to begin drinking, and the craving for alcoholic euphoria is created. These things require rooms, houses and buildings. If it were necessary to make liquor in caves and ravines, and carry it around and sell it secretly, it could be disposed of to those who had acquired the habit, but few new addicts would be made and the business would soon come to an end. Whether liquor is legalized or outlawed, rooms, houses and buildings are absolutely necessary for the creation and gratification of the desire for it. Experience has demonstrated that only by the swift and irrevocable forfeiture of property can its use for such purposes be prevented.

Inadequate Penalties

If anything further was needed to insure the failure of the Volstead Act, it was supplied by the penalties that were prescribed for its violation. After eight years of able and courageous effort to enforce the act, Mrs. Willebrandt refers to them as " the toothless penalties for misdemeanor offenses " and says that prosecutors and judges were only permitted to give violators a "slap on the wrist." United States District Judge William H. Sawtelle said: "Such light penalties do not serve as a deterrent. They are by the lawless element considered as a license to continue in the liquor business. Experience has demonstrated that, if this law is to be enforced, more severe punishment must be meted out to the offenders thereof."[48] These are typical of the statements of all those who were charged with the duty and were actually endeavoring to enforce the law.

No penalties were prescribed for those who purchased and used liquor nor for those who shared the profits of the outlawed business by furnishing materials and supplies to or renting their property for use as breweries, distilleries and speak-easies. The penalties for the manufacture and sale of liquor were as follows:

> Any person who manufactures or sells liquor in violation of this title shall for a first offense be fined not more than $1,000 or imprisoned not exceeding six months, and for a second or subsequent offense shall be fined not less than $200 nor more than $2,000 and be imprisoned not less than one month nor more than five years.

Penalties for importation, exportation, transportation and possession were prescribed in the following blanket clause:

> Any person violating the provisions of any permit or who makes any false record, report, or affidavit required by this title, or violates any of the provisions of this title, for which offense a special penalty is not prescribed, shall be fined for a first offense not more than $500; for a second offense not less than $100 nor more than $1,000, or be imprisoned not more than ninety days; for any subsequent offense he shall be fined not less than $500 and be imprisoned not less than three months nor more than two years.

For manufacture and sale, the first offense was a misdemeanor that might be disposed of by the imposition of a small fine. This was true as to both first and second offenses in the case of importation, exportation, transportation and possession. For subsequent offenses in all cases, there was a minimum penalty of a small fine and a short jail sentence.

The act was so drawn that a vast quantity of liquor was made available, an unlimited market for its sale was provided, the use of property for its manufacture and sale was rendered safe and lucrative, it was given a fictitious value, the bootleg trade was made enormously profitable, large sums of money were made available for the corruption of politics and the bribery of public officials, and powerful elements of the community were induced to consent to and assist in the law's violation and breakdown. Its enforcement was left to a handful of men, some of whom were incompetent and corrupt, and no additional judges were provided to assist in handling the vast amount of new business that was dumped upon the federal courts.

Huge profits and small penalties soon clogged the dockets of the federal courts with liquor cases. As prison sentences required jury trials and no adequate machinery had been provided for such trials, prosecutors were forced either to dismiss a majority of liquor cases or to accept pleas of guilty to misdemeanors under agreements by which small fines would be imposed. Bootleggers and their lawyers soon worked out an effective technique of law evasion. As a rule, it was the little fellows who were arrested and they would accept a fine which was paid for them, go out of court laughing at the prohibition agents, and return to their old pursuits. The fines, court costs and lawyers' fees were simply charged up to expense, like water, light, telephone and similar expenditures. The procedure was to herd the "small fry" into court, and, as Mr. Buckner says, "to call the roll and charge an exit fee."

The following are typical of the statements of those engaged in the administration of the law:

MRS. WILLEBRANDT. Any fine under it was less than a license, compared to the profits of the business. And it was easy for such violators in effect to hire substitutes to go to jail for short terms.[49]

DANIEL D. CRONIN, captain of police, Denver, Colorado. In numerous cases, there are three or four parties involved, and to escape a second offense charge, which always carries a more severe penalty, the real offender gets one of his pals to plead guilty. He then pays the fine.[50]

MR. BUCKNER. I have had almost 3,000 pleas of guilty in the last 12 months. I have collected $265,000 in fines in prohibition cases. That probably would run my entire office. I do not point to it with pride; I am ashamed of it. . . . And I think, gentlemen, that one of the unfortunate features in prohibition enforcement is that when the people read about so many thousand convictions — 3,000 convictions by Buckner last year — it looks as if that connoted efficient law enforcement. In my judgment, that proposition should be changed and the records of the Prohibition Unit and the records of the Department of Justice read: "Escaped on payment of money." Because, don't you see, almost any violator is willing to compound with the prosecutor and pay a small part of his earnings. This business of the enforcement of law paying its way is, in my judgment, a very bad feature to inject into law enforcement of any kind. I will undertake to take over the prosecution of pickpockets in New York city and make that law pay its way.[51]

GUY W. CHENEY, district attorney, Steuben county, New York. The judges are forced, therefore, to encourage pleas of guilty to the indictments found by federal grand juries. If at any term a federal judge becomes severe, begins to announce a jail sentence or really heavy fines, the defendants immediately enter pleas of not guilty. The law gives these defendants the right of a trial by jury. . . . The practical result (which all federal judges, United States attorneys and other persons familiar with the situation know to be the fact), is that in order to make some sort of progress with the criminal cases facing them, judges are absolutely forced to accept innumerable pleas with the tacit understanding that the fines will be nominal.[52]

Insignificant penalties and inadequate legal machinery resulted in one of the major scandals of the Volstead Act era — "bargain day in the federal court." From New York to San Francisco, federal judges were compelled to permit and witness this humiliating spectacle. It was also witnessed by the people with increasing irritation and disgust. The attitude of those engaged in the enforcement of the law toward this congestion of the courts is illustrated by a statement by Harold C. Keyes, formerly in the United States Secret Service:

The federal courts are so disorganized by the number of prohibition cases and the difficulties of dealing with them, that it has become the custom in many federal courts, in order to expedite the handling of prohibition cases, to turn the days for pleading into "bargain days" for those who will plead guilty. The practice is carried over into other kinds of federal cases and federal judges now treat the more serious felonies with greater leniency.[53]

Between the unrestricted legal supply and the unrestricted legal market, there was a no man's land. It was occupied by those who operated illicit breweries and distilleries, diverted industrial alcohol and full-strength beer and ran speak-easies, and by smugglers, rumrunners, hijackers and bootleggers. These men were outlaws but the prizes were so glittering and the dangers so insignificant that the life of the ordinary criminal, who was constantly in the shadow of the penitentiary or the gallows, seemed hard, perilous and unprofitable in comparison. Into this no man's land, therefore, poured burglars, swindlers, bombers, gunmen, gangsters, racketeers and the whole criminal fraternity to compete with the old-fashioned liquor dealers for the profits of crime. Men who had been pariahs, shabbily dressed, working by stealth and gaining a dangerous and precarious living, became the possessors of imperial revenue, associated with millionaires and society people, gave orders to police and other officials, became allies of political bosses, lived in sumptuous homes, drove high-powered cars and appeared in full evening dress at the opera.

So scandalous were the results of imposing petty fines upon men engaged in a criminal business with profits running into the millions that Congress was forced to act. In 1929 it enacted the Jones Law which was signed by President Coolidge. It provided that "for the illegal manufacture, sale, transportation, importation, or exportation of intoxicating liquor, the penalty imposed for each such offense shall be a fine not to exceed $10,000 or imprisonment not to exceed five years, or both."

This made the first offense as well as succeeding offenses a felony and gave the court the power to impose an adequate penalty. But the words "or imprisonment" made it possible for defendants to dicker with the prosecutor for a plea of guilty and a small fine. The law did not prescribe any penalties for those who purchased, possessed or used liquor, furnished materials and supplies, or permitted their property to be used in connection with the outlawed business. Nor did it remove any of the absurd restrictions that had paralyzed all efforts to enforce the law. Furthermore, it introduced an entirely new absurdity into the situation. Under the federal criminal code, if a man has knowledge of the commission of a felony and fails to disclose it to the proper authority, he "shall be fined not more than $500, or imprisoned not more than three years, or both."

Construing the Jones Law in connection with this provision of the criminal code, the court, in U. S. *vs.* Kent, said:

> The effect of the Jones Law is to make an entirely new set of felonies. By reason of this fact, it is now a felony for any person who buys a drink of intoxicating liquor not to report the sale to the proper officers of the United States government; any person who knows that anybody else has transported intoxicating liquor for use as a beverage is now a felon, if he does not report it; any person who knows that anybody else is manufacturing, importing or exporting liquor for a beverage is a felon, if he does not report it, if the Jones Act is constitutional.[54]

What was the new situation? Two men met and a bottle of whisky was transferred from one to the other. The seller was a felon and could be sent to the penitentiary for five years. The buyer was a respectable, law-abiding citizen. But since it was a felony to fail to report a felony of which one had knowledge, the buyer was obliged to turn his bootlegger over to the government or be guilty of a felony for which he could be sent to the penitentiary for three years. If a man rented his property for use as a speak-easy, he was obliged to turn over his tenant to the proper authorities, or become a felon. The result was a new set of unpunished crimes.

The Jones Law, passed after the enemies of prohibition had had ten years in which to perfect their technique of law evasion and create an attitude of defeat and contempt for law, accomplished little. The changes were inadequate and they came too late.

In the past, criminal laws have resulted from the desire for revenge, retaliation or compensation, and cruel and unusual punishments have been resorted to for their enforcement. This theory and practice have been abandoned by modern democratic nations. With us, the purpose of a criminal law is the protection of society and the object of the penalty is the prevention of its violation. Unnecessary severity or sentimental leniency may result in the failure of the law. What constitutes an appropriate and adequate penalty for a particular crime is a question of experience and common sense. Today a great majority of crimes are committed for the sake of financial gain, and in such cases fines are both inappropriate and utterly futile. Experience has demonstrated the fact that such crimes can be prevented only by taking the profit out of them and by prison sentences of such length that they will actually deter men from committing the crimes.

A law making a highly lucrative business a crime and prescribing fines for its violation, is the very essence of futility. But this is precisely what the Volstead Act did. It should have prescribed imprisonment for not more than ten years, and the court could have given a defendant a day, a month or the full term, according to the circumstances of the case and the demands of the situation. In his plan submitted in the Durant contest, C. G. Saunders, assistant superintendent of the Bureau of Identification in the police department, Winston-Salem, North Carolina, said:

> There should be no fines. If a liquor violator can get by for six months, he can pay almost any fine the courts see fit to impose upon him. He can do this for the reason that there is a great profit in the handling of liquor. And for that reason I say, do away with the fines and put a straight road or workhouse sentence on the violator who is caught and convicted.[55]

Not only should the act have made violation a felony punishable in all cases by imprisonment, but its penalties should have been made applicable to all those who made the outlawed traffic possible and shared its profits by knowingly furnishing materials and supplies, or permitting the use of their property, whether personal or real, in connection with any of the prohibited acts. The views of those engaged in enforcement of the law are illustrated by the statement of A. P. Wilson:

> In every prosecution for a violation of the prohibitory law which involves or requires the furnishing of any material or supplies or the use of any property, either real or personal, always make the owner of the property so used, and the person furnishing the supplies or materials used, parties defendant, to be so joined as aiders and abettors of the principal defendant, subject to the same penalty for suffering their property, supplies and materials to have been used in violation of the law.[56]

An Enforcible Amendment

A century of experience has proved that a sound prohibition amendment should have read in substance as follows:

> The manufacture, importation, exportation, transportation, sale, purchase, possession or use of whisky, brandy, rum, gin, wine, ale, porter, beer, cordials, hard or fermented cider, alcoholic bitters, ethyl alcohol, all malt liquors and all other alcoholic liquors for use as beverages, and the use of personal or real property for any of said purposes, is hereby prohibited.
>
> Congress and the several states shall enact appropriate legislation to enforce this article.

A practicable enforcement act to carry out this amendment would have read somewhat as follows:

> Whenever the term " alcoholic liquor " is used in this act, it shall be deemed to include whisky, brandy, rum, gin, wine, ale, porter, beer, cordials, hard or fermented cider, alcoholic bitters, ethyl alcohol, all malt liquors and all other alcoholic liquors.
>
> Whoever shall manufacture, import, export, transport, sell, advertise for sale, barter, deliver, furnish, purchase, receive, possess or use alcoholic liquors for beverage purposes, or knowingly furnish materials or supplies, or permit real or personal property to be used for any of said purposes, shall be imprisoned not more than ten years. The furnishing of such materials or supplies or the use of personal or real property for any of said purposes shall constitute *prima facie* evidence of the guilty knowledge of the person or persons who own or control the same.
>
> Every utensil, contrivance, machine, material, supply, preparation,

compound, tablet, substance, formula, direction or recipe used, advertised, designed or intended for use in the manufacture or sale of alcoholic liquor in violation of this act, and all alcoholic liquor so made, shall be destroyed.

Every vehicle or instrument of transportation of any kind whatsoever, whether operating on water, on land or in the air, which shall be used for the manufacture, storage, sale, transportation or use of alcoholic liquor in violation of this act, shall be confiscated.

Every house, building or other structure of any kind whatsoever in which, or in any part of which, and every lot or tract of land upon which alcoholic liquors are manufactured, kept, possessed, sold, purchased or used in violation of this act, is hereby declared to be a common nuisance. In any action to enjoin said nuisance, it shall not be necessary for the court to find that the property involved was being unlawfully used as aforesaid at the time of the hearing, but on finding that the material allegations of the petition for an injunction are true, shall order the nuisance to be abated and shall further order that said house, building or structure, and said lot or tract of land, shall not be occupied or used for any purpose whatsoever for one year thereafter, or confiscated.

The ordinary citizen could have read this amendment and statute in two minutes, and would have known exactly what they meant without consulting a lawyer. They would have applied to rich and poor alike and meant the same thing to everyone in every part of the country. They would have afforded no loopholes for criminals and no opportunity for their lawyers to confuse the situation by claiming that the transaction in question came within the limits of some exemption, exception or permissive regulation. The prosecution of cases under this statute would have presented few difficulties because it would have involved the exercise of ordinary common sense on the part of the jury and the court rather than an effort to work their way through the intricate mazes of statutory constructions and legal technicalities. Its administration would have become a part of the duties of the regular law enforcing agencies of the government. The coast guard, customs and immigration officials, members of the secret service, marshals, district attorneys, and their assistants, members of the

Department of Justice, judges and others charged with the enforcement of federal laws, were men of ability, training, and experience in dealing with the criminal classes. They knew how to investigate, prepare and present cases, and their traditional honesty, relentlessness and efficiency made them the terror of those tempted to violate the laws of the United States and commanded the respect, confidence and unwavering support of all law-abiding citizens. If the new law had made additional men necessary, they would have been selected in the usual manner, absorbed into the existing system and molded by its traditions. Such action would have given unequivocal notice to all who either directly or indirectly were fattening on public debauchery that their game was at an end, and that in the future, the traffic in and the use of alcoholic liquors would be neither respectable, profitable nor safe.

No one who in 1919 was sufficiently mature to be aware of the intensity of the hatred which the great majority of the American people felt toward intoxicating liquor in its every phase, and the strength of their determination that it should be suppressed, can have the slightest doubt that this was what they had commissioned their representatives in Congress to accomplish, and that they supposed that it was being done.

If the remarkable series of prohibition victories which for a period of twenty years swept every part of the country and culminated in the ratification of the Eighteenth Amendment by the practically unanimous action of the states, had been secured by an adequate amendment and enforcement statute, the liquor traffic would have been given its death blow, and would be no more of a problem today than is the traffic in other narcotic drugs.

NOTES

[1] Durant, *op. cit.*, p. 280.
[2] *Ibid.*, p. 22.
[3] NPL, pp. 94–128, 178–208, 1652–60.
[4] Durant, *op. cit.*, p. 366.
[5] NPL, p. 451.
[6] Durant, *op. cit.*, p. 115.
[7] *Ibid.*, pp. 277–78.
[8] State vs. Fargo Bottling Co., 19, N. D. 326.

[9] Purity Extract Co. vs. Lynch, 226, U. S. 197.
[10] Willebrandt, *op. cit.*, p. 81.
[11] *Ibid.*, p. 79.
[12] Colvin, *op. cit.*, p. 492.
[13] Durant, *op. cit.*, pp. 377–78.
[14] NPL, p. 68.
[15] NPL, pp. 112, 113, 115.
[16] Durant, *op. cit.*, p. 373.
[17] Willebrandt, *op. cit.*, p. 41.
[18] *Alcohol and Man*, edited by Haven Emerson (The Macmillan Co., 1932), pp. 133, 176.
[19] Arthur Dean Bevan, *Alcohol and Prohibition* (Anti-Saloon League), pp. 3, 4, 6, 7, 8.
[20] Haven Emerson, *Alcohol, Its Effects on Man* (Appleton-Century Co., 1934), pp. 55–58.
[21] The statements of Drs. Blumer, Kelly and Cushny are quoted in the *Anti-Saloon Year Book* for 1931, pp. 150, 153, 154.
[22] *Ibid.*, p. 148.
[23] *Ibid.*, p. 149.
[24] See *supra*, pp. 232–33.
[25] NPL, p. 871.
[26] Bevan, *op. cit.*, pp. 7, 8, 9.
[27] NPL, p. 874.
[28] NPL, pp. 118, 119, 120.
[29] Quoted by Willebrandt, *op. cit.*, p. 343.
[30] Colvin, *op. cit.*, p. 265.
[31] *Alcohol and Man*, p. 264.
[32] NPL, p. 1229.
[33] Durant, *op. cit.*, p. 154.
[34] NPL, p. 386.
[35] NPL, p. 659.
[36] See *supra*, pp. 254 ff.
[37] Norris vs. U. S., 34, Fed. (2d.) 839.
[38] *Illinois Crime Survey* (Illinois Association for Criminal Justice), p. 857.
[39] 123, U. S. 623.
[40] Dobbins vs. U. S., 96, U. S. 395.
[41] 26, Fed. (2d.) 189.
[42] 22, Fed. (2d.) 422.
[43] NPL, pp. 188–89.
[44] Durant, *op. cit.*, p. 130.
[45] *Ibid.*, p. 300.
[46] *Ibid.*, pp. 523–26.
[47] *Ibid.*, p. 334.
[48] *Ibid.*, p. 427.
[49] Willebrandt, *op. cit.*, p. 257.
[50] Durant, *op. cit.*, p. 162.
[51] NPL, p. 185.
[52] Durant, *op. cit.*, pp. 126, 127.
[53] *Ibid.*, p. 315.
[54] 36, Fed. (2d.) 401.
[55] Durant, *op. cit.*, p. 424.
[56] *Ibid.*, p. 526. Cf. *supra*, pp. 309–10.

Chapter Ten

The Administration Of The Prohibition Law

THE PRINCIPAL object of the wet propaganda was to deceive the people as to the real reasons for the inadequate enforcement of the prohibition law. Each violation was exaggerated and trumpeted forth by the wet press, and from coast to coast the great Du Pont chorus chanted, " Prohibition is a tragic, ghastly failure and there is no hope except through repeal." Every conceivable effort was made to force upon the people the belief that failure resulted not from the improper administration of the law but from the fact that it prohibited the liquor traffic. The fraudulent character of this propaganda becomes clearly apparent from an examination of the manner in which the law was administered.

Efficient administration of the prohibition law was just as essential as its enactment. The same moral earnestness and persistence that marked the campaign to elect men who would pass the law should have characterized the struggle to elect men who would properly enforce it. As the attitude of the president would exert a profound influence upon the attitude of public officials, both federal and state, and of the public at large toward the prohibition law, it was of the utmost importance that he should be a man whose habits, convictions and character would have made it certain that he would give that law uncompromising and courageous support.

A president of this type would have made it clear at the outset that this law was to be enforced in the same spirit and with the same vigor that marked the enforcement of all other federal laws. He would have appointed to office only men who obeyed it, believed in it, and could be depended upon to enforce it. No liquor would have entered the White House, and its use by a member of the cabinet, a district attorney or any other federal employe, would have resulted in his instant dismissal from the service. A senator or congressman who violated or encouraged and abetted the violation of the law, would have been denied social and political recognition and classed with smugglers and bootleggers. Foreign governments would have been requested to respect the laws of this country, and they would not have been permitted to turn their embassies into barrooms. Washington would have been made a model for the nation in respect for and obedience to law. The president would have called upon Congress to make adequate appropriations of money and to provide a sufficient number of agents, district attorneys and courts to meet the actual necessities of the situation. He would have insisted that the law be purged of its compromises and unusual and senseless restrictions, and put into a form that would command respect and be enforcible. He would very soon have realized that the Volstead Act was based on a fallacious theory and he would have asked for its repeal and the substitution of a simple and comprehensive law prohibiting the manufacture, sale, purchase, possession and use of all alcoholic and malt liquors for beverage purposes, and leaving its enforcement to agencies engaged in the enforcement of other federal laws. If he had given the nation such courageous leadership, the liquor traffic would have been banished to the underworld, where it could have been dealt with as successfully as in the case of other crimes.

Harding, Mellon, Daugherty

The prohibition law went into effect in January 1920. In June of that year, the Republican national convention became hopelessly deadlocked, and a little coterie of old guard politicians, at a midnight meeting in the Blackstone Hotel, Chicago, perfected the political deals that resulted in the nomination of Warren G. Harding for president. He was a member of the "Ohio gang," a political spoilsman of the worst type, a drinker and an opponent of prohibition. He was elected, and for secretary of the treasury and attorney general, the men whose duty it would be to administer and enforce the prohibition law, he selected Andrew Mellon and Harry Daugherty. The manner in which Mr. Harding obeyed his oath to "preserve, protect, and defend the Constitution," and the example of respect for law which he set for his subordinates and the country, is illustrated by the following passage from Alice Longworth's autobiography:

> Though violation of the Eighteenth Amendment was a matter of course in Washington, it was rather shocking to see the way Harding disregarded the Constitution he had sworn to uphold. Though nothing to drink was served downstairs, there were always, at least before the unofficial dinner, cocktails in the upstairs hall outside the President's room and the guests were shown up there instead of waiting below for the President. While the big official receptions were going on, I don't think the people had any idea what was taking place in the rooms above. One evening while one was in progress, a friend of the Hardings asked me if I would like to go up to the study. I had heard rumors and was curious to see for myself what truth was in them. No rumor could have exceeded the reality; the study was filled with cronies, Daugherty, Jess Smith, Alex Moore, and others, the air heavy with tobacco smoke, trays with bottles containing every imaginable brand of whisky stood about, cards and poker chips ready at hand — a general atmosphere of waistcoat unbuttoned, feet on the desk, and spittoon alongside.
>
> I recollect that the first time we went to the White House after the Coolidges were there, the atmosphere was as different as a New England front parlor is from a back room in a speak-easy.[1]

Mr. Mellon was allied with the political machine of Pennsylvania and heavily interested in the distilling business. He had taken no part in the movement to destroy the liquor traffic, did not understand its significance, and was opposed to the law that it was his duty to administer. Mr. Daugherty was a charter member of the "Ohio gang," a spoils politician, a heavy drinker and an enemy of prohibition, who later was saved from the penitentiary by the vote of a single juror.

Harding, Mellon, Daugherty — this was the triumvirate that

was to execute the mandate of the American people that the liquor traffic be destroyed. The manner in which that mandate was executed is indicated by authoritative statements.

Mr. Gifford Pinchot is one of the ablest and most courageous men in the public life of America. As governor of Pennsylvania, he made an honest effort to enforce the prohibition law and, from personal experience, he gained a comprehensive and accurate knowledge of the facts. He said:

> I am . . . convinced that the violation of the Eighteenth Amendment and the racketeering in liquor were both deliberately encouraged by the controlling federal authorities and by many minor authorities. They were encouraged for the purpose, which has been successfully accomplished, of breaking down the national confidence in prohibition, and bringing liquor back.
>
> The wets were put in charge of enforcing the dry law. Whisky was given the job of keeping whisky out. If ever wolves were put in control of the sheepfold, they were in this case. Naturally it was the sheep, and not the wolves, that were eaten up.
>
> When the Eighteenth Amendment went into effect, there was immediate compliance with it on the part of the liquor interests. Years of honest enforcement of the excise law by the federal government had taught them to expect honest enforcement of the prohibition law. They began by respecting it. But almost at once they learned that the authorities at Washington did not respect it themselves, and had no intention of enforcing respect from others.
>
> The treasury department had at its command the highly trained, highly efficient and thoroughly reliable corps of special agents which had made for itself so enviable a record in enforcing the excise law. Authorities who intended to enforce the law would have retained it, and would have been thankful for the chance. Instead of that, these men, with their record, their reputation, and their experience, were dismissed. That in itself was notice to every lawbreaker that he was expected to break the law.
>
> In the place of the invaluable corps of special agents, the treasury department began by installing the scum of the political underworld — men who were totally incapable of enforcing any law, even if they had not been selected, as they were, for the express purpose of nullifying this one.

In state after state, including this one, the federal administrator of the Volstead Law was guilty of breaking the law he was appointed to enforce. In Pennsylvania incompetent after incompetent followed crook after crook in this crucial position, all nominated for wet and political reasons by wet politicians.[2]

The report of the Wickersham Commission said:

The enforcement agents, inspectors and attorneys, as were authorized in Section 38 of the national prohibition act, were appointed without regard to the civil service rules. A force so constituted presented a situation conducive to bribery and official indifference to enforcement. It is common knowledge that large amounts of liquor were imported into the country or manufactured and sold, despite the law, with the connivance of agents of the law. . . . In view of this bad start, of the defective organization, unsatisfactory personnel, and insufficient equipment, and of the want of coordination among the agencies concerned, it is no wonder that there was a steady decline in the enforcement of prohibition from 1921 to 1927. Unfortunately, this steady decline gave an impetus to the illicit traffic which makes it hard for any organization and personnel to cope with it.[3]

In his separate statement filed with the Wickersham Commission Report, Justice Kenyon said:

It has been stated before us by those who should know that at least 50 per cent of the men employed as prohibition agents prior to the time they were placed under civil service were unfit for the position and incompetent as law enforcing officers. . . . Major Chester P. Mills, who honestly tried to enforce the law as prohibition administrator of the second federal district of New York, has told in articles published in *Collier's Weekly* in 1927 the story of an attempted political influence in the appointment of prohibition agents in his district, and has repeated practically the same story before us. In these articles he said that " three fourths of the 2,500 dry agents are ward heelers, and sycophants named by the politicians." Politicians, some of them high in national affairs, attempted to force upon him men with criminal records — some of the very lowest grade of vote-getters — which apparently was the test of the politician for good prohibition agents. Prohibition was expected evidently by some politicians to furnish a fine field for the operation of the spoils system in politics. Their expectations have been largely realized. One of the leading political bosses of New York city informed Mills that he must let him control the patronage in his office or he would have to get out. Another told him that efficiency must give way to patronage. One agent with a criminal record, whom he discharged, was reinstated after Mills ceased to be administrator, and was continued in office until about a year ago, when he was indicted for alleged conspiracy to violate the provisions of the national prohibition act. One of the parties whom it was insisted he should appoint had shortly before shot a man in a row in a speak-easy, another had been found with burglar tools upon him. Major Mills tried to do an honest job and soon discovered, according to his statements, that he was not wanted on the job, and to use his language, was "kicked upstairs to an innocuous zone of supervisorship." [4]

Mrs. Willebrandt in her book on prohibition declares:

That the prohibition force, largely as the result of political influence, was for several years filled with unfit men, is proved by official records. These records disclose that in the six years from 1920 to 1926 more than seven hundred and fifty prohibition agents were dismissed from the force for delinquency or misconduct. Among the charges which brought dismissal were extortion, bribery, solicitation of money, illegal disposition of liquor or other property, intoxication, assault, the making of false reports and theft. Sixty-one officers and employees were dismissed for acts of collusion or conspiracy to violate the very law they had sworn to enforce. . . .

In the beginning and during five or six years following, the prohibition enforcement force was composed very largely of men of the ward heeler class. Appointments of prohibition agents were, until 1926, made as the result of political endorsement. The frequent reward for polling precincts, getting out the votes on election day, marking and stealing ballots, " slugging " the opposition poll watchers, and generally being useful in operating the machinery of politics, was the appointment as a prohibition agent.[5]

In 1923, William Dudley Foulke, president of the National Civil Service Reform League, said:

Among the reactionary exceptions from competition made by the Democratic Congress (though this was without President Wilson's approval) was the bureau for the enforcement of the Volstead Act, and this exception was most disastrous. It inaugurated an era of corruption in this branch of the service unheard of even in the worst days of spoils politics. Every important appointment was the political booty of some congressman, often a spoilsman of the lowest type, and hundreds of these appointees (and perhaps also some of their congressional backers to whom they owed their places) have grown fat on the bribes received from bootleggers and other miscreants engaged in defying the law. . . .

President Harding's administration found the enforcement bureau filled with Democratic spoilsmen, many of them criminals, who have since been indicted and some of them convicted, but instead of changing the system and making these appointments nonpolitical, the same methods were continued. Democratic malefactors were turned out and Republican malefactors were put in their places as part of the recognized plunder of Republican congressmen.[6]

The President had the power by executive order to place the agents of the prohibition bureau in the classified civil service. In 1922, the National Civil Service Reform League urged him to take this action. His reply was: " I am not yet convinced that this is the wisest step to take to promote effective service."

Neither he nor Secretary Mellon made any effort to secure adequate appropriations for prohibition enforcement. When an attempt was made in Congress to increase the appropriations, Mr. Mellon opposed it. Dr. James M. Doran, chief of the chemical division of the Prohibition Bureau, stated that proper enforcement would require $300,000,000 a year, and a proposal was made in Congress to add $256,000,000 to the budget of the bureau. Senator Harris of Georgia proposed as a substitute that the budget of the Prohibition Bureau be increased to the extent of $25,000,000. Secretary Mellon opposed it, on the ground that after years of experience with smaller sums, the Prohibition Bureau would not know what to do with a sudden appropriation of this size.

Washington an Example of Lawlessness

No single influence did more to discredit and destroy prohibition than the spectacle of the flagrant lawlessness of the nation's capital.

The President, the attorney general, cabinet members, senators, congressmen and other government officials openly drank and served liquor that had reached them through smuggler, rum-runner, moonshiner, gangster and bootlegger. They associated with, and helped to enrich and make invincible, the criminals of the underworld, whom it was their duty to put behind prison bars. Trucks filled with liquor went along the streets, and bootleggers, insolent and unafraid, entered the halls of Congress, the Department of Justice and other government offices to ply their criminal trade. This situation, which would have been impossible under a president having proper respect for his oath of office, brought the government, the prohibition law and other laws into public contempt.

One of the influences that contributed largely to the disgraceful situation in Washington was the conduct of the foreign embassies. An attempt by Congress to improve the situation was blocked by Secretary Mellon. Mr. Cramton introduced a resolution calling on the secretary of the treasury to reveal what shipments of intoxicating liquors had been received by the embassies and legations in Washington since January 1920, "giving in connection with each such shipment the name and office of each consignee, the country to which he was accredited, the kind and quantity of liquor, the place from which shipped to the United States, to whom delivered by the customs service, and the date of such delivery to the consignee or his representative." In supporting his resolution, he said:

It is time Congress and the country knew the facts about this, knew whether that which has been permitted as a courtesy is being used as a cover for abuses seriously contributing to scandalous disregard of the fundamental law of our land.

I think no one wants to be overcritical of any of the legations as to what they shall do at their own tables, but we do feel they ought not to make barrooms of their receptions.

In an article in the New York *Times* of February 4, 1923 . . . it is stated that a certain embassy was the first to grasp the full strategic importance connected with prohibition as a social element in their influence, and during the Arms Conference, it is said that this certain embassy laid in a whole cellarful of choice liquors, and that the cellars gave out and had to be restocked, and that at one of the social functions given in honor of the army and navy, a barroom was established in the embassy, with three bartenders in attendance serving Johnny Walkers and other drinks.

Congress is entitled to have authentic facts with respect to such importations. There is no desire on the part of anyone to begin an offensive campaign of overhauling the personal effects of diplomats, but truckload shipments of liquor coming into Washington from Baltimore and coming in daylight through the streets of this city can only lead to confusion in the enforcement of the laws. Since I introduced this resolution, I have had information coming to me from official sources of such incidents, and the statement that they caused great embarrassment to the police authorities of Washington in their endeavor to enforce this law. If one sees a truckload of liquor going through the streets of Washington with cases marked "Whisky" — 14 cases in one instance that I know of — one does not know whether it belongs to an embassy or not, and may easily think that the laws are being put aside by everyone. The information ought to come to us as to the extent to which this is being carried on.[7]

Secretary Mellon declined to comply with the request, saying that it would be incompatible with public interest to divulge this particular information. He should have given the information, and the President should have notified foreign governments that the conduct of their embassies was an affront to the law-abiding people of America. It should, of course, be borne in mind that this situation would not have existed if the officials of our own government had shown proper respect for the law.

Coolidge and Mellon

When Mr. Coolidge became president in August 1923, the technique of law evasion had been well worked out. Bootleggers had acquired great financial and political strength and respect for the law had been undermined in the minds of large numbers of people. If he had understood the real meaning of his oath of office, President Coolidge would have suppressed the rising tide of lawlessness by the prompt destruction of its sources. As a matter of fact, however, he exhibited not a trace of understanding, courage or leadership. He wrote beautiful speeches and messages on law observance, as had Harding and Daugherty. But in the sphere of action he did all the things he should not have done and left undone all the things that he should have done and in the end left the country in a worse condition than it had been in under Harding.

He retained Mellon and Daugherty in the key positions which they held, and when nearly a year later Daugherty resigned, it was because Mr. Coolidge differed from him on a question of procedure, and not because he wished to rid the public service of his presence. At the very beginning, the President refused to issue an executive order placing prohibition officials in the classified civil service, and for his refusal assigned the absurd reason that some future president might rescind the order. He thus condoned and perpetuated the spoils system of the Harding administration.

In 1927, Congress was forced by public opinion to pass a law placing prohibition agents in the classified civil service. How this law fared under the Coolidge administration is illustrated by the following statement by Mrs. Willebrandt:

> So it was on the recommendations of ward and county bosses that congressmen and senators secured the appointment of hundreds of prohibition agents and administrators. And it was the opposition of the politicians, big and little, that prevented the use of civil service examinations to select the enforcement personnel during the first six years after the amendment went into effect.
>
> I have no hesitancy in asserting that it is the continued influence of politicians, little and big, that still keeps in the service either men who have managed to qualify under civil service but who are entirely unfit, or those who have not qualified but are working under temporary appointments that know no end.
>
> The fact is that in March 1929, according to a report made by the acting secretary of the treasury, there were still employed more than six hundred prohibition agents, inspectors, investigators and chemists, who were holding so-called temporary appointments without examination. This was practically one-third of the total number of prohibition employees. . . .

The influence of politicians in defeating real enforcement extends far beyond the appointment of unfit agents. It permeates the courts of justice. Dozens of United States district attorneys and assistants owe their appointments to the favor of not only congressmen and senators, but of the whole political machine ranging up from deputy constable and assistant assessors to mayors and councilmen. . . . We lost cases because politically appointed marshals assembled questionable juries or failed properly to guard juries to prevent tampering and bribery or the exertion of political influence. We failed to obtain convictions, even where the Prohibition Unit furnished us with competent and sufficient evidence, because politically appointed district attorneys, who were less lawyers than politicians, had established definite schedules of fees for what came to be known as nolle-prossing liquor cases. Time after time, they dismissed cases without trial because of the alleged want of proper evidence, disappearance of witnesses, et cetera. Bootleggers in one western state advertised that the standard fee was fifty dollars in ordinary small cases thus dismissed.[8]

It had been repeatedly urged that the enforcement of the prohibition law be transferred from the treasury department to the Department of Justice.

Nevertheless, despite the interest shown in this proposal by two secretaries of the treasury, the senior circuit judges and the chief justice of the United States, neither Mr. Harding nor Mr. Coolidge raised the question of this possible transfer in any of their public statements on the problem of enforcement, discussed its relative advantages and disadvantages in any of their messages to Congress, or expressed an opinion in these messages on the merits of any one of several bills introduced in the Senate and the House, designed to effect a change in the status of the Prohibition Bureau on the initiative of Congress.[9]

In 1926, the report of the Senate Investigating Committee disclosed the innumerable defects of the law, the inadequacy of the enforcement machinery, the inefficiency and corruption of the service, and the rapid growth of liquor lawlessness. President Coolidge could have ignored the propaganda, studied the testimony of General Andrews, Mrs. Willebrandt, the district attorneys, the prohibition agents, and others engaged in the administration of the law, and learned just what the difficulties were. He could then have gone before Congress and the country with a definite and effective program for dealing with the situation. Apparently he did not know that there was a hearing or a report.

In 1926, General Andrews urged Congress to appropriate enough money so that he might have a sufficient number of men to enable him to perform the task imposed upon him. Some of the other requests which he made are stated as follows by Charles Merz in his book *The Dry Decade*:

> For all five of the major sources of production which had flourished despite the best efforts of the Prohibition Bureau, General Andrews recommended the adoption of legislation giving the government new authority.
>
> He urged that the control of the Prohibition Bureau over the distribution of medicinal liquor be broadened. He proposed that all manufacturers of cereal beverages be required to take out a federal permit, give bond, and subject their plants to federal inspection. He asked for power to search American ships beyond the twelve-mile limit, power to confiscate vessels captured by the government, and power to negotiate new agreements with foreign countries, in an effort to reduce smuggling by sea and along the borders. He proposed that Congress permit the Prohibition Bureau to confiscate such industrial alcohol " as does not substantially comply with the formula under which it is authorized to be manufactured." He asked for power to search private dwellings to discover illicit stills, not only on warrants charging sale, as provided in the Volstead Act, but also on suspicion of manufacture for commercial purposes. . . .
>
> Though General Andrews appeared before one committee of Congress or another on eight different occasions in the month of April to urge the adoption of his bills, though he declared that the Prohibition Bureau would be seriously handicapped by the failure of this legislation, and though his efforts to obtain action were reinforced by pleas from the Methodist Board of Temperance and other prohibition organizations, not one of the bills designed to give the government new power to deal with the sources of illicit liquor was adopted by the Congress to which it was submitted with a plea for urgent action.[10]

In this struggle, General Andrews received not the slightest encouragement or help from the President. The result was that spoilsmen, bootleggers, Wall street gamblers, international bankers and big business pirates got just what they wanted and split the proceeds with the politicians. That is the reason that all these elements combined to create the " Coolidge myth " of the " strong, silent statesman in the White House."

Herbert Hoover's Election

In 1928 the clouds lifted. For eight years a law that could have been enforced only by honest and efficient public officials had been administered by incompetent and corrupt political spoilsmen. The liquor interests had carried on a ceaseless campaign of lawlessness, sabotage and fraud. In 1925 they had been joined by the representatives of big business. The allied Tammany organizations, under the leadership of Tammany Hall of New York, had gained control of the Democratic national convention and forced the nomination of Al Smith for president. He was the product and the mouthpiece of Tammany Hall. He had persistently misrepresented and denounced the law. He and his Tammany gang had secured the repeal of the New York enforcement act, and he was the leader of the movement for the modification of the Volstead Act to permit the return of beer and the nullification of the Constitution by congressional action. He had selected as chairman of the Democratic national committee John J. Raskob, a Republican, a millionaire munition maker, a Wall street gambler, an arch-representative of big business, a rabid foe of prohibition and a large contributor to the Association Against the Prohibition Amendment. Al Smith's election would have meant the transference to the White House of the headquarters of Tammany Hall, the liquor interests, and business pirates of the type of Raskob.

On the surface it seemed that the Republican party had taken a stand, on the prohibition question, at the opposite pole of everything represented by Al Smith. Its platform declared that " the people through the method provided by the Constitution have written the Eighteenth Amendment into the Constitution. The Republican party pledges itself and its nominees to the observance and enforcement of this provision of the Constitution."

Far transcending this declaration in importance was the character of the party's candidate for president. Mr. Hoover had not grown up with " one foot on the rail blowing off the foam " in Tammany saloons. He had never been an errand boy for Tammany Hall, and his political ideals had not been formed in the atmosphere of Tammany politics. His background was thoroughly American. As a child, he had seen the people of Iowa banish the liquor traffic from the state. He attended a typically American university. He had gained international recognition through his work as chairman of the Committee for Belgian Relief, and through other great philanthropic undertakings. He had obeyed the prohibition law. He had never been an office-seeker or the spokesman of a political machine.

In his speech of acceptance, he issued the following defiant challenge to the liquor interests, their apologists and their financial and political allies:

> I do not favor the repeal of the Eighteenth Amendment. I stand for the efficient enforcement of the laws enacted thereunder. Whoever is chosen president has under his oath the solemn duty to pursue this course. Modification of the enforcement laws which permit that which the Constitution forbids is nullification. This the American people will not countenance.

The American people believed that in making this declaration, Mr. Hoover had expressed his personal convictions and that he had the insight, the high purpose and the courage necessary to make it effective. This conviction was shared by both the wets and the drys. Everyone believed that the supreme issue of the campaign was: Shall the Eighteenth Amendment be retained and vigorously enforced, or shall it be nullified and repealed and prohibition abandoned as a mistake? The *Christian Century*, one of the ablest exponents of liberal religious and political thought in the country, expressed the situation as follows:

> How dry is the United States? How dry does the United States wish to be? The two questions, endlessly debated, are at last to be answered in a manner that will approximate a clear expression of the national mind.

Go into the street this morning and ask the first half-dozen citizens you meet to tell you the difference between the Hoover plan for farm relief, for superpower development, for foreign relations, and that of Governor Smith. It need not surprise you if not one of the six can make an intelligent distinction. But on prohibition? Hoover's dry and Al's wet. Everybody knows that. And because everybody knows it, it is the issue of issues in this campaign.[11]

It is, of course, true that for partisan reasons many wets voted for Mr. Hoover, just as many drys, particularly in the south, voted for Mr. Smith. How nearly these two elements offset each other it would be impossible to determine. It is also true that a small group of intellectuals supported Mr. Smith. These men had no vital contact with or first-hand knowledge of the realities of our social, economic and political life. With an affectation of intellectual and moral superiority, they sat in their ivory towers and forced their second-hand facts into the pattern of the theories they were weaving. They attracted little attention and their influence was negligible.

Down on the embattled plain, however, where men and women were reacting directly and vigorously to the realities of the situation, there was taking place a great realignment of voters. The underworld, those who were directly or indirectly interested in the liquor business, those who were determined to get rid of the income tax at any cost, newspapers that depended upon the patronage of the masses in wet centers for their circulation and on the big business and financial interests for their advertising and financing, and all other uncompromising wets, lined up solidly with the Tammany organizations from New York to San Francisco, in support of Mr. Smith.

On the other hand, the great body of men and women who were opposed to the return of the liquor traffic rallied to the support of Mr. Hoover. It is true that some people supported Mr. Hoover because Mr. Smith was a Catholic. But a majority of those who raised this question did it to enforce their opposition to Mr. Smith, which was in reality based upon the fact that he was a representative of the liquor traffic and Tammany Hall. If Thomas J. Walsh, the great progressive and dry senator and loyal Catholic, had been the candidate, the religious question would never have been heard of. Its injection into the campaign was a cheap and futile political trick by which Mr. Smith sought to obtain the sympathy of those who were opposed to religious intolerance.

The character of the people who disregarded party lines and supported Mr. Hoover, and their real motives, were well illustrated by a meeting that I attended on the Sunday night preceding the election. It was held in one of the largest and most influential churches in California. The great auditorium was filled to capacity. In the audience there was not a down-and-outer, a millionaire, a brewer, a distiller, a bootlegger or a gangster. There was not a proprietor of a gambling establishment, a brothel or a speakeasy, or a member of a gang of organized criminals. There was not an office-seeker, a ward heeler or a political boss. There were simply intelligent, successful, high-minded and patriotic business and professional men and women. Their responses showed that they were seething with indignation at the threat to American traditions and ideals involved in the possibility of Mr. Smith's election. The speaker was a clergyman of great intelligence and he spoke with solemn earnestness. The substance of his address was as follows:

During the last three months I have traveled from New York to California, speaking daily to audiences such as this. In every part of the country I have talked with and to parents, teachers, members of women's clubs, churches, temperance and prohibition organizations. I know what they are thinking, and I believe that I know what they are going to do and why they are going to do it. The religious question is a red herring. By itself, its influence would have been negligible and it probably would not have been of sufficient importance to receive attention. The millions of intelligent, moral, free and undeceived people who are throwing off party shackles and rallying to the support of Herbert Hoover are determined that a representative of the liquor interests and Tammany Hall shall not be installed in the White House, and that the liquor traffic shall not again become a legal institution in this nation. Their feeling of revulsion is like that of a man who hears the rattle of the serpent that is about to strike and bury its fangs in his body. They are determined that the advance of these menacing forces shall be stopped. Everywhere from set lips come the grim words, "They shall not pass." On next Wednesday morning, the world will know that the moral and patriotic forces of America have accepted the challenge.

Mr. Smith carried 8 states, with 87 electoral votes, and Mr. Hoover carried 40 states, with 444 electoral votes, and received a 6,300,000 popular plurality. According to the statements of dry leaders, who had kept a record of the pledges of candidates for all other offices, the new Congress was dry by a majority of 80 to 16 in the Senate, and 328 to 106 in the House; dry majorities had been elected to nearly every state legislature, and of 48 governors only 5 were wet. So emphatic and unquestionable was the meaning of the popular verdict that between the election and Mr. Hoover's inauguration, Congress passed the Jones Act making all violations of the Volstead Act felonies.

The liquor interests and their political champions and the wet press endeavored to deceive the people as to the true meaning of Mr. Hoover's victory. They said that it was the result of religious fanaticism, prosperity, the strength of the Republican organization, and so on. But the real meaning of the victory was expressed by the dry *Christian Century* and the wet New York *World*. The former said:

The election definitely ushers American prohibition of the liquor traffic into a new dispensation. The people have spoken again. They leave no doubt of their unchanged determination that the saloon shall not be allowed to return to the country from which it was definitely expelled a decade ago. Prohibition was one of the paramount issues in the campaign, made so by the daring championship of its one candidate, and by the decisive support of its constitutional status by the other candidate.

Mr. Hoover therefore will come to the presidency with a clear mandate from the people to maintain the law and to recover it from the odium into which violators, opponents, perfunctory officials, and an indifferent President, have allowed it to fall. He will come at a moment when all the factors in the situation are especially favorable to the success of his earnest purpose.

In addition to the basic fact that he has been elected by so overwhelming a vote, there is the associated fact that in their herculean effort to compass his defeat, the wets have exhausted their case. In the campaign against him, the arsenal of the enemy has been emptied. One has only to scan the metropolitan press of the country to measure the abandon with which the big guns used up their ammunition. The most brilliant correspondents and feature writers were assigned to the Smith entourage. A fortnight before the campaign ended, the cry of one of the most brilliant of them was, " My kingdom for another adjective." And for the last week the riot of rhetoric passed from a hysterical orgy into a condition of groggy exhaustion. The campaign to elect Mr. Smith marked the climax of a ten-year program to discredit prohibition. The wets fought as if fully aware of the desperate phase their long war had now entered upon.

Mr. Hoover is coming to the presidency just at the dark moment which is said to usher in the dawn.[12]

In a spirit of resignation, the New York *World* said: " Since the American people are not ready to modify the law, the best alternative is a real effort to enforce it. Mr. Hoover has his mandate and we shall see what we shall see." [13]

Nullification

When Herbert Hoover took the oath to " preserve, protect and defend the Constitution of the United States," the nation was confronted with dangers of a more fundamental and serious character than those which it faced when Abraham Lincoln first took that same oath. The advantages that would have been sacrificed and the evils that would have resulted from a dissolution of the Union and the perpetuation of slavery, are now recognized by the people of both the north and the south. But if that had happened, the people of both sections would have remained intelligent, moral, law-abiding, and loyal to their respective governments. The foundations of civilization would have remained sound and secure. While the people of the south had announced their withdrawal from the Union, they did not propose nullification, lawlessness, anarchy and the dissolution of the foundations of social order.

In 1832, certain elements in South Carolina had asserted the right to remain in the Union and accept its benefits and to nullify and disregard those provisions of its Constitution to which they were opposed. This proposition was decisively rejected by the foremost leaders of both the north and the south. In his reply to Calhoun, Webster said:

> Nullification, sir, is as distinctly revolutionary as secession; but I cannot say that the revolution which it seeks is one of so respectable a character. Secession would, it is true, abandon the Constitution altogether; but then it would profess to abandon it. Whatever other inconsistencies it might run into, one, at least, it would avoid. It would not belong to a government, while it rejected its authority. It would not repel the burden, and continue to enjoy the benefits. It would not aid in passing laws which others are to obey, and yet reject their authority as to itself. It would not undertake to reconcile obedience to public authority with an asserted right of command over that same authority. It would not be in the government, and above the government, at the same time. But however more respectable a mode secession may be, it is not more truly revolutionary than the actual execution of the doctrines of nullification. Both, and each, resist the constitutional authorities.[14]

The difference between nullification, which is lawlessness and anarchy, and the action of the south in withdrawing from the Union, is clearly stated by Jefferson Davis in the address he delivered on retiring from the United States Senate:

> I hope none who hear me will confound this expression of mine with the advocacy of the right of a state to remain in the Union, and to disregard its constitutional obligations by the nullification of the law. Such is not my theory. Nullification and secession, so often confounded, are indeed antagonistic principles. . . . The phrase " to execute the laws " was an expression which General Jackson applies to the case of a state refusing to obey the laws while yet a member of the Union.[15]

Webster, speaking for the north, conceded " the right of revolution for justifiable cause," and in 1861 the south believed that it had justifiable cause for revolution and revolted. That was the issue involved. But the greatest leaders of both north and south expressed their scorn for the man who would live in a country, accept the protection of its laws and enjoy the other privileges and advantages that it provided, but nullify and flout those provisions of its constitution and laws which he did not wish to obey. Such conduct was branded as nullification, lawlessness, anarchy, revolution, insurrection, treason, as subversive of orderly government and civilized society.

It was precisely this type of insurrection that was convulsing the country in 1929 and that Mr. Hoover had been given a mandate by the law-abiding people of America to suppress. The danger came not from the petty and irresponsible bootlegger and liquor addict. It came from the liquor interests and their business affiliates, from big income taxpayers, their newspapers, lawyers, propagandists and political hirelings. These elements were engaged in open nullification and defiance of the Constitution and of the laws of the country with the deliberate purpose of discrediting and breaking down the law and bringing about such a state of lawlessness and anarchy that the people, in confusion and disgust, would consent to the repeal of the Eighteenth Amendment. Their object was the satisfaction of their lust for liquor profits, liquor revenue and political power. A few statements will illustrate the spirit of this insurrection.

In an article that appeared in *Vanity Fair*, Mr. Corey Ford said:

> Personally, I should like to call on every free-thinking American of my generation, and every American of the older generation who can think at all, to break this law; break it repeatedly, break it whenever he can. Drink what you please, when you please. Urge others to drink. Don't betray the bootleggers who are smuggling liquor for you. In every way possible flaunt your defiance of the Eighteenth Amendment. Render it inoperative; ignore it, abrogate it, wipe it out. While it stands there, let it be disobeyed.[16]

A book entitled *Prohibition Primer* which was widely circulated by the wets, said:

> So if millions and millions of people go on for years and years breaking the prohibition laws and proving that they cannot be made to obey

them, Congress will finally wake up and see how silly prohibition is, and grow ashamed of the harm it is doing the country, by trying to keep them. When Congress does see this, it will repeal all the prohibition laws and amendments and set America free from them. So now you see how important and even patriotic it is to disobey prohibition.[17]

In a book circulated by the wets as a part of their propaganda, Harry Elmer Barnes said:

Sectional nullification, carrying further present tendencies, appears to be the only immediately practicable solution. Let those parts of the country that want an alcoholic desert proceed to make one for themselves, while other regions that prefer to do so can go dripping wet.

He quotes the following statement by Clarence Darrow:

Repeal of the Eighteenth Amendment is pure nonsense. Thirteen dry states with a population less than that of New York state alone can prevent repeal until Halley's comet returns. What we should do is to repeal the Volstead and Jones acts and provide no federal enforcement legislation. . . . If we can't get the Volstead and Jones acts off the books, a continuance of nullification must be our method of relief from oppression and corruption.[18]

The position of the insurrectionists was bluntly stated by the Chicago *Tribune*. For years it had misrepresented prohibition, denounced its supporters as bigots and fanatics, branded those engaged in enforcing the law as tyrants and murderers, and glorified bootleggers as the representatives and martyrs of human liberty. Finally, in a front-page editorial, it announced:

The Eighteenth Amendment will be repealed or nullified. . . . Nullification can end national prohibition but it cannot substitute so well ordered a state as will be made possible by repeal. . . . One house of Congress can refuse appropriations to national prohibition enforcement as it does to other laws on the statute books. The enforcement unit in the department of justice will be closed. Federal agents will be withdrawn, as the army of occupation was withdrawn from the southern states.[19]

Rich and fashionable people summoned the criminal bootlegger to their homes, purchased his contraband liquor, and served it openly. They poured their millions into the hands of smugglers, moonshiners, gangsters and racketeers. They helped elect to office men who would protect these criminals and share their profits. They sent forth their hired propagandists to misrepresent and denounce the law and slander and vilify those who supported and those who were endeavoring to enforce the law. With supreme insolence, they then turned to the law-abiding and patriotic people of America, and said: "You see, you can't enforce prohibition. This is what the country is going to get until you consent to the repeal of the law." In other words, this rebellion could be suppressed only by repealing the law that prohibited the business of debauching people for profit.

When the wets decided that they would not obey the prohibition law, they did not move out of the country or renounce the advantages which they enjoyed because of the existence and enforcement of other laws. On the contrary, they not only consented to but demanded laws that would secure them against every form of violence, protect their property and business, enforce their contracts, safeguard their health, educate their children, protect them on the high seas and in foreign lands, and, at their death, secure the passage of their property to their families or to those designated in their wills. It was only when the law ran counter to their avarice and blocked their greedy design to create and exploit a degrading and destructive appetite and maintain a nuisance and public menace, that they announced that the law "will be repealed or nullified," and openly proclaimed their rebellion.

When Lincoln stood firm for a fugitive-slave law, it was because it was necessary to the enforcement of a provision of the Constitution that had been adopted nearly a century earlier and one which in his time would not have been ratified by three-fourths of the states, but would have been rejected by a decisive majority. Furthermore, the fugitive-slave law established a thing that he hated and caused him to be misunderstood and criticized by many of the best people of the north. Through all the excitement and turbulence of the time, however, he remained steadfast, because it was clear to him that security, liberty, happiness and true progress were possible only under a reign of law and order where even righteous impatience was properly restrained and all change brought about by the orderly procedure provided by the Constitution.

How different was the situation in 1929. The Eighteenth Amendment had been recently adopted by the nearly unanimous action of the states, the enforcement law had been passed by an overwhelming majority of the Congress, every effort to repeal it had failed, and it had been strengthened by amendments. Both the amendment and the enforcement act had been attacked in the courts by leaders of the bar, but had been upheld without qualification by the Supreme Court of the United States. At every election since the ratification of the amendment, the people had sent to Congress increased majorities pledged to its support, and in the great referendum of 1928 they had decisively rejected the candidate of nullification and repeal. The people had taken this action deliberately after the experience of a hundred years had convinced them that in no other way could the evils of the liquor traffic be suppressed. But the most important distinction of all was that prohibition was adopted not to protect, but to destroy, an ancient evil.

Men in positions of the highest responsibility repeatedly called attention to the fact that the insurrection against prohibition threatened the gravest consequences. The following illustrates the nature and spirit of their protest. A federal judge, charging the grand jury, said:

> When they buy liquor somebody else violates the law in order that they may possess it and to that extent they are aiding in this lawlessness, not merely lending their countenance to it, but actually are partners in the crimes being committed. It is not a mark of good citizenship. That conduct is the beginning of anarchy, of class privileges and disrespect for law.[20]

The judicial section of the American Bar Association unanimously adopted a report which contained the following:

> When, for the gratification of their appetites or the promotion of their interests, lawyers, bankers, great merchants and manufacturers,

and social leaders, both men and women, disobey and scoff at this law, or any other law, they are aiding the cause of anarchy and promoting mob violence, robbery and homicide; they are sowing dragon's teeth, and they need not be surprised when they find that no judicial or police authority can save our country or humanity from reaping the harvest.[21]

Senator Borah said:

The " red " sits in his darkly lighted room, around his poorly laden table, and denounces the provisions of the Constitution placed there to protect property. The " white " sits in his brilliantly lighted room, about his richly laden table, and defies or denounces the provisions of the Constitution placed there in the belief that they would protect the home. I leave it to all good citizens whether it is not true that both are traveling the road to lawlessness, both sowing the seed of destruction, both undermining the whole fabric of law and order.[22]

Judge Kenyon, in his separate statement appended to the Wickersham Report, said:

This government will continue to be a government of law or it will cease to be a government at all. The representatives of great property interests who are well within their rights in seeking repeal of laws go far beyond such rights when they defy the law enforcement. The day may come in this country when representatives of great property interests will realize that they need the protection of the law for the properties they represent more than other people may need it. . . . That the Eighteenth Amendment is now nullified in many of the large cities of the country cannot be denied by anyone willing to face the facts, and this very nullification is producing public sentiment against the prohibition laws and affecting the judgment of those who earnestly believe that it is a dangerous proposition for a country to permit its laws to be nullified.[23]

President Harding said:

Whatever satisfaction there may be in indulgence, whatever objection there is to so-called invasion of personal liberty, neither counts when the supremacy of the law and the stability of our institutions are menaced. With all good intention, the majority sentiment of the

United States has sought by law to remove strong drink as a curse upon the American citizen, but ours is a larger problem now to remove lawless drinking as a menace to the republic itself.[24]

President Coolidge, in his message to Congress in 1926, said:

> Some people do not like the amendment, some do not like other parts of the Constitution, some do not like any of it. Those who entertain such sentiments have a perfect right to seek through legal methods for a change. But for any of our inhabitants to observe such parts of the Constitution as they like, while disregarding others, is a doctrine that would break down all protection of life and property and destroy the American system of ordered liberty.

In accepting the Republican nomination for president in 1928, Mr. Hoover said:

> Modification of the enforcement laws which would permit that which the Constitution forbids is nullification. This the American people will not countenance. Change in the Constitution can and must be brought about only by the straightforward methods provided in the Constitution itself. There are those who do not believe in the purposes of several provisions of the Constitution. No one denies their right to seek to amend it. They are not subject to criticism for asserting that right. But the Republican party does deny the right of anyone to seek to destroy the purposes of the Constitution by indirection.

In his address at the annual luncheon of the Associated Press reported in the New York *Times*, April 22, 1929, he expressed the same convictions:

> What we are facing today is . . . the possibility that respect for law as law is fading from the sensibilities of our people. No individual has the right to determine what law shall be obeyed and what law shall not be enforced. If a law is wrong, its rigid enforcement is the surest guaranty of its repeal. If it is right, the enforcement is the quickest method of compelling respect for it. I have seen statements published within a few days encouraging citizens to defy a law because that particular journal did not approve of the law itself. I leave comment on such an attitude to any citizen with a sense of responsibility to his country.

In an article in the New York *Herald Tribune* in which he discussed the legality of the sit-down strikes of 1937, Walter Lippmann said:

> Never in the history of the law has rebellion been made lawful. Only the rights demanded by the rebels have been legalized. Thus, for example, the Volstead Act was nullified by an act of rebellion in which a large part of the American people conspired with bootleggers and smugglers. The result of that rebellion was the repeal of the Volstead Act and the legalization of the sale of liquor. But bootlegging was not legalized by repeal. Smuggling was not legalized by repeal. The lawless acts of the rebellion by which prohibition was challenged have not received the sanction of the law.[25]

President Hoover's Action

When Mr. Hoover took his oath of office, ten years of experience, investigation, study and discussion had brought to light all the facts of the situation. Newspapers, magazines, the Civil Service Reform League, congressional investigations, plans submitted in the Durant contest, books by Commissioner Haynes, Mrs. Willebrandt and others, had shown the conditions that existed, the defects in the prohibition law and its administration, the source of the wet propaganda, and just what steps were necessary to restore law and order and re-establish the authority and dignity of the government of the United States. Although the wets controlled the most important instruments of publicity, they could not smother the voice of the president of the United States. Mr. Hoover was in a position to command attention and carry the truth to the people.

In view of the circumstances of his election, there can be no doubt as to the course he should have pursued. He should have called a special session of Congress and submitted to it a message dealing in a comprehensive manner with the problem of prohibition enforcement. He should have exposed the sources and the falsehoods of the wet propaganda, and made it clear that the rebellion had not originated with the people, but was being fomented by the liquor interests and those who were seeking to escape the payment of taxes on their incomes. He should have demanded the repeal of the Volstead Act and the enactment of a short, clear enforcement statute, making every aspect of the liquor business a crime and its penalties applicable to all who either directly or indirectly participated in its violation. He should have purged the federal service of the weaklings and crooks that were making a farce of the law, and replaced them by men who could be relied on to perform their duty. He should have decreed social and political ostracism to all politicians, high and low, who dealt with bootleggers or in any other manner aided or abetted the commission of crime. He should have announced with absolute finality that from that time forward, the Eighteenth Amendment would be treated as a part of the Constitution, which he had taken an oath to "preserve, protect and defend." Experience had demonstrated the necessity for this course of action, every legal obstruction had been cleared away by the Supreme Court, Congress was fresh from the people and overwhelmingly dry, and the country was impatient with the lawlessness and insolence of the wets. As a result of his extraordinary popular and electoral victory Mr. Hoover possessed great prestige and power. If he had launched a campaign to put down the liquor rebellion with the authority and courage of a true leader, he would have electrified the nation and rallied all its moral and patriotic forces to his support.

But in that great hour of opportunity and duty, President Hoover gave an exhibition of lack of comprehension, timidity and inability to lead that is disheartening to contemplate. His first blunder had been committed during the campaign, when he referred to the Eighteenth Amendment as a "noble experiment." We had been experimenting for a hundred years with different methods of dealing with the liquor traffic and the purpose of the Eighteenth Amendment was to put an end to experimentation and make prohibition the established policy of the nation. But since the President elected by the drys had called it an experiment, the wets were able to argue that it had failed, and since it was only an experiment, it should be abandoned. And so the phrase "the noble experiment" became the triumphant theme song of all the elements that had opposed Mr. Hoover.

In his inaugural address, he pointed out clearly the dangers that would result from lawlessness and nullification, just as Mr. Harding and Mr. Coolidge had done. He then appointed a cabinet of ten men, six of whom were wet, according to the statement of the head of the Association Against the Prohibition Amendment. One of the six was a member of the board of directors of that organization. As the man to have charge of prohibition enforcement, he reappointed Mr. Mellon, a wet, and one of the men chiefly responsible for the breakdown of the law. When public opinion forced Mr. Mellon to resign, he was replaced by Ogden Mills, a dripping wet New York politician and office-seeker, who had spent years competing with Tammany Hall for the support of New York's underworld and liquor element, and who, because of his great wealth, would profit by the return and taxation of the liquor traffic. Mr. Hoover appointed a wet political spoilsman to the important position of postmaster general. He then asked these gentlemen if they would please not serve liquor in their homes.

The man whom the President appointed as attorney general was conscientious in the performance of the routine duties of his office, and, in a small way, made a sincere effort to enforce the prohibition law. But either he did not have the ability and vision or he was not authorized to make the drastic cleaning and reorganization of the district attorneys' offices of the country that the situation so urgently demanded.

Mr. Hoover took no effective steps to end the conditions that prevailed in the national capital, to secure the loyalty of every man engaged in the federal service, to expose and dissipate the propaganda with which the people were being deceived and inflamed, to secure adequate appropriations and the needed strengthening of the enforcement machinery, or to obtain the passage of the additional laws which experience had shown were indispensable. What did he do? He appointed a commission to investigate.

The Wickersham Commission

Appointment of a commission was the very essence of ineptitude and futility. It was more — it was a national tragedy. Under a corrupt and supine government, sinister forces had taken things into their own hands and were offering the nation the alternative of repeal or rebellion. American civilization was confronted by the same conditions that have made history a dreary record of civilizations destroyed through a coalition of avarice, corruption and irresponsibility at the top, and dependence, appetite and degeneracy at the bottom. The situation demanded action as prompt, as realistic and as uncompromising as that of Andrew Jackson in 1832 and of Abraham Lincoln in 1861. The people had given Mr. Hoover a mandate to take just such action — not to waste years in a futile, academic investigation.

What was the commission to find out? Was it to find out whether the law was being violated, and, if so, to what extent? It was common knowledge that in every part of the country there were certain elements that were openly flouting the law. Was it to investigate the sufficiency of the Volstead Act? Its long record of failure and the testimony of those charged with its administration showed that the act was inadequate. Was it to find out what changes should be made in the law? This had been repeatedly and authoritatively pointed out by men who, as a result of years of effort to enforce the law, had gained first-hand and exact knowledge of its defects and of the amendments needed. Was it to find out whether the prohibition bureaucracy was efficient and honest? The record showed conclusively that it was inefficient and corrupt, and, as a member of the cabinet, Mr. Hoover had had eight years in which to gain first-hand knowledge of that fact. Was it to help him make up his mind? He had already told the people that his mind was made up and that it was his intention to enforce the law.

If, after his election, he had made a careful examination of the official and authoritative investigations and reports that were then available, he could have learned more about the subject in two weeks than his commission reported to him after two years of solemn investigation. If he had appointed to the commission people of the type of Mrs. Willebrandt, General Andrews, Major Mills, Mr. Buckner, Mr. Chase, Mayor Dever and Governor Pinchot, his action would have had at least one element of realism. He would have had the assistance of men and women who had been charged with the enforcement of the law and from long and intimate experience knew the difficulties that had been encountered. He chose instead ten men and one woman, none of whom, with the exception of Justice Kenyon, had participated in the struggle for the enactment and enforcement of prohibition laws in a manner that gave them special qualification for the work they were to undertake. The Republican platform, Mr. Hoover's speech of acceptance and the vote of the people had eliminated every question except that of effective enforcement.

The act under which the commission was appointed stated that its purpose was to make " a thorough inquiry into the problem of the enforcement of prohibition under the provisions of the Eighteenth Amendment of the Constitution and laws enacted in pursuance thereof, together with the enforcement of other laws." Notwithstanding these limitations, the commission assumed that it was authorized to roam at large, open up every closed question and, finally, to enter what the lawyers call judgment *non obstante veredicto* — that is, any judgment they saw fit notwithstanding the solemn verdict of the American people. So they decided, as they stated later in their report,

> to go into the whole subject of enforcement of the Eighteenth Amendment and the national prohibition act; the present condition as to observance and enforcement of that act and its causes; whether and how far the amendment in its present form is enforceable; whether it should be retained, or repealed, or revised, and a constructive program of improvement.

In the meantime, Mr. Hoover waited for two years while his commission, in complete isolation from the realities of the situation, engaged in an academic and futile threshing of old straw.

The wets, who had read the doom of their cause in the Republican platform, in Mr. Hoover's speech of acceptance, in the vote of the people both for president and for the Congress, and in the prompt passage of the Jones Act, gave a long sigh of relief and indulged in Homeric laughter as they realized that they had only seen a ghost.

When Mr. Hoover's term of office was half over and his great opportunity had passed, the commission submitted its report. After reading it, Nicholas Murray Butler, quoting Horace, said that "the mountain had labored and brought forth a funny little mouse." This was flattery. The mouse was not funny; it was pitiable and absurd. It gave a long and solemn parade of liquor lawlessness, with all of which everyone was familiar and thoroughly sick of hearing about. In this part of the report there was nothing that was new, enlightening or helpful. In fullness and definiteness it did not compare to the exposure of those abuses that had been made by the Senate Investigating Committee of 1926. In a timid and meaningless way, it stated that prohibition had got off to a bad start, that there had been corruption, and that politics had interfered with enforcement. But there was no searching and courageous exposure of the corruption and betrayal of the Harding and Coolidge administrations, which was so essential to an adequate understanding of the problems confronting the country. A few minor changes in the law were suggested, but no reference was made to the great fundamental changes that experience had shown to be essential and that had been repeatedly recommended by those actually administering the law.

In the previous year, the Senate Lobby Investigating Committee had laid bare the files of the Association Against the Prohibition Amendment. Documents in those files gave direct and conclusive proof of the fact already established by circumstantial evidence, that for purely financial reasons, a small body of millionaires had entered into a conspiracy to destroy the Eighteenth Amendment. Their campaign was the greatest obstacle to the enforcement of prohibition and the most sinister phenomenon of the time. It was the duty of the commissioners to make an exhaustive and uncompromising exposure of this conspiracy. They did not have the courage to mention it. They should have pointed out that the nation was not confronted simply with petty and occasional violations of the liquor laws by people who had to have a drink, but with an organized rebellion against the Constitution and the laws of the country by men determined to obtain billions of dollars of liquor profits and liquor revenue. They should have pointed out that, in such a situation, making periodic raids and arresting and fining subordinates was like going against heavy artillery and tanks with bows and arrows. These and the other really vital aspects of the problem of enforcement which they were appointed to consider they ignored.

After two years of gestation, the commission announced to a waiting world that it was " opposed to the repeal of the Eighteenth Amendment," " to the restoration in any manner of the legalized saloon," " to the federal or state governments, as such, going into the liquor business " and " to the proposal to modify the national prohibition act so as to permit manufacture and sale of light wines or beer," and " that if the amendment is revised," it should give Congress the power to regulate or prohibit the liquor traffic. These were questions that were not submitted to the commission; they had been settled by the American people. They were not open to official consideration, and it was an act of presumption for the commission to make pontifical pronouncements in regard to them. The commission further announced that although there had been some improvement since the enactment of the bureau of prohibition act of 1927, " there is yet no adequate observance or enforcement," and that " the present organization for enforcement is still inadequate." These were facts that everybody knew and it was unnecessary for the commission to discover them or to proclaim them.

What did the commission offer on the subject of enforcement, which it was appointed to consider? It recommended removal of restrictions on the medical profession. Since it did not recommend the thoroughgoing revision or repeal of the Volstead Act, this simply amounted to giving unlimited bootlegging privileges to physicians. It recommended increasing appropriations, elimination of the provision in regard to cider and fruit juices, increase in the number of enforcement officials, permission to trace specially denatured alcohol to the ultimate consumer, prohibition of independent denaturing plants, codification of prohibition laws, making more effective the procedure in padlock injunction cases and a mode of prosecuting petty offenses in the federal courts. It opposed allowing more latitude for federal searches and seizures. With the exception of the last two mentioned, these were good suggestions and had all been made many times before.

As to the most important and fundamental things necessary to the enforcement of prohibition, the report was either brief and vague or silent. As Mr. Merz says:

> Having recognized that the attitude of the public was a fundamental factor in the enforcement of the law, and having recognized the total inadequacy of existing federal agencies of investigation and prosecution, the commission made no recommendations whatever on either of these points. The one new proposal which it made was concerned not with the large problem of "observance" and "enforcement," but with the small problem of handling petty cases in the courts.[26]

To this report, each of the eleven commissioners added an oracular separate statement. They simply threshed over again the old straw of abuses and difficulties; they threw no new light whatsoever on the question of enforcement. They did, however, make many statements that made it possible for the wets to discredit the recommendation of the commission that the amendment should not be repealed.

Thus Newton D. Baker signed the report which said that "the commission is opposed to the repeal of the Eighteenth Amendment" and "all the commission agree that if the amendment is revised, it should give to Congress full power to regulate or to prohibit the liquor traffic." In his separate report, Mr. Baker said: "In my opinion, the Eighteenth Amendment should be repealed and the whole question of policy and enforcement with regard to intoxicating liquors remitted to the states."

Henry W. Anderson forgot all about " a thorough inquiry into the problem of prohibition enforcement," the only thing that he had any authority to consider. He decided to supersede the President, the Congress and the American people, and to work out a beautiful new solution of the whole liquor problem that would be all his own. His practical insight and prophetic vision told him that " the saloon is gone forever. It belongs as completely to the past as the institution of human slavery." With this comfortable assurance, he put on his dressing gown, sat down in his easychair, lit his pipe and, as the smoke curled upward, he dreamed a dream. It seemed that the Eighteenth Amendment had been repealed and Congress given full authority over the liquor traffic. A law had been passed restricting the manufacture of liquor to corporations having federal charters, and their profits were limited to seven per cent. The liquor could be distributed only by the states and sold only in state liquor stores and could not be consumed at the place of purchase. Sales were " limited to persons holding license books " and " the amount of high alcoholic liquors . . . limited to a reasonable quantity in any month." There were no profits to private individuals and the revenue went into the state treasury and was " used for educational purposes, especially as to the evils resulting from the use of alcoholic beverages and for the eradication and prevention of those conditions which cause excessive drinking, or which tend to create a demand for intoxicating beverages."

With a sophomoric display of superficial and irrelevant learning, Mr. Anderson launched this dream with the approval of five of his fellow commissioners. Of course, this " plan " contributed absolutely nothing to the solution of the problem of enforcement. It did, however, furnish the wets with a powerful weapon for use in their campaign to destroy the Eighteenth Amendment. Millions of people were opposed to repeal because they believed that it would result in a return to all the evils of pre-prohibition days. It was the strategy of the wet propaganda to convince these people that all those evils had resulted not from the liquor traffic but from the saloon, and that all existing evils resulted not from the liquor traffic but from prohibition. They said, therefore, that if the Eighteenth Amendment was repealed and the liquor traffic was taken over by the state, all the evils of the saloon and the prohibition era would be abolished and the millennium would be at hand. Their immediate objective was to break down opposition to repeal and get rid of the Eighteenth Amendment. They knew that when this was accomplished, they would be in a position to prevent the fulfillment of their promise and the adoption of any plan that would prevent them from exploiting the liquor traffic for profit. The Anderson plan fitted perfectly into this part of the wet strategy, and, embodied in the widely heralded report of the commission appointed by a President pledged to the retention and enforcement of the Eighteenth Amendment, it had the greatest possible publicity value.

At first the wets criticized the report of the commission because it opposed repeal of the Eighteenth Amendment and modification of the Volstead Act to legalize wine and beer. But they soon saw that it was better strategy to suppress these findings and exploit all the evils and abuses that were paraded in the report, praise the Anderson plan, and deceive the people and make them believe that the President's commission had pronounced the Eighteenth Amendment a failure and recommended its abandonment. After repeal became effective, I met one of the attorneys of the prohibition unit. He was an intelligent and honest young man who had struggled faithfully to enforce the law. I asked him what the greatest obstacles to enforcement had been, and he said:

> The loopholes, technicalities and restrictions of the Volstead Act, and the Wickersham Report. The wet press garbled from that report all the statements that tended to discredit prohibition and gave them daily and universal circulation. From that time on, the attitude of the people became increasingly indifferent or hostile, and juries let bootleggers go regardless of the evidence.

If Mr. Hoover had had true insight and courage, he would have clarified the situation with a message to Congress which the wet press could not have suppressed. He would have stated frankly that the Wickersham Report was superficial and presumptuous. He would have pointed out that the evils mentioned in it were not the result of the Eighteenth Amendment, but of the activities of those seeking to profit by the liquor traffic. He would have shown that the report of the commission, signed by nine out of eleven of its members, had declared against the repeal of the Eighteenth Amendment, the modification of the Volstead Act, the return of the saloon and the surrender of federal jurisdiction, and for the strict enforcement of the law, and that these findings were being suppressed and distorted by the wet propagandists. He would then have submitted the enforcement program that should have been proposed two years earlier. Instead of this, he let them "get away with it." In the meantime, without "dramatic displays" and "sensational raids," and by "legal methods," a "steady pressure" was maintained against the little fellows, and prominent citizens were occasionally notified in dignified language that it was their duty to obey the law. While Raskob, Shouse and Michaelson carried on their "smear Hoover" campaign in order to discredit and destroy his power to enforce prohibition, he "took it lying down," not even daring to emit a groan.

A week before the report was submitted to Congress, the *Christian Century*, which had struggled bravely to find some good reason for supporting Mr. Hoover, said:

Mr. Hoover's formula of prohibition as "a noble experiment" leaves it undetermined as to whether he is a wet or a dry. A dry does not believe that prohibition is an experiment. He believes that it is the end of an experiment — a long, patient, resourceful and thorough experiment in dealing with the liquor traffic as a legalized economic entity. We do not suggest that Mr. Hoover is a wet. His formula, however, is not a dry formula. It is a wet formula. Mr. Hoover, we believe, has deeper thoughts on the subject than he has yet expressed, more definite thoughts, more leaderlike thoughts. The nation is waiting to know what these thoughts are. It earnestly wishes to know whether its President is a wet or a dry.

The Wickersham Commission is, we are told, about to make its report. Will it be wet or will it be dry? No one knows. The public will judge as to its merits. The press is preparing the public for a

" moist " report. We know in advance that a report which the wet press will label " moist " is a wet report. The public has one fundamental question under which to examine the Wickersham Commission's reports: Does it recommend at any point, in any degree, the relegalization of the liquor traffic? If it does, it is wet. If it does not, directly or indirectly, it is dry. There are innumerable details in connection with the enforcement in which the essential wet and dry issue is not involved. Upon these there will be harmless and inevitable differences of opinion. But the great issue is Democracy versus the Liquor Traffic. A wet report, confessing the inability of democracy to enforce its own laws and therefore making concessions to the liquor traffic, will weaken democracy. A dry report will strengthen democracy by justifying the delegalizing of the liquor traffic and pointing out wise methods by which the sovereign will of the people may be more fully effectuated.[27]

A month later the same journal declared:

This, then, is the situation. The daily press, led by the metropolitan papers of large circulation, is out to make the nation " wet-minded," and it is rapidly succeeding. How can this peril to the hope of an ultimately dry nation be conquered? If the President of the United States would come to the front to defend and champion the cause of federal prohibition before the country, the weight of the wet press could and would be overcome. For there are no journalistic devices able to smother the voice of a President. If he would do it, Herbert Hoover could place the case for prohibition before his fellow citizens in such a fashion that they would see the realities of the situation which the wet press keeps hidden from them.[28]

The fact is that, so far as prohibition was concerned, Mr. Hoover's actions were futile. During his administration, a law was enacted transferring responsibility for the enforcement of the prohibition law from the treasury to the Department of Justice. But as this was a mere patch on the Volstead Act, its results were unimportant. The attorney general issued pamphlets on law observance which nobody read, and prosecuted privates who had strayed beyond the protection of the heavy wet artillery. His efforts were comparable to those of the celebrated Mrs. Partington with her broom.

Mr. Hoover did nothing to secure the repeal of the Volstead Act and the enactment of an adequate enforcement law. When the wet propagandists were telling the people that the criminal conditions which had been steadily growing worse for half a century, the economic and moral dislocations of the World War, the political corruption and betrayal of the Harding and Coolidge administrations, the Tammany rule of our cities, and the lawlessness of the liquor business, were all the results of the Eighteenth Amendment, he did nothing to expose the fraud or its source. When the Senate Lobby Investigating Committee laid bare the evidence of a scheme to destroy prohibition for the sake of liquor revenue, he remained dumb. When the wet rebellion was daily becoming more open, insolent and menacing, and the millions of moral and patriotic people who had elected him president looked eagerly to him for vital and courageous leadership, he not only was as helpless as a figure of straw, but even his well-wishers could not tell whether he was a wet or a dry.

Republican National Convention of 1932

For months prior to the national conventions of 1932, the politicians, the press and the people discussed nothing but the question of repeal. The wets were elated with the prospect of their return to power, the removal of every barrier to their greed, and the realization of billions of dollars of profits and revenue. The drys were alarmed and oppressed by the prospect of a great moral catastrophe and were fighting desperately to avert it. During this period, a number of Republican leaders conferred with Mr. Hoover on the question. As they left the White House after the conference the drys denied that he was wet, and the wets denied that he was dry, but no one could say what he really was, and he remained silent on the subject. There was a general feeling, however, that the President was simply looking about for a winning formula.

As the delegates assembled in Chicago, the wets staged a frenzied orgy of propaganda which was sheer political blackmail. There were beer parades, the galleries of the convention hall were packed with riff-raff instructed to stampede the convention for repeal, and every reference to prohibition was greeted with jeers, groans and boos. At the same time, thousands of men and women from every part of the country, representing business, churches, social workers, women's organizations, parent-teacher associations and patriotic bodies, were holding meetings day and night, praying, beseeching and demanding that the convention take a firm stand for the maintenance and enforcement of the Eighteenth Amendment. Mr. Hoover remained silent, but he had appointed as his manager and spokesman Ogden Mills, the millionaire New York politician and ardent wet.

While the convention was in session, the *Christian Century* gave an accurate statement of the quality of Mr. Hoover's leadership:

Mr. Hoover has been the leader of the drys. They elected him President. They trusted him. He used words about prohibition which sounded as if he were a dry, but which skirted the issue so cleverly as to commit him to nothing but law enforcement, to which his oath bound him. Since the day he became President, he has uttered no syllable of leaderlike or responsible interpretation. His reputation as a dry became a sacred myth and held the personnel of the dry organization under its spell. The myth was sustained by Mr. Hoover's silence. He has remained silent to this day. But meantime, Mr. Hoover has had a monopoly of the dry constituency. The liquor issue was Mr. Hoover's issue. No one could take it from him. He was the leader. The rewards of leadership were not available for any other statesman so far as this issue was concerned. Therefore, no other leadership emerged. Prohibition's eggs were all in Mr. Hoover's basket.

Behind his silence and evasion, the wets have been able to carry on their campaign. On the wet side the prizes of leadership were open and obtainable. Therefore, leadership was forthcoming. . . . The drys' morale weakened because they had no leaders. They had no leaders because it was Mr. Hoover's issue. And Mr. Hoover failed to lead.

For the trust which the drys have placed in Mr. Hoover, we shall soon see the quality of his requital. The prohibition plank in the Republican platform will disclose it.[29]

When that plank appeared, it disclosed that Mr. Hoover did not have the courage to declare either for or against repeal or even to use the word. After much high-sounding verbiage on the subject of observance and enforcement of law and the mechanism of "change," it proposed to submit the question to the states:

We, therefore, believe that the people should have an opportunity to pass upon a proposed amendment the provision of which, while retaining in the federal government power to preserve the gains already made in dealing with the evils inherent in the liquor traffic, shall allow states to deal with the problem as their citizens may determine, but subject always to the power of the federal government to protect those states where prohibition may exist and safeguard our citizens everywhere from the return of the saloon and attendant abuses.

Such an amendment should be promptly submitted to the states by Congress, to be acted upon by state conventions called for that sole purpose in accordance with the provisions of Article V of the Constitution and adequately safeguarded so as to be truly representative.

Apparently the Republican convention believed that this was a pill that would be swallowed by both wets and drys. But the desertion of the Eighteenth Amendment and the proposal to submit an amendment for its repeal disappointed and disgusted the drys. The proposal to retain federal jurisdiction to "preserve the gains already made" and to "prevent the return of the saloon" enraged the wets because it would give to a dry Congress the power to interfere with their plans for profits and revenue. The reaction of the wets was expressed by the Chicago *Tribune* as follows:

The plank on the Eighteenth Amendment concocted by the majority members of the resolutions committee and approved by the Republican convention is the product of political cowardice and hypocrisy. It deserves the indignant repudiation of every opponent of federal prohibition and the contempt of every supporter of that sorry experiment. . . . The proposal is a flagrant fraud devised to conciliate the dry vote while offering to the opponents of prohibition a promise which cannot be realized if the demands of the federal prohibitionist are obeyed. The plank is a fraud. It is an offense to the Republican party and to the American people, wet and dry. It is a declaration of political bankruptcy upon this great issue, for it is as futile as it is fraudulent.[30]

In a speech in the Senate, Mr. Borah, as a leader of the drys, declared that the plank simply provided for the repeal of the Eighteenth Amendment and the return of the liquor traffic and the saloon. What were the gains and how were they to be preserved? If the liquor traffic was legalized and it was left to the " states to deal with the problem as their citizens might determine," how would the federal government prevent the return of the saloon? How would it go into every city and village of the land and supervise the method of sale of a lawful article of commerce? How would it " safeguard " the state conventions to which the repeal amendment would be submitted?

The Reverend James K. Shields, superintendent of the New Jersey Anti-Saloon League, said: " The worst part is the discouragement. It seems strange that four years ago, on a dry platform, Herbert Hoover received the greatest electoral vote ever given to any man. Now Mr. Hoover is running on a platform nearly the same as Al Smith ran on then." [31]

That platform invited from Mr. Hoover's opponent, Franklin D. Roosevelt, the following contemptuous remarks: " I suspect that those who wrote that plank thought that it would sound dry to the drys and wet to the wets. But to the consternation of the high priests, it sounded dry to the wets and wet to the drys. This was very serious." [32]

Some drys were in favor of supporting Mr. Hoover. The party was not committed to repeal, but to a resubmission of the question to the states. It proposed not the submission of the question of flat repeal but of a substitute. This might result in important advantages to the dry cause. It was thought possible " that the difficulties in the way of formulating a substitute upon which the wets themselves can agree will prevent resubmission." The *Christian Century* took this position, but added:

With the adoption of an unqualified repeal plank by the Democratic party and its unqualified acceptance by Mr. Roosevelt, the nominee, that party and its ticket are definitely ranged on the absolute wet side of the liquor issue. The Democratic convention reached the conclusion that the dry constituency can be ignored in the election, and it chose not only to disregard it, but to affront and defy it. . . .

The Republican plank offers something different. But here the wise voter raises the question as to how much dependence is to be put on party platforms. Is the Republican liquor plank merely a device to hold the dry voter until after November, or does it represent the intelligent purpose of the Republican leadership? Particularly, does it represent the intelligent purpose of Mr. Hoover? It is Mr. Hoover's responsibility to say what degree of life is to be given to the Republican plan. His treatment of it will tell whether it is a hypocritical vote-catcher or the formulation of a serious policy. After all, we are more concerned with Mr. Hoover's interpretation of this plank than with the plank itself. . . .

Does Mr. Hoover propose to run on this Republican plank, as Mr. Roosevelt challengingly announces that he proposes to run on his Democratic plank? And will Mr. Hoover, in his acceptance speech, tell the country that has been misled as to the meaning of the Republican plank just what it does mean? And will he make it clear in his case, as Mr. Roosevelt did in his, that he can be counted upon to perform what his plank proposes? If Mr. Hoover will do this, in words as ringing as Mr. Roosevelt's, he will not only win back the now departing drys, but they will return to his banner with enthusiasm and the courage of victory.[33]

Hoover's Speech of Acceptance

In his address accepting the nomination, Mr. Hoover said:

I have always sympathized with the high purpose of the Eighteenth Amendment, and I have used every power at my command to make it effective over the entire country. I have hoped it was the final solution of the evils of the liquor traffic against which our people have striven for generations. . . .

The Republican platform recommends submission of the question to the states that the people themselves may determine whether they desire a change, but insists that this submission shall propose a constructive and not a destructive change. It does not dictate to the conscience of any members of the party. . . . The Constitution gives the president no power or authority with respect to changes in the Constitution itself; nevertheless my countrymen have a right to know my conclusions upon this matter. They are clear and need not be misunderstood. They are based upon the broad facts I have stated, upon my experience in this high office and upon the deep conviction that our purpose must be the elimination of the evils of this traffic from this civilization by practical measures.

It is my belief that in order to remedy present evils a change is necessary by which we resummon a proper share of initiative and responsibility which the very essence of our government demands shall rest upon the states and local authorities. That change must avoid the return of the saloon.

It is my conviction that the nature of this change, and one upon which all reasonable people can find common ground, is that each state shall be given the right to deal with the problem as it may determine, but subject to absolute guaranties in the Constitution of the United States to protect each state from interference and invasion by its neighbors, and that in no part of the United States shall there be a return of the saloon system with its inevitable political and social corruption and its organized interference with other states.

The only language in that statement that had any actual and definite meaning was the clause, " that each state shall be given the right to deal with the problem as it may determine," and in spite of the other deceptive verbiage, that meant the complete abandonment of prohibition and the return of the liquor traffic, saloons, liquor control of politics, and all the other familiar evils. Mr. Hoover further declared that he would not only favor the submission of such an amendment, but that he would advocate its adoption. The *Christian Century* commented:

Mr. Hoover has now justified Senator Borah's assumption and disappointed those drys who trusted him to stand on his party's plank. The President has gone far beyond his platform. He not only favors the submission of a substitute but declares himself in favor of the substitute. Those drys who, unlike the senator from Idaho, have been disposed to take the Republican plank as the reflection of the President's mind in the present stage of the prohibition controversy, and to give him their support on that basis, cannot avoid the feeling of having been " taken in " by the clever device of breaking the bad news in two installments.

The mood of these drys in the present situation can be made clear if we place ourselves back at the time of the Republican convention and assume the adoption of a liquor plank identical with the position taken by Mr. Hoover in his acceptance speech. Does anyone believe that such a plan would have caused a single dry organization or organ to hold in abeyance for six weeks its decision as to its attitude in the campaign? The adoption of such a plank by the Republican convention would have dispelled dry illusions instantly. Their leaders would have agreed that the dry stake in the success of the Republican party was so confused, and so inconsiderable, that there was not sufficient reason for them, as drys, to take sides in the presidential contest. They would at once have concentrated their energies upon the congressional campaign, while those of more extreme temperament would have flocked to the standard of a third party. It would hardly have occurred to any among them to await Mr. Hoover's acceptance speech before making their decision.

As it now turns out, whether as the result of deliberate strategy or otherwise, the interim between the adoption of the Republican platform and Mr. Hoover's speech of acceptance has been improved by many of the more reasonable drys to commit themselves more or less tentatively to Mr. Hoover, in the faith that the Republican platform was his personal platform. . . .

The drys have no one else to vote for but Mr. Hoover. Manifestly, as drys, they cannot vote for Mr. Roosevelt. But if they elect Mr. Hoover, they help to swell a popular presumption against the retention of the Eighteenth Amendment. Had the President stood squarely on the Republican plan, the drys, as well as all patriotic wets, could have supported him with ardor and complete consistency. And both the voters and Mr. Hoover himself could have postponed the necessity of taking an affirmative position on any substitute for federal prohibition to the time when such a substitute should be formulated by Congress and submitted to the states.[34]

In a later issue, the same journal said:

So far as the presidential campaign is concerned, the question of prohibition is a washed-out issue. The retreat of President Hoover from his position of hopeful faith in the Eighteenth Amendment and of hearty commitment to the vigorous enforcement of the prohibition law, leaves him practically side by side with Mr. Roosevelt. . . .

But Mr. Hoover himself dissolved this issue between his candidacy and that of Mr. Roosevelt. In his acceptance speech, he declared that he personally would be in favor of the substitute when it was proposed, and strongly advocated the return of the liquor problem to the several states. His personal expression thus marked a distinct retreat from his party platform in the direction of the Democratic position. . . . Is there any difference on the prohibition question between the Democratic party and the Republican party that is worth making a fight over? Our answer is that the prohibition question, so far as the presidential contest is concerned, is practically a washed-out issue.[35]

" Return the problem to the states " was the slogan by which the wets endeavored to conceal their real purpose, which was to lift the national floodgates to an unrestrained liquor traffic. Now that the drys had no other choice, Mr. Hoover inscribed upon his banner this deceptive wet slogan. Will Rogers expressed it exactly when he said:

Well, he did it. Mr. Hoover held his handkerchief up and saw which way the old " noble experiment " was blowing and joined in the parade. You can talk " morals " and all that, but when the votes lay the other way, why they sho' go with 'em.

Now the question is where are the drys going? Both sides are wet and the poor old dry hasn't got a soul to vote for. He is Roosevelt's " forgotten man."[36]

The drys, betrayed by their leader, and disfranchised, took no further interest in the prohibition aspect of the campaign.

NOTES

[1] *Crowded Hours* (Charles Scribner's Sons, 1933), p. 324.

[2] Quoted by Lucy W. Peabody, *Kidnapping the Constitution* (N. A. Lindsey, Inc., 1934), pp. 45–46.

[3] Wickersham Report, pp. 13, 79.

[4] *Ibid.*, pp. 118, 119.

[5] Willebrandt, *op. cit.*, pp. 111, 132.

[6] Quoted by Lamar T. Beman, *Prohibition — Modification of the Volstead Act* (H. W. Wilson Co., 1924), pp. 117–18.

[7] *Congressional Record,* Vol. 64, Part 4, 67th Congress, 4th Session, pp. 3789–91.

[8] Willebrandt, *op. cit.,* pp. 135–38.

[9] Merz, *op. cit.,* p. 108.

[10] *Ibid.,* pp. 186–89.

[11] Sept. 6, 1928.

[12] Nov. 15, 1928.

[13] Quoted in *Literary Digest,* March 16, 1929.

[14] *Speeches of Daniel Webster,* edited by B. F. Tefft (Porter & Coates, 1854), p. 468.

[15] David J. Brewer, *The World's Best Orations* (Fred P. Kaiser, 1899), p. 1652.

[16] May 1930.

[17] *Op. cit.,* p. 67.

[18] Harry Elmer Barnes, *Prohibition vs. Civilization* (Viking Press, 1934), pp. 118–19.

[19] June 14, 1932.

[20] Quoted by Roy A. Haynes, *Prohibition Inside Out* (Doubleday, Page & Co., 1923), p. 229.

[21] *American Bar Association Journal,* VII (1921), 484.

[22] Quoted by Irving Fisher, *Prohibition Still at Its Worst* (Alcohol Information Committee, 1928), p. 310.

[23] Wickersham Report, pp. 132–33.

[24] Haynes, *op. cit.,* p. 260.

[25] April 7, 1937.

[26] *Op. cit.,* p. 256.

[27] Jan. 14, 1931.

[28] Feb. 25, 1931.

[29] June 15, 1932.

[30] June 16, 1932.

[31] *Literary Digest,* Aug. 27, 1932.

[32] Chicago *Tribune,* Aug. 28, 1932.

[33] July 13, 1932.

[34] Aug. 24, 1932.

[35] Sept. 21, 1932.

[36] Los Angeles *Times,* Aug. 13, 1932.

Chapter Eleven

Prohibition And Crime

IN HIS book *The American Mind,* published by the Columbia University Press in 1930, Professor Peter Odegard of Ohio State University said:

> A prominent wet member of Congress once told the writer the principle upon which the wets base their propaganda: Every time a crime is committed, they cry prohibition. Every time a girl or a boy goes wrong, they shout prohibition. Every time a policeman or politician is accused of corruption, they scream prohibition. As a result, they are gradually building up in the public mind the impression that prohibition is a major cause of all the sins of society.[1]

One of the most effective broadcasters of this propaganda was that great high priest of temperance, virtue and political purity, William Randolph Hearst. On Sunday, March 20, 1932, he devoted an entire page to exhibits from his chamber of prohibition horrors. In a cartoon, Uncle Sam was pictured as bowed down and in chains. A man labeled " The American People " was lying flat on his face, and on his back was a huge fist labeled " Gangster Crime." In the distance, women, terror-stricken, were fleeing with their children in their arms. Underneath in heavy black type, were four columns of statements like these:

> If Americans do not like this picture, let them change it.
>
> They have the power, for they have the ballot. Their ancestors fought for it.
>
> They are flat on their stomachs, with the fist of the gangster on their backs, and the mothers of the country are in fear of kidnapers.
>
> The dreadful kidnaping of the Lindbergh baby, the humiliating spectacle of a father and a mother, driven to appeal for help to the criminal class, because the law and its representatives are helpless, should stir up SOME ACTION in this country.

Only a fool could doubt that our crime wave, racketeering, bootlegging, kidnaping, as established industries, all result from prohibition.

Statements of this kind were being constantly reiterated by the newspapers in every part of the country. It was this fact that inspired the Association Against the Prohibition Amendment's eulogy on the " liberal press " quoted earlier in this book. It was the AAPA that inspired the propaganda and caused it to be broadcast on a national scale. The association determined to make the people believe that political corruption, gangsters, racketeers, gang warfare and crimes of violence were the result of prohibition; that repeal would destroy the bootleg profits which were used to corrupt politics and for the possession of which criminals were fighting, that it would convert bootleggers, rumrunners, hijackers, gangsters and racketeers into lawful and peaceful liquor dealers, end corruption and crime, establish order and restore respect for the law.

This propaganda was a fraud. All students of history know that " appalling conditions of political corruption " existed prior to the adoption of the Eighteenth Amendment. They know the story of Tweed, Croker and Murphy of New York; Sullivan, Brennan, Thompson and Cermak of Chicago; McManes, Durham and Vare of Philadelphia; Magee and Flum of Pittsburgh; Cox of Cincinnati; Butler of St. Louis; Ames of Minneapolis; Ruef of San Francisco, and men of their type in other cities. They are familiar with the alliance that existed between politics, the under world and business whereby the politicians received their graft, the underworld was granted the wide-open town, and business was given franchises, public contracts, exemption from taxes and the privilege of exploiting the people in any way it desired. They are familiar with the results of this alliance as exposed by Lincoln Steffens in his *The Shame of the Cities* and by many other writers. They know the story of the giving away of the public domain, of pork-barrel legislation and tariff scandals, and the malodorous record of Hanna, Aldrich, Gorman, Platt, Quay, Penrose, Foraker and others.

Every informed person knows that the gangster and the racketeer put in their appearance fifty years before the adoption of the Eighteenth Amendment, and that crimes of violence increased steadily during that period. In the bitter struggle between laborers and employers that began in the middle of the last century, the employers hired strikebreakers and detectives and sluggers to protect their property, and the laborers accepted this method of warfare. The gangsters and racketeers were born of this struggle, although they were not exploited and dramatized until they became the heroes of the wet propaganda. In his exhaustive survey of the conflict between employers and laborers, Louis Adamic says:

> One should bear in mind that gangsterism was a vital factor early in the American class struggle, first on the capital side, and then on the side of labor; and that its history is inextricably bound up with the history of organized labor. . . . I have indicated how criminals were drawn into the struggle between the haves and the have-nots; how they were organized on a large scale by detective agencies, and hired out, by the hundreds, as gunmen to powerful industrialists, to protect their property and scabs, and to attack strikers; and how, later, labor organizations, taking their cue from capital, began to hire professional strong-arm men to slug scabs, assassinate employers and foremen, and dynamite mills, mines and uncompleted bridges and buildings. . . .
>
> Of course, the gang takes control of the liquor business in the section. It opens speak-easies, night clubs, gambling joints, dance halls and brothels. It also "gets in on" the dope business. In all of these rackets they have practically a free hand; all they have to watch is some other gang of "wise guys" who may have their eyes on the "territory."[2]

As Professor Thrasher shows,[3] for many years gangs have been forming among the victims of economic injustice who lived in slums in close proximity to vice and crime. Many of these were engaged in robbery, burglary, theft and other forms of crime. They have furnished recruits for the mercenary armies employed by the leaders of the industrial struggle. In the course of time, these professional criminals began to realize their effectiveness and power and to look for other sources of revenue. They took control of gambling, vice, dope, larceny and other underworld activities; they levied blackmail on legitimate business; they sold their services to politicians for the control of elections; they were engaged by business men to destroy competitors. With the adoption of the Eighteenth Amendment, they took control of the illicit sale of liquor and added greatly to their wealth and power. They were abetted by men and women who complacently regarded themselves as good citizens.

In 1926, the Illinois Association for Criminal Justice began "a state-wide survey of the administration of criminal justice and of the causes and conditions of crime within the state." It had the cooperation of Northwestern University, the University of Chicago, the Chicago Crime Commission, the Illinois Chamber of Commerce, the Illinois Federation of Labor, the Illinois Manufacturers' Association, the Illinois Federation of Women's Clubs and many other organizations, and of a large committee composed of the state's leading citizens. Three years were spent in making the survey, and the report of over eleven hundred pages that resulted is one of the most comprehensive studies of the causes and conditions of crime that have been made in this country.

The report shows that the tide of crime had been steadily rising for years and that the characteristic features of the crime situation existed before the adoption of the Eighteenth Amendment. It points out the many factors that have contributed to the growth of crime: the vanishing of the frontier, which has caused the "reckless and the lawless" to congregate in "our great metropolitan centers"; the coming to this country of millions of immigrants, especially from southern Europe, with "alien ways, alien notions, alien psychology of crime, punishment and revenge"; the bitter racial hatreds and conflicts that have followed the movement of large numbers of Negroes to northern cities; the wars between rival gangs that sought to control the vast revenues derived from gambling, vice and dope; the alliance between politics and crime and the use of gunmen and sluggers to control elections; the use of sluggers and bombers by small business enterprises to get rid of competitors; the development of a large body of professional gunmen and sluggers in the warfare between laborers and employers; the fact that men of this class have obtained control of many labor unions and also levy blackmail upon many kinds of legitimate business; the organization of criminals for the purpose of intimidating the police, public prosecutors, juries and witnesses. These are only a few of the causes of crime set forth in the report. It continues:

Organized crime is not, as many think, a recent phenomenon in Chicago. A study of vice, crime and gambling during the last twenty-five years shows the existence of crime and vice gangs during that period and how they have become more and more highly organized and powerful. . . . Bombing, combined with window smashing, slugging and shooting, has become a profession practiced by specialized crews or gangs. . . . A study of over three hundred cases of bombings in the last quarter-century seems to justify the following classification by motive: gambling wars, " black hand," political bombing, interracial conflict, labor union (" direct action "), and merchant association (" racketeering "). . . . Within organized gambling, however, many of the characters and all of the patterns of violence and anarchic warfare have been developed. . . .

Finally, with the coming of prohibition, the personnel of organized vice took the lead in the systematic organization of this new and profitable field of exploitation. All the experience gained by years of struggle against reformers and concealed agreements with politicians was brought into service in organizing the production and distribution of beer and whisky.[4]

Criminals took advantage of the violations of the prohibition law just as they did of other forms of vice and lawlessness, and a large part of the profits over which the most spectacular battles were waged came from the men who were carrying on the wet propaganda and crying out against liquor lawlessness.

How repeal fulfilled their sweeping promise that it would end crime is shown by John Edgar Hoover, director of the Federal Bureau of Investigation of the Department of Justice, in an address which he delivered before the Round Table Forum on March 11, 1936:

Crime has reached a pinnacle of appalling heights. It lives next door to us. It rubs elbows with us. Its blood-caked hands touch ours. A lackadaisical attitude now has resulted in a crisis.

No American home is free of its shadow. Aggravated robbery, theft, arson, rape, felonious assault or murder annually is visited upon one of every 16 homes in America. Last year in this supposedly enlightened, advanced, civilized country, there was a minimum of 12,000 murders and an estimated total of 1,445,581 major crimes. Thus one of every 84 persons in the United States was subjected to injury or death through the workings of this tremendous crime aggregate.

Beyond this there is a constant toll of the rackets; here no home is exempt. The criminal toll is taken upon food and services, and actual physical violence includes the loss of life itself. The American home and every person in it is today in a state of siege. . . . The crime problem in America is something which should take precedence before any subject other than that of livelihood itself. Even then it becomes a correlated subject because it is costing each American citizen a minimum of $120 a year. This is the per capita tax which must be assessed to pay our annual crime bill, estimated to be more than $15,000,000,000. If the entire cost of crime could be eliminated for 2 years, that saving would pay off our entire national debt. Freedom for 3 years would pay the entire cost of America's share in the World War, plus an enormous bonus.

Such, then, are the facts concerning the relation between prohibition and crime. Prohibition did not give birth to the criminal element. Indeed it is more than probable that proper enforcement of the prohibition law would have struck a mighty blow at the world of crime and vice, would have done much to eradicate them. But the " respectable " men and women who openly flouted the law and the greedy politicians and financiers who strove against it by means chiefly foul must be held responsible for the growth of evil which, by their aid, penetrated every part of American life.

NOTES

[1] *Op. cit.*, p. 180.
[2] *Dynamite* (Viking Press, 1931), pp. 349, 355.
[3] *The Gang* (University of Chicago Press, 1927).
[4] *Illinois Crime Survey*, pp. 845, 935, 867, 863.

Chapter Twelve

The Depression

WE COME now to the most dishonest and shameless phase of the entire wet propaganda — its capitalization of the depression. For years it had been charged that drunkenness, lawlessness, racketeering and everything of which the people disapproved were the results of prohibition. Now the depression was declared to be the result of the "appalling economic waste" and "frightful cost" of national prohibition, and we were solemnly warned that there would be no recovery until we were rid of this incubus. We were told that it had destroyed a billion-dollar industry, crippled many others affiliated with it, thrown hundreds of thousands of men out of employment, cut off one of the largest markets for the products of the farm, reduced the business of the railroads, diminished the purchasing power of laborers and farmers, depressed the market for real estate, increased taxes, dried up one of the greatest sources of revenue for governments, local, state and national, and set up an endless chain of disasters. We were told that repeal would re-establish a great industry, increase the prosperity of its affiliates, re-employ labor, bring relief to the farmers, enlarge the business of the railroads, bring about a boom in real estate, increase the purchasing power of the masses, supply an ample source of easily collected revenue, take from the backs of the people a "staggering load of taxation," balance the budget, revive industry, and set us on the road to prosperity. The only ones to suffer would be the opulent bootleggers.

Those responsible for these statements said nothing about the fact that under prohibition we had had ten years of unexampled prosperity, that the depression was world-wide and due to causes with which prohibition had nothing to do, and that it had come earlier and was more severe in countries like England and Germany which were not " afflicted with prohibition." They were as little concerned with consistency as with honesty. By their own logic, if prohibition had not reduced the amount of liquor consumed, it had not caused the asserted economic waste, and if it increased consumption, by the same logic it resulted in economic gain. This is true because a given amount of liquor requires the same amount of raw materials, labor and other elements for its production and distribution, whether we have license or prohibition. When making their economic argument, therefore, they had to assume a great reduction in the amount of liquor consumed. To admit a reduction, however, would be to admit that prohibition was succeeding. This, of course, had to be denied. How they talked when making their moral argument is shown by this statement from a pamphlet issued by the AAPA in 1932:

> Under prohibition we are probably spending $2,848,000,000 a year on drink. This exceeds the most liberal estimate of what we should have been spending if the Eighteenth Amendment had never been enacted.

Professor Carver states this inconsistency as follows:

> " More liquor is being drunk than before we had prohibition! " " If we could only get rid of the Eighteenth Amendment, the liquor business would put a million men to work! " Both statements are being repeated by wets, sometimes by the same wet. To an uninspired dry they would seem to be contradictory. If more liquor is being drunk, is must take more men to produce and dispense it. If getting rid of prohibition would promote " true " temperance and reduce the quantity of liquor consumed, it would obviously not put more men to work. Those who worked in the liquor business would be legally employed, it is true, but there would be fewer of them.
>
> People who make such statements should have good memories. They should not say, as did one writer, that more liquor is drunk here than in Europe, and, in the next paragraph, affirm that Europe is full of American tourists who are fleeing from the Sahara on this side of the Atlantic.[1]

A few statements will illustrate the way in which the depression argument was used. A pamphlet entitled *The Vicious Circle,* which was given national circulation, said:

There is no getting away from the actuality of the Eighteenth Amendment. It is concrete. It is no exaggeration to say that it is in a large measure responsible for the chaotic economic situation in which we as a nation find ourselves today. If traced back, the roots and causes of our present depression lead, with a directness that will surprise, to the law passed by Congress on January 16th, 1919. The Eighteenth Amendment contains less than a hundred words. On the surface, it is innocent enough. Superficially considered, it is a social measure, not an economic one. But its effects lie beneath the surface. *Without mentioning it the Eighteenth Amendment automatically abolished the excise tax and that which we have had foisted upon us in place of the excise tax has led slowly and surely to the depression which now grips us.* We are trying to find a way out, but it is depressing to see that the remedies suggested will but lead us deeper into the mire.

The AAPA distributed a pamphlet entitled *Prohibition and the Deficit,* which declares:

By the end of 1931 annual liquor tax collections since 1920, if national prohibition had not intervened, should have totaled practically eleven billion dollars. This money might have been used (if all other sources of revenue had been availed of) to reduce our 1931 indebtedness from $16,801,000,000 to $5,801,000,000.

If we continue our estimate of liquor revenue through 1933, a total of $13,035,000,000 would by that time have been available. By the end of 1933 we should have a balanced budget and a public debt of $7,306,000,000 instead of $20,341,000,000.

In 1932, when the wet propaganda had reached the peak of its frenzy, Malvern H. Tillett published a book which gave elaborate "statistical dressing" to every fake that that propaganda had put forth. The book was acclaimed by the wets and touted by all their publicity agencies, and undoubtedly it netted its author a pretty penny. It pretended to be an original survey of the results of national prohibition. Anyone familiar with the documents issued by the liquor interests, the AAPA, the Crusaders, the Moderation League and other wet organizations, will recognize at once that this book is simply a rehash of the stuff ground out by the propaganda hacks of these organizations.

The author presents a table which purports to show that without prohibition the annual liquor " Revenue Which Would Have Accrued from 15 Wet States " would have been $1,163,432,580, and says that this was

> an annual loss in federal revenues of a billion dollars or more — a loss of revenues approximately equal to the total individual income taxes paid to the U. S. government in 1930 and equivalent to three times the total U. S. customs receipts in 1931.
>
> This mammoth loss in federal revenues represents a per capita loss of more than $8 — which, directly or indirectly, falls on every man, woman and child in the United States. And it is a loss that taxpayers must make up. Employer and employed, farmer and business man, tenant and landowner, producer and consumer — all must bear this burden that has thus been cast upon them by national prohibition.[2]

Tillett asserted that " 700,000 jobs are to be counted as the measure " of direct and indirect employment represented by liquor production.

On December 6, 1932, the WONPR adopted and broadcast the following resolution:

> *Whereas*, the unemployment of approximately 12,000,000 people and a deficit in the national treasury estimated at $2,000,000,000 create a national emergency; and,
>
> *Whereas*, the passage of a beer bill would provide immediately alleviation of both these conditions; be it therefore
>
> *Resolved*, that for economic and humanitarian reasons, the WONPR, while reaffirming its stand for the unequivocal repeal of the Eighteenth Amendment, pending this latter action by the Congress, lend its support to the immediate passage of a beer bill.

Experience has shown that all these statements were false. The depression was not overcome, but became more severe. During the years immediately following repeal, approximately two and a half billion dollars were spent for liquor. The diversion of this vast sum from the purchase of milk, bread, meat, clothing, automobiles and other useful and necessary things, and its expenditure in saloons, night clubs, cocktail lounges and brothels, depressed every kind of legitimate industry and business and prolonged the depression. It brought no relief to the farmers and the railroads, the real-estate markets remained depressed, foreclosures increased in number, the budget remained unbalanced, and taxes continued to soar. How the promise was fulfilled that repeal would immediately put a million men to work in the liquor and allied industries and relieve unemployment, is shown by the following statement which appeared in the press a year and three months after repeal became effective:

> Federal Relief Administrator Hopkins announces that the number of people on government relief has passed 20,000,000, a new all-time high. The most recent published estimate of the number of unemployed is 10,671,000, an increase of more than half a million over that of the same time a year ago.

That the pompous tables showing the revenue to be realized from repeal were fakes is shown by the fact that for the calendar year 1934, when liquor was legalized, when its production and sale were being pushed by every means that greed could devise and the government was squeezing from the traffic every possible dollar by means of taxation, the total internal revenue receipts from liquor taxes were $374,506,232.50. This sum did not represent a gain in national wealth, a saving of " mammoth loss in federal revenues " or the lifting of a " burden " from " employer and employed, farmer and business man, tenant and landowner, producer and consumer," but the transfer of that amount of taxes from the incomes of individuals and corporations to the purchasers of liquor — in the language of the AAPA, to " workingmen and others who would willingly pay a tax of three cents per glass." The reason they estimated the revenue to be derived at from one to two billions of dollars annually was not that they believed it, but that they wanted to make the people think the budget was to be balanced and the government given enough money to pay the bonus and provide for relief and other expenses, while they themselves would be relieved of a large part of the taxes they were compelled to pay. Du Pont and his associates knew that while the revenue would not be as large as they predicted, it would be very large, and that they would profit by it through the saving in their income taxes. The only people who have benefited by repeal have been liquor dealers, large income taxpayers, the underworld and wet politicians.

The election of Mr. Hoover and the enactment of the Jones Act marked the turning of the tide in the battle for national prohibition. There cannot be the slightest doubt that it was the abnormal conditions resulting from the depression that made repeal possible. When people are ill and discouraged by the slow process of recovery, they are disposed to turn from the honest physician and listen to the confident assurances of the quack. So when the people were in the throes of a severe and prolonged depression, their business failing, their income and wages diminishing, facing unemployment and want, harassed by insecurity and oppressed by worry and fear, they were ready to listen to almost any confident voice of hope. Economists, financiers and statesmen differed widely as to what should be done and the masses were confused and bewildered and unable to comprehend the situation. This presented a golden opportunity to the wet fakers. They had only to make the sweeping assertion that to bring back the liquor traffic would revive business and help to overcome the depression, repeat the assertion everywhere and incessantly, and make its denial impossible, and they could put it over on millions of people. The effectiveness of this propaganda was illustrated by the statement of an honest and intelligent carpenter. I asked him how he was going to vote on repeal, and he answered: "I am going to vote for it. I have always been for prohibition, but I have been out of work so much and I don't think we will get over the depression until we get rid of the Eighteenth Amendment."

The official history of the WONPR was written, when the facts were fresh in her memory, by a woman who had taken an active part in the repeal campaign. She says:

Not enough emphasis can be laid upon the help given to the repeal cause by the nation's hope that bad times would turn to good times through the economic betterment which the end of prohibition would bring about. The promise of re-employment and of the conversion of the profits of the bootleggers into taxes paid to the government was a matter of deep concern in those gray days to millions of voters who cared little whether the Eighteenth Amendment did or did not belong in the Constitution.[3]

Depression Propaganda Exposed

The economic aspect of prohibition was made the subject of exhaustive investigation by many men who were honest, competent and disinterested. They found that prohibition brought about a great decrease in the amount of liquor consumed, increased the dependability and efficiency of labor, reduced industrial accidents and losses; that the loss to the farmers was more than offset by the increased sale of milk, bread, vegetables, meat and other farm products; that the closing of the saloons had increased the value of adjacent real estate; that it greatly increased the power of the people to purchase necessary and useful articles and stimulated every line of legitimate industry; and that it increased the national wealth and promoted the prosperity of all classes not directly or indirectly interested in the liquor business.

As to some of these men, critics may say that although they had no financial interest that would influence them knowingly to misrepresent the facts, still their conviction that prohibition had brought about a great moral improvement might cause them to overestimate its economic advantages. But against many of these investigators of the economic aspects of prohibition this charge could not possibly be brought. To this class belonged such men as Thomas Nixon Carver, professor of political economy in Harvard University; Irving Fisher, professor of economics in Yale University; Herman Feldman, professor of industrial relations in Dartmouth College; Samuel Crowther, economist and experienced investigator; and Whiting Williams, scholar, welfare worker and author. They are men of great acknowledged ability and masters of the scientific method of investigating social and economic phenomena, and their impartiality and intellectual integrity are not open to question even by wet propagandists.

Professor Fisher was not originally in favor of prohibition but came to support it through his observation of the effects of the liquor traffic and his exhaustive studies of the results of prohibition. Professor Feldman limited his investigation to the economic and industrial aspects of prohibition. He spent nine months interviewing and corresponding with men in every part of the country who were in a position to give original and accurate information on the question. Mr. Crowther made an equally exhaustive and impartial investigation of the subject, and his book is equally illuminating and convincing. Mr. Loring A. Schuler, editor of the *Ladies' Home Journal*, said: "I believe that the facts revealed by Mr. Crowther in this book are the most important contribution that has been made to the discussion of prohibition." The New York *Times* said: "Mr. Crowther writes with forcefulness and presents his impressive array of evidence and his arguments in concise language that is wholly without the taint of emotionalism or of propaganda." Mr. Williams donned the clothes of a laborer and lived and worked with the workmen of America, Europe, and Central and South America. His articles, which appeared in the *Survey Graphic* early in 1931, furnish vivid, first-hand and authentic information.

Referring to the amount of alcohol consumed, the conclusions of these men were as follows:

PROFESSOR FISHER. From all this, it is evident that the total consumption of alcohol today in beverage form is less than 16 per cent of pre-prohibition consumption and probably less than 10 per cent.[4]

MR. CROWTHER. The actual amount spent for liquor today can hardly amount to more than half a billion dollars, but whether it be half a billion or a billion, the amount is paid for a volume of liquor certainly not exceeding 20 per cent of that sold in the pre-war trade.[5]

PROFESSOR FELDMAN. As we see it, the wage earners are paying out a great deal less on drink and all that went with it than they did before prohibition, or than they would spend today if we did not have it. . . . It appears to us most likely that the great mass of the people, however, are spending much less on drink today than in pre-prohibition days.[6]

In 1930, Whiting Williams, effectively disguised, investigated workers' speak-easies in a number of places and compared the drinking he found there with the drinking in the saloons in the same places in 1919, when, disguised as a laborer, he was living and working with laborers. He says:

Nevertheless, putting together all the hours and all the days in all these wetter-than-average places, the fact remains: In the old days, more intoxicated men than I discovered this year could have been encountered in two or, possibly, three saloons within a few blocks in a single one of the whole list of communities visited. . . .

All that day in Homestead I kept recalling how, in the winter of 1919, hundreds of us would come trooping out, the very instant the six o'clock whistle ended our thirteen hours of pick and shovel night work, and, after all but shoe-horning ourselves into any one of the five or six saloons opposite the various plant gates, would inch our way through the jam up to the bar. . . . All the speak-easies of Homestead are not handling in a whole average day of 1930 as much of either alcohol or money as crossed a single average saloon bar in Homestead during a single morning of 1919. . . .

Whatever the causes of its demise, the fact is plain that the saloon is not only dead but its soul is not marching on in the speak-easies.[7]

Mr. Crowther says: "The wage earner who formerly frequented the saloon is not buying either in speak-easies or from bootleggers."[8]

The investigators found that a great increase in the national wealth had been brought about through the greater efficiency and dependability of labor. Professor Feldman says:

Summarizing several chapters dealing with the industrial effects of prohibition, we find that employers and executives are, on this matter, overwhelmingly favorable to prohibition as far as it affects production and business. . . . Judging from interviews and questionnaires, which they returned, we can say with confidence that the great majority of employers report that:

1. The disciplinary problem of dealing with inebriates has become much less serious since prohibition and the number of discharges for intoxication is markedly smaller.

2. The age-old difficulty of keeping a full force at work after paydays is now a thing of the past, having disappeared entirely in many plants and been reduced considerably in most.

3. While there are no statistics showing the part played by intoxication as a cause of accidents, the whole subject of the relation of drunkenness to accidents has become passé since prohibition. Not a single employer claimed that conditions were worse in this respect, while many asserted that they could see decided improvements resulting from the abolition of saloons.

4. As a group the workers are of higher type, steadier, stronger, clear-headed, more alert, and more efficient, because removed from the temptations which worked havoc with men unable to resist the demoralizing social influences of the saloon.

5. In spite of home brewing, plenty of available speak-easies, bootleggers and other evidences of lax enforcement and uncertain workings of the law, the mass of wage earners are much better off because of the abolition of the saloon. . . .

That the abolition of the saloons has increased dependability seems to be borne out in our survey. We have pointed out the decreased proportion of charity cases attributed to drink, the general testimony that garnishments of wages have been markedly fewer, and the increase in attendance and morale reported by employers.[9]

Professor Feldman states that in 1926 a nation-wide survey of the effects of prohibition was carried on by the National Federation of Settlements. From the report he quotes the following: "Employers everywhere are agreed that the law is a great benefit to the workingman and a great aid to efficient operation of industry. They are for it."[10]

Professor Fisher estimated that since "the human machine is the most important machine in industry," the effect of prohibition was to "speed up industry" and increase national production approximately $3,000,000,000 annually. For the twelve-year period this would amount to $36,000,000,000. Professor Feldman and Mr. Crowther did not believe that it was possible to arrive at definite figures but stated that their investigation showed that prohibition increased the dependability and efficiency of labor, increased our productive capacity, and added greatly to our national wealth. Mr. Williams stated that his investigations showed "that our present effort to control John Barleycorn has provided a cushioning of vast proportions against the impact of current unemployment."

Prohibition's Contributions to Welfare

Important as were the effects of prohibition on production, it made a greater and more definitely ascertainable contribution to our economic and industrial welfare through its effect on consumption. These investigations showed that from two to four billions of dollars that would have been wasted annually on liquor were spent for other things. Disregarding its physical and moral effects, liquor was neither necessary nor useful, and from an economic standpoint it was sheer waste. A man with an ample income could buy both liquor and necessities. If, however, a man of small means bought liquor, he was forced to that extent to curtail his expenditures for things that were useful and necessary. Since, under prohibition, drinking was confined largely to the well-to-do, it did not seriously interfere with the consumption of other things. At the same time, the absence of saloons, the high prices of liquor, and the fact that its sale was unlawful, caused wage earners, people with small salaries and law-abiding people generally — in fact the great body of the American people — to reduce their expenditures for liquor to a minimum. The result was that billions of dollars which would have been spent by the masses for liquor were used to purchase bread, milk, meat, shoes, clothing, small homes, automobiles, radios, washing machines, books, tickets to the movies, or were deposited in savings banks for use in emergencies. This greatly enlarged and stabilized the market for necessities and many luxuries, helped to solve the problem of consumption, gave employment to labor, and was one of the most important factors in the extraordinary and exceptional prosperity that we enjoyed during the first ten years of prohibition.

Stating the results of his nation-wide survey of the problem, Professor Feldman says:

It may be stated as a fact, testified to by numerous employers, that the cashing of pay checks in saloons has been, to all practical purposes, eliminated, and the speak-easies have not taken over this function. Employers and savings banks have in many instances made arrangements for the cashing of checks, while, on the other hand, retail stores have been obliged to provide this service. A typical reply from employers is the following: "During the pre-Volstead days, a large number of our employees would get all their pay checks cashed at saloons. Today, the endorsers of these checks are the groceries, the meat markets, and the dry-goods stores." . . .

If the widespread observations of people who have been interested in this problem are worth anything at all, movies, autos, touring, radios and other forms of recreation having an economic basis have been satisfying a good part of the desire for relaxation which the "poor man's club" met. . . . While drink ended in drink, buying something else awakens desires for other things and sends out ripples of purchasing power over a large number of other industries. . . .

There has been a huge increase in the quantity of milk consumed in this country during the past few years. As estimated by the U. S. Department of Agriculture, milk for beverage and household purposes produced in 1917 amounted to 36,500,000,000 pounds, while by 1924 it had risen to 54,325,800,000 pounds, or almost 50 per cent more, an increase far exceeding that in population. Prosperity and increased advertising of the food values of milk partly explain this marked increase, but do not, in the opinion of persons in official position, account for all of it.

That prohibition has been an important factor in promoting the popularity of milk, is a view supported by every study and survey of the milk question made, and by every authority with whom the writer has corresponded. Those well informed in this field are not merely confident but emphatic on the matter. An example is the reply of the executive secretary of the International Association of Milk Dealers: "There can be no denying the fact that the cutting off of beer has diverted a great deal of thirst to the drinking of milk." Similar information was secured from the U. S. Department of Agriculture and other government departments. . . .

Postal savings are one source of information as to the thriftiness of the poor, since the depositors in these are the humblest in the economic scale. The most impressive fact in the U. S. postmaster's figures is the increase in the average principal per depositor from $111.83 in 1914, to $336.03 in 1926. . . . As compared with an average of 12,378,909 savings bank depositors in the five-year period 1912–1916, the average for 1922–1926 was 39,155,499, culminating in 1926 with 46,762,240 depositors, the highest number ever recorded. . . . A letter was addressed to twenty-five savings banks in various parts of the country. The majority of the banks are certain that prohibition has aided in increasing their business.

Giving the results of his comprehensive survey, Mr. Crowther says:

We shall entirely disregard, for the moment, any possible effects of the liquor on [the purchaser] and think of it only as a way of spending money. But a purchaser of liquor sets in motion a very small chain of purchasing, while, if the family of the man has that twenty dollars to spend, they will put it out into goods which require a deal of labor and start many chains of purchasing. Or the same effect will be had if they save part of the money.

The difference in the effect on the country of a man laying out twenty dollars a month over a bar and a wife laying out the same sum over a store counter is so great that giving the money to the wife amounts to an increase of family buying power of nearly twenty dollars a month. To all intents and purposes, money diverted from drink to goods can be counted as new money. . . .

There is an absolute unanimity of opinion that the wage earners are spending more on their families than ever they did and that the standards of living are constantly growing higher. . . . Prohibition, it appears from the letters which I have received, has definitely switched the spending of wages for drink to the spending of wages for goods. These letters in themselves present a really remarkable record — and it is an unprejudiced, first-hand record having to do only with the effects of spending on prosperity. All of the writers are in a position to know what they are talking about. . . . The answers from everywhere in the country are the same — the workingmen are spending little or nothing for drink and a great deal on their families. . . .

The diversion of spending is even larger, however, than appears because the drink which is being bought today is by the classes with higher incomes who can afford to buy without cutting into their general expenditures. . . .

> The principal consumption of the country comes from the wage earners. If they were spending the same proportion of their wages for drink today that they spent before prohibition, then at least three billion dollars would be withdrawn from buying power. That would take the edge off the high consumption which makes high production possible. We have seen consumption and consequently production increase steadily ever since the money that used to go into liquor started to go into goods. . . .
>
> By the rerouting of at least two-thirds of the money which formerly went for drink into the buying of useful goods, a higher level of general living has been established in this country. The higher level has brought higher wages and still higher levels of living.
>
> We have as a nation been infinitely more prosperous since prohibition than ever before. We are definitely going forward. It would seem that prohibition is fundamental to our prosperity — that it is the greatest blow which has ever struck poverty.

In 1927, Professor Fisher stated that the diversion of money from liquor to other things represented an economic gain of $3,000,-000,000 annually, which added to the $3,000,000,000 increase in production gave a total economic gain of $6,000,000,000 annually. Based upon this estimate, the economic gain to this country for the prohibition period was $72,000,000,000. Professor Fisher cites Dr. Paul H. Nystrom, professor of marketing in the school of business of Columbia University, who in an address to the National Retail Dry Goods Association in 1929 said:

> Place whatever estimate you like on the amount of bootleg liquor sold in this country and I am sure you will admit, as I have been forced to admit, that a return to the liquor consumption of the pre-Volstead days would mean several billions of dollars less business in home furnishings, automobiles, musical instruments, radio, travel, amusements, jewelry, insurance, education, books and magazines.[11]

Mr. Samuel G. Blythe, distinguished author and journalist, in an article in the *Saturday Evening Post* of July 9, 1927, says:

> A new and gigantic purchasing power has developed in this country since we have had prohibition that accounts for the prosperity of our railroads, our manufactories, our trade in all directions. That, in a

large measure, is a purchasing power derived from the diversion of former booze money into economic channels. It does not come from the very rich, nor from the very poor, although it has decreased the number of the very poor, as any student of economics knows. It comes from the great average American citizen, the blood and bones of this country, and it comes in part because booze is no longer an article of legal merchandise in this country, because the saloons are gone, because liquor, to the average American, is not worth the money and the effort required to secure it nor worth taking the risks that go with the drinking of it. Hence, the individual, his family and general trade, get the benefit of the wages and profits that formerly went to the nonproductive saloon-keeper.

At the 1926 annual meeting of the American Economic Association, there was a round table discussion of prohibition and not an economist in the United States could be found who would oppose prohibition on economic grounds. Professor Fisher, who presided, says:

> I got a list of the economists who are supposed to be opposed to prohibition, and wrote to them; they all replied either that I was mistaken in thinking that they were opposed to prohibition or that, if we were going to confine the discussion to the economics of prohibition, they would not care to respond. When I found that I was to have no speaker representing the opposite point of view, I wrote to all American economists listed in " Minerva " and all American teachers of statistics. I have not received from anyone an acceptance.[12]

Prohibition a Benefit to Farmers

One of the chief objectives of wet propaganda was to make the farmers believe that prohibition was ruining them and that their only hope was the repeal of the Eighteenth Amendment. Professor Feldman called attention to the fact that in May 1926, wet congressmen " had interrupted a speech on farm relief by assertions that enforcement of the federal dry law was responsible for the economic plight of the American farmer, and that he could expect no substantial relief until the law was either modified or repealed."

He made a careful study of this question and found that before prohibition "the production of alcoholic drinks consumed an insignificant fraction of one per cent of the country's total" production of wheat and oats, "slightly more than one per cent of the total national production" of corn, 8 per cent of the rice, 7.5 per cent of the rye, and 32 per cent of the barley. How insignificant an item barley was is shown by the fact that the pre-prohibition production was 184,812,000 bushels as against 7,461,219,000 bushels of wheat, oats, corn, rice and rye. At the same time, prohibition greatly increased the power of the masses to buy bread, vegetables, milk, fruit, meat and all the other staple products of the farm. Summarizing the results of his investigation, Professor Feldman says:

> The very fact that enormous excesses in certain crops occur six years after prohibition indicates that fundamental economic conditions, many of a world-wide character, and many obvious defects in production and marketing, are the basic problem. . . . From a national standpoint, modification of the liquor laws would help some barley farmers, and provide a profitable market for hop growers, but would not be a general aid to the farming industry as a whole, and could not affect the farm relief issue in any important way.

Discussing the assertions of the wet propagandists that prohibition caused the depression, Professor Carver said:

> The depression is world-wide. The countries which do not have prohibition are worse off than we are. Some of them are practically bankrupt. They owe us money which they cannot repay. England went off the gold standard. Wages are now paid in a depreciated currency. . . . This was probably necessary in order to save British industries from wholesale bankruptcy. It was not prohibition that put Great Britain in such a position.
>
> If prohibition produced the depression in this country, it worked as a very slow poison. Wartime restrictions on the liquor traffic were adopted in 1918 as economic measures. Liquor was prohibited to soldiers and sailors. Wartime prohibition came in 1919, practically without opposition. The Eighteenth Amendment became operative in January 1920. For ten years this country enjoyed unexampled prosperity under prohibition. We were able to lend billions of dollars to

other countries after the war was over. This helped them to rehabilitate their industries and set their men to work. In spite of that they now claim that they are unable to pay us back. In other words, they plead bankruptcy. We may have to accept that plea and forgive their debts. That would put us in the position of a rich creditor forgiving a poor debtor. Yet every one of those countries is spending enough on drink to more than pay what they owe us.

It was not prohibition that put them in such a position. It is not prohibition that makes them such poor customers for what we have to sell. It does not seem that prohibition in this country could cause a world depression.[13]

A Sample of Depression Propaganda

In December 1932, the Crusaders issued a statement that was blazoned on the front pages of the wet press with scare headlines. It is reproduced below, as it appeared, except that numbers have been placed before the various items for convenience of reference:

MONEY COST OF PROHIBITION, 1920–1932

1.	Appropriated by Congress for prohibition enforcement bureaus	$ 132,958,530
2.	Appropriated by states for enforcement (8 years' figures only available)	5,585,850
3.	Assessed value of property seized	186,867,322
4.	Cost to taxpayers of merely keeping violators in jail	128,000,000
5.	Cost of putting or trying to put federal violators in jail and then trying to keep them there	111,103,870
6.	Coast Guard appropriations by Congress for enforcement	152,503,464
7.	Customs service expenditures for enforcement	93,232,230
8.	Cost of criminal justice to state, municipal and local governments for prohibition cases	2,922,622,980
9.	Loss in rentals to owners of padlocked property	303,615,000
10.	Loss in liquor revenue to federal government	11,988,000,000
11.	Loss in liquor revenue to states, counties, cities	6,540,620,000
12.	Loss to consumer in excessive liquor bill, bootleg profits and protection, etc.	12,000,000,000
		$34,565,109,246

Based on official reports, the total cost of the Eighteenth Amendment to the American public has been $34,565,109,246, as shown by the accompanying table.

TWICE THE NATIONAL DEBT

The tremendous effect exerted by these huge sums upon the economic fabric of the United States almost staggers comprehension. The 12-year cost is more than twice the national debt of 16 and a half billion dollars. It is more than two and a half times the total amount owed the United States by foreign governments.

In twelve years, prohibition has cost the United States nearly ten billion dollars more than the total net war cost of $26,361,096,001 (1917 to 1921).

Difficult as it is to believe, the cost of prohibition in 12 years nearly equals the total continuing cost to the United States of the war, which was $37,873,908,499 as of June 30, 1930.

EXCEEDS INCOME TAXES

The average annual cost of prohibition to the taxpayers is ten times the yearly payments scheduled to be received by the United States on foreign debts; it is more than one-half the federal budget for 1932. During each of the last ten years the cost of prohibition has exceeded the amount of federal income tax collected.

The combined interest-bearing debt of all the municipalities, township, county and state governments in the United States is $16,500,000,000. The national debt is about the same figure. It makes a total of 33 billion dollars as the funded governmental debt — federal, state and local. In 12 years the cost of prohibition has been a larger sum than the total debt of federal, state and local governments.

Interest on this aggregate funded government debt is approximately $1,350,000,000 a year. The cost of prohibition each year is more than twice this sum.

Average men and women and those far above the average did not have the information, training and time necessary to analyze and understand this statement and they were disposed to turn in wrath against anything that seemed to be the source of their financial troubles, their anxiety and their despair. This statement, therefore, which pretended to state exact figures and purported to be based on official reports but in its entirety was an absolute swindle, was well calculated to deceive and inflame them and cause them to join the wet parade.

Items 1 to 8 of the table, with the exception of number 3, refer to the cost of prohibition and enforcement. The appropriation and expenditure of money represent not two but one cost to government. This statement enters that cost as two items, thereby swelling the totals. If, therefore, the figures were correct, which they are not, the totals would be fictitious. The state and local governments maintained the machinery for the administration of their criminal laws and there is no way of telling whether prohibition added to that expense, and, if it did, of even estimating how much. The liquor traffic has always been one of the principal sources of crime and whether prohibition increased or decreased the actual cost of crime from that source we do not know. The probabilities are that there was a decrease. The $2,922,622,980 cost to the states was taken out of the air and is a pure fake.

This talk about the cost of enforcement of prohibition was a repetition of statements which had been repeatedly made by the AAPA propagandists. Replying to one of their pamphlets, Dr. J. M. Doran, commissioner of prohibition, on June 15, 1929, said:

> During the nine years since the effective date of prohibition the expenditures for the Prohibition Bureau, coast guard and customs incident to the enforcement of the Eighteenth Amendment total $141,179,485. The collections from fines and penalties and the revenue from taxes on distilled spirits and fermented liquors total $460,502,792.76.
>
> It is apparent that the collections by far overbalance the expenditures. Even if $72,000,000 estimated in the pamphlet as the cost to the Department of Justice for the enforcement of prohibition should be added, there would still be a balance of $247,324,307.76 over and above the total expenditures accredited to the enforcement of the prohibition laws.[14]

If item number 3 refers to real estate seized, it is fictitious because the property was ultimately returned to its owners and was not lost. If it refers to liquor, stills and similar articles, it is equivalent to saying that the destruction of counterfeit money and the tools for making it is a loss to the United States. If the figures in item 9 were correct, they would simply represent the temporary loss of men who had had their partnership with criminals dissolved by law.

Items 10 and 11 purport to show that state and federal governments lost a total of $18,528,620,000, and that this should be treated as a part of the cost of prohibition. The amount is a palpable absurdity, but if it had been justified it would have represented neither a loss nor a cost " to the American public." Money raised by taxation does not represent an addition to the national wealth. It is a tribute on wealth to defray the expense of government. The fact that it is levied on one class of people rather than on another does not change its character or its relation to our total wealth. If this amount had been raised by a liquor tax, it would have meant simply that it would have been shifted from people of taxable incomes to the consumers of liquor. Mr. Crowther comments in this connection:

> The taxes which were once paid by the workman over the bar are now shifted to the income taxpayers — who are far better able to pay them. So the whole argument that the government loses taxes because of the passing of the liquor trade shows a profound ignorance of the nature of the taxes.[15]

Professor Fisher says:

> A tax comes out of the individual pocket and goes into the common pocket of the nation; so it does not get anywhere to talk about the " loss " sustained by the government which surrenders a tax or shifts the form in which it is applied. This argument is on all fours with the ridiculous assumption of " loss " recoverable by repealing the prohibition of sales of narcotic drugs and placing that traffic under a license tax. The fact that it is a mischievous and parasitic business is, of course, ignored. For every million dollars recovered in taxes by restoring the saloon the nation would pay many millions more in impaired efficiency of its workers and in productive business replaced by a destructive traffic.[16]

Item number 12 is for losses from three sources, amounting to twelve billion dollars. The first loss is for " excessive liquor bill."

As a matter of trade, what a purchaser of liquor lost, the seller gained. To say, therefore, that the difference between what a man paid to his bootlegger and what he would have paid to a saloon-keeper, was a cost to the United States, is too absurd to warrant further comment.

The next loss is "bootleg profits." This is very interesting. A profit to the steel industry would not be treated as an appalling loss to the nation. From a purely economic standpoint, the bootleggers' profits can be regarded as a loss only on the assumption that the consumption of alcoholic liquors is waste. That being true, the loss would have been the same whether the sale was legal or illegal. If we had not had prohibition, the amount of liquor sold and the profits to those engaged in the liquor business would have been much greater. By their own logic, therefore, prohibition represented a great saving to the nation rather than a loss.

The third loss is "protection." Disregarding the moral question involved and viewing the matter merely in its economic aspect, the passing of money from one person to another in the form of a bribe does not represent a cost to the United States.

Items 10, 11 and 12, amounting to $30,528,620,000 out of the total of $34,565,109,245, are brazen frauds.

It was by propaganda of this kind, prepared by the AAPA and put out through its kept politicians and through the organizations it had formed for the purpose, and broadcast by the newspapers and magazines which its members owned or controlled, that the liquor rebellion was fomented. It was by such methods that the liquor traffic was forced back upon this country, and it will be by such methods that it will be retained, if that is to be our fate.

NOTES

1 *Christian Science Monitor,* July 27, 1932.

2 *The Price of Prohibition* (Harcourt, Brace & Co., 1932), p. 67.

3 Root, *op. cit.,* p. 105.

4 Fisher, *Prohibition at Its Worst,* p. 44.

5 Samuel Crowther, *Prohibition and Prosperity* (John Day Co., 1930), p. 57.

6 Herman T. Feldman, *Prohibition, Its Economic and Industrial Aspects* (D. Appleton & Co., 1927), pp. 118, 124.

[7] *Survey Graphic*, Feb. 1, 1931.
[8] *Op. cit.*, p. 60.
[9] *Op. cit., passim.*
[10] *Op. cit.*, p. 254.
[11] Fisher, *The Noble Experiment*, p. 142.
[12] *Ibid.*, p. 147.
[13] *Christian Science Monitor*, Aug. 18, 1932.
[14] Quoted by Fisher, *The Noble Experiment*, pp. 145–46.
[15] Crowther, *op. cit.*, p. 77.
[16] *The Noble Experiment*, pp. 144–45.

Part Three

The Liquor Problem Of Today

Chapter Thirteen

The New Era

AT THE beginning of the repeal era, it seemed that the triumph of the liquor traffic had been complete and final. It had been legalized and taxed by the federal government. This had given it the badge of respectability and enlisted in its defense the most powerful financial interests in the country. The mails, the columns of newspapers and magazines and the channels of the air had been made available for liquor advertising and promotion. State and local governments were repealing their prohibition laws and engaging in a scramble for liquor revenue. Opponents of the traffic had been driven from public life and the politicians of both parties reduced to a state of vassalage. The moral forces of the country had suffered a defeat that appeared to be decisive and they were scattered and demoralized. Confident that prohibition had breathed its last, men were investing hundreds of millions of dollars in the manufacture and distribution of liquor, it was being sold not only in saloons, night clubs and roadhouses, but in groceries and drugstores and at lunch counters, and was easily available to everyone everywhere. Millions of people had been deceived as to the nature and effect of alcohol and their intellectual and moral resistance to its use had been weakened or destroyed. Deceptive propaganda, alluring and misleading advertising, the use of liquor at social functions, its service and use by parents in the presence of their children, the representation in the movies of drinking as the symbol of gaiety and true hospitality, cocktail lounges, cocktail parties, cocktail hours and the equipment of sales places with all the enticements of food, music, dancing, gambling, barmaids, hostesses and sexual excitement, were encouraging drinking by men and women of every class and every age.

While with general acquiescence everything conceivable was being done to promote the use of liquor, there existed what amounted to a nation-wide taboo against opposing its use or even discussing the question. A group of people who regarded themselves as model citizens and leaders of society would sit down to dinner and discuss freely the New Deal, Hitler, Mussolini and Stalin; but if one of their number had called attention to the fact that in their own community and under their very noses the liquor dealers were ruining lives, wrecking homes, spreading poverty and vice and corrupting politics, a sudden and awkward silence would have ensued — just as if the speaker had tucked napkin into collar and proceeded to drink his soup out of his plate — and there would have been a nervous and concerted effort to divert the conversation to some other subject. In a group of politicians such a suggestion would have been followed by a frigid silence and the speaker would have been forced to abandon the role of a statesman and seek some other occupation. Many of the religious leaders of the country remained silent or referred to the subject in such a brief and furtive manner that their words were meaningless. It seemed that they were trying to ease their conscience without being caught in the act.

All the elements having a direct or indirect financial interest in the liquor traffic were confident that at long last they had realized their dream of conditions under which the use of intoxicating liquors would become both universal and habitual.

The Awakening

This confidence was destined to be short-lived. The wets had spread the belief that by some form of magic, repeal would usher in a new type of liquor traffic that would be not only innocuous but an economic and moral boon. It was soon discovered, however, that the nature of alcohol had not changed and that its effects were precisely the same as they had been before and during prohibition and at all times and under all circumstances.

It was also found that the application of machinery to the production of raw materials, more efficient methods of manufacturing, storing and transporting liquor, high-pressure salesmanship, the removal of legal and moral restrictions, the extension of drinking habits to women and to boys and girls of school age, the increased use of dangerous machinery not only in manufacture and transportation but on the farms and in the homes, and the fact that on our crowded highways automobiles operated by drinking drivers become veritable engines of death — that all these caused the evil results of the use of alcohol to become more widespread and disastrous than at any previous time.

Experience very soon demonstrated the fact that the entire repeal propaganda had been a tissue of fakes and falsehoods; that the wets had not been interested in true temperance, law and order, personal liberty and the Constitution, but in liquor profits and revenue; that alcohol is not a socializing and civilizing agent but a habit-forming, narcotic drug; that beer is not a temperance beverage but an intoxicating liquor and that it is chiefly responsible for the creation of the drink habit, the debauchery of youth and the multiplication of saloons and other vicious sales places; that the evils of the liquor traffic had not resulted from prohibition but from the sale and consumption of alcohol; that repeal did not lessen the use of hard liquor, decrease drunkenness and crime, do away with bootlegging, end unemployment, restore prosperity to the farmer and "lick the depression." It became evident that the promise that the saloon would not be permitted to return and that a new and constructive method of handling the liquor traffic would be worked out, under which all its historic evils would be eliminated, was simply a part of a scheme to defraud. It was established by unimpeachable evidence that the false statements of the repeal campaign had not been made as a result of error or mistake; that although many honest people were led to believe and repeat them, those who fabricated them and put them into circulation knew that they were false, and that it was their deliberate purpose to deceive and mislead the people.

As the truth emerged from the fog of propaganda, it became

clear to those who could see that the nation was confronted with precisely the same stubborn, ultimate facts that had caused the adoption of the Eighteenth Amendment. They saw that the same results follow the use of alcohol and are in proportion to the amount consumed regardless of the name of the liquor, the sales agent or the law that may exist at any time or place; that the liquor business invariably falls into the hands of the antisocial and lawless elements of the community; that as long as it is permitted, it cannot be controlled or confined to particular localities or states; that in the fight against it there can be no peace without victory; that in the end it will be expelled from or fastened upon every part of the country; and that the only alternative to absolute surrender is an amendment to the federal Constitution under the terms of which complete prohibition will become the settled policy of the entire nation, all the agencies of government, local, state and national, will be made available for its enforcement, and the whole question eliminated from politics and removed forever from the sphere of legitimate discussion.

As the facts and lessons of experience became more and more obvious and the blighting effects of the liquor traffic were constantly forced upon the attention of the people, the taboo began to lose its power. Millions of sincere men and women who, under the spell of the wet propaganda, voted for repeal in the hope that it would bring relief from intolerable liquor conditions, realized that they had been deceived. Disillusionment gave way to indignation, the fighting spirit revived and the truth was courageously proclaimed. The nature and extent of this change of attitude are illustrated by the facts and statements set out in the chapter on "Results of Repeal."

As those engaged in the liquor industry witnessed this renewal of public antagonism, their attitude of swaggering confidence changed to one of alarm. Their leaders and journals began to send out warnings that the tide had turned, that prohibition was on its way back, and that unless it was stopped, the liquor traffic, having returned from Elba, was on its way to Waterloo.

Their attitude is illustrated by the following statements. In its issue of May 11, 1936, *Tap and Tavern* warns its readers that " a powerful drive to wipe out repeal " is in progress. " The evidence is discouragingly preponderant. Its gathering weight reflects the size of the opponent the liquor industry will be called upon to meet in the future unless something effective is done to stunt the growth of the stubborn antagonist now." In its issue of June 20, 1938, the same journal has a sensational editorial entitled " Local Option Sweeps On — Call to Arms," in which it says: " Anyone not seeing the danger in the local option deluge is so blind that he will not see anything. It is up to the liquor dealer to become doubly alert to the onsweep of local option."

In the *Brewers' Journal* for December 1937, a leading brewer discusses the growth of public resentment against the liquor traffic, and says, " The time has arrived when more than just a feeble effort must be made to stem this oncoming tide of adverse sentiment."

Collier's Weekly, a leading advocate of repeal, in its issue of December 4, 1937, devotes a full-page editorial to the discussion of liquor conditions. Referring to the situation in Pennsylvania, it says: " Two out of three communities which have had local option elections have voted dry. The dry majorities have been large, running up to four and five to one. The same people who voted so exuberantly against prohibition four years ago are now expressing impatience with the products of repeal."

An editorial that appeared in the *Beverage Retailer Weekly* in its issue of October 3, 1938, under the heading " Action Needed — Now! " said:

The most impressive speaker at the recent convention of the New Jersey Licensed Beverage Association, we thought, was Captain William H. Stayton, affectionately known as the " father of repeal." When the white-haired director of Repeal Associates stood up and warned the industry that it must defend itself, for it could never recover from another prohibition era, he put his finger on the crying need of the trade.

Too long have the slimy accusations and false charges of the drys gone unanswered, said Captain Stayton. We agree. Those liquor men who feel it wise not to dignify these falsehoods with a reply had best look around them and notice how the public has reacted. Of 7,000 local option elections throughout the country last year, 5,000 ended in victories for the drys. How long can this continue without reaching a situation similar to that immediately preceding national prohibition?

A central public relations agency to co-ordinate the industry's manifold arguments in favor of its continued existence and to point out clearly the base reasoning and emotional illogic of the drys is what we need—*right now.* British spirits vendors have a joint "defense fund." Why not the United States? The man or woman who rallies the industry to such a goal is indeed worthy of the highest honor and tribute.

Mobilization

Experience has taught the liquor forces the meaning of an aroused public sentiment. It has taught them that, whatever the cost, it would be cheaper to prevent the enactment of prohibition laws than to bring about their nullification and repeal. They have learned that it would require less money and effort to keep their enemies out of office than to dislodge them after they had attained positions of influence and power. They know that they cannot achieve these results by eliminating the evils from the liquor traffic because those evils are inherent in and inseparable from the business of creating and exploiting a degrading appetite and habit and promoting public debauchery for profit. They know that the return of prohibition can be prevented only by employing all the methods that were used to destroy it.

With a realism and efficiency characteristic of men having billions at stake, representatives of the liquor interests, manufacturers and jobbers furnishing materials and supplies to the industry, large income taxpayers and other elements having a financial interest in the perpetuation of the liquor traffic have mobilized all their forces and launched a campaign "on a huge, nation-wide scale" to "stop prohibition." They are determined that the protection of the liquor industry by systematic, ceaseless, fraudulent propaganda, social pressure, financial coercion and the domination of politics shall be a permanent feature of American life.

For the accomplishment of this result, four powerful organizations have been formed: Repeal Associates, United Brewers' Industrial Foundation, Distilled Spirits Institute, and National Institute of Manufacturers and Distributors. They are modeled after the great repeal organizations and are fully equipped to perform the same functions and employ the same technique in the fight to preserve the achievement of the parent organizations — a dripping wet nation. Their war chests are filled and their payrolls are adorned with the names of the familiar brood of publicity experts, holders of academic degrees, professors, criminologists, statisticians, well known authors, prominent women and influential politicians. With a pretense of lofty motives and accuracy of statement, they are flooding the country with propaganda which by its cynical and shameless disregard for truth consigns the lies and fakes of the repeal struggle to the horse-and-buggy age of public deception. There is no great difference among these four organizations, but we shall treat each of them in some detail.

Repeal Associates

Referring to the Repeal Associates, Captain Stayton says:

> I believe that none opposed to the theory of prohibition or materially concerned in the legal traffic of liquor can afford to shut his eyes to the growing danger in the dry activities. Naturally the more the public can be led to pooh-pooh the efforts of the drys, the better the drys can accomplish their purpose. Nothing will play more into their hands than to have the thinking public look on them as futile fanatics.
>
> Repeal Associates, the successor to the Association Against the Prohibition Amendment, is keeping tab on what the drys are doing, and is working now to prevent the return of national prohibition, instead of doing what was done before — avoiding the fight in the beginning, suffering from intolerable conditions and then going through a long period of work and sacrifice to bring about repeal.

The following appears on the organization's stationery:

REPEAL ASSOCIATES
Otis Building
Washington, D. C.

Advisory Committee

Pierre S. du Pont, *Chairman*	W. H. Stayton, *Executive Director*
Robert K. Cassatt	Elizabeth Livingston, *Executive Secretary*
Benedict Crowell	Carey Jarman, *Treasurer*
Grayson M. P. Murphy	W. H. Stayton, Jr., *General Counsel*
Ralph M. Shaw	
W. H. Stayton	
James W. Wadsworth, Jr.	

The fundamental purpose of Repeal Associates is to help bring about observance of constitutional principles in connection with the conduct of the liquor traffic in the United States. Its working program will change from time to time as circumstances dictate, but its activities will always conform to its fundamental purpose — protection of the Constitution.

The motives, methods and resources of the organization are shown by the following statements appearing in its official organ, *Repeal Review*:

Repeal Associates is a Citizens' Council for Liquor Control. It was organized early in 1934, upon the dissolution of the Association Against the Prohibition Amendment and by resolution of the national board of directors of the old association.

Consistent with its fundamental purpose, the most important work of Repeal Associates is to stand sentry duty and give warning if there should be any probability of a return to national prohibition.

Since legalization of beer April 7, 1933, up to and including May 1937, the federal government had collected $1,759,537,879.77 in revenue on alcoholic beverages.

Exact figures on revenues collected by state and local governments are not available, but they aggregate more than a billion dollars. These revenue figures show that the three classifications of government — federal, state, and municipal and local — have taken the major profits of the legalized alcoholic beverage industries.

A horde of bootleggers yet remains to harass enforcement officials, to undermine and discredit the legal liquor industry, to foster crime and rackets, and to rob the country of millions in evaded taxes. . . . If bootleggers could be wiped out . . . large sums, now being stolen by tax evasion, would go to federal and state treasuries, thereby giving an opportunity for reduction of other taxes.

The drys would have us forget that the greatest depression the United States has ever known came in the national prohibition era, and that the economic upswing did not begin until revenues from the legal liquor traffic — which had been going into the hands of criminals for thirteen years — began to flow into the federal and state treasuries.

Statements issued by Repeal Associates to the public through newspapers and periodicals have been given dignified and excellent editorial and news treatment.

The clearinghouse department steadily is becoming better known as a source of information concerning state control laws, conditions prevailing during national prohibition and since repeal, and the activities of the drys.

As an important part of its future program, Repeal Associates is establishing at strategic points throughout the country "Listening Posts." . . . Although the work of forming Listening Posts is only well begun, indications are that at least 500 members are ready and able to serve in this work.

Members of Listening Posts will —

Keep watch on dry activities and report them to headquarters;

Keep watch on proposed liquor control legislation and report developments to headquarters;

When dangerous or unwise legislation is pending, or when new legislation is required, will appear before legislatures or Congress — as disinterested citizens representing no industry — to urge proper legislative action.

The pioneers in this movement [repeal] who stayed with it until its successful finish naturally gained invaluable experience and knowledge which now enable them to see the renewed threat of dry domination, and the ways of destroying that threat.

Many of those who fought for repeal are members of Repeal Associates; others are its friends and are ready, when necessary, to become its allies.

The influence of such people will be great in solving the problem of

control of the liquor traffic, and in keeping the issue from again becoming a political football and a national scandal.

THE MINIMUM ANNUAL VALUE

Experience, leadership and prestige of advisory committee and officers	$ 250,000
Service of Listening Posts personnel	500,000
Surveys through members	10,000
Value of local publicity sponsored by leading members and given out in their names	50,000
Experience and training of officers in the fight for repeal; records, contacts and good will of Association Against the Prohibition Amendment	100,000
Friendly contact with liquor law administrators, trade associations and trade papers, and with anti-prohibitionists throughout the country, including many of the 15,000,000 whose votes brought repeal	90,000
	$1,000,000

Here is a store of energy potentially worth $1,000,000 a year. This energy can be converted into tremendous power; or it can be allowed to go to waste. . . . The end of the year [1937] finds your association with funds to meet all outstanding obligations.[1]

The liquor interests are enthusiastic about the assistance they are receiving from Repeal Associates. An editorial in *Tap and Tavern* says: "One of the best weapons used by Repeal Associates for the promotion of temperance and the smashing of dry fallacies is *Repeal Review*. There is ammunition enough for a hundred Big Berthas to be pointed against the drys." [2]

The 1937 convention of the New Jersey Beverage Association adopted the following resolution:

Whereas, Repeal Associates is constantly watching and combatting dry activities. . . . be it

Resolved, that the New Jersey Licensed Beverage Association lend its every effort toward perpetuating and aiding the work of Repeal Associates and be it further

Resolved, that this association undertake to cooperate with Repeal Associates in contacting not only all branches of the alcoholic beverage trade but all allied industries.

The United Brewers' Industrial Foundation

The high-sounding title of the United Brewers' Industrial Foundation cannot lend dignity to its aims. These are the circumstances under which it was organized: Jacob Ruppert, then president of the United States Brewers' Association, in his opening address to the 1937 convention of that organization, said: "I am not unduly alarmed when I say that if we fail to stand together for mutual protection, we shall again be driven out of business. Short of memory indeed must be the brewer who fails to recognize the dangers that constantly confront the industry."

Conscious of the truth of this statement, the brewers determined to resist the return of prohibition with a campaign that would be commensurate with the interests involved and the dangers to be overcome. They decided to put their business on exhibition attired in sheep's clothing with a halo attached, to extol the use of beer in the home and cover up the fact that without the inducements to drink provided by the saloon, the beer hall, the night club and the roadhouse, brewery profits would disappear and the industry would dwindle to insignificance.

The United Brewers' Industrial Foundation was organized to conduct the campaign. Jacob Ruppert was made chairman and Edward L. Bernays, America's professional propagandist number one, was made director of publicity. Mr. Bernays was given a salary of $75,000 a year and was charged with generating the industry's odor of sanctity. Plans were made for the annual expenditure of $1,000,000 or more.

Mr. Bernays knew, of course, that it would be foolish to send out statements signed by his clients. They were too thoroughly discredited in the public mind. He selected, therefore, men and women who, theoretically, were free from the odor of the brewery and who had high-sounding academic degrees and titles, and hired them to sponsor the beer propaganda. Soon "booklets" and

" manuals " began to pour out from the great propaganda machine and were distributed with an effectiveness possible only to " America's most resourceful public relations counsel." Among the first to appear were: *Beer and Brewing in America, An Economic Study,* by Warren M. Persons, Ph.D., former professor of economics, Harvard University; *Beer in the American Home,* by Eloise Davison, B.S., Ohio State University, M.S., Iowa State College; *It's Smart to Serve Beer, Menus and Recipes to Assist the Gracious Hostess,* by Helen Watts Schreiber, B.S., Iowa State College; *References, Ancient and Modern, to the Literature on Beer and Ale, A Selective Bibliography,* by Isabell M. Cooper, B.A., M.A., B.L.S.

These " booklets " make Baron Munchausen seem like the honest man of Diogenes' search. *The Economics of the Beer Industry* presented a pompous array of figures, omitted every fact that would show their true economic significance, and presented a picture that was absolutely false. *Beer in the American Home* suppressed every fact having any bearing on the real relation of beer to the American home. It was a wild rhapsody on the glories of beer and the statements it contained were either false or totally irrelevant to the actual problem beer presents to the American people. The attention of the reader is diverted from saloons, beer halls, barmaids, hostesses and the debauchery of boys and girls and he is told that this " golden beverage of the gods and the fortunate has sparkled on civilized tables " in every age and land.

The effectiveness of this propaganda is shown by a booklet that was given wide distribution, *Comments on the United Brewers' Industrial Foundation, Its Purposes, Functions and Activities, by Leaders of American Thought and Opinion.* It contains statements by a long list of professors, business men, labor leaders, editors, mayors, congressmen and others, showing that they had been converted to the idea that beer is America's way to prosperity, health and true temperance.

The Distilled Spirits Institute

The third of these propaganda organizations, the Distilled Spirits Institute, was formed to mobilize all the elements interested in the distilling business to resist the return of prohibition. The circumstances of its formation indicated the kind of campaign it would conduct. W. Forbes Morgan was made director with a salary of $100,000 a year. At the time of his selection, he was treasurer of the Democratic national committee, had directed the raising of $2,700,000 for the 1936 campaign, and was an uncle by marriage of Mrs. Franklin D. Roosevelt. He was in a position to bring pressure to bear upon the politicians of the dominant party wherever it might be needed, whether in the nation's capital or in the smallest community where a local option election was pending.[3] James M. Doran was made technical director. He was an influential Republican, had been prohibition commissioner, and knew his way behind the scenes. Norman W. Baxter was chosen as public relations director. He was a veteran newspaper man and had been press relations officer of the Reconstruction Finance Corporation. Leonard V. Harrison, an academic criminologist, was employed and given the title of director of research. His job was to sponsor the propaganda. The "releases" to which his name is attached amply justify his salary.

The National Institute of Manufacturers and Distributors

In his *Economic Study,* Professor Persons completely ignores the fundamental economic aspects of the liquor problem. He ignores the vast economic loss resulting from waste, inefficiency, illness, idleness, destruction of purchasing power, diversion of billions of dollars annually from useful enterprise and investment and the heavy load of taxation laid upon every community by the liquor traffic. He states that in the fiscal year 1937, the people spent $2,011,598,000 for beer and that this promoted national recovery and contributed to the prosperity of allied industries, farmers, laborers and taxpayers. He says, in part:

The rehabilitation of plants, installation of machinery and equipment, and the purchase of materials for the manufacture of beer constituted the first real stimulus to the general recovery of American business. . . . The relegalization of the brewing industry in April 1933, provided not only a new legalized market for beer and ale, but also new markets for its allied industries as well. . . . The brewers alone have contributed at least $21,000,000 to the revenues of the motor industry. . . . 1,500,000 steel beer barrels have been purchased up to 1937 at a cost in excess of $10,000,000. . . . White oak stumpage, reduced from timber to staves and heading pieces, amounted to 310,300,000 feet of lumber. . . . According to the Associated Cooperage Industries of America, Inc., the total expenditures for these barrels by the brewers was $31,490,000. . . . The total number of bottles shipped to brewers up to the end of 1936 totaled 8,948,000 gross, valued at $21,311,900. . . . With 58,000,000 barrels as the estimated consumption for 1937, and about 40 per cent of it, or 23,200,000 barrels, packaged, this will mean that 2,552,000 barrels of this refreshing beverage will go into American homes via 842,160,000 cans. . . . It is estimated that about 18,000,000,000 bottles of beer have been sold from relegalization in 1933 to August 1937, which would give identical figures for labels and very slightly higher figures for closures. . . . Dispensing equipment is a part of every restaurant and hotel serving beer, its total value running into many millions of dollars.

Of course, nothing was said about the fact that these industries had shared the unusual prosperity that had prevailed for the ten years under prohibition or the fact that they would continue to prosper with the return of prohibition. These figures were paraded for the purpose of making those connected with "allied industries" believe that they were threatened with heavy financial loss and, in many cases, with ruin.

As a result of propaganda and agitation of this kind, the fourth post-repeal wet organization, the National Institute of Manufacturers and Distributors, was formed. Its secretary, strategist and propagandist is Mr. C. D. Cecil. His statements leave no doubt as to the reasons for its organization and its methods:

The first prohibition wave was between the years 1847 and 1858; the second during the period 1867 to 1889; the third from 1907 to 1919.

We are now in the early stages of the fourth, as the drys are re-engaged in their old tactics, of promoting local option as a means to state-wide and ultimately national prohibition. . . . The revival of the brewing industry was an immediate and prime factor in industrial recovery from the past depression. . . . The National Institute of Manufacturers and Distributors is composed of manufacturing and jobbing firms selling equipment and supplies to the brewery, but virtually all of our members sell products to various other industries. . . . Activities of the National Institute are premised on endeavors in the best interests of the brewing industry and to the benefit of the allied industries. . . . Individually, you can do little to offset the constant menace to the economic security of the brewing industry and to your own business. Collectively, with those who are similarly situated, you can do much. . . . Foremost among the activities of the National Institute is the dissemination of educational facts concerning beer and the brewing industry; both in the nature of regular publicity, releases and literature that deals especially with the social and economic importance of the industry and the value of beer in furthering true temperance.

In his annual report of 1937, Mr. Cecil says:

During the year we have continued our educational publicity releases that met with such favorable reaction when that service to the industry was initiated. Wider use has been made of this material in the past twelve months than in the previous year, resulting in the placing of factual information before the public in every state. . . . Also, we very often get requests for our literature from various individuals and groups representing a cross section of the country. Particularly has this been true with regard to the pamphlets recently made available — one being a general treatise on beer, outlining its historical development and early recognition as a temperance beverage as well as its social and economic importance; the other a summary of the revenue obtained from beer by each state during the years 1935 and 1936 and the educational and welfare purposes for which used. Among those requesting this material were a number of college students who advised that they were seeking information concerning the economic position of the brewing industry and its relation to other industries. . . .

Our publicity service alone, in my opinion, is an accomplishment that more than justifies the existence of the National Institute. . . . We now have in preparation a leaflet that will clearly depict the staggering costs to the nation, both in dollars and demoralized social conditions, of the past era of prohibition.

In his annual report for 1938 he says:

> Our statistical material and pamphlets are now distributed in large quantities throughout the United States. Thousands of copies of this data have gone this year into those states where the prohibitionists are seeking referenda on repeal of the beer laws at the coming elections, most of these requests reaching us from breweries or wholesalers. It should be of interest to you to know that the district representatives and salesmen of the largest breweries of the country often make distribution of our material on the direction of their home offices. That, in my opinion, is very definite recognition of the National Institute and the service you gentlemen are rendering through the maintenance of this organization.[4]

The indefatigable labors and the fanatical attitude of Mr. Cecil leave no doubt that he is simply the agent of the brewers. This fact is emphasized by the following editorial that appeared in the *Brewers' Journal* for October 1937:

> In the September 15th issue of *Brewers' Journal* appeared a full page that related in succinct form the accomplishments of the National Institute of Manufacturers and Distributors during the two years' stewardship of Curtis D. Cecil, secretary. . . . We are sure we are not betraying a confidence when we say that a great deal that the National Institute has accomplished has never been made public. It would not have been prudent, and would have served no good purpose. But you can take our word for it — the " under-cover " work that Mr. Cecil has accomplished, through his excellent contacts, and by his tact and good judgment, would bring the plaudits of every brewery executive and master brewer in America, if it were made known.

The Army of Occupation

These organizations are the four great divisions of the army of occupation which has been established in this country to determine what the people shall hear, think and do about the liquor traffic. They have superb leadership and unlimited financial resources, and are unencumbered by moral scruples that would interfere with efficiency in action. They regard truth, fair play and public welfare precisely as Old World dictators do treaties, international law and the rights of other nations.

An adequate consideration of the methods that are being employed to control politics and public opinion would require an additional volume. Only a few illustrations can be given.

The liquor strategists agree that national prohibition was preceded by local option prohibition, that history is repeating itself, and that the most important task confronting them is to prevent the spread of this movement. The purpose of " Listening Posts " is to flash news of these contests to headquarters the moment they start in any part of the country. Repeal Associates have six lurid pamphlets ready for immediate shipment and distribution. They are filled with statements like the following:

> In the first place, the dry community loses the revenue from licenses which goes to a neighboring place.
>
> Increased taxes and decreased general business are a poor reward for local option — actually prohibition which fails to prohibit.
>
> What local option actually means is a return to all of the evils which disgusted the entire nation during 15 years of prohibition.
>
> Professional prohibitionists do not support local option movements because they believe it to be an effective method of control but because they believe that local option is a means to prohibition — with its control by criminals.

In an address delivered at the 1937 convention of the United States Brewers' Association, its secretary, C. D. Williams, said: " Our local option department started about a year ago, has gradually built up a monthly reporting system covering practically all counties in which elections can occur in the United States and in many cases districts and parishes in regard to which systematic reports go to interested groups."

The plan of campaign was described by George W. Eads, publicity director for Anheuser-Busch Brewing Company, in an address to the Virginia Malt Beverage Association on November 30, 1937. The following statements from this address illustrate the tactics employed:

. . . When local option elections are called, thoroughly experienced organizers and research and publicity men will be sent to the assistance of the local people. With such help, campaigns will be organized for getting the facts to the voters and the voters to the polls. . . . Through the organization we are now in process of creating, we hope to be able to render this kind of service in every community in which local option elections are held. . . .

In the city of Chicago last year local option elections were called in 88 precincts, each precinct having the population of an average county. Our national organization, Brewing Industry, Inc., in cooperation with local organizations, arranged a meeting with all the retail dealers and distributors in 44 of these precincts. We were unable to get such an organization meeting in the other 44 precincts. We found out from these dealers the number of persons they employed, the amount of wages paid them, and an estimate of the expenditures of these wage earners in the immediate neighborhood. We made up a statement of the property and license taxes paid by all the dealers. Also a statement of the rentals, and payment for water, gas, heat, power, etc. In other words, this statement showed the exact economic value of the business in these precincts.

An organization was formed for the purpose of getting facts into the hands of all the voters in these 44 precincts. Our national organization supplied all the necessary facts pertaining generally to the prohibition question. . . . We prepared a model speech for use in the campaign, in which the entire subject was pointedly reviewed and emphasis given to the vital and important factors. The local committee created to handle the campaign employed young ladies to leave the literature issued at every home in these 44 precincts. In the other 44 precincts, owing to the indifference of the retail dealers, and to some outside interference, we were unable to get any organization. The result was that we won 44 precincts in which we were organized, and lost practically all in which there was no organization.

The kind of work that was done in these Chicago precincts is exactly the kind of work that should be done in every community in which local option elections are called.[5]

Another fruitful field for the propagandist is that of liquor and its relation to taxes. The Distilled Spirits Institute issued a booklet entitled *Public Revenue from Alcoholic Beverages for the Year 1936*, signed by Mr. Harrison as director of research. In his *Economic Study*, Professor Persons has a chapter on liquor taxes. Both these documents contain elaborate tables showing the revenue received by the federal government and each of the forty-six wet states and the District of Columbia. Mr. Harrison says: "The grand total of revenues derived by the United States government for 1936 stands at $612,581,000. . . . The aggregate net profit obtained by the forty-six states and the District of Columbia totaled more than one-quarter billion dollars — $252,345,476. The combined federal and state collections amounted to $864,927,355." Professor Persons says: "The federal treasury collected on or about August 10 [1937] its billionth dollar from beer tax."

All the implications of these documents are false. They are so worded that the impression is conveyed that the people do not pay the taxes but that in some miraculous way these vast sums of money were brought from some other planet and presented to the states and the nation by the liquor industry. The people are led to believe that liquor revenue is "net profit" and reduces their taxes to the extent of nearly a billion dollars annually.

As has already been pointed out,[6] this revenue is not profit of any kind and does not reduce taxes to the extent of one dollar. It shifts taxes from incomes and other sources to the purchasers of liquor, but the total amount to be raised is not affected, that being determined entirely by cost of government. From beginning to end, the documents are appeals to ignorance and cupidity. Income taxpayers are to realize their dream of escape through a sales tax, abstainers are to shift their taxes to consumers of liquor, occasional drinkers are to see the principal burden borne by the constant drinkers, and the latter are to believe that they are not paying taxes at all but realizing a net profit.

To this false interpretation of the facts given is added the distortion of truth by omissions. The glowing prospectus sets out a balance sheet which states purported assets, but omits the liabilities. Nothing is said about the heavy burden of taxation that is imposed upon every community as a result of the vice, disease, dependence, political corruption and crime caused by the liquor traffic.

But worse than that, the propaganda distorts the question of public welfare. The United Brewers' Industrial Foundation is circulating a booklet entitled *American Beer and Ale, a Handbook of Facts and Figures.* The chapter on "Taxes and Allocation" says:

> Fifteen states used all or part of their beer revenue for educational purposes in 1936. . . . Of the taxes accruing to the states and their political subdivisions in 1936 about 50 per cent was used for public schools and public welfare. . . . Eighteen states used all or part of their beer revenue for public welfare purposes in 1936.

Tables are given showing the amounts contributed for these purposes by the various states.

The April-June 1938 number of *Repeal Review* contains elaborate tables showing the amount of liquor revenue received by each of the states and the purposes to which it was allocated. The following are some of the purposes designated: Old age pensions, social security and welfare, unemployment relief, state fund for the needy, fund for the indigent, hospitals, county welfare boards, tuberculosis fund, aid to the blind, crippled children's services, children's home, child welfare service, emergency school fund, public school teachers' retirement fund, police pension fund, firemen's benefit fund, employes' compensation fund, mothers' aid, maternity and child health.

Tap and Tavern gives the situation the following dramatic setting:

> A little child is playing happily in the streets of a big city. With all the strength of a twelve-year-old, he throws a ball against the side of a building. It bounces off his hand on the rebound. Quickly the youth runs after the ball into the middle of the street.
>
> Brakes screech wildly. One anguished scream rends the air. Johnny lies unconscious beneath the wheels of a big truck, his two legs broken.
>
> Were it not for alcoholic beverages, Johnny might go through life

a helpless cripple. Thanks to the revenue derived from liquor taxes, however, the state has been able to build and maintain a large hospital just for cases like his.

And this is only one of the many splendid causes to which liquor revenue is put. Much publicity has been given in the past to the so-called evils of liquor while its sale has been, and is, attacked vigorously by varying numbers of drys. Small stress, on the other hand, is given to the enormous benefits derived from liquor taxes.[7]

Taxes come out of the pockets of the people and go into a common fund from which the expenses of government are met. The application of receipts from specific taxes to specific expenditures is a mere bookkeeping transaction and has not the slightest significance. The amount of money to be spent for a particular purpose depends upon the amount appropriated for that purpose and not upon the source from which it is derived. If liquor revenue is used for education and welfare work, gasoline, property and other taxes must be used to pay the other expenses of government. The allocation of liquor revenue to education and welfare work does not make an additional penny available for those purposes. It is a pure sham. The success of the trick depends upon the inability of the readers to detect the deception.

The purpose is obvious. Those engaged in educational, religious and humanitarian work have been the traditional enemies of the liquor traffic and are its greatest menace today. If they can be made to believe that not merely their salaries but the work in which they are engaged is dependent upon the liquor traffic, it is thought that they will withhold their support from the prohibition movement. It is simply a cheap swindle that is being perpetrated by the liquor interests and their political retainers.

By every means that professional propagandists can devise, the doctrine is being proclaimed that through business affiliations, the collection of taxes or the allocation of public revenue, every citizen has a vested financial interest in the liquor traffic which he should do everything in his power to protect.

The Golden Beverage of the Gods

As we have seen, in 1926 Du Pont and his asssociates decided that the quickest way to abolish the income tax would be to get around the Constitution and legalize beer. So they started a great propaganda campaign to convince the people that beer is not intoxicating, that the Eighteenth Amendment did not apply to it, and that it would be legal to modify the Volstead Act. This doctrine having been approved by Congress and the President, it was used to circumvent the constitutions of the states that remained dry after repeal. This has paved the way for the propaganda the brewers are now carrying on to make the people believe that beer is not an intoxicating liquor but a liquid food and a true temperance drink.

The strategy of this campaign was suggested by Ralph T. Kettering, secretary of the American Brewers' Association. He said:

> The time is at hand, so it appears to me, to begin a concentrated campaign to sell beer to the housewife. . . . Surely the importance of the housewife is a thing to conjure with, and never more important than at this time, when juvenile protective leagues and others are attacking the methods pursued in the distribution of beer in its relation to American home life.
>
> Why not enlist the brewers of the nation in a campaign to place beer in its rightful place, alongside of the bread and other foodstuffs, in the pantry of the homes? After all, it is the housewife who holds the family purse strings and, once you sell her the idea that beer is a necessity to American family life, you have gone the whole distance in defeating those now active in bringing prohibition once again upon our country. Surely, the memories of that sad hiatus have not faded so soon that the brewers are content to drift once again into those swift currents of public opinion that could lead but in one direction. To my mind, there is one great way to halt its march forevermore, and that is to sell beer, and all it means, to the housewife, and, through her, to the family. . . .
>
> Let her fight the battles as she surely will, when once we have convinced her of the healthful, necessary qualities of good beer. Let her

give back an answer to the blue-noses by the red cheeks of her healthy youngsters, the happy smile of her good husband, and the serene family fireside where *all* the family gathers to drink that temperance beverage of a winter evening. Do this and you will sell more beer in the winter as well as in the summer and you will scatter the shadows of prohibition and all that it stands for. Sell beer to the housewife now! [8]

Beer in the American Home, which is being widely distributed by the United Brewers' Industrial Foundation, is filled with statements such as the following:

When Colonial ladies in their embroidered mulls sat in the shade of the mulberry to talk, as women will, of what things pleased their lords — they spoke in a reverent way, mentioning how Mrs. Ferris at the tavern cooked a Virginia ham with beer in a manner that the gentlemen liked. They spoke of a new slaw made with a dressing tanged with beer. " The way to a gentleman's heart," and they nodded gravely at the thought. . . . Down through the eons from fig leaves to dinner jackets, beer, the golden beverage of the gods and the fortunate, has sparkled on civilized tables. . . . Under their Egyptian taskmasters, they learned the brewing art, and afterwards set up breweries under their own direction in the land of Canaan. There was milk, honey and beer in the promised land. . . . Those blond, powerful fighters, the Vikings, were devoted to beer. . . . All the earliest European breweries were operated by the monasteries. . . . The monks made the beer-making a fascinating business. Churchmen especially were active in the improvement of malt liquors. . . . Royal tables served beer on all occasions. . . . It has been prescribed for the old and infirm both as a food and for its stimulating effect. . . . Beer combines the value of tea and coffee, which act as stimulants, with that of milk, which is merely a food. . . . Breathe deep of its aromatic essence, touch the foam with the tip of your tongue. Is it smooth? Does it tingle to the touch? Then there is health . . . exhilarating always, no doctor needs to tell you that. . . . Here are old palate-teasing recipes brought up to date, with modern ingredients.

Then follow the recipes with directions for making Chocolate Beer Cake, Beer Bread, Ham Cooked with Beer, Beef Kidney with Beer, Sweet Potatoes and Beer, Beer Cabbage Slaw, and other kinds of food with beer as an essential ingredient. Referring to the food value of beer, the booklet says:

The caloric value of one pint of beer would thus approximately be equivalent to the caloric value of:

1	ounce of butter, or	11½	ounces lean fish meat, or
11¼	ounces potatoes, or	4	ounces medium fatty beef, or
10	fluid ounces milk, or	5	ounces lean beef, or
3¼	ounces bread, or	3	average eggs
16	ounces apples		

Dr. Haven Emerson, speaking not as an employe of the brewers but as an outstanding representative of modern scientific medicine, says:

When comparing the food value of beer with that of milk, it is well to remember that milk is in itself almost a complete, balanced food, containing all the food elements the human body needs, including essential vitamins, while beer contains only water, alcohol, starch, a very small amount of protein, some minerals, and no vitamins. The poisonous effects of the alcohol in beer make even its narrow nutritional uses strictly limited and of little value even to an adult.[9]

Dr. William Healy has thrown the clear light of science on the relationship between this " golden beverage of the gods and the fortunate " and " the red cheeks of healthy youngsters and the serene family fireside." Dr. Healy was professor of nervous and mental diseases in Chicago Policlinic from 1903 to 1916, and from 1909 to 1917 was director of the Psychopathic Institute of the Juvenile Court of Chicago. Since 1917, he has been director of the Judge Baker Foundation of Boston and lecturer at Harvard, Yale and other universities. He has made a scientific study of thousands of cases of youthful delinquency. In his book, *The Individual Delinquent*, he says:

The effect of a little wine or beer upon an adolescent girl in breaking down her normal social and moral inhibitions is notorious. The effect is produced by premeditation of companions of both sexes who desire to lower the intended victim's levels of behavior. Many well founded social studies of the connection between drinking in dance halls and saloons and beginning prostitution are now available. One of the most simple and direct is to be found in the report of the Vice Commission of Chicago. In our own study of cases, we have learned the facts over and over again; and they amount to just this: there was a desire for company and pleasure on the part of the girl; even in bad company there would be resistance to the many suggestive influences thrown about her, except for the directly decisive part played by a physio-psychological condition with the use of liquor to which she was unaccustomed, a feeling of not caring possessed her, and the step was taken.[10]

The Minneapolis *Star* for May 21, 1936, says:

Two-thirds of youth crime and juvenile delinquency in Minneapolis can be traced to beer parlors and taverns. As the breeding ground of crime and immorality, beer parlors have taken the place of corner poolrooms from which mothers guarded their sons a generation ago. Beer parlors offer undesirable social contacts which were impossible in the blind pigs of prohibition or the saloons of pre-war days.

Thousands of dollars are spent annually in the city to apprehend, prosecute and punish or supervise boys and girls who get into trouble from drinking or from undesirable associations in beer parlors.

Mrs. Blanche Jones, head of the police department women's bureau, reported a sharp increase in the number of minor girls and young women who have come to her attention since repeal of prohibition. County Attorney Ed. J. Goff, stated 70 per cent of the youthful criminals prosecuted by his office admitted that they were intoxicated when they committed crime. Approximately 90 per cent of the illegitimate births in the county result from acquaintances formed in drinking places, according to Assistant County Attorney Lucien Selover. Most girls involved in such cases are between 18 and 22 years old. Frank P. Forestal, superintendent of police, said 70 or 75 per cent of police calls after 11 P.M. are to beer parlors and bars. Many of the fights and disorders involve boys and girls, he said.

Referring to his experience in the Boys' Court of Chicago, Judge J. M. Braude said:

The surprising thing to me is that boys are under the impression that beer is not intoxicating. When I question a lad about his delinquent acts, I ask him if he had any liquor. His answer invariably is, "No, sir, I just had a couple of beers." They don't seem to realize that beer is intoxicating. About 40 per cent of the boys coming into my court today are beer drinkers.[11]

Mr. W. S. Alexander, federal alcohol administrator, declared in his annual report filed with Congress on January 5, 1938:

It is the conclusion of the administration after more than two years' experience with the problems, that the brewers of malt beverages should be placed under permits and regulated in the same manner as the distillers of distilled spirits. The administration is cognizant of the effort by certain brewers to distinguish malt beverages from alcoholic beverages, but feels that there is no just reason whatever for any such classification. It is a scientific fact that malt beverages as generally understood in the United States are alcoholic beverages, and are sold and consumed with that understanding. It is further true in the opinion of the administration that the social aspects of the beer and ale industry demand as much regulation as do distilled spirits or wines. . . .

The administration feels that certain amendments in respect to advertising would be desirable to more effectively regulate this phase of its activities, and that radio advertising of distilled spirits, wine or malt beverages should be prohibited, and advertising in Sunday magazines or newspapers carrying Sunday date lines should also be prohibited. . . . That all advertising, referring directly or indirectly to the value of alcoholic beverages, either as a medicine, tonic or food, should be prohibited.

What a complete fake this beer-food propaganda is, is illustrated by the fact that near-beer looks and tastes exactly like real beer and possesses all the same ingredients except alcohol. And yet Professor Persons solemnly announces:

Since the relegalization of beer in 1933, the production of cereal beverages, or near-beer (less than one-half of 1 per cent alcohol) has been a negligible part of the brewing industry. . . . Thus the grand total is a production of 119,000 barrels of cereal beverages by 18 plants in the United States for the fiscal year 1936. This figure, less than one-fourth of 1 per cent of the production of malt beverages in that year, definitely indicates that consumers do not demand cereal beverages when beer is available.[12]

Which, of course, proves that people drink beer not for its food value, but for its intoxicating effect.

Drunken Driving

From the grand headquarters of these propaganda organizations, there is issuing a steady stream of releases, reports, leaflets and booklets comparing conditions before and after repeal. These documents are formidable in appearance, contain imposing tables and graphs and make a solemn pretense to detachment, impartiality and statistical accuracy. They purport to show that since repeal, there have been fewer motor accidents caused by the use of alcohol, that the number of arrests for drunken driving has decreased and that crime has diminished.

The research departments of a number of organizations opposed to the liquor traffic have subjected these statements to careful and exhaustive analysis. They have shown that figures, localities and times have been so selected and emphasized that they appear to support the conclusions given. They also show that figures, facts and circumstances necessary to complete the picture and show the real situation have been suppressed or distorted and that the results are false and misleading.

Most people lack the time, information and training necessary for an analysis of these statements. All they can do is to gaze at the fancy statistical dressing and read the sweeping conclusions. As newspapers and "popular" magazines having large circulation and receiving millions of dollars from liquor advertising broadcast this propaganda and ignore its refutation, the truth is effectively suppressed.

There is one fact, however, which is so obvious that no special training is necessary in order to grasp it, and that is that the purpose of these statements is public deception. If it be granted that the figures are fairly selected and honestly stated, they do not sustain the conclusion that all efforts to suppress the liquor traffic should be abandoned. They establish just the opposite conclusions.

In July 1935, Captain Stayton issued a statement in which he said that "Repeal Associates made a survey to find out" whether arrests for drunken driving had increased since repeal. He added:

> The chiefs of police of 323 cities of a population of more than 36,000,000 cooperated by furnishing official records of arrests of drunken drivers. The average for the 323 cities for the four prohibition years was 24,306 and 20,927 for beer and repeal years. That was a decided improvement.

If he had selected sections of the country in which prohibition had been properly enforced, an entirely different showing would have been made. He seeks to discredit prohibition by selecting communities that did not have prohibition. He says nothing about the fact that one of the principal causes of these arrests for drunken driving prior to repeal was that he and his associates were doing everything men controlling forty billions of dollars could do to prevent the enforcement of the law and bring about its breakdown.

Putting aside considerations of this nature, what does this statement amount to? It is a bald admission that the liquor traffic is a source of drunkenness and that it is a menace to our people as they use the public highways. The fact that during a period of four years, when the manufacture and sale of liquor was prohibited by law, there were 100,000 arrests for drunken driving in 323 cities, is a complete confirmation of the verdict of history that "the liquor traffic is criminal by nature." These facts do not sustain Captain Stayton's solemn conclusions that we should continue to tolerate a legalized and unrestricted liquor traffic, and that all who oppose this course are fanatics.

Crime Since Repeal

The Distilled Spirits Institute has given national distribution to a booklet entitled *Crime Since Repeal*, by Leonard V. Harrison, director of research. It contains complicated tables, ornamental graphs and other paraphernalia usually employed to impress ordinary mortals. It purports to give the major crime rates for the three years before and the three years following repeal and to show that there has been a reduction in crime during the latter period. It says: "The unescapable conclusion is that legalization of liquor under suitable regulations and control, contributes to a reduction of crime, while prohibition contributes to its increase."

The academic detachment and impartiality that the author affects are a transparent sham. It is evident that the purpose of his investigation was not to discover the truth but to find some way of giving plausibility to a conclusion he had been hired to sponsor.

That crime was steadily increasing is established by the testimony of those who are in a position to know the facts. We have seen [13] that in 1936 J. Edgar Hoover, director of the Federal Bureau of Investigation of the Department of Justice, stated that "crime has reached a pinnacle of appalling heights." In February 1938, Mr. Hoover told a committee of Congress that in the first nine months of 1937 there had been a 7 per cent increase in such classes of crime as murder, negligent manslaughter, criminal assault, aggravated assault, robbery, burglary, larceny and automobile theft.

On February 18, 1938, Congressman Tarver, discussing the annual appropriation for federal prisons, pointed out that the director of the Bureau of Prisons had testified before a committee of the House that federal prison population reached its high point in July 1937, when there was an aggregate of 16,600 prisoners, and that his chart showed a steadily increasing prison population ever since about the time of the repeal of the Eighteenth Amendment. Discussing this testimony, Mr. Tarver said:

> He [the director of the Bureau of Prisons] further testified that the estimated increase in federal crime for the present fiscal year would be in excess of 7 per cent and that he anticipated that there would be an increase for the next fiscal year in excess of 8 per cent. It thus becomes apparent to anyone who is willing to read the evidence relating to this subject matter with an impartial mind that the adoption of the Twenty-

first Amendment not only did not decrease crime, as was so confidently claimed for it by its proponents, but that the exact reverse of that proposition is true.[14]

If it were conceded that the figures given are accurate, still *Crime Since Repeal* is simply a red herring drawn across the trail. The wets are constantly assuring us that there was more drinking and drunkenness before repeal than since. If, therefore, we bring the two parts of their propaganda together, it appears that crime increases or decreases according to the amount of liquor consumed. Nothing is said on this subject. But there is a still more glaring defect. Mr. Harrison is heralded as a great criminologist and yet he sponsors a statement dealing with liquor and crime from which are omitted all statistics and facts that would throw light on the question of the fundamental relationship between liquor and crime, and which parades figures that, if correct, are totally irrelevant.

For generations, informed and disinterested people have recognized the fact that whether its manufacture and sale were legal or illegal, intoxicating liquor has been the greatest single source of crime. This has been the conclusion of all competent and unsubsidized criminologists. Dr. Gustav Aschaffenburg was professor of psychiatry in the Cologne Academy of Practical Medicine and editor of the *Journal of Criminal Psychology and Criminal Law Reform*. After one of the most exhaustive scientific studies of the subject ever made, he published his great work *Crime and its Repression*, which has become a classic. Throughout this book the close relationship between alcohol and crime is emphasized. He says:

The baleful influence of alcohol is one of the best known and most transparent causes of crime. It is true that the effect of alcohol can be fairly calculated only when the crime is the direct consequence of alcoholic indulgence. And yet it is just the indirect effect of alcoholism that is of so much greater importance and is so much more distressing, because those who are affected are by no means always drunkards. . . .

Supposing that with one blow we could do away with the abuse of alcohol, the number of annual convictions would be reduced by one-fifth, with the omission of the cases of aggravated assault and battery, or at least by one-tenth if only half of such cases can be attributed to alcohol. . . .

To many, the effort to do away with the abuse of alcohol, especially to oppose the "occasional drink," seems to be merely a fad, a sort of hobby of uninvited national philanthropists. They are not so to the man who has recognized the relation between the occasional drink and crime, who knows that the pleasure of a convivial evening may have to be paid for by years of suffering, who has seen the extent of the injury that is inflicted on our national prosperity by crimes committed while the criminal is intoxicated.[15]

Dr. William Healy says:

The many-sided relationship of the use of alcoholic beverages to criminalism is so completely established that we hardly need to dwell on the general question important though it is. All court officials are well acquainted with the concrete facts, and many statisticians and others have gathered the larger data. . . . Impossible though it may be to accurately determine the influence of alcohol in the production of this or that especially attributed condition, still taken either *en masse* or studied in connection with the individual offender, which is our special point of view, the facts will easily justify the cold assertion of Aschaffenburg that if we could by one blow do away with the use of alcohol, the number of annual convictions would be reduced one-fifth.[16]

The Committee of Fifty of which Seth Low, president of Columbia University, was president, and which had on its executive board such men as Charles W. Eliot, Carroll D. Wright, Francis G. Peabody and Richard T. Ely, spent years in the minute study of every phase of the liquor problem. In its report, it said that "nearly 50 per cent of crime is referred to intemperance as one cause and in 31 per cent it appears as a first cause."

The grand jury of Cuyahoga county, Ohio, in the report cited earlier in this book,[17] said:

The whole question of the improper use of liquor in our community is perplexing and discouraging. This jury has found partial or complete intoxication to be an important element in many types of crime and charges of criminality. These include arson, attempted burglary, sex offenses, shooting, stabbing, robbery, manslaughter, defrauding an innkeeper, carrying concealed weapons, assault, and violation of the auto law. . . .

Crimes committed by persons while under the immediate influence of liquor constitute only a small part of the crime chargeable to alcohol. Aschaffenburg, Healy and others have pointed out that still more important factors are the steady downward pull, the inevitable physical, mental and moral deterioration, disease, poverty, broken homes, degrading surroundings and vicious associates, and the destructive habit of depending on a " chemical kick " rather than on normal and wholesome activity for satisfaction and happiness.

Mr. Harrison is silent on another aspect of the question. Not only has the consumption of alcohol resulted in crime, but the business of furnishing it to the consumer always has been and always will be a criminal business. The age-old struggle to curb and suppress its evils will continue unless society should reach a state of moral stagnation. All laws enacted for that purpose have been defied. Liquor has been sold to minors and intoxicated persons; it has been sold on Sundays, holidays and after closing hours; all prohibition laws have been flouted; politicians have been purchased; and everywhere there has been systematic bribery of the police and other public officials having power over the liquor traffic. The business has left a trail of crime across the pages of American history.

Alibis

It is said that the present revulsion against the liquor traffic is the result of the activities of professional prohibitionists.

A score of professional prohibition organizations are vigorously soliciting campaign contributions from an emotional public to support their political and propaganda campaign. Their slogan is: " Repeal has failed; prohibition must be re-enacted." [18]

The prohibitionists are having a heyday, both in promoting and carrying local option elections. . . . Much of all this scurrilous propaganda is disseminated by the professional dry — one who makes his living from fomenting intolerance, begging money from those easily swayed to any cause zealously presented to them, especially when the one appealing hypocritically wraps himself in a cloak of assumed piety.[19]

Statements of this nature are addressed to the emotions of people of moronic intelligence. A different kind of propaganda is used for those who are intelligent enough to know that liquor evils exist outside the minds of "dry agitators." The evils are admitted, but it is said that they result from the failure of public officials to enforce the law. This argument runs as follows:

> Lax law enforcement, or perhaps in some instances, no law enforcement at all, is responsible for the adverse criticism directed against the industry. . . . Today lax law enforcement slowly but surely is creating a prejudice against an industry, which, unless rectified, will again bring the country face to face with an issue for some form of prohibition.[20]
>
> Unless the public is willing to take some part of the responsibility for bringing about proper liquor control and demands the enforcement of appropriate control laws and regulations, unsatisfactory conditions in connection with the liquor traffic are sure to develop.[21]

If the powers of government and the vigilance of citizens are required to enforce decency on the liquor business, it is evident that its right to exist rests upon precarious foundations. This is especially true since the products it dispenses are disastrous to the individual and society. It is evident, therefore, that the "law enforcement" argument will appeal to a limited number of people.

But another alibi is ready. The retailers are responsible for liquor evils. Brewing and distilling are great and honorable industries and should not be destroyed because of the shortcomings of their distributors.

> In their abuse of the beverage traffic, the prohibitionists make no distinction between the manufacturer and the local distributor. . . . This state of mind which fails to recognize the distinction between the manufacturer and the local dispenser is a dangerous one, and for it the prohibitionists are wholly responsible. . . . Yet plain common sense

will convince anybody that the locality need not be at all responsible for the manufacturer, the distiller or the brewer who may live thousands of miles from the particular locality in question. But before we can have proper conditions, the people of that locality *must take* responsibility for the man who sells beverages in their towns.[22]

The unlawful conduct of business on the part of some retailers is the cause of the criticism and condemnation appearing in national editorials.[23]

Where formerly the enemies of the industry were outsiders working for the establishment and enforcement of prohibition, now the greatest liability and danger comes from within the industry itself — from chiseling, smart-aleck, unscrupulous retailers who conduct their establishments by a code of ethics which puts them on a par with the lowest dives of the " speak-easy " era.[24]

Liquor is made to be sold for a profit. The retailer is, therefore, an integral part of the liquor business. Moreover, there are only a few hundred brewers and distillers and nearly half a million retailers. As the business of the retailers is to create, foster and exploit a degrading appetite, they are inevitably what they are. The attempt of the brewers and distillers to wrap themselves in the robes of respectability and hide behind their retailers is absurd.

Mr. D. Frederick Burnett, commissioner of the Department of Alcohol Control of New Jersey, has stated the truth very bluntly. Addressing the 1937 annual convention of the United States Brewers' Association, he said:

You know as well as I do that however straight you keep your own house in order, the public judges the whole industry by the things which it sees, and that is natural. So would you or I if we were on the outside. . . .

Calling spades spades, that is the saloon, the restaurant, the hotel, the night club. That is where your problem lies today; that is to say, in the place where the products of your brewery are dispensed. It is a problem in distribution and that is the thing that has to be brought under control, and that is the problem which I want to speak to you about this morning. . . .

Now, then, what are these problems about distribution and dispensation? This is what I see. I wonder whether you see the same thing? You probably do. I see in the licensed places overdrinking, excess of drinking which leads to drunken driving. I see sales to minors. I see the employment of hostesses, women who are paid a commission to sit down with men and induce them to drink, and on every drink which is sold they get a commission. I see prostitutes and open solicitation. I see lewd performances and indecent advertising. Those are the things which are going on in the licensed places and which are giving a bad name.[25]

Another favorite alibi is that present-day evils are the result of "our disastrous experience under prohibition." We are solemnly reminded that we have faced the task of clearing

away the wreckage of corruption and disrespect for law left by the devastating storm of national prohibition.[26]

We hear complaints today about bootleggers and chiselers and cheats and crooked politicians. Many of us have overlooked the fact that the people can get rid of these hangovers from prohibition days if they put their minds to it.[27]

Before prohibition, the evils had become so intolerable that they brought about a national uprising against the liquor traffic. If it is true, as is said, that those evils continued under prohibition and exist today as a "hangover," it is evident that they are the result of alcohol and liquor lawlessness rather than of the effort of the people to suppress them.

We are told that the appalling conditions that prevail throughout the country do not result from alcohol, but from the folly and lack of self-control of those who use it. It is said that the problem can be solved only by teaching the people the importance of moderation and true temperance. This type of propaganda is illustrated by a book that is being widely circulated by a large distillery. It employed a prominent author to write a book, the purpose of which is "to help you insure the health and happiness of your precious middle years." There are fourteen chapters having such titles as "The Cheerful Outlook and How to Acquire It" and

" Man's Worst Enemy — Fear." As if it were merely a part of a treatise on health, there is a chapter on " Moderation in Drinking " which contains the following:

> Intelligent, modern medical men have discarded completely the notion that total abstinence from alcohol is either necessary or desirable. On the contrary, there is an abundance of medical testimony to the effect that the moderate drinker is not only likely to live a more cheerful, contented and happy life, but that he will actually live longer.[28]

The Voice of Science

It is refreshing to turn from the voice of greed-inspired propaganda to the findings of science as stated by men whose authority cannot be questioned. In their standard work on psychiatry, Strecker and Ebaugh say:

> Alcoholism may be a symptom of other psychoses but in itself it accounts for from five to ten per cent of all mental disease. Even in moderate doses, alcohol lessens motor activity, increases reflexes, diminishes physical strength, lowers the fatigue point, interferes with clarity of ideation, impairs capacity for judgment and mental work, interferes with the sharpness of memory and the stability of the emotions. It is a direct poison to the cortical cells, and in acute intoxication Nissl found they were destroyed or damaged with shrunken and displaced nuclei.[29]

Dr. Emil Bogen is pathologist and director of research at the Los Angeles County Tuberculosis Sanitarium. He has been on the medical faculties of the University of Cincinnati and New York University and has achieved national distinction for his research work in the field of toxicology, the study of poisons. He was selected by the editor of *Alcohol and Man* to write the chapter on " The Human Toxicology of Alcohol." He says:

> Alcohol, in the form of some type of beverage, has been known from the earliest times, each country having some national drink containing it. No other poison causes so many deaths or leads to or intensifies so many diseases, both physical and mental, as does alcohol in the various forms in which it is taken. . . . In short, both in its immediate effects

and in its slower and more chronic manifestations, alcohol is the most dangerous poison widely included in the human diet, affecting nearly every tissue of the body, but having a particularly toxic action upon the tissues of the central nervous system. Recognition of this fundamental fact must underlie consideration of any other aspect of the alcohol problem.[30]

Dr. Adolph Meyer, professor in Johns Hopkins University, a psychiatrist of international standing, says in the same volume:

Alcohol clearly enters in many ways as a *pathogenic factor* into disturbances of the health, happiness and efficiency of man, as a disturber of the normal individual and of social and economic equilibrium, before one focuses on specifically medical and even more specifically psychiatric pathological developments. And yet, it is in these beginnings that both functional pathology and preventive hygiene have their first important fields. . . .

Statistical curves of arrests and admissions to hospitals give but the final results of alcoholism, but little of the real meaning of the problem for the individual and the community or of the actual frequency of drunkenness and delinquencies. What does it mean to the person involved and to the family and social group? What were the conditions under which the persons became drunk and sick? What else did it bring about, besides the arrest and admission to the hospital? How much was the diversion of money and work from where both were needed? How much was there an involvement of other persons. . . ?

The non-dependability of inhibitions, the shallow sham euphoria, exaggerated bragging and vanity, and the effort to cover up and avoid situations that bring one to a test, the ease of producing excuses and of attributing failures to the situation all lead to vitiations, to dishonesty, to anticipations and mistrust and suspicions in the less optimistic moods. The frequent shifts from good intentions to incapacity to live up to them entails an increasing duplicity. It becomes very difficult to say what is psychopathic background and what a consequence of drinking. . . .

In all this, a social conscience has to face the attitude toward a kind of questionable " right to be sick," to lower one's standards, to seek solace in the double-edged boon of " sedative stimulants " i.e. stimulants working by virtue of reduction of the higher human capacities. . . . One cannot help feeling that the alcohol industry and the alcohol traffic are practically bound to favor what one might properly designate as a *sabotage of human health,* ranking with the exploitation of other appetites capable of overstimulation. . . .

A vast amount of human happiness and misery is at stake, with alcohol the essential component that is absolutely within the control of man, more than is the case of any other form of illness and mental disease, of a type that mankind can eliminate if it wants to. It would be incomparably easier than will be the elimination of the "social" diseases, the crucial factors of which are dependent on the sex impulses, which are a product of growth and not merely a product of adult work.[31]

In 1932, there was held at Washington the First International Congress on Mental Hygiene, which was attended by the outstanding psychiatrists of all the nations of the world. Dr. K. Herman Bouman, professor of psychiatry and neurology in the University of Amsterdam and director of the Clinic for Psychiatry and Neurology, Wilhelmina Gasthuis, was selected to present the subject of "Alcohol as a Mental Hygiene Problem." He said:

Among the three great diseases — alcoholism, syphilis and tuberculosis — the first occupies a very peculiar position from the point of view of prevention and treatment. In contradistinction to the other two, alcoholism is a condition of which we know accurately the composition, distribution and effects, and the problem is one for which man himself is responsible. Nothing would seem simpler than to do away with the cause of this particular evil as soon as the community is convinced that the mental life of the individual, as well as that of his offspring, is injured by it. And yet the mental hygienist hardly anywhere finds so many difficulties in his path as when fighting alcoholism. . . . Social conditions and prejudices of all kinds block his way. . . .

Alcohol has long been known to be a chemical substance with a great affinity for exactly those cells of our organism which have either a highly developed and specialized function — such as the cells of the central nervous system, particularly those of the brain cortex — or which are in a state of growth. In a sense, this applies also to the procreation cells of the sexual glands.

The way in which the cells of the tissues mentioned are injured by the presence in the blood of even small quantities of alcohol much resembles the effect of an insufficient supply of oxygen.

While the cells of the tissues are in a state of growth, and an intensive metabolism is taking place, even very small quantities of alcohol suffice perceptibly to injure this metabolism. Nobody — not even those who think small doses of alcohol not too injurious to adults — can doubt the danger of giving alcoholic drinks to young children.

So far as the functions of the psychic life in adults are concerned, the effects of the consumption of greater or smaller quantities of alcohol have been long sufficiently well known. Laboratory experiments (in which all disturbing influences can be eliminated) have taught us that even very small doses of alcohol injure the receptive functions — as perception, memorization, conception and attention — in such a way as to cause the appearance of errors. As a result of the appearance of superficial associations without inner contact, the thinking faculty itself becomes incapable of serving as the basis of any higher mental life and degenerates. The action that springs from this defective thinking takes place too quickly and results in a great many errors. It is important to observe that even in these conditions of slight intoxication, self-criticism becomes less active, and the person tested has the subjective feeling that he has done his work much better than the experiment actually indicates. The result is, therefore, that less accurate perception and more superficial thinking are followed by hasty and inefficient action, which the person tested cannot himself adequately criticize, because he has the illusion that he can do his work more easily and better than would be the case in a state of perfect sobriety.

Even these very small quantities of alcohol produce a condition that has all the essential characteristics of a delirium. For the symptoms of delirium are not really different, though they may be more pronounced. When the condition of intoxication reaches the degree that is usually called a " drunken fit," the picture is not essentially altered.[32]

Dr. Haven Emerson says:

The most successful artificial or drug excitant to sexual excess is alcohol. More instances of syphilis and gonorrhea in youths of both sexes, whose sober good intentions are to avoid extramarital sexual connection, have been due to alcoholic abuse than to any other one cause.

Alcohol in moderate amounts suffices commonly to lower self-restraint and self-control in situations of sex temptation so that exposure to the hazards of sexual diseases is undertaken thoughtlessly and without care of the consequences.

The following quotation from an eminent specialist in venereal diseases expresses the usual opinion of observant physicians:

" Alcohol paralyzes the inhibitions, renders the physical urges more obvious, disarms the critical faculty, breaks down reasonableness and prudence, blurs fineness of perception and taste, without necessarily creating the state socially recognized as intoxication.

" Alcohol is the best salesman and procurer known, and is a constant and essential stock in trade for the promotion of prostitution." [33]

Dr. Richard C. Cabot, for many years chief of the medical staff of the Massachusetts General Hospital and professor of clinical medicine in the Harvard Medical School, states the matter for the layman as follows:

We ordinarily speak of alcohol as a " stimulant." It is worth realizing that it is universally agreed among physicians now, that it is never a stimulant, always a narcotic. The reason it seems to be a stimulant is because after dinner it narcotizes our inhibitions, our modesty, so that our tongues move very freely and often very fast. Certain activities come to light and so seem to be stimulated; but in fact the brakes are taken off of natural self-restraint. A man who is dead drunk and snoring with liquor is narcotized in an obvious way; the man who is supposed to be brilliant after dinner is also narcotized, only less obviously.[34]

In the detachment of the clinic and the laboratory, the modern scientist reaffirms the wisdom of Solomon which was expressed three thousand years ago and has been confirmed by the experience of each succeeding generation:

Who hath woe? Who hath sorrow? Who hath contentions? Who hath complaining? Who hath wounds without cause? Who hath redness of eyes? They that tarry long at the wine; they that go to seek out mixed wine. Look not thou upon the wine when it is red, when it giveth its color in the cup, when it goeth down smoothly. At the last it biteth like a serpent and stingeth like an adder. Thine eyes shall behold strange things, and thine heart shall utter froward things. Yea, thou shalt be as he that lieth down in the midst of the sea, or he that lieth upon the top of a mast. They have stricken me, shalt thou say, and I was not hurt; they have beaten me, and I felt it not. When shall I awake? I will seek it yet again.[35]

The Last Line of Defense

Those engaged in the defense of the liquor traffic know that their propaganda is contrary to the facts of history, experience, science and common sense. They know that the very fact that they must organize on such a vast scale, raise huge sums of money, subsidize the press, purchase and intimidate politicians and spend millions of dollars upon fraudulent propaganda to save the liquor traffic from destruction, is itself conclusive proof that it should be destroyed. They realize that when the people are again aroused and ready for action, these tactics will be as futile as they proved to be in 1919. They are, therefore, after the manner of Hitler, defying their enemies and endeavoring, by a showing of strength, to force them to surrender without giving battle.

Supported by their powerful allies, the liquor interests now issue to the American people a defiance which, if stripped of the verbiage of the public relations counsel, would declare frankly:

> We have demonstrated the fact that we are stronger than you are, that you cannot destroy us, and that whenever and wherever we cannot operate under the law, we can and will operate in defiance of the law. After a prolonged struggle, you adopted a national prohibition law and made available for our destruction all the powers of the local, state and national governments. We flouted this law just as we had flouted every prohibition law of the past. In the end, we forced you to accept repeal as the only alternative to a reign of lawlessness. Since repeal, you have passed laws prohibiting the sale of liquor in the neighborhood of schools and churches, on Sundays, election days, and after stated hours, to minors and intoxicated persons. You have endeavored by law to prevent dishonest advertising and the alliance of liquor, gambling and vice. In the usual manner, we are disregarding these laws, and, in the usual manner, you are becoming indignant and are passing prohibition laws by local option and demanding a return of state-wide and national prohibition. What is the use of passing another law against the liquor traffic when you cannot enforce those that you have?

A prohibition law would simply mean another law for us to ignore. We demand that you admit that you are helpless and that you give up and make the best of it.

In one of the pamphlets which Repeal Associates distributes in districts where local option contests are in progress, this defiance is expressed as follows:

What guarantee is there that local option can be enforced? Decent and respectable citizens are sometimes persuaded that conditions growing out of inadequate enforcement can be cured by local option prohibition. But if legal control has failed, how can it be expected that illegal sales can be controlled?

This is the challenge of the underworld, the liquor traffic and its business affiliates and political allies, the large income taxpayers, the big business and financial interests and a subsidized press to the intelligence, social conscience and patriotism of the American people.

NOTES

[1] *Repeal Review,* Dec. 1936, July-Sept. 1937 and Oct.-Dec. 1937, *passim.*

[2] Quoted in *Repeal Review,* Oct.-Dec. 1937, p. 17.

[3] An exhaustive analysis of the political significance of Mr. Morgan's selection is given in an editorial in the *United States News,* March 8, 1937.

[4] These statements by Mr. Cecil were made in reports and addresses during the years 1937–38, and can be found in the issues of the *Brewers' Journal* for those years.

[5] American Business Men's Research Foundation Monthly Reference Service, No. 1, 1938.

[6] See *supra,* p. 394.

[7] Oct. 10, 1938.

[8] *Brewers' Journal,* June 15, 1937.

[9] Emerson, *op. cit.,* pp. 28, 30.

[10] P. 267 (Little, Brown & Co., 1915).

[11] Quoted in *Union Signal,* April 22, 1939.

[12] Persons, *op. cit.,* p. 23.

[13] See *supra,* pp. 373–74.

[14] *Congressional Record,* Vol. 83, Part 2, 75th Congress, 3rd Session, p. 2169.

[15] Pp. 69, 228 (Little, Brown & Co., 1913).

[16] Healy, *op. cit.,* p. 262.

[17] See *supra,* p. 198.

[18] *Repeal Review,* July-Sept. 1937, p. 7.

[19] C. D. Cecil in an address at Richmond, Va., Nov. 30, 1937.

[20] C. F. von dem Bussche in *Brewers' Journal,* Dec. 15, 1937.
[21] *Repeal Review,* Oct.-Dec. 1937, p. 7.
[22] *Ibid.,* April-June 1937, pp. 6, 7.
[23] C. F. von dem Bussche in *Brewers' Journal,* March 15, 1938.
[24] *Coors' Courier,* Dec. 1937.
[25] *Brewers' Journal,* Dec. 1937, pp. 30–31.
[26] *Repeal Review,* Dec. 1936, p. 10.
[27] *Ibid.,* Oct.-Dec. 1937, p. 8.
[28] Frank Parker Stockbridge, *You'll Feel Better* (Seagrams-Distillers' Corporations), p. 34.
[29] *Clinical Psychiatry* (P. Blackiston's Sons & Co., 1928), p. 152.
[30] *Alcohol and Man,* pp. 126, 150, 151.
[31] *Ibid.,* pp. 277, 278, 281, 285, 300, 307.
[32] *Proceedings of the First International Congress on Mental Hygiene,* pp. 444–46.
[33] Emerson, *op. cit.,* pp. 82, 83.
[34] *A Layman's Handbook of Medicine* (Houghton Mifflin Co., 1916), p. 416.
[35] Prov. 23:29–35.

Index

Index